Rethinking the Judicial Settlement of Reconstruction

American constitutional lawyers and legal historians routinely assert that the Supreme Court's state action doctrine halted Reconstruction in its tracks. But it didn't.

Rethinking the Judicial Settlement of Reconstruction demolishes the conventional wisdom – and puts a constructive alternative in its place. Pamela Brandwein unveils a lost jurisprudence of rights that provided expansive possibilities for protecting blacks' physical safety and electoral participation, even as it left public accommodation rights undefended. She shows that the Supreme Court supported a Republican coalition and left ample room for executive and legislative action. Blacks were abandoned, but by the president and Congress, not the Court. Brandwein unites close legal reading of judicial opinions (some hitherto unknown), sustained historical work, the study of political institutions, and the sociology of knowledge. This book explodes tired old debates and will provoke new ones.

Pamela Brandwein is professor of political science at the University of Michigan. She is the author of *Reconstructing Reconstruction: The Supreme Court and the Production of Historical Truth.*

CAMBRIDGE STUDIES ON THE AMERICAN CONSTITUTION

SERIES EDITORS

Maeva Marcus, *George Washington University*
Mark Tushnet, *Harvard University* and *Georgetown University Law Center*
Melvin I. Urofsky, *Virginia Commonwealth University*
Keith Whittington, *Princeton University*

Cambridge Studies on the American Constitution publishes books that examine the American Constitution and offers a range of interpretations and approaches, from traditional topics of constitutional history and theory, case studies, and judicial biographies, to more modern and often controversial issues dealing with gender and race. While many estimable series have incorporated constitutional studies, none has done so exclusively. This series seeks to illuminate the implications – governmental, political, social, and economic – of the relationship between the American Constitution and the country it governs through a wide array of perspectives.

TITLES IN THE SERIES

Mark A. Graber, Dred Scott *and the Problem of Constitutional Evil*
Christian G. Fritz, *American Sovereigns: The People and America's Constitutional Tradition Before the Civil War*

Rethinking the Judicial Settlement of Reconstruction

PAMELA BRANDWEIN
University of Michigan

CAMBRIDGE
UNIVERSITY PRESS

32 Avenue of the Americas, New York NY 10013-2473, USA

Cambridge University Press is part of the University of Cambridge.

It furthers the University's mission by disseminating knowledge in the pursuit of education, learning and research at the highest international levels of excellence.

www.cambridge.org
Information on this title: www.cambridge.org/9780521887717

© Pamela Brandwein 2011

This publication is in copyright. Subject to statutory exception and to the provisions of relevant collective licensing agreements, no reproduction of any part may take place without the written permission of Cambridge University Press.

First published 2011

A catalogue record for this publication is available from the British Library

Library of Congress Cataloguing in Publication data
Brandwein, Pamela.
   Rethinking the judicial settlement of Reconstruction / Pamela Brandwein.
     p. cm. – (Cambridge studies on the American Constitution)
   Includes bibliographical references and index.
   ISBN 978-0-521-88771-7
   1. Civil rights – United States – States – History.   2. Blacks – Legal status, laws, etc. – United States – States – History.   3. Discrimination – Law and legislation – United States – States – History.   4. Civil rights – United States – History.   5. Discrimination – Law and legislation – United States – History.   6. Civil rights – United States – History.   7. Reconstruction (U.S. history, 1865–1877)   I. Title.
   KF4757.B655   2011
   342.7308´73–dc22   2010030600

ISBN 978-0-521-88771-7 Hardback

Cambridge University Press has no responsibility for the persistence or accuracy of URLs for external or third-party internet websites referred to in this publication, and does not guarantee that any content on such websites is, or will remain, accurate or appropriate.

Contents

Acknowledgments		*page* ix
1	Abandoned Blacks?	1
2	The Emergence of the Concept of State Neglect, 1867–1873	28
3	The Civil/Social Distinction: An Intramural Republican Dispute	60
4	The Birth of State Action Doctrine, 1874–1876	87
5	A Surviving Sectional Context, 1876–1891	129
6	The *Civil Rights Cases* and the Language of State Neglect	161
7	Definitive Judicial Abandonment, 1896–1906	184
8	Twentieth-Century Receptions	206
9	Conclusion	240
Bibliography		245
Index		261

Acknowledgments

I have accrued many debts in the course of writing this book, and it is a great pleasure to thank the colleagues and friends who have lent their support. My deep gratitude goes to Sandy Levinson, who offered reflections and advice at both a 2002 talk at the University of Texas at Austin and a 2008 conference at Harvard Law School. Many thanks to Mark Graber for providing early encouragement, as well as feedback on the entire project that advanced my thinking about the Waite Court and its relationship to the executive branch. Rogers Smith was a sounding board on numerous occasions and I am grateful for his skepticism, which gave me the opportunity to refine my analysis. I am also indebted to Robert C. Post for his enthusiasm and critical commentary at an early and vital time. Julie Novkov read multiple versions of chapters, provided detailed and insightful comments on the complete manuscript, and offered a steady stream of support. I am very pleased to acknowledge a long-running debt to Julie, whose work has helped me to think about white supremacy and legal change.

I owe special thanks to Richard M. Valelly, whom I had the great good fortune to meet as I worked on the project. I am deeply grateful to Rick for his intellectual generosity and support as for well as a set of comments on the full manuscript from which I profited greatly. My deepest appreciation also goes to Michael Les Benedict, whose reflections and insights were enormously helpful. An extended conversation with Les at the 2008 meeting of the American Society for Legal History buoyed me as I neared completion of the work. In their different ways, Les and Rick have made it seem obvious that the study of constitutional development during the post–Civil War decades is a joint endeavor between legal history and political science, and for that I am thankful.

Three of my steepest debts are to political theorists, all wonderful friends. Douglas C. Dow provided invaluable criticism during the early years of the project and later saw the work through a formative stage of development. I am deeply grateful for his insights and energy. It is a very special pleasure to thank Don Herzog, whose close attention to the full manuscript yielded comments,

x   *Acknowledgments*

questions, and friendly provocations that substantially improved the book. I owe an enormous debt of gratitude to Don for his support, which sustained me during a turbulent time. At a late hour in the production process Elizabeth Wingrove gave an extraordinary amount of time to an intensive reading of the entire manuscript, making it better in ways large and small and too numerous to count. I am profoundly grateful for her critical interventions, editorial skill, and generosity of spirit.

The long process of writing and revising was aided by comments and suggestions from Richard Aynes, David Bogen, Mark Brandon, John Brigham, John Chamberlin, Lisa Disch, Lynda G. Dodd, Lauren Edelman, Sam Erman, Daniel Ernst, Bryant Garth, Deborah Hellman, Bob Kagan, Paul Kens, Charles Lane, George Lovell, Joe Lowndes, Jonathan Lurie, Wayne Moore, Amnon Reichman, Kim Scheppele, Daniel Sharfstein, Christopher Waldrep, Joe Wells, G. Edward White, Bryan Wildenthal, Dan Wirls, and Mariah Zeisberg. My thanks to them all. I want to particularly acknowledge Ronald Kahn and Ken Kersch, who gave me the opportunity to develop some core ideas in a chapter I contributed to their edited volume, *The Supreme Court and American Political Development*. I thank Ron and Ken for their engagement with the project at its early stages. Thanks also to Chris Waldrep for generously sharing with me copies of the indictment in *United States v. Harris* and several letters in the Joseph Bradley Papers.

I would like to gratefully acknowledge a number of institutions. The University of Michigan provided course relief to work on the project. I presented papers at Harvard Law School, the University of Califonia at Berkeley, the University of North Carolina School of Law, American University's Washington College of Law, the University of Maryland School of Law, the University of Oregon, and the University of Iowa. Portions of Chapters 5, 6, and 8 appeared as "A Judicial Abandonment of Blacks? Reconsidering the 'State Action' Cases of the Waite Court," *Law & Society Review* 41 (2007): 343–86, and appear here in revised form by permission of Wiley-Blackwell. A very early version of Chapter 6 appeared as "The *Civil Rights Cases* and the Lost Language of State Neglect" in Ronald Kahn and Ken Kersch, eds., The *Supreme Court and American Political Development* (Lawrence: University Press of Kansas, 2006), 275–325. A small portion of a book review appears by permission of H-Law: "Review of Labbé, Ronald M.; Lurie, Jonathan, *The Slaughterhouse Cases: Regulation, Reconstruction, and the Fourteenth Amendment* and Ross, Michael A., *Justice of Shattered Dreams: Samuel Freeman Miller and the Supreme Court during the Civil War Era*," H-Law, H-Net Reviews (May 2004). I presented pieces of the argument at the American Society for Legal History, the American Political Science Association, the Western Political Science Association, the Law and Society Association, and the Southeastern Association of Law Schools, and I benefited greatly from comments, questions, and criticisms in those sessions.

It is a privilege to be included in the Cambridge Studies on the American Constitution series; my thanks to Maeva Marcus, Mark Tushnet, Melvin I.

Acknowledgments xi

Urofsky, and Keith Whittington. Special thanks to Howard Gillman for his support of the project as he was stepping down from the series board. I am also grateful to an anonymous referee for Cambridge University Press for comments that allowed me to refine my argument and sharpen various disagreements. Lew Bateman supported the project and kept tabs on me over a long stretch during which I was absent, and I am appreciative on both scores. Russell Hahn was a patient copy editor, and I thank him as well.

I want to extend a very personal thank you to Anisha Mandol, who gave support and encouragement as I devoted time and energy to the project over the past many years. I hope she will accept an uncomplicated expression of gratitude for that support, which at times came with costs to her. I remain ever grateful for her love and care.

One final expression of thanks: In the months following the Supreme Court's ruling in *United States* v. *Morrison* (2000), I was startled by a brief passage in the dissenting opinion of Justice Stephen Breyer. Justice Breyer suggested that the canonical 1883 decision, the *Civil Rights Cases*, never considered the kind of claim advanced by the federal government in the *Morrison* case, namely, that Congress was authorized under the Fourteenth Amendment to remedy the failure of state actors to punish gender-motivated violence. My first thought was that Breyer must be wrong. I knew the *Civil Rights Cases*, and I was sure it blocked that kind of claim. After all, scholars widely condemn the decision for putting state failures to punish Klan violence outside the reach of the Fourteenth Amendment. But I reread the decision and was amazed to find that the text could support Breyer's reading. Such was the initiating event that led to this project and book. Justice Breyer, of course, bears no responsibility for the results.

I

Abandoned Blacks?

Reconstruction – America's second revolution[1] – was dead by 1877, and the fatal blow was inflicted by the Supreme Court. This has been the common wisdom since the dawn of the civil rights era, when a story about the Court's dismantling of Reconstruction spread across law, history, and political science.[2] In this story, the Court stands accused of crippling the national government and forsaking the former slaves. The end of Reconstruction meant "the abandonment of the freed slaves to the prejudices of their former owners,"[3] and the vehicle for abandonment was a legal rule known as "state

[1] Eric Foner, *Reconstruction: America's Unfinished Revolution, 1863–1877* (1988). Reconstruction has also been called "America's Second Founding." See Barry Friedman, "Reconstructing Reconstruction: Some Problems for Originalists (and Everyone Else, Too)," 11 *Journal of Constitutional Law* 1201, 1205, 1207.

[2] See, e.g., C. Vann Woodward, *Reunion and Reaction: The Compromise of 1877 and the End of Reconstruction* (1951), 245; Robert J. Cottrol, "Civil Rights Cases," in Kermit Hall, ed., *The Oxford Companion to the Supreme Court* (1992), 149; Harold M. Hyman and William Wiecek, *Equal Justice Under Law* (1982), 488; Eugene Gressman, "The Unhappy History of Civil Rights Legislation," 50 *Michigan Law Review* 1323, 1336–7 (1952); Robert J. Harris, *The Quest for Equality* (1960), 82–91; Peter Magrath, *Morrison R. Waite: The Triumph of Character* (1963), 130–49; William Gillette, *Retreat from Reconstruction, 1869–79* (1979), 295, 310, 346; Robert Kaczorowski, *The Politics of Judicial Interpretation* (1985), 217; Michael Kent Curtis, *No State Shall Abridge: The Fourteenth Amendment and the Bill of Rights* (1986), 179–80; Foner, *Reconstruction*, 587; J. Morgan Kousser, *Colorblind Injustice: Minority Voting Rights and the Undoing of the Second Reconstruction* (1999), 49–50; Rogers M. Smith, *Civic Ideals* (1997); Rayford Logan, *The Negro in American Life and Thought, The Nadir, 1877–1901* (1954); Loren Miller, *The Petitioners* (1966), 158; Walter Murphy, James Fleming, and William Harris, *American Constitutional Interpretation* (1986), 744; Laurence H. Tribe, *American Constitutional Law* (2000), 922; David O'Brien, *Storm Center* (2000), 1290; Charles Lane, *The Day Freedom Died: The Colfax Massacre, the Supreme Court, and the Betrayal of Reconstruction* (2008); Lou Faulkner Williams, *The Great South Carolina Ku Klux Klan Trials, 1871–1872* (1996), 142; Howard Gillman, "How Political Parties Can Use the Courts to Advance Their Agendas: Federal Courts in the United States, 1875–1891," *American Political Science Review* 96 (2002): 516.

[3] See Melvin I. Urofsky and Paul Finkelman, *A March of Liberty: A Constitutional History of the United States*, vol. 1 (2002), 480.

action" doctrine. Elaborated by the Court in a series of decisions from 1876 to 1883,[4] this rule is said to have put Klan violence and intimidation beyond the reach of the Fourteenth and Fifteenth Amendments, rendering those amendments largely useless in the federal effort to protect the physical safety and voting rights of blacks.

In this book, I elaborate an alternative account of the judicial settlement of Reconstruction. State action doctrine, I argue, was not a definitive abandonment. Indeed, an entire jurisprudence of rights and rights enforcement has been lost to twentieth-century observers. This jurisprudence included a Fourteenth Amendment concept of "state neglect" and a voting rights theory built from the Fifteenth Amendment and Article 1, Section 4.[5] Constructed from legal categories that have long since disappeared, this jurisprudence contained broad possibilities as well as constraints and ambiguities, and modern observers have perceived its contours in only partial and inchoate ways. I recover this jurisprudence and attend to the consequences of its recovery. One consequence is a shift in the periodization of definitive judicial abandonment: it begins with *Plessy v. Ferguson* (1896),[6] the infamous decision that put the Court's imprimatur on legal segregation, and culminates ten years later with *Hodges v. United States* (1906),[7] an under-studied decision that gutted the Civil Rights Act of 1866.

A second consequence of recovering this lost jurisprudence is its highlighting of the limitations of realist-inspired approaches to Court decision making in political science. My account shows that these dominant approaches' focus on outcomes leads to a misunderstanding of the state action cases. The misunderstanding is compounded by an inability to explain subsequent, rights-friendly decisions handed down by the same Court, decisions whose theory of rights traces back to the state action cases. Only by investigating the jurisprudential context – the discursive and institutional world in which concepts were shaped, debated, and deployed – can we understand the Court's role in the transition from Reconstruction to Jim Crow. Otherwise put, my study reveals that in order to properly understand judicial outcomes, we must invest in the historical study of ideas and political regimes.

My new account dispenses with the cinematic terms that characterize the accepted narrative of judicial abandonment. In that narrative, the forces of good (Republicans) are vanquished by the forces of evil (Democrats) and Court justices (with the exception of Justice John Marshall Harlan) are aligned with the latter. On my reading, the protagonists – the Republican actors who built and circulated an eclipsed jurisprudence of rights and rights

---

[4] *United States v. Cruikshank*, 92 U.S. 542 (1876); *United States v. Harris*, 106 U.S. 629 (1883); *Civil Rights Cases*, 109 U.S. 3 (1883).

[5] U.S. Constitution, Article 1, Section 4: "The times, places and manner of holding elections for Senators and Representatives, shall be prescribed in each state by the legislature thereof; but the Congress may at any time by law make or alter such regulations, except as to the places of choosing Senators."

[6] 163 U.S. 537 (1896).

[7] 203 U.S. 1 (1906).

Abandoned Blacks?

enforcement – are neither heroes in the mold of Fredrick Douglass nor villains like the Democrats. These Republicans believed in white superiority and rejected what was termed the "social equality" of blacks, often scorning the public accommodation provisions of the Civil Rights Act of 1875. But they also supplied broad possibilities for the federal protection of black physical safety and voting rights. Indeed, in the 1880s the federal government succeeded in several important cases that relied on a Court-supplied theory of voting rights. If these doctrines creatively devised by the Waite Court had been consistently exploited by the executive and subsequently institutionalized, the legal edifice that undergirded Jim Crow would not have existed. Certainly a two-tiered system of citizenship rooted in white supremacy could and no doubt would have emerged. But it would have required the explicit overturning of Waite Court precedent. Or it would have required extra-legal sources of authority and thus enforcement. Whether or not such a counterfactual system of political and economic racism would have led to the same degree of black subjugation, the path to such a system – and so opportunities for resisting it – would have looked profoundly different.

Twentieth-century interpretations of the *Civil Rights Cases* and precursor decisions have been guided by assumptions about what follows from or is necessarily produced by racism. Justice Bradley and his brethren cannot be absolved of racism, and they are not pardoned here. What follows from their racism is the crucial question. Assumptions about such entailments carry a risk: misapprehension of the state action cases and the political and legal opportunities and resources that flow from them. As I show here, the rejection of black property, contract, safety, and voting rights does not follow inevitably from derision for black claims to public accommodation rights, though the assumption has been otherwise. In the wake of the Civil War, after the republic had nearly been destroyed, a resurgent commitment to rule of law, which now encompassed blacks, combined in mainstream Republicans with a belief in white superiority. In recovering the legal concepts and rights theories that were generated in the 1870s by mainstream Republican jurists – which could support the federal protection of blacks' physical safety and voting rights but not public accommodation rights – my goal is not to rescue Bradley. Rather, it is to elaborate the stakes that attach to the use of faulty assumptions about what follows from racism in the Reconstruction and post-Reconstruction eras.

Let me now turn to a more detailed introduction of state action doctrine. This doctrine holds that the Fourteenth and Fifteenth Amendments[8] protect

---

[8] U.S. Constitution, Fourteenth Amendment, Section 1: "No State shall make or enforce any law which shall abridge the privileges or immunities of citizens of the United States; nor shall any State deprive any person of life, liberty, or property, without due process of law; nor deny to any person within its jurisdiction the equal protection of the laws." U.S. Constit. Amend. XV, Section 1: "The right of citizens of the United States to vote shall not be denied or abridged by the United States or by any State on account of race, color, or previous condition of servitude."

individuals against the government; the "merely private" wrongs of individuals are beyond the reach of the amendments. "The provisions of the Fourteenth Amendment have reference to State action exclusively,"[9] the Court explained. "The first section of the Fourteenth Amendment...is prohibitory in its character and prohibitory upon the States.... That Amendment erects no shield against merely private conduct, however discriminatory or wrongful."[10] "Individual invasion of individual rights," the Court summed up, "is not the subject-matter of the Amendment."[11] While all of the Court's explications of state action doctrine cited the Fourteenth Amendment, jurists and scholars have assumed that the Court applied the doctrine to the Fifteenth Amendment as well, since prohibitory language is a feature of both amendments.

As scholars understand it, state action doctrine decisively closed the door on Reconstruction because it answered a critical question about the power of Congress to protect black rights. Did Congress have the power to punish private individuals, such as Klansmen, whom states failed to punish? The answer has been a firm and decisive *no*: the failure or refusal of state officials to punish Klansmen did not count as state action, and so there was no federal remedy for their rampant and brutal violence.

This answer was, of course, devastating. As Eric Foner explains in his standard history of Reconstruction, state action doctrine gave "a green light to acts of terror where local officials either could not or would not enforce the law."[12] Legal historians agree: a state's failure to protect its citizens "could not be construed as a reason for the federal government to intervene."[13] This view appears in the *Oxford Companion to the Supreme Court*, where Robert Cottrol explains that the *Civil Rights Cases* – the canonical expression of state action doctrine – "largely mandated the withdrawal of the federal government from civil rights enforcement."[14] In Derrick Bell's words, the promised protections for blacks were rendered "meaningless in virtually all situations."[15] Leonard Levy sums it up perhaps most bluntly. State action doctrine, he declares, "shaped the Constitution to the advantage of the Ku Klux Klan."[16]

---

[9] *Virginia v. Rives*, 100 U.S. 313, 318 (1880).

[10] 109 U.S. at 11.

[11] 109 U.S. at 11. The Court had earlier stated that the Fourteenth Amendment "adds nothing to the rights of one citizen as against another." (*United States v. Cruikshank*, 92 U.S. 542, 544).

[12] Foner, *Reconstruction*, 531.

[13] Williams, *The Great Klan Trials*, 141. See also Kaczorowski, *The Politics of Judicial Interpretation*, xiii (the decision "relegated Southern blacks...to the protection of local law and law enforcement agencies"); Michael Kent Curtis, *No State Shall Abridge* (1986), 179 ("Republican judges were abandoning a commitment to enforcement of...the rights of blacks"); Loren Miller, *The Petitioners* (1966), 158.

[14] Robert Cottrol, "Civil Rights Cases," in Kermit Hall, ed., *The Oxford Companion to the Supreme Court* (2005), 174.

[15] Derrick Bell, *Race, Racism, and American Law* (1992), 58.

[16] Leonard W. Levy, *United States v. Cruikshank*, in Leonard W. Levy and Kenneth L. Karst, eds., *Encyclopedia of the American Constitution* (2000), 733.

Abandoned Blacks?

And as scholars have emphasized, the Court did not have to exclude state failure to punish Klan violence from its concept of *state action*. The text of the Fourteenth Amendment does not demand this exclusion. The language of the equal protection clause can be read to include the unequal enforcement of the law, where violence against whites is punished but violence against blacks is not. Moreover, there is substantial evidence that Congress understood the equal protection clause in precisely this way.[17] In addition, then, to imposing a reading that is not demanded by the text, the Court appeared to be betraying the original understanding.

In need of a historical and political explanation for state action doctrine, scholars have seized upon long-standing wisdom about the Compromise of 1877. The Compromise is central to historical accounts of the disputed 1876 election and its aftermath. The conventional account tells of the removal from the South of the last Union troops, which had remained in South Carolina and Louisiana. Republican President Rutherford B. Hayes removed these troops in the wake of the 1876 election, and the troop withdrawal is part of the reason that scholars take 1877 to mark the end of Reconstruction.

But more broadly, the Compromise is seen as "a pivotal moment in national policy."[18] As told in the classic work of C. Vann Woodward,[19] a political deal was struck between Republicans and Democrats in which the nation's economic and rights enforcement policies hung in the balance. Republicans got control of the White House and the national economic program. In return, "the Democrats got a free hand to implement of policy of reaction in the South.... [W]ith scarcely a shrug, Republicans abandoned the freedpeople of the South to their fate, freeing themselves to pursue a policy of economic development unencumbered by moral baggage."[20] The Compromise is thus taken to mark the definitive abandonment of blacks by the Republican Party.[21]

---

[17] See, e.g., studies of the passage of the Ku Klux Klan Act of 1871 by Michael Zuckert (1986) and Frank Scaturro (2000).

[18] William M. Wiecek, *The Lost World of Classical Legal Thought* (1998), 77, citing C. Vann Woodward, *Origins of the New South, 1877–1913* (1951).

[19] C. Vann Woodward, *Reunion and Reaction: The Compromise of 1877 and the End of Reconstruction* (1951).

[20] Wiecek, *The Lost World of Classical Legal Thought*, 77. See also Howard Gillman, *Constitution Beseiged* (1993), 84 (the Compromise gave the Republicans "the presidency and southern support for their policy of rapid industrialization in exchange for southern internal improvements and an end to the federal commitment to the protection of black civil rights in the South"). Gillman cites C. Vann Woodward, *Reunion and Reaction: The Compromise of 1877 and the End of Reconstruction* (1951), and Eric Foner, *Politics and Ideology in the Age of the Civil War* (1980), 126.

[21] This view of the Republican Party also appears in the American political development literature. See, e.g., Richard Bensel, *Sectionalism and American Political Development, 1880–1980* (1984); Richard Bensel, *The Political Economy of American Industrialization, 1877–1900* (2000).

6 Rethinking the Judicial Settlement of Reconstruction

The standard view is that the Court followed and cemented the policy shift of the Republicans.[22] By remitting blacks to "home rule," state action doctrine was an instrument to consolidate the party's definitive political abandonment of blacks.

A portrait of President Grant's judicial appointees, dominant since the Progressive era, buttresses this explanation of state action doctrine. These biographical sketches present Grant's appointees as railroad attorneys who cared only for the interests of large corporations and were happy to facilitate the party's turn to big business.[23] One of Grant's appointees, Justice Joseph P. Bradley, is a key figure in the abandonment narrative. Material interest and political regime neatly converge in the portrait of Bradley: in addition to having a reputation as a railroad lawyer, Bradley served on the Electoral Commission that gave the disputed 1876 election to Hayes.

But it is Bradley's authorship of the *Civil Rights Cases*, a prominent postwar decision, that secures his role as a central player in that narrative. Making the link between the Compromise and the *Civil Rights Cases*, Woodward called the decision the Court's own "bit of reconciliation" between North and South, "which sacrificed blacks in order to cement reunion."[24]

The *Civil Rights Cases* invalidated the public accommodation provisions of the Civil Rights Act of 1875, which guaranteed to individuals "full and equal" enjoyment of inns, public conveyances, and places of public amusement, regardless of race.[25] Black plaintiffs, excluded from theaters and a ladies' railway car, argued that these exclusions were "badges of slavery" and a denial of the equal protection of the law. Justice Bradley rejected these arguments. "It would be running the slavery argument into the ground," he declared, "to make it apply to every act of discrimination which a person may see fit to make as to the guests he will entertain, or as to the people he will take into his coach or cab or car, or admit to his concert or theatre."[26] Such access was among "the social rights of men and races in the community"[27] and not among the essential rights of freedom. Bradley also cautioned against treating blacks as the "special favorite of the laws."[28] This comment, in conjunction with the

---

[22] See, e.g., Magrath, *Morrison R. Waite*, 132–4; Ruth Ann Whiteside, *Justice Joseph P. Bradley and the Reconstruction Amendments* (1981), 223, 284; Walter Murphy, James Fleming, and William Harris, *American Constitutional Interpretation* (1986), 744; John A. Scott, "Justice Bradley's Evolving Concept of the Fourteenth Amendment," 25 *Rutgers Law Review* 565–9 (1971).

[23] See Gustavus Myers (1912) and, more recently, James MacGregor Burns, *Packing the Court: The Rise of Judicial Power and the Coming Crisis of the Supreme Court* (2009).

[24] Woodward, *The Strange Career of Jim Crow* (1950), 71.

[25] 18 Stat. 336 (1875).

[26] 109 U.S. at 24–5.

[27] 109 U.S. at 22.

[28] "When a man has emerged from slavery, and by the aid of beneficent legislation has shaken off the inseparable concomitants of that state, there must be some stage in the progress of his elevation when he takes the rank of a mere citizen, and ceases to be the special favorite of the laws, and when his rights as a citizen, or as a man, are to be protected in the ordinary modes by which other men's rights are protected" (109 U.S. at 25).

Abandoned Blacks? 7

case outcome, its elaboration of state action doctrine, and Bradley's professional history, make the decision look like an archetypical example of judicial retrenchment.

The story of abandonment winds down by sliding quickly from the *Civil Rights Cases* to *Plessy v. Ferguson*, where the story ends.[29] The 1896 *Plessy* decision, of course, stands symbolically for America's embrace of racial apartheid. The *Civil Rights Cases* dealt with black exclusion from public accommodations, not with legal segregation, but the abandonment narrative presents the Jim Crow regime as a short step from the Court's invalidation of the public accommodation provisions. The narrative links the decisions, moreover, through the lone dissenting opinions of Justice Harlan. Justice Harlan wrote sharp dissents in both cases, arguing that exclusion and legal segregation were indeed badges of slavery and a deprivation of equal treatment. His arguments rang true to the twentieth-century civil rights generation, who cast him as the egalitarian-minded racial hero opposite the racist–railroad lawyer Justice Bradley.

So goes the conventional wisdom, accepted across multiple academic disciplines. For legal historians and law professors, the abandonment narrative is standard constitutional history. Conducting a rearguard action against Reconstruction, the Court ushered in the long nightmare of Jim Crow. For political scientists, the constitutional history provides a stock example of the "political" as opposed to "legal" nature of Court decision making. State action doctrine was an instrument for enacting the policy shift of the ruling regime.

Unraveling the threads of this tightly interwoven account entails attention to a multitude of interpretive errors. My own point of entry takes its bearings from a series of recent historical studies that look anew at political events between 1877 and the early 1890s. Read together, these works provide a new political history that challenges standard wisdom about the *political* (party) abandonment of blacks. On this reading, it was the failure of the Lodge Elections bill in 1890–91 that marked definitive political abandonment.

THE NEW POLITICAL HISTORY

In the past dozen years, an emerging literature has shown that the Republican Party maintained a genuine and principled effort to protect black voting rights between 1877 and the early 1890s, though this effort matched neither the vigor nor the effectiveness of the early 1870s.[30] Revealing conventional

---

[29] 163 U.S. 537 (1896). See, Friedman, "Reconstructing Reconstruction," 1232.

[30] Charles W. Calhoun, *Conceiving a New Republic: The Republican Party and the Southern Question, 1869–1900* (2006); Charles W. Calhoun, *Benjamin Harrison* (2005); Richard M. Valelly, *The Two Reconstructions: The Struggle for Black Enfranchisement* (2004); Richard M. Valelly, "Partisan Entrepreneurship and Policy Windows: George Frisbie Hoar and the 1890 Federal Elections Bill," in S. Skowronek and M. Glassman, eds., *Formative Acts: American Politics in the Making* (2007); Richard M. Valelly, "The Reed Rules and Republican Party Building: A New Look," *Studies in American Political Development* 23

8   *Rethinking the Judicial Settlement of Reconstruction*

wisdom about the Compromise of 1877 to be myth, this work identifies the disputed election of 1876 and its immediate aftermath as more complex and ambiguous than Woodward imagined.[31] These studies replace the standard image of 1877 (as a falling curtain) with a new story about political transition and uncertainty. Beginning with the economic Panic of 1873 and ending with the failure of the Lodge Elections bill in 1890–91, scholars trace a period of transition separating the height of Reconstruction from the establishment of Jim Crow.

This revisionist work has never been directly challenged, but neither has it been grappled with nor integrated into accounts of post–Civil War constitutional development. And notably, it aligns with older work that has been anomalous in past generations. These older political studies, for example, concern the southern disfranchisement movement,[32] the Republican Party's southern policy after 1877,[33] and national election patterns.[34] Studies of other social developments also emphasize a period of transition. Trends in black migration north and west[35] and trends in northern acceptance of Southern "Lost Cause" versions of Civil War history[36] indicate that the mid-1870s through the late 1880s were years of decline and increasing violence, but the nadir of postwar black subjugation was not reached until the early decades of the twentieth century.

These older works and revisionist studies of Republican Party development together comprise a critical mass of scholarship that forces a rethinking of the conventional wisdom. I bring these diverse studies together for the first time under the label the *new political history*, emphasizing its uncontested but nonintegrated reception in constitutional history.

The economic Panic of 1873, as we will see, triggered a steep and long-running economic depression, and it altered the politics of rights enforcement in ways that have been unattended by legal scholars. Complicating assessments of the Republican commitment to rights enforcement, the Panic and depression hurt white labor, made Republicans vulnerable at the polls, and made rights enforcement both expensive and politically risky. Bearing out the political axiom that voters turn their wrath on the party in power after an

---

(October 2009): 115–142; Xi Wang, *The Trial of Democracy: Black Suffrage and Northern Republicans, 1860–1910* (1997); Robert M. Goldman, *A Free Ballot and a Fair Count: The Department of Justice and the Enforcement of Voting Rights in the South, 1877–1893* (2001). See also Michael F. Holt, *By One Vote: The Disputed Presidential Election of 1876* (2008).

[31] Historians have raised questions about Woodward's thesis. See, e.g., Allan Peskin, "Was There a Compromise?" *Journal of American History* 50 (1973): 63–75; Keith Ian Polakoff, *The Politics of Inertia: The Election of 1876 and the End of Reconstruction* (1973). These critiques have not been transported into the legal literature on Reconstruction.

[32] J. Morgan Kousser, *The Shaping of Southern Politics* (1974).

[33] Stanley P. Hirshson, *Farewell to the Bloody Shirt* (1962).

[34] Joel H. Silbey, *The American Political Nation, 1838–1893* (1991).

[35] James R. Grossman, *Land of Hope: Chicago, Black Southerners, and the Great Migration* (1989). See also Klarman, "The Plessy Era," 309–312, 374.

[36] David Blight, *Race and Reunion: The Civil War in American Memory* (2001).

Abandoned Blacks? 9

economic shock, Democrats gained control of the House in the 1874 election. Now in charge of appropriation bills, Democrats could set low appropriations for rights enforcement, jamming government machinery, as inadequate as it already was.[37] Following the panic, too, was a burgeoning of new organizations such as the White Leagues, which were more threatening and menacing than predecessor Klans.[38]

It is not a coincidence, I suggest, that the year 1873 marked the high point in the number of federal voting rights prosecutions brought in the South under the Enforcement Acts of 1870 and 1871.[39] But after reaching a low in 1878, voting rights enforcement resurged with the 1880 election of Republican President James A. Garfield,[40] an election marked by the sectional antagonism between North and South of a decade earlier. This resurgence, which was sustained throughout the Garfield and Arthur administrations (1880–85), carries enormous significance for our understanding of the state action decisions and the role of the Court in politics. Though enforcement rates never approached that of the early 1870s, this resurgence provides the context not only for the *Civil Rights Cases*, but also for the little-studied voting rights decisions, *Ex parte Siebold* (1880) and *Ex parte Yarbrough* (1884). The strongly worded decisions sent election officials and Klansmen to jail and endorsed a broad theory of voting rights, the contours of which have been missed in the legal literature. These tools lay unused by the next administration, but that is unsurprising as a Democrat, Grover Cleveland, won the 1884 election.

The larger point is that the Panic of 1873 and election of 1874 marked the beginning of a transitional period during which national politics was uncertain, unstable, and fluctuating. Neither of the major political parties and no faction in the Republican Party had full control at the national level and national elections were decided by razor-thin margins. The Republican Party was no longer what it had been, but it was not yet what it would become. Still committed to building a southern wing for both pragmatic and principled reasons – but facing profound constraints – the party strategically experimented with a variety of means, including conciliation, internal improvements (regional infrastructure), and alliances with Independents. These strategies held out the possibility of circumventing the difficulties that plagued rights enforcement: massive resistance, inadequate administrative machinery, lack of funds, jury nullification, and fear of voters' reprisals. As even proponents of the abandonment thesis acknowledge, "federal election enforcement had never worked well."[41] But after each of these alternative

---

[37] Gillette, *Retreat from Reconstruction*, 293, 357.

[38] Gillette, *Retreat from Reconstruction*, 229.

[39] Wang, *Trial of Democracy*, 300–1 (Appendix 7).

[40] Leading scholars have stated that enforcement ended in 1873 if not 1876. Among legal historians, see Kaczorowski (1987), 67. Among political scientists, see Gillman (2002), 516. According to Gillette, Republicans had largely given up on the southern question by 1875; see Gillette, *Retreat from Reconstruction*, 317, 333, 371, 374.

[41] Gillette, *Retreat from Reconstruction*, 292.

strategies failed – Democrats responded with violence and fraud to each of them, making gains in national elections that pushed Republican power to the precipice – Republicans returned to rights enforcement. As the elections of 1880 (and 1888, which returned Republicans to power) show, northern distrust of Democratic political strength remained, and northern ire could still be sparked. Each of the party's renewals of rights enforcement brought some success, but the returns were diminishing.

Scholars are fond of quoting *The Nation*, which sounded the death knell for Reconstruction in 1877. "The Negro will disappear from the field of national politics," the newspaper declared. "Henceforth the nation, as a nation, will have nothing more to do with him."[42] But *The Nation* was wrong. Blacks did not completely disappear from the field of national politics in 1877, and the Republican Party did not change so thoroughly between the early 1870s and 1876.

And while black electoral inclusion of course suffered as violence and fraud increased, its collapse, as Richard Valelly notes, "was far from becoming a complete certainty."[43] J. Morgan Kousser observed years ago that "[t]he notion that disfranchisement was simultaneous with the textbook end of Reconstruction in 1877[44] and that the South became 'solid' immediately after that date are myths."[45] Indeed, the first wave of the disfranchisement movement, which turned the Deep South solidly Democratic and inaugurated the reign of lynch law, was launched in the wake of the Lodge bill defeat in 1890–91. It was only after this defeat that the political coalition that gave us Reconstruction was finally destroyed.

The new political history matters – quite a lot – when it comes to understanding state action doctrine and the judicial settlement of Reconstruction. For if the Republican Party did not definitively abandon blacks until the early 1890s, then state action doctrine *cannot be explained as a judicial consolidation of the party's definitive policy shift*. The relationship between case law and political context suddenly looks unclear. So how can state action doctrine be explained?

One tempting answer is that the judicial and political branches were working at cross-purposes: the Court tried to dismantle Reconstruction, while the Republican Party held to the project of building southern Republicanism.[46]

---

[42] *The Nation* 24 (April 5, 1877): 202. This line is often quoted in the Reconstruction literature as evidence that federal civil rights enforcement was over. Most recently, see Charles Lane, *The Day Freedom Died: The Colfax Massacre, the Supreme Court, and the Betrayal of Reconstruction* (2008), 249.

[43] Valelly, *The Two Reconstructions*, 121.

[44] This claim was advanced by Charles Warren, *The Supreme Court in US History* (1922), 604.

[45] Kousser, *Shaping of Southern Politics*, 11; Kousser, *Colorblind Injustice*, 20. See also Valelly, *The Two Reconstructions*, 121–48.

[46] The Republican Party was split into factions during this transitional time, but none of them sought to abandon the project of building southern Republicanism. The struggle was over the best strategy to achieve this end; support for rights enforcement, when the party

Abandoned Blacks?

The judicial branch, after all, has worked at cross-purposes with ruling political elites on multiple occasions.[47] We could thus retain the view of state action doctrine as a legal abandonment of blacks, but we would have to jettison the "regime" understanding of the state action cases, which conceives of the Court as enacting the policy shift of the ruling coalition.

The legal abandonment view does seem initially plausible. "No state" language is present in the texts of both the Fourteenth and Fifteenth Amendments. Private individuals were involved in major state action cases, and none were punished. Indeed, as cited above, the Court stated that "merely private" conduct was beyond the reach of the Fourteenth Amendment. The Court also never explicitly stated, for example, that "[d]enying includes inaction as well as action, and denying the equal protection of the laws includes the omission to protect, as well as the omission to pass laws for protection."[48] This statement issued from a circuit court in 1871, but never appeared in a Supreme Court opinion. The outcomes in Court decisions are also notable, as when the justices struck down several sections of Reconstruction legislation[49] and let Klansmen walk free.[50] It therefore seems plausible to conclude that the Court dismantled federal power to protect the voting rights and physical security of blacks. But the standard legal reading is not the best reading.

CONTEXTUALIZING THE STATE ACTION DECISIONS

Historians of political discourse have long warned that a typical danger in reading historical texts is that alien elements will be "dissolve[d] into a misleading familiarity."[51] My approach draws from this insight to explore a jurisprudence of rights and rights enforcement that included a concept I call "state neglect." Initially formulated in legislative debates and later revised by courts, the concept permitted the federal government to punish private individuals whose race-based violence and intimidation went unpunished by states. The jurisprudence I recover also included a rule I call the "Fifteenth Amendment exemption" (from state action doctrine), which permitted the federal government to directly prosecute private, race-based interferences in voting, regardless

---

circled back to this policy, would come from across the factions. See Calhoun, *Conceiving a New Republic.*

[47] The main example is the *Lochner* era, when the Court resisted regulatory policies. See also the discussion of "reconstructive presidents" and executive-Court conflict in Keith Whittington, *Political Foundations of Judicial Supremacy* (2007), 28–81.

[48] *United States v. Hall*, 26 F. Cas. 79, 81 (C. C. S. D. Ala. 1871). This language first appeared in a letter from Justice Bradley to Circuit Judge William B. Woods, author of the opinion.

[49] *United States v. Reese*, 92 U.S. 214 (1876) (invalidating Sections 3 and 4 of the Enforcement Act of 1870); *United States v. Harris*, 106 U.S. 629 (1883) (invalidating Section 5519 of the Ku Klux Klan Act of 1871); *Civil Rights Cases*, 109 U.S. 3 (1883) (invalidating Sections 1 and 2 of the Civil Rights Act of 1875).

[50] *United States v. Cruikshank*, 92 U.S. 542 (1876) (throwing out the federal indictments of three men involved in the bloodiest massacre of Reconstruction).

[51] Quentin Skinner, *Visions of Politics, Vol. 1, Regarding Method* (2002), 76.

of state behavior. The standard for defining "race-based," articulated by C. J. Waite in the under-studied 1877 decision *United States v. Butler*,[52] did not appear onerous, and the federal government successfully prosecuted several such cases under the Fifteenth Amendment.

Both the concept of state neglect and the Fifteenth Amendment exemption provided protection against race-based interference, but white Republicans gained a measure of protection from a federal elections jurisprudence authorized by Article 1, Section 4 of the Constitution, the "times, places, and manner" clause.[53] Under this constitutional provision, the federal government could prosecute private and official interference in national elections, whatever the motive.

The Fifteenth Amendment exemption and federal elections jurisprudence made up a two-pronged voting rights jurisprudence wholly unencumbered by state action doctrine. The jurisprudence provided the federal government with broad possibilities for rights enforcement, and the Grant, Hayes, Garfield, and Arthur administrations all turned to it.

I turn now to introduce these legal concepts in more detail.

THE CONCEPT OF STATE NEGLECT

When the Court issued its decision in the *Civil Rights Cases*, the Republican *Chicago Tribune* expressed support for the decision, condemning the public accommodation provisions. But consider how the *Tribune* explained state action doctrine:

> The negro citizen enjoys everywhere the same political and civil rights under the law which the white citizen enjoys. Any person who interferes with these rights is subject to the same penalties as if he had interfered with the rights of a white citizen. If there are State or local laws anywhere which decree otherwise, *or if there are State or local officers who refuse to extend to black citizens the protection to which they are entitled as citizens*, it is the function of the United States courts and authorities to defend their citizenship and their rights....[54]

This is clear evidence that the *Tribune* read the decision in the *Civil Rights Cases* as accepting a "state neglect" conception of state action. Indeed, the *Tribune* also perceived a concept of state neglect in Justice Bradley's circuit court opinion in *United States v. Cruikshank* (1874).[55] There, Bradley threw out federal charges against Klansmen who had perpetrated one of the worst massacres of Reconstruction. But Bradley also supplied the government with a blueprint for bringing future charges. That blueprint is of central importance, and Bradley presented it again in the *Civil Rights Cases*, housing it in the

---

[52] *United States v. Butler*, 25 F. Cas. 213 (C. C. D. S.C.) (1877).
[53] *Ex parte Siebold*, 100 U.S. 371 (1880).
[54] *Chicago Tribune*, October 17, 1883, p. 4 (emphasis added).
[55] *Chicago Tribune*, June 28, 1874, p. 16.

Abandoned Blacks? 13

phrase "under color of law...or custom," which appeared in the enforcement provision of the Civil Rights Act of 1866.

Accordingly, the federal government had the power to prosecute private individuals under the equal protection clause if (1) the individual interfered in *civil rights*, which Bradley defined using the rights listed in the Civil Rights Act of 1866 and federal statutes deriving from it,[56] (2) the interference was motivated by the race of the victim, and (3) state remedies for such interference were not available or in "full force." When state remedies were not available, such interference gained the "color of law...or custom" and was subject to federal prosecution. It is the unequal execution of the law that transforms the "merely private" wrong (which is under state jurisdiction, only) into a wrong having the "color of law...or custom" (which is amenable to federal punishment). It is thus incorrect to understand the rule as permitting the federal government to punish *private action*. The rule permits the federal government to punish *private individuals*, whose race-based wrongs gain the "color of law...or custom." The constitutional wrong is the states' unequal enforcement of the law.

This was not an irregular legal construction. The corpus of Waite Court Fourteenth Amendment cases, which includes the jury and removal cases,[57] supplied a larger framework for conceptualizing state neglect as a form of state action. Likewise, Bradley's concept of state neglect was not new. Earlier, Justice Miller noted in the *Slaughter-House Cases* (1873) – conventionally read as hostile to Reconstruction – that after the passage of the Thirteenth Amendment, southern states were not yet in their proper relationship to the Union. This was because the lives of blacks "were at the mercy of bad men, either because the laws for their protection were insufficient or were not enforced."[58] In 1874, Bradley wrote to longtime friend Republican Senator Frederick Frelinghuysen: "To have redress for injuries the same as all others have" is "to have and enjoy the equal protection of the law."[59]

Chapter 2 examines the emergence of the state neglect concept in the Reconstruction Congresses and the federal courts as a centrist Republican solution to the problem of unpunished Klan violence. The systematic failure to

---

[56] These were the rights "to make and enforce contracts, to sue, be parties, and give evidence, to inherit, purchase, lease, sell, hold, and convey real and personal property" and to "equal benefit of all laws." The 1874 Revision of Statutes reorganized Reconstruction legislation, and statutes deriving from the 1866 act included the right to vote. While Bradley would have likely put Bill of Rights freedoms in the civil rights category – and indeed, legal historians have adduced compelling evidence that the Civil Rights Act of 1866 applied the Bill of Rights to the states (Curtis 1986) – the *Slaughter-House Cases* and *Cruikshank* excluded most Bill of Rights freedoms from federal enforcement.

[57] I pay particular attention to *Virginia v. Rives*, 100 U.S. 313 (1880), and *Neal v. Delaware*, 103 U.S. 370 (1880).

[58] *Slaughter-House Cases*, 83 U.S. 36, 70 (1987). This comment is nowhere, to my knowledge, quoted in the Reconstruction legal literature.

[59] Joseph Bradley to Frederick Frelinghuysen, July 19, 1874, Bradley Papers, Box 18, New Jersey Historical Society.

punish violence against blacks and white Republicans was a breakdown of the rule of law: the legal and the extra-legal had become undifferentiated. Facing a new and unprecedented threat to republican government – a threat created by the same forces that had nearly wrecked the Union – Republican congressmen sought a remedy, crafting a vocabulary to define, deploy, and limit the concept of state neglect in consistent ways. Importantly, while Republican congressmen defined the concept to include unpunished race-based and politically based violence, Bradley (and the Court) filtered out political violence. In a partial rebuff to Congress, the Court indicated that only race-based interferences would be covered.

But what about the *Tribune*'s support for the outcome in the *Civil Rights Cases* and Bradley's famously hostile mention of blacks as the "special favorite" of the laws? This hostility has been interpreted as Bradley "ceremoniously wash[ing] his hands of the freemen's problems."[60] Such antagonism reaches less far juridically than generally imagined. Across multiple realms – legislative, journalistic, and judicial – Republicans used a distinction between *civil rights* and *social rights* to debate among themselves the status of public accommodation rights and, more broadly, the meaning of freedom.[61] Chapter 3 traces this intramural debate. While more radical Republicans identified public accommodation rights as *civil rights* and essential for freedom, centrist Republicans typically identified public accommodation rights as *social rights* (belonging to "men and races in the community," as Bradley said in the *Civil Rights Cases*) and nonessential for freedom. "For most Republicans," Calhoun notes, the "good society entailed [civil and] political equality but not social equality."[62] But centrist Republicans gave unquestioned support to the Civil Rights Act of 1866 and later to voting rights. When Justices Bradley and Harlan disputed the nature of public accommodation rights in 1883 (Bradley said *social*; Harlan said *civil*), they were continuing a debate that had begun a decade earlier, a debate in which Harlan's position had always been marginal. By recovering the intramural dispute, I show that a seemingly contradictory mix of positions combined in centrist Republican thought: support for the concept of state neglect – a notion rooted deeply in rule-of-law commitments – and derision for public accommodation rights. Twentieth-century interpreters have assumed that the racist beliefs that generated derision for public accommodation rights necessarily produced tepid or minimal support for voting rights and physical safety. But this was not the case.

---

[60] Williams, *The Great Klan Trials*, 143.
[61] These categories were part of a Reconstruction-era typology of rights. A number of scholars have outlined this typology in rough terms, though a genealogy has not yet been written, and the use of the typology in debates bearing on the state action cases has not been investigated. See, e.g., Mark Tushnet, "The Politics of Equality in Constitutional Law: The Equal Protection Clause, Dr. Du Bois, and Charles Hamilton Houston," *Journal of American History* 74 (1987): 884–90; Hyman and Wiecek, *Equal Justice Under Law*, 395–6; Herman Belz, *A New Birth of Freedom* (1976), xii–xiii.
[62] Calhoun, *Conceiving a New Republic*, 13.

Abandoned Blacks?

THE FIFTEENTH AMENDMENT EXEMPTION

A generation ago, Michael Les Benedict argued that Court cases from the 1870s and 1880s permitted the federal government to prosecute private, race-based interference in voting under the Fifteenth Amendment, regardless of state (in)action.[63] His argument never gained institutional traction, but a lack of evidence was not the reason. He wrote during a time when the abandonment narrative was cresting. He also never supplied a solution to a central puzzle: By what theory could the Court exempt the Fifteenth Amendment from state action rules? Since both amendments contain "no state" language, this looks unprincipled and therefore dubious.

I provide a solution by recovering a conventional nineteenth-century distinction between *secured* rights and *created* rights.[64] The former had their source in natural law and were *declared* or *recognized* by the Constitution. The latter had their source in the Constitution or federal statute; these were positive rights granted or *given* by the Constitution or federal law. A view of the Constitution as a hybrid document, protecting both kinds of rights, is a key feature of nineteenth-century jurisprudence, and it is a view expressed routinely in cases pertaining to federal enforcement of rights as late as 1892.[65] In order to follow the justices as they shuttle back and forth in their opinions between these two types of rights, we must recover the vocabulary they used to designate them – and, importantly, the manner in which Congress might protect them.

Chapter 4 looks closely at Bradley's 1874 circuit opinion in *Cruikshank*, where he worked with this rights distinction to develop a coordinated theory of all three Reconstruction amendments. This rights distinction was the basis for Bradley's exemption of the Fifteenth Amendment from state action doctrine, that is, his view that the federal government could directly punish private, race-based interference in voting, regardless of state behavior. Indeed, state action doctrine emerged in its fullest development – as including the concept of state neglect and as applying only to the Fourteenth Amendment – coincident with Bradley's attempt to build a coordinated theory of the Reconstruction amendments.

As we will see, C. J. Waite explicitly articulated the Fifteenth Amendment exemption in an 1877 circuit opinion, *United States v. Butler*, which grew out of a voting-related massacre that drew national attention during the run-up to the 1876 election. A unanimous Court accepted it in 1884.[66] As late as 1900

---

[63] Michael Les Benedict, "Preserving Federalism: Reconstruction and the Waite Court," *Supreme Court Review* (1978): 39–79. See also Ellen Katz. "Reinforcing Representation (2003).

[64] A variety of words were used to designate each type of right. *Secured* right were also referred to as *declared, recognized,* or *guaranteed. Created* rights were also referred to as *conferred, granted,* or *given.*

[65] *Logan v. United States,* 144 U.S. 263 (1892).

[66] *Ex parte Yarbrough,* 110 U.S. 651 (1884).

and 1901, federal district courts applied the Fifteenth Amendment exemption, quoting Bradley's 1874 opinion for authority.[67]

Justice Bradley's circuit opinion in *Cruikshank* is an unrecognized milestone in American constitutional development, and the opinion carried unusual authority. Bradley consulted with his brethren in the course of writing the opinion. He also gave it a wide circulation upon completion.[68] In fact, Bradley's circuit opinion was frequently cited instead of the Supreme Court opinion as the authoritative expression of the *Cruikshank* decision.[69] This is remarkable, and its significance has yet to be appreciated.

Bradley's opinion gestured, likewise, to Article 1, Section 4 as a source of federal power to punish private and official interference in national elections, whatever the motive. *Ex parte Siebold* (1880) and *Ex parte Yarbrough* (1884) represent the culmination of a developmental process that includes successful federal prosecutions under Article 1, Section 4 launched after the *Cruikshank* decision. While federal elections cases have not been regarded as part of the judicial settlement of Reconstruction, they should be.

In Chapters 4 and 5, I show how the Supreme Court used shorthand – an abbreviated form permitted by the authority and wide circulation of Justice Bradley's circuit opinion in *Cruikshank* – to signal the availability of this two-pronged voting rights jurisprudence in *Cruikshank* and its companion case, *United States v. Reese*. The two decisions are conventionally viewed as devastating to blacks, but these chapters reveal a more complex legacy. The decisions were issued during the run-up to the 1876 presidential election, where Republicans looked vulnerable and where a strong endorsement of black rights appeared harmful to party prospects. In this political context, Waite used shorthand, a significant feature of these opinions. This shorthand was comprehensible to political and legal actors at the time, and Republican administrations seized upon it. Attorney General Taft issued a circular to federal marshals several months before the 1876 election, instructing them on their duties and citing for authority Article 1, Section 4 and the Court's recent decisions. Taft also interpreted the clause to cover political assemblies, a key need for Republican Party building in the South.

---

[67] *United States v. Lackey*, 99 F. 952, 957–8, 967 (District Court, Kentucky, 1900); *United States v. Miller*, 107 F. 913, 915 (District Court, Indiana, 1901).

[68] When Bradley was hearing *Cruikshank* on circuit, he took two weeks to return to Washington and consult with his fellow justices. When Bradley finished his opinion, he circulated it among prominent cabinet members and senators, his brethren, federal district judges throughout the South, and the editors of three legal periodicals.

[69] See, e.g., *LeGrand v. United States*, 12 F. 577 (1882) (written by Justice William B. Woods); *United States v. Harris*, 106 U.S. 629 (1883); *Presser v. Illinois*, 116 U.S. 252 (1886); *United States v. Sanges*, 48 F. 78 (1891); *Green v. Elbert*, 63 F. 308 (1894); *Lackey v. United States*, 99 F. 952 (1900); *United States v. Morris*, 125 F. 322 (1903); *Karem v. United States*, 121 F. 250 (1903); *Ex parte Riggins*, 134 F. 404 (1904); *United States v. Powell*, 151 F. 648 (1907).

Abandoned Blacks?

By telling the story of Taft's circular and showing that the voting rights theories used successfully by the federal government in *Siebold* and *Yarbrough* trace back to Justice Bradley's 1874 opinion, I complicate the legacy of *Cruikshank*. Indeed, once the *Civil Rights Cases* – its rejection of the public accommodation provisions and its maintenance of the state neglect concept – is situated in the midst of these voting rights decisions and the upsurge in voting rights prosecutions, the Waite Court appears to be playing a far more complex role in politics than the abandonment narrative suggests. Seen in relation to the rights victories that occur after *Cruikshank* and *Reese*, Waite's shorthand becomes understandable as a form of cueing or signaling about the rights theories that remained available for building southern Republicanism, if Republican administrations wanted to use them. In short, it becomes apparrent that the Court was trying to help the Republican Party.

The judicial settlement of Reconstruction was a mixed and complicated affair. In my account, the points are always nuanced: state action doctrine did not inflict mortal blows against Reconstruction, but the Court also blocked certain avenues for rights enforcement and did not offer a strong and full defense of black rights; *Cruikshank* let Klansmen who perpetrated a coldblooded massacre walk free, but also signaled a voting rights jurisprudence in a shorthand that Republican administrations understood and later acted upon, though sporadically and with limited effectiveness; the *Civil Rights Cases* kept a concept of state neglect available, but also expressed hostility to public accommodation rights and defined them as nonessential for freedom; in general, the Court provided tools for the practical enforcement of black voting rights and physical safety, but the declining use of these tools in a transitioning political environment limited their impact.[70]

THE STAKES

My examination of interpretive errors in the abandonment narrative carries stakes that are most clear in legal history, for what emerges is a new understanding of the judicial settlement of Reconstruction and a new periodization of definitive judicial abandonment. But there are stakes, as well, that pertain

---

[70] For experts on this subject, the *Slaughter-House Cases* (1873) will loom large here. Conventionally understood as the Court's first blow against Reconstruction, this decision blocked the Republican effort to apply the Bill of Rights to the states. The decision has been reinterpreted to powerful effect by Michael Ross (2003) and Labbe and Lurie (2003), and I discuss *Slaughter-House* in Chapter 2. I show how the Court narrowed Reconstruction to race (not only in *Slaughter-House* but also in other cases), how political assembly rights could be protected within the limits set up by *Slaughter-House*, and how the concept of state neglect coupled with the Court's electoral federalism jurisprudence had the capacity to support a vision of biracial democracy that was mainstream or centrist by Republican party standards of the Reconstruction era. I argue that *Slaughter-House* did less damage to black rights than generally imagined.

to conceptions of Supreme Court decision making (in political science), lost legal resources (in constitutional law), and understandings of how distortions get built into scholarship in the first place (sociology). I turn now to briefly present these stakes.

A New Periodization of Definitive Abandonment

There is a story here about the definitive legal abandonment of blacks, but it is a reconfigured story with a new periodization. Scholars have gotten right the idea that the definitive judicial abandonment of blacks followed and consolidated the Republican Party's definitive political abandonment of them. But scholars have gotten wrong the timing and vehicles of definitive abandonment.

My new story of definitive judicial abandonment focuses on the Court under Melville W. Fuller (1888–1910), and Chapter 7 identifies the many ways this Court shut down options provided or left open by the Waite Court. This story begins, rather than ends, with *Plessy v. Ferguson*[71] and the Court's endorsement of legal segregation. The question of legal segregation was one Justice Bradley left hazy in the *Civil Rights Cases*. *Plessy* also posited an impermeable boundary between the "civil" and "social" spheres that blacks, by their nature, could not cross. The *Civil Rights Cases* was marked by ambiguity on this matter. *Plessy* substituted a social Darwinist vision for vagueness, and this was just the first step in shutting down options left open by the Waite Court.

The story of definitive abandonment continues with a series of voting rights cases that includes *James v. Bowman* (1903),[72] which silently ignored the Fifteenth Amendment exemption and instituted a state action requirement for its application. The story culminates with *Hodges v. United States* (1906),[73] a decision that gutted the crucial Civil Rights Act of 1866 and turned away from Justice Bradley's treatment of the Act of 1866 in the *Civil Rights Cases*. In *Hodges*, the concept of state neglect became obscured in fateful ways.

Waite-era legal concepts were given their last, residual expression during the Fuller era, and Chapter 7 examines these last expressions as well. In a few cases, Klansmen lost and temporarily went to jail. In *United States v. Lackey* (1900),[74] a lower federal court applied the Fifteenth Amendment exemption, citing Bradley's circuit opinion in *Cruikshank* for authority. In *Ex parte Riggins* (1904),[75] a federal court ruled that black prisoners in lawful

[71] 163 U.S. 537 (1896).
[72] 190 U.S. 127 (1903).
[73] 203 U.S. 1 (1906).
[74] 99 F. 952 (District Court, Kentucky, 1900).
[75] 134 F. 404 (C. C. N. D. Ala. 1904).

Abandoned Blacks?

state custody had the right to protection from white mobs under both the Thirteenth Amendment and the due process clause. *Riggins* also articulated the legal concept of state neglect. But these cases not only were reversed, they were lost to institutional memory.

At the time, a handful of judges and scholars took notice. One of them was Justice Harlan, who identified the Fuller Court's departure in the critical *Hodges* decision. It was there that Harlan identified a key matter of consensus between himself and Justice Bradley in the *Civil Rights Cases* on the matter of the Civil Rights Act of 1866. This consensus, significantly, pointed to the opposite result in *Hodges*. But it didn't matter. The Fuller Court shifted course.

One of my central points is that the most rights-friendly elements of the judicial settlement of Reconstruction did not stick. There was no "lock in," to use the phrase of political scientist Paul Pierson.[76] In examining the rise and decline of the concept of state neglect, the Fifteenth Amendment exemption, and federal elections jurisprudence, I build on and modify Richard Valelly's suggestion that party building and jurisprudence building are tandem and reinforcing processes.[77] The transitional years between 1874 and 1891 indeed witnessed a tandem process. But the political and legal events that made up this tandem process have not yet been properly specified. This process included a role for relatively autonomous "legal" elements. Dynamics of building and unwinding also occurred simultaneously: the building of rights-friendly jurisprudential elements continued to take place as late as 1884, even as the Reconstruction coalition weakened.[78] A weakened Republican coalition remained strong enough to support this jurisprudence building, but not strong enough to allow these rights-friendly elements to be fully institutionalized. This left them vulnerable, and a reconstituted party and Court quietly discarded them at the turn of the twentieth century. Thus, while party building and jurisprudence building were tandem processes, building and unwinding took place simultaneously during the transitional period of the 1870s and 1880s; distinctively legal dimensions, moreover, were a part of this tandem process.

Reconstruction lasted long enough to witness the creation and circulation of a new rights framework, but the rights-friendly elements of this jurisprudential framework were incompletely institutionalized, and they declined and collapsed. And when they disappeared, they left few conceptual or intellectual legacies. When Justice Hugo Black asserted in 1970, for example, that broad

---

[76] Paul Pierson, "Increasing Returns, Path Dependence, and the Study of Politics," *American Political Science Review* 94 (2000): 253–4.

[77] Valelly, *The Two Reconstructions.*

[78] The first modification of Valelly pertains to the specification of events during this transitional period. The second pertains to the role of relatively autonomous legal elements. The third pertains to the simultaneity of dynamics of building and unwinding.

Rethinking the Judicial Settlement of Reconstruction

federal powers over national elections existed under Article 1, Section 4, not a single member of the Court joined him.[79]

Methodology and the Conceptualization of Supreme Court Decision Making

My dismantling of the abandonment narrative speaks to methodological problems in dominant approaches to the study of Supreme Court decision making, more specifically, in attitudinalism and a strategic-rational choice variant.[80] Both descend from legal realism, which made it conventional to conceive of judicial behavior in almost wholly instrumental terms, and both apply a methodology that focuses on votes, judicial ideology (scaled along a liberal-conservative continuum),[81] and prediction.

When we look at votes and outcomes in the state action decisions, we find the dismissal of federal indictments against Klansmen (*Cruikshank*) and the invalidation of federal civil rights legislation (*United States v. Reese, United States v. Harris, Civil Rights Cases*). How would these votes/outcomes be scaled on a liberal-conservative continuum? The attitudinal and strategic models agree: as conservative.[82]

But these outcomes can be the result of either of two visions: a vision of congressional power that is centrist Republican in character, which would leave the door open to future indictments, or a vision of congressional power that is Democratic in character, which would shut the door to future indictments. Conventional methods, which look only at vote/outcome, provide no way of telling which vision might be operating.

Does the focus on prediction at least work here? No. There are many cases during the 1870s and 1880s that attitudinal and rational choice models would fail to predict. Justices vote in seemingly contradictory ways. Even if *Cruikshank* is understood as conservative, how do we explain *Butler*, which was written by the same justice (Waite)? Even if the *Civil Rights Cases* is understood as conservative, how do we explain *Siebold*, which was written by the same justice (Bradley)? The unanimous *Yarbrough* decision, moreover, was written by the author of the *Slaughter-House Cases* (Miller), a decision widely understood as the Court's first blow against Reonstruction. And judicial acceptance of the Fifteenth Amendment exemption survived in the District Courts until 1901. The repeated efforts of Democrats to repeal Reconstruction-era voting rights

---

[79] *Oregon v. Mitchell*, 400 U.S. 112 (1970). Black cited (at 121) the following cases: *Ex parte Siebold*, 100 U.S. 371 (1880); *Ex parte Yarbrough*, 110 U.S. 651 (1884); *Swafford v. Templeton*, 185 U.S. 487 (1902); *Wiley v. Sinkler*, 179 U.S. 58 (1900).

[80] According to attitudinalists, judges vote their policy preferences almost all of the time. See Segal and Spaeth (1993, 2002). According to the strategic-rational choice model, judges maximize their personal policy preferences amid constraints imposed by their colleagues and the other branches of government. See Epstein and Knight, *The Choices Justices Make* (1998).

[81] For a more detailed picture, see the Spaeth Supreme Court Databases as well as Benesh (2002).

[82] See, e.g., Epstein and Walker (2004), 656–61, 793.

Abandoned Blacks? 21

legislation, which finally succeeded in 1894, are yet additional anomalies. Why spend so much energy trying to repeal a dead statute?

My approach, which blends historical institutionalism[83] with an attention to discursive context,[84] reveals a cohesive pattern in these decisions. All of the various "inconsistencies" dissolve.

My approach also points to difficulties with the "regime" conception of Court decision making. Taking a cue from Robert Dahl,[85] political scientists have advanced the notion of an affiliated Court, where justices associated with a ruling coalition "can be expected to articulate the constitutional commitments of the dominant coalition."[86] As I have indicated, the Waite Court, nearly all of whose members were appointed by Presidents Lincoln and Grant,[87] acted at times to support the ruling Republican coalition (or at least the Grant-Garfield-Arthur wing of the party). The Court upheld the constitutionality of Reconstruction legislation against strong Democratic opposition.[88] The Court also supplied a voting rights theory that the party used successfully in *Siebold* (1880) and *Yarbrough* (1884). But the Court issued rebuffs as well. It invalidated pieces of Reconstruction legislation that passed with the strong support of the ruling coalition,[89] and it likewise threw out federal indictments brought by that regime.[90]

[83] See, e.g., Rogers M. Smith, "Political Jurisprudence, the 'New Institutionalism' and the Future of Public Law," 82 *American Political Science Review* 89–108; Mark Graber, *Transforming Free Speech* (1991); Howard Gillman, *The Constitution Beseiged* (1993); Ken I. Kersch, *Constructing Civil Liberties: Discontinuities in the Development of American Constitutional Law* (2005); Ronald Kahn and Ken Kersch, *The Supreme Court and American Political Development* (2006); Julie Novkov, *Racial Union* (2008).

[84] See, e.g., Skinner, *Visions of Politics, Vol. I, Regarding Method*: J. G. A. Pocock, *Virtue, Commerce, and History: Essays on Political Thought and History* (1985); Terence Ball and J. G. A. Pocock, *Conceptual Change and the Constitution* (1988).

[85] In his classic exposition of the "regime" model, Robert Dahl conceives of the Court as a national policy maker, emphasizing the significance of presidential appointments. "The main task of the Court," Dahl explains, "is to confer legitimacy on the fundamental policies of the successful coalition." Robert Dahl, "Decision-Making in a Democracy: The Supreme Court as a National Policy-Maker," *Journal of Public Law* 6 (1957): 294.

[86] Whittington, *Political Foundations of Judicial Supremacy*, 24.

[87] Lincoln appointed Noah Swayne (1862), Samuel F. Miller (1862), David Davis (1862), Stephen J. Field (Democrat, 1863), and Salmon P. Chase (Chief Justice, 1864). Grant appointed Joseph P. Bradley (1870), William Strong (1870), Ward Hunt (1872), and Morrison R. Waite (Chief Justice, 1874).

[88] *Cruikshank* treated Section 6 as constitutional, despite the urging of Democratic lawyers to rule it unconstitutional.

[89] *Reese* invalidated Sections 3 and 4 of the Enforcement Act of 1870. *Harris* invalidated Section 2 of the Ku Klux Klan Act of 1871. I am not including the Court's invalidation of the public accommodation provisions of the Civil Rights Act of 1875 because this measure did not have the strong and principled support of the party, a point I examine in Chapter 3. I leave to the side the matter of incorporation. While there is compelling evidence that the Fourteenth Amendment originally incorporated the Bill of Rights, and while the *Slaughter-House Cases* and *Cruikshank* blocked this (excepting various First Amendment rights), revisionist scholarship on *Slaughter-House* and findings reported here have convinced me that the jury is still out regarding the Court's purpose in rejecting incorporation.

[90] *United States v. Cruikshank* (1876).

What are we to make of this mixed behavior, which is high-profile and high-stakes? Is the Waite Court not really an affiliated Court? Or is the current conception of an affiliated Court unduly simple? I argue the latter. The Waite Court was affiliated with the ruling coalition, but the concept *affiliated* needs reworking to include the presence of specifically legal elements. Judge Hugh L. Bond, for example, was a Grant appointee and widely viewed as deeply committed to Reconstruction. Yet he threw out multiple counts of federal indictments in the South Carolina Klan trials, providing principled and consistent reasons. *Affiliated* cannot mean accepting any theory or any indictment the government puts forward. These rebuffs, moreover, had an impact on political development. While the regime model posits causal arrows that run in only one direction, from the ruling coalition to the Court, I reveal a more dynamic relationship in which legal actors and their coalition partners are mutually affecting.

Keith Whittington has recently examined the political logic of judicial authority, advancing a model of collapse where legal frameworks break down under the force of, in his phrase, a reconstructive president's challenge.[91] The legal framework developed by the Waite Court, however, collapsed not under the force of a reconstructive president but under the pressure of political reaction and retrenchment. The political logic of judicial authority, therefore, must also be reworked to capture this major episode in constitutional development.

RESOURCES IN CONSTITUTIONAL ARGUMENTATION

To put the Fourteenth Amendment into operation, a distinction between state and private action must be made. This opposition is built into Section 1, which contains the "no state" prohibition. But while this opposition is necessary to get the amendment off the ground, the text does not say how to draw the line and no line exists in nature. We know from law and society scholars that law touches individual lives in the most subtle of ways.[92] Moreover, we can conceptually obliterate the state/private distinction by pointing to the ubiquity of state regulations and the judicial enforcement of contracts.[93]

My interest lies not in troubling over the best place to draw the line. Rather, my point is that standard knowledge about the state action cases has played a key role in maintaining the operational utility of a rigid boundary around "private action." This boundary aided opponents of the civil rights movement. Even liberal legal actors and courts adhered to this line, which attests to its felt necessity.

Even "wins" for civil rights were more narrow than they might have been. As the federal government renewed its commitment to black rights in the 1940s,

---

[91] See Whittington, *Political Foundations of Judicial Supremacy*, 28–81.
[92] See Patricia Ewick and Susan S. Silbey, *The Common Place of Law* (1998).
[93] In *Shelley v. Kraemer*, 334 U.S. 1 (1948), the Court held that judicial enforcement of restrictive covenants (private contracts restricting housing sales to, typically, blacks, Jews, or Asians) counted as state action under the Fourteenth Amendment. The Court immediately backed away from *Shelley*.

Abandoned Blacks?

Justice Department lawyers perceived the state action cases as an obstacle. Working in the newly established Civil Rights Section, the lawyers believed that state action doctrine blocked the federal punishment of Klansmen who remained unpunished by state officials. They acted against their policy preferences, declining to bring cases of this nature.[94] Amassing the legal authority to punish sheriffs who murdered defenseless blacks in their custody also proved difficult. All of this could have been otherwise.

Civil rights victories achieved through analytical reasoning were also unnecessarily restricted. During the 1960s, lower federal courts extended the meaning of state action to include police failures to protect civil rights protesters from violent retaliation.[95] Holding officers and/or city governments civilly liable for these failures, courts made the protesters' exercise of constitutional rights under the First Amendment and the Commerce Clause the trigger for federal protection.[96] Thus, marchers from Selma to Montgomery had a right to police protection when exercising their rights of speech and assembly.[97] The failure to provide protection was a violation of Section 1983,[98] a statute that derives from the Civil Rights Act of 1866. But even as the statute contained the "color of law" language that Justice Bradley used to house the state neglect concept, federal judges in the 1960s and 1970s used analytical reasoning, not case precedent, to define these police failures as a form of state action. To be sure, the use of analytic reason is a commonplace practice. Its use in twentieth-century civil rights cases, I suggest, was made necessary by standard knowledge about state action precedent. The Supreme Court did not put its imprimatur on the 1960s and 1970s decisions, a perhaps telling indicator of the power of juridical "common sense." Indeed, a historically attuned reading of Bradley's "color of law" construction could supply warrants for police protection, even when First Amendment or Commerce Clause rights were not exercised – thus providing broader protections than those supplied in the 1960s/70s cases – but standard knowledge about the *Civil Rights Cases* made Bradley's construction inaccessible.

Today, the federalism jurisprudence of the Supreme Court has returned the *Civil Rights Cases* to legal prominence.[99] Relying on the *Civil Rights Cases* as a central source of authority, the Rehnquist Court invalidated a variety of

---

[94] See Robert K. Carr, *Federal Protection of Civil Rights: Quest for a Sword* (1947). I offer a more detailed discussion in Chapter 8.

[95] See Don Herzog, "The Kerr Principle, State Action, and Legal Rights," 105 *Michigan Law Review* 1 (2006).

[96] *United States v. U.S. Klans, Knights of Ku Klux Klan et al.*, 194 F. Supp. 897, 901–2 (1961); *Cottonreader v. Johnson*, 252 F. Supp. 492 (M. D. Ala. 1966); *Wolin v. Port of New York Authority*, 392 F. 2d 83 (1968); *Smith v. Ross*, 482 F. 2d 33, 37 (6th Cir. 1973); *Glasson v. City of Louisville*, 518 F. 2d 899 (1975); *Dunlap v. City of Chicago*, 435 F. Supp. 1295 (1977).

[97] *Williams v. Wallace*, 240 F. Supp. 100 (1965).

[98] 42 U.S.C. 1983. According to the statute, persons who "under color of law...or custom" deprived individuals of rights secured by the Constitution were liable for civil damages.

[99] The legal stakes that attached to interpretation of the state action cases were lowered in 1964 when the Court approved the Civil Rights Act of 1964, i.e., approved Congress's power to protect civil rights, under the Commerce Clause.

civil rights laws as beyond Congress's power under Section 5 of the Fourteenth Amendment. One of these laws was Section 13981 of the Violence Against Women Act, which imposed penalties against private individuals who committed gender-based violence. The Court invalidated this law in *United States v. Morrison* (2000),[100] ruling that Congress lacked the power to pass Section 13981 under Section 5. According to Chief Justice William Rehnquist, the statute ran afoul of state action doctrine. This outcome, Rehnquist stated, was "controlled by"[101] the *Civil Rights Cases*, the canonical expression of state action doctrine, and *United States v. Harris*,[102] a precursor decision.

The outcome, however, did not follow inevitably from those decisions, a point emphasized by Justice Breyer in his dissenting opinion. The recovery of the state neglect concept can provide guidance for rewriting the statute. While there was extensive testimony that states were failing to provide adequate remedies for violence against women, the statute was not predicated on this failure. But it is also true that the recovery of the state neglect concept would not demand the validity of Section 13981, even if it were rewritten. The concept would have to be extended to include protected categories other than race, such as gender (and what about disability?). Threshold questions, moreover, remain most pressing. How would the practice of state neglect be established? District by district? State by state? How would an insufficient remedy be defined? It is unclear how these threshold questions could be handled, and history cannot provide an answer. There were ambiguities in the state neglect concept from the beginning, and the concept was undertheorized.

The point to stress is that the concept of state neglect is not a silver bullet; no originalist assumptions reside here. New avenues of historical argumentation are opened up by the recovery of the state neglect concept – and this is no small thing – but its recovery determines no legal results today.

The state/private distinction has been and will always remain a judicial artifice. The point here is that standard knowledge about the state action cases has imposed powerful felt restrictions on where (even liberal) legal actors draw that line. A more historically attuned reading of the state action cases would provide resources for drawing that line in a different place. Perhaps even more far-reaching: space for analytic reason – without recourse to history – is opened up by an account of how distorted knowledge about the state action cases came to win institutionally.

THE RISE OF DISTORTED KNOWLEDGE

Retracing the interpretive errors in the abandonment narrative raises a matter of interest to sociologists: If standard knowledge about the state action cases

---

[100] *United States v. Morrison*, 529 U.S. 598 (2000). The case involved the gang rape of a student at Virginia Tech.
[101] 529 U.S. at 602.
[102] 106 U.S. 629 (1883).

Abandoned Blacks? 25

does not flow inevitably from the text of the opinions – if it is not necessary – how was it established in the first place? How did we get here?

The story about the rise of these distortions is, at bottom, a story about a loss of context. Much of the context of the state action cases has been stripped away or has fallen away, such that later interpreters have had difficulty reading the juridical language of state action. These later interpreters, moreover, span the ideological spectrum and are located across multiple institutional sites, including Congress, the Justice Department, law schools, and history departments.

In Chapter 8, I examine episodes in the twentieth-century reception of Waite-era cases. I offer a suggestive but not conclusive exploration of legal and political practices that stripped the contexts from these cases, the recovery of which my book supplies. My anatomizing of two episodes in the reception history could point either to the highly instrumental use of history in law or to the possibilities for argumentation opened up by my historical corrective. But because legal practice has always involved the mobilization of precedent, one can be a so-called "realist" or not and still have to grapple with the opportunities and constraints generated by each jurisprudence, lost or otherwise.

The developments I examine include the rise of the scientific or "case" method of legal education, a highly decontextual reading practice that was pioneered at Harvard Law School in 1870 but not institutionally established until the second decade of the twentieth century. The 1891 creation of the U.S. Circuit Courts of Appeals matters here, too, for the establishment of permanent circuit seats marked the end of Supreme Court justices "riding circuit" and diminished the significance of circuit opinions. Bradley's all-important circuit decision of 1874 could fade more easily in the new context where circuit opinions were viewed as a place for disagreements to pool to be resolved by the Court.

More important is the decline and collapse of nineteenth-century legal frameworks during the Progressive and New Deal years. *Lochner v. New York* (1905) figures here in an important way. This decision invalidated a maximum-hour law passed by the New York legislature, and it came under extensive criticism at the time. An obstacle to Progressive-era efforts to respond to the rapid industrialization of the late nineteenth century, *Lochner* used a natural law concept (the right to contract) to invalidate the maximum-hour law. As criticism of *Lochner* mounted, natural law became delegitimated. Scholars began to think about rights and rights protections in reformulated ways, and a new rights framework emerged in legal scholarship. When *Lochner*-era jurisprudence finally collapsed under the weight of the Depression, the New Deal Court enshrined this new language of rights. While the decline and collapse of *Lochner* has drawn enormous scholarly energy, I reveal an unnoticed dimension: erosion in the capacity to read the old legal language of state action.

During the Progressive and New Deal eras, too, materialist histories of post–Civil War America were written which cast the postwar Court as the tool of big business. These histories made no distinction between Republican justices in the 1870s and 1880s, who were part of the Civil War generation, and those in the 1890s, who were not. The histories cast Grant's judicial appointees as railroad lawyers, though as C. Peter Magrath (Waite's biographer) has pointed out, working for the railroads in the 1850s and 1860s was quite a different matter than working for them in the 1880s. Lincoln, after all, worked for the railroads. In general, these materialist histories projected the political and economic developments of the 1890s backward onto the postwar years.

C. Vann Woodward's account of the Compromise of 1877 was part of a wave of revisionist scholarship that swept through history departments in the 1950s. Scholarship threw off overtly racist Dunning School histories of Reconstruction that were written during the Progressive era and that cast the Klan as heroes of the period. Scholarship also revised Beardian materialist histories of Reconstruction, which portrayed Reconstruction-era Republicans as voices of the corporate class. Recovering the antislavery origins of the Reconstruction Amendments, this scholarship re-presented Republicans of the era as genuine and principled supporters of black rights. Understanding the liberalizing and corrective role played by this 1950s scholarship helps us to understand its durability. But in constructing a myth about the Compromise of 1877 and by leaving in place Progressive-era portraits of Republican justices on the Supreme Court, this scholarship (i.e., its success) cemented older distortions and left a legacy of new ones.

My chapters are organized in a loosely chronological way. Chapter 2 explores the unfolding of the concept of state neglect as a centrist Republican remedy for the problem of unpunished Klan violence. Chapter 3 examines the civil/social distinction as it was used by centrist and radical Republicans to debate Charles Sumner's Supplementary Civil Rights bill. Chapter 4 focuses intensively on the circuit and Supreme Court decisions in *Cruikshank*, identifying the decision as the birthplace of state action doctrine in its fullest development. Chapter 5 begins the story of the reception of *Cruikshank*, telling the story of Attorney General Taft's circular to federal marshals and the post-1876 enforcement of voting rights by the Justice Department. Chapter 5 also tells an untold story about *United States v. Harris*, a case in the state action pantheon. There is a drama to this case that contains ineptitude, mystery, and one big surprise: the victims in the episode that gave rise to the case turn out to be white. Chapter 6 arrives at the *Civil Rights Cases* and examines Justice Bradley's discussion of "under color of law...or custom," which housed the concept of state neglect. Chapter 7 provides a new periodization of definitive abandonment and explores the residual expressions of Waite-era concepts during the Fuller era. Chapter 8, finally, examines episodes in the twentieth-century reception of the state action cases. The Conclusion returns briefly to the contemporary constitutional stakes that attach to this analysis.

Concerning the sources gathered and presented here, I have included all district, circuit, and Supreme Court cases interpreting the Reconstruction

Abandoned Blacks? 27

Amendments from 1865 to 1910. Charges to grand juries are also covered. I include, as well, congressional debate over the Civil Rights Act of 1866, the Enforcement Act of 1870, the Ku Klux Klan Act of 1871, and the Civil Rights Act of 1875. Finally, to access newspaper coverage and political commentary, I have used the ProQuest Historical Newspapers database,[103] the American Periodicals Series Online (APS Online),[104] and the African-American Nineteenth Century Newspapers Collection.[105]

---

[103] The ProQuest Historical Newspapers Database includes the following newspapers from the Reconstruction and post-Reconstruction eras: the *Chicago Daily Tribune* (1849–1946), the *New York Times* (1851–2005), the *Washington Post* (1877–1992), and the *Los Angeles Times* (1881–1986),.

[104] APS Online chronicles developments in the United States across 150 years, including the Civil War and Reconstruction eras. Included are 118 periodicals published during the Civil War/Reconstruction, early professional journals, popular titles such as *Scribner's*, newspapers (e.g., *The Independent* and *Harper's Weekly*), and several legal periodicals (e.g., the *Selected Digest of State Reports*).

[105] The African-American Nineteenth Century Newspapers collection includes only one black newspaper from the Reconstruction and post-Reconstruction eras, the *Christian Recorder* (1861–1902). This four-page weekly offered both secular and religious material.

2

The Emergence of the Concept of State Neglect, 1867–1873

After the passage of the Civil Rights Act of 1866, one thing was perfectly clear: Democrats needed another plan to reestablish control over the freedmen. After the passage of the Thirteenth Amendment in 1865, Democrats had responded by passing the notorious Black Codes, reinstituting black subordination through formal rules that differentiated between blacks and whites. Reacting with outrage, Republicans passed the Civil Rights Act of 1866, which rendered the Codes inoperative. A year later, Democrats were also forced to contend with the passage of the Reconstruction Act of 1867, which granted suffrage to black men in the South and put Republicans in charge of southern legislatures. Thrown out of state capitols and now facing a black electorate, ex-Confederates could not rely on the passage of restrictive laws and the strength of the Democratic vote to resist Reconstruction. But Democrats still retained control of local law enforcement. And they could refuse to enforce the law when the Klan terrorized blacks or white Republicans. While sheriffs had ignored violence against blacks since the earliest days of Reconstruction, a pattern materialized and spread in the wake of the acts of 1866 and 1867: the local and systematic refusal to punish Klan violence and intimidation aimed at blacks, white Republicans, and Freedmen's Bureau agents. This was the practice of state neglect.

The legal concept of state neglect arose from these practices and from the dilemma they posed for republican government. My exploration of state (in)action and of centrist Republicans' response to it calls to mind what Quentin Skinner characterizes as a "Collingwoodian approach"[1] to the history of political thought, in which political actors seek out new political concepts

---

[1] Quentin Skinner, "Meaning and Understanding in the History of Ideas," J. Tully, ed., *Meaning and Context: Quentin Skinner and His Critics* (1988), 64–6; and Skinner, "The Rise of, Challenge to, and Prospects for a Collingwoodian Approach to the History of Political Thought," in D. Castiglione and I. Hampsher-Monk, eds., *The History of Political Thought in National Context* (2001), 176–7. See also R. G. Collingwood, *An Autobiography* (1939), 29–43.

The Emergence of the Concept of State Neglect, 1867–1873

and languages as a response to new and apparently intractable problems. The political and legal history of state neglect that I retrace in this chapter reflects such a "question-and-answer" dynamic:[2] was the systematic nonenforcement of laws against perpetrators of violence against blacks and white Republicans a violaton of rights, and if so, what remedies should be provided?

The systematic nonenforcement of law reflected Democrats' adaptation of resistance to Reconstruction. Republicans perceived local failures or refusals as a violation of republicanism, but there was no ready vocabulary to identify or discuss it. Centrist Republicans responded by crafting a vocabulary of state neglect. In other words, they used the vocabulary to "think" the new problem – to define it and demarcate it from other problems as well as to define a remedy. For Republicans, state neglect was a rights denial and a form of *state action* within the meaning of the Fourteenth Amendment.

In developing a new vocabulary, Republicans drew on background principles. I call these the principles of state neglect. Such principles formed the philosophical framework out of which the new problem was identified and a remedy conceived. These principles were drawn from the antebellum era, and they pertained to the role of government, the harms of special burdens to citizenship, and the reciprocal duties of government protection and citizen allegiance. Included was the Jacksonian principle that public power must be used in a disinterested way. As Thomas Cooley put it, "[t]he State can have no favorites."[3] What was new was the recognition of blacks as proper subjects of such principles as members of the national collective.

Significantly, the concept of state neglect emerged in the course of an intramural Republican dispute. Centrist and more radical Republicans disagreed over how to respond to the new political problem of nonenforcement. While more radical Republicans argued that the federal government could punish Klansmen without regard to state action/neglect, centrists insisted that state failure to punish Klan violence was a necessary condition or predicate for federal intervention. So concerns about federalism were central in the intramural dispute.

As centrists explained it, the duty to equally administer the law created correlative rights, so that dereliction of the duty counted as a rights denial. Accordingly, if a state punished violence against whites and Democrats but failed to punish violence against blacks or Republicans, the failure was a denial of the equal protection of the law. Failure to punish racial or political violence[4] permitted the federal government to provide a corrective. The

---

[2] The phrase belongs to Douglas C. Dow. See Dow, "Decline as a Form of Conceptual Change: Some Considerations on the Loss of the Legal Person," *Contributions to the History of Concepts* 4 (2008): 11.

[3] *People v. Salem*, 20 Mich. 452, 486 (1870). Michigan Supreme Court Justice Thomas Cooley's concern here was the use of state power to benefit already privileged individuals and corporations (Jones 1967: 765).

[4] Congressmen did not utilize a distinction between "political" and "racial" violence because they aimed to reach unpunished violence against blacks and white Republicans. The federal

government could therefore prosecute individuals if three conditions were met: (1) there was interference in *civil rights* or *political rights*, all-important categories here; (2) interference was on account of race or politics; and (3) the state systematically failed to punish such interference.

Federal courts accepted most but not all of this centrist solution. Congressmen identified both racial and political violence as part of the practice/problem of state neglect, but courts filtered out political violence, that is, violence motivated by the politics/political beliefs of the victim. Only interference "on account of race, color or previous condition of servitude" (hereinafter "race &c.") would be covered. What emerged in the federal courts, then, was a more limited legal concept of state neglect. These federal circuit decisions constitute the beginnings of a legal doctrine of state action, with state neglect treated as a form of state action.

The legal concept of state neglect, in sum, refers to a set of commonly assumed principles held by Republicans in Congress and in the federal courts, which, when combined in light of the problem of systemic nonenforcement of law, produced an overlapping consensus about the power of the federal government to remedy unpunished interference on account of race &c. in *civil rights* and *political rights*.

The creators of the state neglect concept never addressed threshold questions. In other words, they never defined the point at which state neglect was "established," thereby permitting federal intervention. How many instances of failure or refusal were enough to permit intervention? And how much time had to elapse after a crime occurred before it could be said that the state failed to provide a remedy? Thirty days? Sixty days? A Collingwoodian approach explains why these important threshold questions were never addressed: the problem at hand concerned the broad and systematic refusal to remedy Klan violence. The violence was massive, as was the scale of nonenforcement. The nature of the problem, therefore, did not require careful attention to thresholds. Moreover, while the concept circulated long enough to be reiterated in the *Civil Rights Cases*, the weakening of the Reconstruction coalition meant that the federal government was not enough of what political scientist Charles Epp calls a repeat player to generate the judicial demarcation of thresholds.

As a *legal* concept, state neglect lacked autonomy, beginning its "life" as a political concept. Federalism concerns were evident at multiple points in its development. I have already underscored how they surfaced in centrist congressmen's insistence on a state action/neglect predicate for the federal enforcement

---

courts introduced the distinction, ruling that the federal government could reach racial violence, that is, violence "on account of" the race of the victim; political violence remained under exclusive state jurisdiction. Such a distinction of course was difficult to maintain as violence against blacks was both racial and political. The courts viewed violence against white Republicans as politically motivated, though such violence could be conceived as racial: as motivated by "inappropriate" race behavior.

The Emergence of the Concept of State Neglect, 1867–1873

of rights. Such concerns are also critical to understanding how the courts filtered the state neglect concept. Historians have long noted Republicans' attachment to federalism.[5] Less remarked on are the diverse positions held by Republicans: in insisting on plenary federal enforcement, radicals were willing to jettison federalism concerns altogether, while centrist Republicans' notion of state neglect pushed the notion of state action to its outer limits. There was also a diversity of positions among centrist Republicans: while centrist congressmen and justices shared the insistence on a state action/neglect predicate, the two groups differed on whether the denial of equal protection pertained to both unpunished political and racial violence (congressmen) or only to racial violence (justices).

Two final prefatory notes: The first pertains to my use of the term "centrist" rather than moderate Republican.[6] While the label *moderate Republican* was used at the time (and is the term of choice among historians), *centrist* is descriptively accurate and more neutral. The same centrists who gave strong and principled support to the act of 1866 and black voting rights never gave strong and principled support to what they called *social rights*, often scorning public accommodation rights and rejecting "race mixing." This is an effort to contextualize the thought of centrist Republican legal actors. The term *moderate* carries positive connotations, and so I avoid it.

Second, I have been referring to the concept and the practice of state neglect. The term itself is my own, as a singular term never emerged from Congress or the federal courts. The reconstruction of political and legal discourse shows that political and legal actors could communicate clearly and consistently about the state neglect concept, without the need for a unique term. The practice of state neglect was labeled unequal protection, a rights denial, and state action. But while the relevant historical actors had a perfectly sufficient vocabulary to debate the new problem, contemporary interpreters have had a harder time: the lack of a single term for state neglect helps to explain why the concept has been lost to twentieth-century observers.

FIGHTING THE "KU-KLUX"

The savagery and brutality of the Klan horrified U.S. Attorney General Amos T. Akerman. Himself a southerner, Akerman became convinced that no community, "nominally civilized, has been so fundamentally under the domination of systematic and organized depravity."[7] Klan violence was often election-related though Klansmen also brutalized blacks who made good wages in railroad construction, driving them back to farming, where earnings were significantly lower.[8]

---

[5] See, e.g., Foner, *Reconstruction*, 243.
[6] Thanks to Les Benedict for suggesting the centrist label.
[7] Williams, *The Great Klan Trials*, 44. See generally Allen W. Trelease, *White Terror* (1971).
[8] Williams, *The Great Klan Trials*, 30.

The failure of state authorities to protect blacks and white Republicans was widespread.[9] Eyewitness accounts "confirmed again and again the enormity of the problem and the complete failure of the state governments to restore order."[10] In her study of the South Carolina Klan trials, for example, Lou Faulkner Williams explains, "It was almost impossible to find whites loyal to the state government. Questioned whether he would obey the governor as commander in chief in the event of an armed collision resulting from an attempt to enforce the laws, the captain of a white company responded, 'In case of difficulty, I will go with my race.'"[11] Williams reports a total breakdown of the criminal justice system in South Carolina:

> Because the majority of white South Carolinians supported the goals of the Ku Klux Klan, the state's criminal justice system was inadequate to stop the violence. Blacks who dared to report the crimes perpetrated against them often found that the local trial justices turned a deaf ear to their complaints. Some of these magistrates, appointed by the governor, were white Democrats personally involved in Klan activities. Others acquiesced silently to the goals of the Klan, refusing to use their authority to investigate outrages or issue warrants.[12]

Attorney General Akerman was convinced that "the local law is utterly unable to cope with the criminals."

Attempts to conduct judicial proceedings were also met with violence. "Republican trial justices, whether black or white, were threatened, intimidated, and sometimes even murdered when they attempted to uphold the rights of freemen." When Klan terror was at its peak, local magistrates "did not dare to take up the cases and proceed with them."[13] Of course, when blacks were accused of crimes the behavior of local law enforcement was very different. "Retribution against black criminals was apt to be swift and terrible, whether it was informal and extralegal or within the state's judicial system."[14] Major Lewis Merrill documented 11 murders and more than 600 whippings in York County, South Carolina, yet the civil authorities in the county were

[9] See, e.g., Hyman and Wiecek, *Equal Justice Under Law*, 416, 419, 422, 425. See also Robert J. Kaczorowski, "To Begin the Nation Anew: Congress, Citizenship, and Civil Rights after the Civil War," 92 *American Historical Review* (1987): 45–68. ("Local officials in the South sanctioned and legitimized the defiant behavior of individuals and the racial and political customs of communities dominated by whites. In their constitutions and laws, Southern states refused to recognize that blacks were citizens possessing the natural rights of free people. State officers commonly failed or refused to protect the personal safety and property of blacks. They similarly refused to extend this protection to whites who were political allies or federal agents of blacks. When Southern blacks and politically unpopular whites were the victims of crimes, they could not get sheriffs to arrest, courts to try, or juries to convict the perpetrators.")

[10] Williams, *The Great Klan Trials*, 42.

[11] Ibid. at 23.

[12] Ibid. at 37.

[13] Ibid.

[14] Ibid. at 38.

The Emergence of the Concept of State Neglect, 1867–1873

unwilling to address the problem. Local civil officials all over the upcountry were "either in complicity with the Ku-Klux conspiracy, or intimidated by it." Major Merrill labeled grand jury proceedings "so broad a farce that it was very distasteful to be forced in contact with it."[15]

In Southern practice, the legal and extra-legal had become undifferentiated. This was a problem pertaining to the rule of law and republican government, and a new concept was needed to identify and discuss it. The crafting of the state neglect concept by Republicans – most of whom held beliefs in white superiority and rejected "social equality" – can be understood with reference to rule-of-law and republican commitments.

The *Chicago Tribune* regularly reported incidents of Klan violence, citing the failure to punish the "Kentucky Ku Klux"[16] and observing that the state government was "failing to protect."[17] The paper reported on whippings of U.S. officers by the Klan, as well as a northerner's change of mind regarding the level of Klan violence upon visiting the South.[18] As late as 1883, the *Chicago Tribune* was reporting on such murders, pointing to the failure of local authorities to punish such violence. Responding to the Montgomery (Alabama) *Advertiser*, which asserted that white men had been punished for crimes against blacks, the *Tribune* challenged the *Advertiser* to "name one white man who has been hanged or lynched or in any way troubled in the last two years for murdering a negro? If not during the last two years, is there any reason to presume that one has suffered during the last eighteen years?"[19] (The *New York Times*, the leading Republican newspaper in the East, did not generally report on this violence. Democratic papers like the *Washington Post* ignored it completely.)

In 1870, Gen. Benjamin F. Butler approached President Ulysses S. Grant to seek his support for powerful new anti-Klan legislation. The Enforcement Act of 1870 was already on the books, but this act lacked the mechanisms (e.g., a presidential prerogative to call out federal troops) that Republicans now deemed necessary for protecting both blacks and white Republicans. Grant did not need convincing. He understood that local southern authorities were failing or refusing to remedy the violence. "The power to correct these evils is beyond the control of State authorities,"[20] Grant declared. In his proclamation of May 4, 1871, he stated, "The failure of local committees to furnish

---

[15] Ibid. at 39. Williams reports, "No serious investigation of Klan atrocities in South Carolina was attempted until the U.S. Army sent Major Lewis Merrill to York County. Initially skeptical concerning the level of both Klan brutality and community consensus among the whites, Merrill soon learned that the violence surpassed anything the Republican national government had imagined" (ibid. at 37).

[16] *Chicago Tribune*, March 20, 1871, p. 2.

[17] *Chicago Tribune*, March 25, 1871, p. 1.

[18] *Chicago Tribune*, May 6, 1871, p. 2.

[19] *Chicago Tribune*, November 20, 1883, p. 4. The *Christian Recorder* made mention of the Tribune's numbers and challenge (December 6, 1883).

[20] *Chicago Tribune*, April 2, 1871, p. 2.

34   *Rethinking the Judicial Settlement of Reconstruction*

such means for the attainment of results so earnestly desired imposes upon the National Government the duty of putting forth all its energies for the protection of its citizens, of every race and color and for the restoration of peace and order throughout the entire country."[21] Under President Grant, the national government launched the most extensive federal involvement in the administration of criminal justice up to that time.[22]

CREATING THE VOCABULARY OF STATE NEGLECT

The Reconstruction debates were a continuation of the Civil War by other means. Republicans and Democrats contested the meaning of the war and slavery's destruction. While Democrats insisted that the slavery problem had ended with formal emancipation and the repudiation of secession and the southern war debt, Republicans viewed the failure to control and remedy Klan violence as a continuation of the slavery problem that nearly destroyed the Republic.[23] The systematic failure to punish Klan violence was a violation of republicanism. During an extensive investigation, Congress accumulated a mountain of evidence about the failure and refusal of southern officials to control and punish violence against both blacks and white Republicans. The congressional report on this unpunished violence, known as the KKK Report, was published in thirteen volumes.[24] It was in the course of the investigation and in the debates that culminated in the passage of the Ku Klux Klan Act of 1871 that centrist Republicans developed a vocabulary of state neglect to address the issue.

In this section, I provide a chronological look at key moments in the history of Reconstruction legislation, focusing on the Civil Rights Act of 1866, Rep. John Bingham's 1866 prototype Fourteenth Amendment, and the Enforcement Acts of 1870 and 1871. A main question is whether Congress authorized primary and plenary federal enforcement of rights, regardless of state behavior. One group of scholars, led by the legal historian Robert Kaczorowski, answers yes, advancing what I call the plenary enforcement theory.[25] Another

---

[21] *Chicago Tribune*, May 5, 1871, p. 1.

[22] Kaczorowski, *Politics of Judicial Interpretation*, 53.

[23] See Pamela Brandwein, *Reconstructing Reconstruction: The Supreme Court and the Production of Historical Truth* (1999), 23–60; Blight, *Race and Reunion*, 31–63.

[24] *Report of the Joint Select Committee to Inquire into the Condition of Affairs in the Late Insurrectionary States*, 13 vols. (hereinafter cited as KKK Report) (Washington, 1872), *House Reports*, 42nd Cong., 2nd sess., No. 22 (serial 1529–41). "On the typical Klan visit recounted time and time again in the two thousand pages of testimony in the South Carolina Klan reports, night riders forced their way into the freedman's home, demanded to talk to the man of the house, questioned him about his political activities, ordered him to renounce the Radical party, dragged him outside, then delivered a severe whipping. Almost every Klan visit included a search for weapons." Williams, *The Great Klan Trials*, 29.

[25] Robert Kaczorowski, "The Supreme Court and Congress's Power to Enforce Constitutional Rights: A Moral Anomaly," 73 *Fordham Law Review* 154 (2004); see also Kaczorowski, "The Enforcement Provisions of the Civil Rights Act of 1866: A Legislative History in Light of *Runyon v. McCrary*, 98 *Yale Law Journal* 565 (1989); Amicus Curaie Brief of Historians,

The Emergence of the Concept of State Neglect, 1867–1873

group answers no,[26] arguing that federal enforcement was made contingent on state denial of rights. I align myself with the latter group.

The answer matters for our assessment of Supreme Court decisions and the extent to which their decisions departed from, narrowed, or betrayed the vision of the Republican framers of Reconstruction legislation. If the framers provided for plenary federal enforcement of rights, charges of narrowing are more warranted. But if the framers always predicated federal rights enforcement on state rights infringement and identified the practice of state neglect as a form of rights infringement, the Court narrowed the congressional vision to a lesser extent than is generally imagined. By reviewing these key features of legislative history, my goal is to begin a recovery of the discourse of state neglect and reveal its presence in multiple institutional sites: Congress, the lower federal courts, and newspapers.

The Civil Rights Act of 1866 and the *Prigg* Analogy

Congress originally passed the Civil Rights Act of 1866 to enforce the Thirteenth Amendment. While the language of that amendment does not include a "no state" prohibition – it declares that "Neither slavery nor involuntary servitude…shall exist within the United States" – the absence of a state action limitation is not sufficient evidence that the plenary enforcement theory attached to the act of 1866. Introducing the 1866 bill, Sen. Lyman Trumbull stated, "It shall be understood that it is the policy of the Government that the rights of the colored men are to be protected by the States if they will but by the Federal Government if they will not."[27] He continued, "So long as the states did [not deny rights], the national government had no more power in the areas of traditional state jurisdiction than it had before the war."[28] The effort to remove doubt about the constitutionality of the act of 1866, moreover, produced the Fourteenth Amendment, which contains the "no state" limitation.[29] If the Fourteenth Amendment introduced a state action predicate for federal enforcement that was not previously there, presumably congressmen would

---

in *CBOCS West v. Humphries* (2008). Historians signing include Mary Frances Berry, Paul Finkelman, Robert Kaczorowski, Stanley Katz, Leon Litwack, James McPherson, and William Wiecek.

[26] See, e.g., Michael Les Benedict, *Preserving the Constitution: Essays on Politics and the Constitution in the Reconstruction Era* (2006), 3–22; Michael P. Zuckert, "Congressional Power under the Fourteenth Amendment: The Original Understanding of Section 5," 3 *Constitutional Commentary* 123 (1986).

[27] Quoted in Benedict, "Preserving the Constitution: The Conservative Basis of Radical Reconstruction," *Journal of American History* 61 (1974): 81.

[28] Quoted in ibid., 77.

[29] Rep. John A. Bingham raised questions about the constitutionality of this act, and it is the consensus view of historians that Republicans passed the Fourteenth Amendment in part to remove all doubt about its constitutionality. Bingham's concern centered on the incorporation of the Bill of Rights contemplated/accomplished by the Civil Rights bill. See the sources cited in Kaczorowski 2004: notes 284 and 310.

have said something. Nobody did. Moreover, the same Congress passed the act of 1866 and the Fourteenth Amendment a mere three months apart. The seamlessness that characterizes the language used in debates on both matters[30] strongly suggests the consistent presumption of a state action predicate for federal rights enforcement.

Historians advancing the plenary enforcement theory attach considerable importance to the decision *Prigg v. Pennsylvania* (1842).[31] In this antebellum case, a unanimous Court held that Congress could enforce the constitutional right to the rendition of fugitive slaves and punish private individuals who interfered with this right. Rep. James Wilson of Iowa was the floor manager of the Civil Rights bill, and he pointed to *Prigg* as authority for the Civil Rights bill of 1866. Wilson was

> not willing that all of these precedents, legislative and judicial, which aided slavery so long, shall now be brushed into oblivion when freedom needs their assistance. Let them now work out a proper measure of retributive justice by making freedom as secure as they once made slavery hateful. I cannot yield up the weapons which slavery has placed in our hands now that they may be wielded in the holy cause of liberty and just government. We will turn the artillery of slavery upon itself.[32]

Wilson read from Justice Joseph Story's opinion in *Prigg*:

> [T]he fundamental principle applicable in all cases of this sort would seem to be that where the end is required the means are given; and where the duty is enjoined the ability to perform it is contemplated to exist on the part of the functionaries to whom it is intrusted.... The [Fugitive Slave] clause is found in the national Constitution and not in that of any State. It does not point out any State functionaries or any State action to carry its provisions into effect.[33]

Wilson's reliance on *Prigg*, however, did not cohere with another facet of his position on the Civil Rights bill: his view of the type of right the bill protected. Wilson explained that the type of right protected in the Civil Rights bill had its source in nature. Quoting Chancellor Kent, Wilson stated:

> 'The absolute rights of individuals may be resolved into the right of personal security, the right of personal liberty, and the right to acquire and enjoy property. These rights have been justly considered, and frequently declared, by the people of this country, to be natural, inherent, and inalienable.' Now, sir, I reassert that the possession of these rights by the citizen raises by necessary implication the power in Congress to protect them.[34]

---

[30] See, e.g., Brandwein, *Reconstructing Reconstruction*, 42–60.

[31] 41 U.S. 539 (1842).

[32] *Cong. Globe*, 39th Cong., 1st sess., 1118 (1866) (Rep. Wilson). Wilson made similar remarks about a week later (ibid. at 1295).

[33] *Cong. Globe*, 39th Cong., 1st sess. at 1294 – Rep. Wilson, quoting *Prigg v. Pennsylvania*, 41 U.S. (16 Pet.) 612, 615 (1842).

[34] Ibid. at 1118–19 (Rep. Wilson). Senator Trumbull also quoted Blackstone and the same passage from Kent. See ibid. at 1757 (Sen. Trumbull). On the Republican view that the Civil

The Emergence of the Concept of State Neglect, 1867–1873

In the *Prigg* decision, Justice Story emphasized that the right to own slaves and hence the right to rendition was a *created* right, a creature of positive law. The right to property in slaves did not exist in nature.[35] The right to rendition was a new right bestowed by the Constitution, and because the right owed its "origin and establishment"[36] to the Constitution, federal enforcement power was plenary. "It [is]...a new and positive right, independent of comity, confined to no territorial limits, and bounded by no state institutions or policy."[37] The theory of plenary enforcement in *Prigg*, therefore, was explicitly based on the type of right at issue: a right created by the Constitution. Because the rights protected by the Civil Rights bill of 1866, by contrast, had their source in nature, as Rep. Wilson himself recognized, the *Prigg* analogy does not establish a plenary enforcement theory of the Civil Rights bill. In short, *Prigg* is not the foursquare analogy that some historians have presumed.

Prigg could still be used to defend the view that the federal government could *ultimately* protect constitutional rights in a corrective capacity if states defaulted. Sen. Trumbull referred to *Prigg* for the general proposition that the federal government could protect freedom: "Surely we have the authority to enact a law as efficient in the interest of freedom, now that freedom prevails throughout the country, as we had in the interest of slavery when it prevailed in a portion of the country."[38] Recall that it was Trumbull, manager of the Civil Rights bill in the Senate, who stated, "It shall be understood that it is the policy of the Government that the rights of the colored men are to be protected by the States if they will but by the Federal Government if they will not.... so long as the states did [not deny rights], the national government had no more power in the areas of traditional state jurisdiction than it had before the war."[39] *Prigg* is thus invoked as authority for a *corrective* model of federal power. It is true that in writing the Civil Rights Act of 1866, Republicans copied some of the machinery of the Fugitive Slave Act of 1850, legislation that embodied the plenary enforcement theory.[40] But they didn't copy all of it. Section 2 of the act of 1866 (the enforcement provision) had the key restriction that persons must act "under color of law...or custom" – a state action term – in order to be subject to federal prosecution.

Rights bill protected natural rights, see the sources cited in Kaczorowski, "A Moral Anomaly," 225–6 (footnote 311).

[35] Kaczorowski notes this (see 2004: 186, footnote 134) but does not perceive the significance of the *created rights* category for Justice Story's theory of federal enforcement.

[36] *Prigg v. Pennsylvania*, 41 U.S. (16 Pet.) at 623.

[37] Ibid. See also 41 U.S. (16 Pet.) at 612 (The Fugitive Slave Clause "manifestly contemplates the existence of a positive, unqualified right on the part of the owner of the slave, which no state law or regulation can in any way qualify, regulate, control or restrain").

[38] *Cong. Globe*, 39th Cong., 1st sess., 475, cited in Kaczorowski 2004: 212. See also the statements cited in Kaczorowski 2004: 205–9.

[39] Quoted in Benedict, "Preserving the Constitution," 77.

[40] See Kaczorowski 2004: 232–41.

The Bingham Prototype

Additional support for the consistent congressional use of a state action/neglect predicate comes from a key episode during the framing and passage of the Fourteenth Amendment. Rep. John A. Bingham, the primary draftsman of the Fourteenth Amendment, offered a prototype of the Fourteenth Amendment: "The Congress shall have power to make all laws which shall be necessary and proper to secure to the citizens of each State all privileges and immunities of citizens in the several States, and to all persons in the several States equal protection in the rights of life, liberty, and property."[41] Bingham's fellow Republicans balked at the proposal, in part because it would permit Congress to pass municipal codes of civil and criminal law. In other words, Bingham's proposal would permit Congress to take primary and full control over rights and preempt the states. This was unacceptable to centrist Republicans.[42] Trying again, Bingham introduced "no state" language into his next draft, which made state denial of rights a predicate for federal civil rights enforcement. Congress quickly approved this language, and there is no indication in the debates that congressmen shifted to a state action theory from a plenary enforcement theory. Such a shift would have been momentous, and it is implausible that they would make such a shift without comment.

In claiming that Republicans gave the federal government "primary legal authority to...enforce the rights of the citizens and inhabitants of the United States"[43] and that federal enforcement power was plenary, Kaczorowski obscures how corrective/remedial power was conceptualized as addressing the practice of state neglect, mis-specifying the distinction between primary/plenary federal power and corrective/remedial power.[44]

A point here bears repeating: it is important to be clear about the vision of federalism associated with the concept of state neglect. Republicans are frequently described as possessing a "nation-centered" vision, but this is because they sought a more robust conception of national citizenship[45] and believed

---

[41] *Cong. Globe*, 39th Cong., 1st sess., 1034 (1866).

[42] For discussion of the Bingham prototype, see Zuckert, "The Original Understanding of Section 5" and his analysis of the debates, including especially the remarks of Rep. Giles Hotchkiss.

[43] Kaczorowski, *Politics of Judicial Interpretation*, xi.

[44] For example, Kaczorowski presents the Republican senator from Indiana, Henry S. Lane, as expressing the view that federal power to enforce civil rights is primary and plenary. But this is what Lane says: "Neither the judge, nor the jury, nor the officer as we believe is willing to execute the law.... We should not legislate at all if we believed the State courts could or would honestly carry out the provisions of the Thirteenth Constitutional Amendment; but because we believe they will not do that, we give the Federal officers jurisdiction" (1987, 60). This is not a view of primary and plenary federal power. It is a view of corrective federal power. The pattern also exists in Kaczorowski, "The Enforcement Provisions of the Civil Rights Act of 1866."

[45] Radical Republicans and centrist Republicans both sought a more robust conception of national citizenship rights (compared to the antebellum definition), but the radical vision was even broader than that of the centrists. See Foner, *Reconstruction*, 243–5.

The Emergence of the Concept of State Neglect, 1867–1873

that the national government had the power to vindicate these rights. But confusion lurks within this idea of a nation-centered federalism. The confusion pertains to the difference between primary and corrective federal power to enforce rights. Centrist Republicans – who held the balance of power – sought a robust definition of national citizenship, but they did not give the federal government primary and plenary power to enforce this new body of rights. This federal power to enforce rights was corrective, that is, contingent upon state rights denials, and so Republican federalism can also be described as "state-centered." Justice Bradley, who argued that the Fourteenth Amendment applied the Bill of Rights to the states, stated clearly in his dissenting opinion in the *Slaughter-House Cases* that federal power to protect these rights was corrective, only.[46]

The Enforcement Acts of 1870–1871

In addition to the *Prigg* analogy and Bingham's prototype, evidence for the consistent presence of a state action/neglect predicate in Reconstruction legislation comes from congressional debate over the Enforcement Act of 1870 and the Ku Klux Klan Act of 1871. It is here, however, that supporters of the plenary enforcement theory find their strongest evidence.

Authorized under the Fourteenth and Fifteenth Amendments, the act of 1870[47] was passed "to enforce the rights of citizens of the United States to vote in the several states of this union, and for other purposes."[48] Comprised of twenty-three sections, Section 6 was the only one to lack a state action/neglect predicate. It provided:

> if two or more persons shall band or conspire together, or go in disguise upon the public highway, or upon the premises of another, with intent...to injure, oppress, threaten, or intimidate any citizen with intent to prevent or hinder his free exercise and enjoyment of any right or privilege granted or secured to him by the Constitution or laws of the United States, or because of his having exercised the same, such persons shall be held guilty of a felony....

The language of Section 6 has been taken as evidence that Republicans embraced a plenary enforcement theory. Before taking up that claim, let us first look at how Republicans debated the acts. Endorsing the act of 1870, Sen. John Pool of North Carolina stated: if "a State, by omission neglects to give

---

[46] Discussing the situation prior to the passage of the Fourteenth Amendment, Bradley stated, "the protection of the citizen in the enjoyment of his fundamental privileges and immunities...was largely left to State laws and State courts, where they will still continue to be left unless actually invaded by the unconstitutional acts or delinquency of the State governments themselves." *Slaughter-House Cases*, 83 U.S. at 121. Note his inclusion of "delinquency" as a form of state violation.

[47] 16 Stat. 140 (Act of May 31, 1870).

[48] Among the "other purposes" of the act were to extend to aliens the protections of Civil Rights Act 1866. Section 18 also reenacted the Civil Rights Act of 1866.

40   *Rethinking the Judicial Settlement of Reconstruction*

to every citizen within its borders a free, fair, and full exercise and enjoyment of his rights," it would be the duty of the federal government to "supply" protection for those rights.[49]

In debate over the Ku Klux Klan Act of 1871, which was far more extensive than debate over the act of 1870, Republicans made it abundantly clear that they were responding to a breakdown in local and state law enforcement. The framers of the Klan Act were overwhelmingly the same group that had passed the Fourteenth Amendment.[50] They rejected plenary enforcement, that is, direct federal punishment of private violence aimed at constitutional rights, regardless of state behavior. Sen. Pool, for example, expanded upon his previously expressed views. According to Pool, the Fourteenth Amendment guaranteed to all U.S. citizens the right to the equal protection of the laws: "If the States shall *fail* to secure and enforce this right of the colored man...then, the United States...must and will, by appropriate legislation, by all the power of its courts, by its land and naval forces, extend over him within the States the shield of the national authority."[51]

During debate over the Klan Act, centrist Republican Rep. (and future president) James A. Garfield helped develop the vocabulary of state neglect:

> But the chief complaint is not that the laws of the State are unequal, but that even where the laws are just and equal on their face, yet, by *a systematic maladministration of them, or a neglect or refusal to enforce their provisions,* a portion of the people are denied equal protection under them. Whenever such a state of facts is clearly made out, I believe the last clause of the first section [of the Fourteenth Amendment] empowers Congress to step in and provide for doing justice to those persons who are thus denied equal protection. Now if the...pending bill can be so amended that it...shall employ no terms which assert the power of Congress to take jurisdiction of the subject *until such denial be clearly made*, and shall not in any way assume the original jurisdiction of the rights of private persons and of property within the state – with these conditions clearly expressed...I shall give it my hearty support.[52]

Rep. Garfield identified both the problem and the remedy, making the remedy clearly contingent on the practice of state neglect. Pool and Garfield spoke for the majority of Republicans. Rep. Coburn, for example, identified the practice of state neglect as a denial of equal protection, identifying it as "the rule...and not the exception."

> How much worse is it for a State to enact that certain citizens shall not vote, than allow outlaws by violence, unpunished, to prevent them from voting?... A systematic failure to make arrests, to put on trial, to convict, or to punish offenders against the rights of a great class of citizens is a denial of

---

[49] *Cong. Globe*, 41st Cong, 2nd sess., 3613.
[50] See Zuckert, "The Original Understanding of Section 5."
[51] *Cong. Globe*, 42nd Cong., 1st sess., pt. 2, 609, emphasis added.
[52] *Cong. Globe*, 42nd Cong., 1st sess. 153 (Appendix) (1871), emphasis added. See also Frelinghuysen's speech of April 6 on the "Ku Klux" bill.

The Emergence of the Concept of State Neglect, 1867–1873   41

equal protection in the eye of reason and the law, and justifies, yes, loudly demands, the active interferences of the only power that can give it. ... The arresting power is fettered, the witnesses are silenced, the courts are impotent, the laws are annulled, the criminal goes free, the persecuted citizen looks in vain for redress. This condition of affairs extends to counties and States; it is, in many places, the rule, and not the exception.

It may be safely said, then, that there is a denial of the equal protection of the law by many of these States. It is therefore the plain duty of Congress to enforce by appropriate legislation the rights secured by this clause of the fourteenth amendment of the Constitution.[53]

Many more statements along these lines can be cited. Rep. George F. Hoar, who twenty years later took a leading role in trying to secure the Lodge Elections bill of 1890–91, stated, "Suppose ... that the constitution of the State all the time declaring that there shall be punishment of crime, to a particular class of citizens there is no criminal remedy enforced for any crime committed upon them. Is that form of government on paper, enrolled on parchment, truly a form of government?"[54] Rep. Horatio C. Burchard of Illinois agreed: "[I]f secret combinations of men are allowed by the Executive to band together to deprive one class of citizens of their legal rights without a proper effort to discover, detect, and punish the violations of law and order, the State has not afforded to all its citizens the equal protection of the laws."[55] Added Rep. Sheldon: "Shall it be said that the citizen may be wrongfully deprived of his life, liberty, and property ... and the national arm cannot be extended to him because there is a State government whose duty is to afford him redress, but refuses or neglects to discharge that duty?"[56]

Writing in 1909, the political scientist John Mabry Mathews identified as incorporated into the Ku Klux Klan Act the rule that state failure to punish the Klan was a denial of rights. "The doctrine that the failure of a State to protect rights guaranteed by the Constitution amounts to a denial of them was expressly incorporated into the [Ku Klux Klan] Act of April 21, 1871."[57]

---

[53] 42nd Cong., 1st sess., 459 (1871).

[54] 42nd Cong., 1st sess., 333 (1871).

[55] 42nd Cong., 1st sess., App. 315. See, too, 42nd Cong., 1st sess., App. 315 (Rep. Hoar); ibid. at 182 (Rep. Mercur); 41st Cong., 2nd sess., 3611 (Sen. Pool); 42nd Cong., 1st sess., App. 251 (Morton); 42nd Cong., 1st sess., 375 (Lowe); ibid. at 514 (Poland); ibid. at 459 (Colburn).

[56] 42nd Cong., 1st sess., 368. See also, ibid. at 459 (remarks of Rep. George F. Hoar) (where the state does not protect a particular class of its citizens from violence, the state denies equal protection); ibid. at 428 (remarks of Rep. Beatty) (the state denied equal protection by failing to "bring the guilty to punishment or afford protection or redress to the outraged and innocent"); ibid., App., at 79 (remarks of Rep. Perry) (the equal protection clause commands that "no State shall fail to afford or withhold the equal protection of the laws"); ibid., App., at 182 (remarks of Rep. Mercur) ("the word 'deny' ... means to refuse, or to persistently neglect or omit to give that 'equal protection' imposed upon the State by the Constitution"); ibid. at 506 (remarks of Sen. Pratt); ibid., App., at 251–2 (remarks of Sen. Morton); ibid. at 608 (remarks of Sen. Pool); ibid. at 409 (remarks of Sen. Frelinghuysen).

[57] John Mabry Mathews, *The Legislative and Judicial History of the Fifteenth Amendment* (1909), 94. Mathews cited, among others, "Pool of NC, *Cong. Globe*, 41st Cong., 2nd sess., 3611.

Notable here is the absence of a singular term to identify this doctrine. Mathews understood that Republicans identified as a rights denial the "failure to make arrests, to put on trial, to convict or punish offenders,"[58] and he described the doctrine using a particular vocabulary. He did not identify this doctrine with a single label or phrase, but he did not need to.

The wording of all seven sections of the Klan act, passed "to enforce the provisions of the Fourteenth Amendment to the constitution of the United States, and for other purposes,"[59] largely tracks the state neglect understanding expressed during debate by Sen. Pool, Rep. Garfield, and the others. Each of its seven sections aimed to remedy the breakdown of law enforcement in the southern states. Section 1 provided that "any person who, under color of law ... or custom, shall subject or cause to be subjected, any person within the jurisdiction of the United States, to the deprivation of any rights, privileges or immunities secured by the Constitution of the United States... be liable to the party injured... in the... courts of the United States." The "color of law ...or custom" language, which originally appeared in the enforcement provision of the act of 1866, thus appeared again. Sections 3 and 4 provided the president with specific powers to remedy the practice of state failure/neglect. For example, Section 3 permitted the president to call out the militia

> in all cases where insurrection, domestic violence, unlawful combinations, or conspiracies in any State so obstruct or hinder the execution of the laws thereof, and of the United States, as to deprive any portion or class of the people of such State of any of the rights, privileges, or immunities, or protection, named in the constitution and secured by this act, and the constituted authorities of such State shall either be unable to protect, or shall, from any cause, fail in or refuse protection of the people in such rights, such facts shall be deemed a denial by such State of the equal protection of the laws.

Section 5 aimed at jury nullification, a common southern practice that aided such lawlessness. Section 6 provided another form of remedy for the practice of state neglect. It provided

> That any person or persons, having knowledge that any of the wrongs conspired to be done and mentioned in the second section of this act are about to be committed, and having power to prevent or aid in preventing the same, shall neglect or refuse to do so, and such wrongful act shall be committed, such person or persons shall be liable to the person injured... for all damages caused by any such wrongful act which such first-named person or persons by reasonable diligence, could have prevented.

Supporters of the plenary enforcement theory point to Section 2 of the act. This section was packed with provisions. It made it a crime for two or more persons to conspire to overthrow the U.S. government, to resist U.S. law, to intimidate U.S. officers, or to intimidate witnesses and jurors in U.S. courts.

---

[58] Mathews, *Legislative History*, 94.
[59] 17 Stat. 13 (Act of April 20, 1871).

The Emergence of the Concept of State Neglect, 1867–1873

The provision in Section 2 on which scholars focus made it a crime for two or more persons to conspire "for the purpose, either directly or indirectly, of depriving any person or any class of persons of the equal protection of the laws, or of equal privileges or immunities under the laws."[60] This single provision in the omnibus Section 2 of the seven-section act of 1871, along with Section 6 of the twenty-three-section act of 1870, supplies the best evidence for the plenary enforcement theory.

When set beside the overwhelming thrust of debate over the acts, as well as evidence pertaining to the act of 1866 and Bingham's prototype, the statutory texts cannot carry the burden of evidence for the plenary enforcement theory. It seems more likely that the absence of a state action predicate was the result of the first-time challenges of drafting enforcement legislation.

Consider finally that opponents of the Klan Act did not attack a plenary enforcement theory. Rather, they attacked the act for its state neglect theory of enforcement. Stated Rep. Francis Blair, Democrat of Missouri:

> The new principle asserted in the bill is that the Government may interfere to put down insurrection in a State without the application of the State authorities, when the State being unable to do so shall fail, neglect or refuse to apply for aid.... It is alleged that great disorders exist in a section of our country, and that numerous crimes are committed with impunity by a secret organization which pervades that community.[61]

The vocabulary of state neglect was commonly understood. But like all Democrats, Rep. Blair rejected state neglect theory as constitutionally invalid. Congress could do nothing even if crimes were "committed with impunity." And again like all Democrats, Blair denied or downplayed the reality of Klan violence.[62] He used the vocabulary of state neglect to challenge Republican claims that Klan violence was widespread

The overview of debate on enforcement legislation clearly shows both that Republicans crafted a vocabulary to define a concept of state neglect and that no singular term for the concept emerged. As Quentin Skinner has remarked, "The surest sign that a group or society has entered into the self-conscious possession of a new concept is that a corresponding vocabulary will be

---

[60] Section 2 also prohibited conspiracies "for the purpose of preventing or hindering the constituted authorities of any State from giving or securing to all persons within such State the equal protection of the laws" and "for the purpose of in any manner impeding, hindering, obstructing or defeating the due course of justice in any State or Territory with intent to deny any citizen of the United States the due and equal protection of the law..." These clauses make direct reference to state officials and state process, as do other clauses that refer to interference in the "discharge of official duty."

[61] 42nd Cong., 1st sess., App. 72, 117.

[62] See, e.g., David Blight's discussion of the Democrats' minority report from the Klan hearings of 1871, which "fashioned an elaborate version of the victimized and oppressed South, and argued vehemently that most of the alleged Klan violence simply had not occurred." *Race and Reunion: The Civil War in American Memory* (2001), 121.

developed, a vocabulary which can then be used to pick out and discuss the concept with consistency."[63]

The vocabulary used by congressmen was also used by newspapers in discussing politics and policy. Having condemned the practice of state neglect and supported the federal remedy fashioned by centrist Republicans, the *Independent* supported the Klan Act.[64] The *Independent* understood the act as a response to the practice of state neglect. "The local authorities have been either unwilling or unable to suppress [the Klan]," declared the *Independent*, "and hence their failure has furnished precisely the case which the Enforcement Act was designed to meet."[65] While the *Independent* would later condemn the public accommodation provisions of the Civil Rights Act of 1875,[66] such an apparently contradictory combination of positions (by today's standards) located the *Independent* in the mainstream of the Republican Party.

Generally speaking, press coverage of the Klan Act is notable for criticism of the habeas corpus and martial law provisions, but not the other provisions. These sections generated the most controversy because they gave the president power to suspend the writ of habeas corpus (Grant suspended the writ in nine counties in South Carolina) and impose military rule when state governors requested aid. Regarding the constitutionality of the Klan Act, the *Chicago Tribune* did not editorialize at the time of its passage. It did print a letter from Henry B. Stanton to Gerrit Smith asserting that the law was "unauthorized" because the "offenses in question are not included among those prohibited by the amendment." (While Stanton is generally remembered as an abolitionist, after the Civil War he contributed regularly to the Democratic and inflammatory New York *Sun*.) Stanton heaped scorn on the habeas corpus and martial law provisions, while also threatening blacks who supported the Republican Party's use of the Fourteenth Amendment as "cover for such oppressive legislation."[67] In 1874, the *Tribune* editorialized that the "the Ku-Klux law is unconstitutional,"[68] though the basis for its conclusion was a charge to a grand jury by District Judge Bland Ballard in Kentucky, which left the door open to future legislation reaching Klan violence.

The *Chicago Tribune*'s view of the habeas and martial law provisions was co-extensive with its hatred for the radical Benjamin Butler, author of the Klan Act. The newspaper spewed vitriol at Butler, saying he had the "power for evil." Along with the radical Sen. Oliver Morton, the "two men [had] a lower class of partisans than any public characters in the North." The paper,

---

[63] Quentin Skinner, "Language and Political Change," in Terence Ball, James Farr, and Russell L. Hanson, eds., *Political Innovation and Conceptual Change* (1989), 8.
[64] *Independent*, March 16, 1871, p. 4.
[65] *Independent*, November 9, 1871, p. 4.
[66] *Independent*, January 29, 1874; February 5, 1874; February 26, 1874.
[67] "Do they forget that these two amendments can be stricken from the Constitution by the same means through which they were engrafted upon it?" *Chicago Tribune*, May 8, 1871, p. 1.
[68] *Chicago Tribune*, October 19, 1874, p. 4.

The Emergence of the Concept of State Neglect, 1867–1873

however, doled out praise to Rep. James Garfield, who "set forth the views of the more moderate Republicans."[69] Garfield, as we have seen, was a major proponent of the state neglect concept. What was most important to the *Tribune* was that Garfield "argued with much power against those features of the pending bill which refer to suspending the habeas corpus and the use of military forces." The *Tribune*'s regard for Garfield, then, appears to align the paper with centrist forces in the party, a point that will become relevant again in understanding the *Tribune*'s reportage on the *Civil Rights Cases*.

That the centrist Republican position accommodated racism is evident in the *Tribune*'s reporting on Klan violence. While the newspaper gave extensive coverage to the issue and pointed to states' failure to punish,[70] it also at times called accounts "exaggerated" and blamed some of the violence on misuse of power by blacks.[71] The paper called "absurd" the charge that the Klan set out to kill or intimidate enough blacks that Democrats could win elections. Indeed, the paper seemingly could not understand the brutal attack on a black mail carrier on the Lexington & Louisville Railroad.[72] So even as the *Tribune* endorsed the state neglect concept, this position was accompanied by views that were racist and reactionary. Our inability to readily imagine such a combination arises from anachronistic assumptions.

STATE NEGLECT IN THE FEDERAL CIRCUIT COURTS

The federal circuit courts accepted most of the federal legal remedy fashioned by centrist Republicans in Congress, turning the political concept of state neglect into a *legal* concept. The courts, however, filtered the concept, limiting it to violence and interference on account of the race of the victim. Using the vocabulary of state neglect, the federal circuit courts thus identified a new type of legally cognizable harm – state failure to punish violence on account of the race or color of the victim – permitting the federal government to prosecute offenders.

Circuit court decisions between 1867 and 1873 represent an important stage in the development of the state neglect concept and the doctrine of state action. During this time, there were thirty references to the Reconstruction Amendments and enforcement legislation. These thirty references appeared

---

[69] *Chicago Tribune*, April 5, 1871, p. 1.

[70] The *Tribune*'s coverage of Klan violence was far more extensive than that of the *New York Times*. However, the *Times* gave more extensive coverage than the *Tribune* to Judge Ballard's complex but ultimately pro-voting rights reasoning in 1874 and Attorney General Taft's voting rights circular in 1876. The *Times* expressed initial concern over Ballard's charge to the grand jury (on October 9, before reporting on Ballard's reasoning) and strongly supported Taft's circular from the outset. The *Tribune* did not examine Ballard's charge and gave strong support to Taft's circular only after the Democratic press called for violent resistance. See the discussion on Ballard and Taft in Chapters 4 and 5, respectively.

[71] *Chicago Tribune*, April 3, 1871, p. 2. See also April 21, 1871, p. 2; August 6, 1872, p. 4.

[72] *Chicago Tribune*, March 26, 1871, p. 2.

46   *Rethinking the Judicial Settlement of Reconstruction*

in twenty cases, written by nine justices and judges.[73] There were two references to the Thirteenth Amendment,[74] five references to the Civil Rights Act of 1866,[75] seven references to the Fourteenth Amendment,[76] five references to the Fifteenth Amendment,[77] five references to the Enforcement Act of May 31, 1870,[78] and six references to the Ku Klux Klan Act of April 20, 1871.[79] Justice Bradley authored three of these circuit court opinions.[80]

In none of these thirty circuit court references to Reconstruction legislation was the concept of state neglect questioned. Nonperformance of duty, courts agreed, was one way that states could deny equal protection and the right to vote. A dual conception of "denying rights" was apparent in the handful of decisions that discussed the issue at length; a denial of rights could take one of two forms: (1) a positive invasion of rights, or (2) omission to protect rights, that is, refusal to perform duties or give requisite relief.

---

[73] The Supreme Court justices were Chase, Swayne, Bradley, and Strong. The circuit judges were Woods and Bonds. The district judges were Busteed, Erskine, and Drummond.

[74] *In re Turner*, 24 F. Cas. 337 (Case No. 14,247) (C. C. D. Md.) (1867); *United States v. Rhodes*, 27 F. Cas. 785 (Case No. 16,151) (C. C. D. Ky.) (1867).

[75] *United States v. Rhodes*, 27 F. Cas. 785 (Case No. 16,151) (C. C. D. Ky.) (1867); *Live-Stock Dealers' & Butchers' Assn. v. Crescent City Live-Stock Landing & Slaughter-House Co.*, 15 F. Cas. 649 (Case No. 8,408) (C. C. D. La.) (1870); *In re Hobbs*, 12 F. Cas. 262 (Case No. 6,550) (C. C. N. D. Ga.) (1871); *Harrison v. Hadley*, 11 F. Cas. 649 (D. D. E. D. Ark.) (1873); *Gaughan v. Northwestern Fertilizing Co.*, 10 F. Cas. 91 (Case No. 5,272) (C. C. N. D. Ill.) (1873).

[76] *Griffin's Case*, 11 F. Cas. 7 (Case No. 5,815) (C. C. D. Va.) (1869); *Live-Stock Dealers' & Butchers' Assn. v. Crescent City Live-Stock Landing & Slaughter-House Co.*, 15 F. Cas. 649 (Case No. 8,408) (C. C. D. La.) (1870); *Ins. Co. v. New Orleans*, 13 F. Cas. 67 (Case No. 7,052) (C. C. D. La.) (1870); *Marsh v. Burroughs*, 16 F. Cas. 800 (Case No. 9,112) (C. C. S. D. Ga.) (1871); *United States v. Hall*, 26 F. Cas. 79 (Case No. 15,282) (C. C. S. D. Ala.) (1871); *In re Hobbs*, 12 F. Cas. 262 (Case No. 6,550) (C. C. N. D. Ga.) (1871); *Northwestern Fertilizing Co. v. Hyde Park*, 18 F. Cas. 393 (Case No. 10,336) (C. C. N. D. Ill.) (1873).

[77] *Live-Stock Dealers' & Butchers' Assn. v. Crescent City Live-Stock Landing & Slaughter-House Co.*, 15 F. Cas. 649 (Case No. 8,408) (C. C. D. La.) (1870); *In re Hobbs*, 12 F. Cas. 262 (Case No. 6,550) (C. C. N. D. Ga.) (1871); *Kellogg v. Warmouth*, 14 F. 257 (Case No. 7,667) (C. C. D. La.) (1872); *Harrison v. Hadley*, 11 F. Cas. 649 (D. D. E. D. Ark.) (1873); *United States v. Collins*, 25 F. Cas. 545 (Case No. 14,837) (C.C. S. D. Ga.) (1873).

[78] *United States v. Crosby*, 25 F. Cas. 701 (Case No. 14, 893) (C. C. S.C.) (1871); *Belding v. Turner*, 3 F. Cas. 84 (Case No. 1,243) (C. C. D. Conn.) (1871); *Gaughan v. Northwestern Fertilizing Co.*, 10 F. Cas. 91 (Case No. 5,272) (C. C. N. D. Ill.) (1873); *Northwestern Fertilizing Co. v. Hyde Park*, 18 F. Cas. 393 (Case No. 10,336) (C. C. N. D. Ill.) (1873). *United States v. Given*, 25 Fed. Cas. 1324 (No. 15, 210) (C. C. D. Del.) (1873).

[79] *In re Lindauer*, 15 F. Cas. 550 (C. C. S. D. N.Y.) (1870); *Ex parte McIllwee*, 16 F. Cas. 147 (C. C. D. Va.) (1870); *United States v. Canter*, 25 F. Cas. 281 (C. C. S. D. Ohio) (1870); *United States v. Hall*, 26 F. Cas. 79 (Case No. 15,282) (C. C. S. D. Ala.) (1871); *United States v. Clayton*, 25 F. Cas. 458 (C. C. E. D. Ark.) (1871); *Harrison v. Hadley*, 11 F. Cas. 649 (D. D. E. D. Ark.) (1873).

[80] *Live-Stock Dealers' & Butchers' Assn. v. Crescent City Live-Stock Landing & Slaughter-House Co.*, 15 F. Cas. 649 (Case No. 8,408) (C. C. D. La.) (1870); *Marsh v. Burroughs*, 16 F. Cas. 800 (Case No. 9,112) (C. C. S. D. Ga.) (1871); *United States v. Collins*, 25 F. Cas. 545 (Case No. 14,837) (C.C. S. D. Ga.) (1873).

The Emergence of the Concept of State Neglect, 1867–1873

An early case, *United States v. Rhodes*, upheld the federal indictment of white individuals under the Civil Rights Act of 1866. They aimed to steal from the dwelling of Nancy Talbot, a black citizen, but the state of Kentucky barred blacks from testifying. Aside from its approval of the federal charges, the importance of *Rhodes* lies in Supreme Court Justice Noah Swayne's identification of the constitutional problem remedied by the act:

> The difficulty was that where a white man was sued by a colored man, or was prosecuted for a crime against a colored man, colored witnesses were excluded. This in many cases involved a denial of justice. *Crimes of the deepest dye were committed by white men with impunity. Courts and juries were frequently hostile to the colored man, and administered justice, both civil and criminal, in a corresponding spirit.* Congress met these evils by giving to the colored man everywhere the same right to testify "as is enjoyed by white citizens," abolishing the distinction between white and colored witnesses, and by giving to the courts of the United States jurisdiction of all causes, civil and criminal, which concern him, wherever the right to testify as if he were white is denied to him or cannot be enforced in the local tribunals of the state.[81]

The idea that white men could commit crimes with impunity, that is, exempt from punishment, is central in *Rhodes*. As Justice Swayne explained, to bar blacks from testifying in court was to administer justice in a hostile spirit, for such bars permitted whites to commit crimes against blacks free from punishment or penalty. State action/maladministration had occurred, and so federal punishment of the white defendants was thus valid federal intervention.

The case, *United States v. Hall*,[82] was the first decision to respond to the recently enacted Enforcement Act of 1870.[83] The case involved two white men, John Hall Jr. and William Pettigrew, who were indicted under Section 6 on two counts for breaking up an election-related political meeting in Eutaw, Alabama. The meeting was largely composed of blacks; two individuals were killed and more than fifty were wounded. The first count charged conspiracy to interfere in the right of freedom of speech, and the second charged conspiracy to interfere in the right to peaceable assembly. Conspiracy to interfere in voting rights under the Fifteenth Amendment was not charged.[84] Hall and

---

[81] 27 F. Cas. at 787, emphasis added.

[82] *United States v. Hall*, 26 F. Cas. 79 (Case No. 15,282) (C. C. S. D. Ala. 1871). For one of the earliest discussions of Hall, see Ruth Ann Whiteside, *Justice Joseph Bradley and the Reconstruction Amendments* (1981), 174–82.

[83] Laurent B. Frantz, "Congressional Power to Enforce the Fourteenth Amendment Against Private Acts," 73 *Yale Law Journal* 1353 (1964), 1362.

[84] In his personal papers, Justice Bradley indicated his certainty that such charges might have been brought: "If this dastardly and savage act was the result of a conspiracy to intimidate the persons attending the meeting from voting at the coming election, it seems to me that it was a violation of the foregoing act [of 1870], and punishable as a felony under the 6th section thereof." Quoted in Whiteside, "Justice Joseph Bradley," 180. Section 6 prohibited conspiracies against "granted or secured" rights, which covered voting as well.

48 *Rethinking the Judicial Settlement of Reconstruction*

Pettigrew argued that no federal rights were at issue and that they could not therefore be charged by the federal government.

Judge William B. Woods, who would later be elevated to the Supreme Court, wrote the opinion in close consultation with Justice Bradley, and the Woods-Bradley correspondence[85] has been of great interest to scholars. The case is important not just because Bradley regarded the Fourteenth Amendment as applying the First Amendment to the states (that is, he viewed the Fourteenth Amendment as prohibiting states from denying First Amendment guarantees).[86] Bradley also perceived the problem of insufficient or incompetent state behavior. In his 1871 letter to Judge William B. Woods, Bradley wrote:

> Denying includes inaction as well as action. And denying the equal protection of the laws includes the omission to protect as well as the omission to pass laws for protection.... [T]o guard against the invasion of the citizen's fundamental rights, and to ensure their adequate protection, as well against state legislation as state inaction or incompetency, the [fourteenth] amendment give Congress power to enforce the amendment by appropriate legislation. And as it would be unseemly for Congress to interfere directly with state enactments and as it cannot compel the activity of state officials, the only appropriate legislation it can make is that which will operate directly on the offenders and offences and protect the rights which the amendment secures.[87]

Judge Woods used Bradley's language nearly verbatim in his *Hall* opinion:

> Congress has the power, by appropriate legislation, to protect the fundamental rights of citizens of the United States against unfriendly or insufficient state legislation, for the fourteenth amendment not only prohibits the making or enforcing of laws which shall abridge the privileges of the citizens, but prohibits the states from denying to all persons within its jurisdiction the equal protection of the laws. Denying includes inaction as well as action, and denying the equal protection of the laws includes the omission to protect, as well as the omission to pass laws for protection.[88]

The language in *Hall* was neither isolated nor unique, and it appeared again in the cases that were among the famous Klan trials of South Carolina. The Klan trials were the first sustained effort at federal rights enforcement, and U.S. attorneys were working in largely uncharted constitutional territory. They experimented, framing long indictments. Their intent was to "stretch the limits of the state-action concept, and to nationalize the Second and Fourth

---

[85] Bradley to Woods, March 12, 1870; Bradley to Woods, January 3, 1871. Bradley Papers, New Jersey Historical Society. See, e.g., Justice Goldberg's discussion of the Woods-Bradley correspondence in *Goldberg v. Maryland* (1964), 81–2.

[86] Bradley would repeat his view that the Fourteenth Amendment applied the Bill of Rights to the states in his dissenting opinion in the *Slaughter-House Cases* (1873).

[87] Letter of Joseph P. Bradley to William B. Woods, March 12, 1871. Bradley Papers, New Jersey Historical Society.

[88] 26 F. Cas. at 81.

The Emergence of the Concept of State Neglect, 1867–1873

Amendments through the Fourteenth to secure for blacks rights to bear arms and be safe in their homes from illegal search and seizure."[89] U.S. Attorney General Amos T. Akerman noted that some experimentation was necessary. Knowing "what should be the theory of the prosecution" would emerge with time. Their goal was to frame a variety of charges and "see how they will stand the scrutiny of a trial."[90]

One of the Klan trials, *United States v. Crosby*,[91] involved the federal prosecution of private individuals under Section 1 of the Enforcement Act of 1870, which "declares that all citizens shall be allowed to vote at all elections, who are qualified by law to vote, without distinction of race, or color, or previous condition of servitude."[92] Circuit Judge Hugh L. Bond of Maryland, a Grant appointee, quashed nine of eleven counts of the indictment. Sustaining the first count, Bond made clear that the federal government could prosecute private individuals under Section 1 if they "intimidated or hindered" the victim Amzi Rainey "from voting because of his race, color, or previous condition of servitude."[93] It was unclear, however, if Bond was applying a state action/ neglect rule or exempting Fifteenth Amendment prosecutions from that rule:

> [T]he constitution has declared that the states shall make no distinction on the grounds [of race &c.]. And, by this legislation, congress has endeavored, in a way which congress thought appropriate, to enforce it.... Congress may have found it difficult to devise a method by which to punish a state which, by law, made such distinction, and may have thought that legislation most likely to secure the end in view which punished the individual citizen who acted by virtue of a state law or upon his individual responsibility.[94]

It is unclear what Bond means by "a state which, by law," makes a racial distinction. A state law that formally differentiates on the basis of race? The unequal application of a formally neutral statute? As Bond presents it, state wrongdoing seems to be a predicate for federal prosecutions of private individuals, but with his reference to "individual responsibility" he might also

---

[89] Williams, *The Great Klan Trials*, 61.

[90] Ibid. at 64.

[91] 25 F. Cas. 701 (Case No. 14,893) (C. C. S.C. 1871).

[92] 25 F. Cas. at 703.

[93] 25 F. Cas. at 704. Judge Bond invalidated indictments drawn up by U.S. Attorney Northrup; he sustained a new set of pleadings drawn up by U.S. Attorneys Ker and Saunders. Goldman, *Free Ballot and a Fair Count*, 94.

[94] 25 F. Cas. at 704. In his 1874 circuit opinion in *United States v. Cruikshank*, Justice Bradley states more clearly that federal enforcement of the Fifteenth Amendment is exempt from state action/neglect limitations. As I explain in Chapter 4, Bradley uses a distinction between granted and secured rights, a conventional nineteenth-century distinction and one contained in the language of Section 6 of the Enforcement Act of 1870 (which prohibited conspiracies to hinder any right "granted or secured" by the Constitution or federal laws) to draw the Fifteenth Amendment exemption. In *Crosby*, Bond offered no rights theory to warrant or undergird his Fifteenth Amendment ruling, relying on a pragmatic argument about enforcement.

50 *Rethinking the Judicial Settlement of Reconstruction*

be exempting Fifteenth Amendment prosecutions from state action/neglect limitations. It is unclear.

The same ambiguity characterized Bond's opinion in *United States v. Petersburg Judges of Elections* (1874).[95] Here, the indictment was drawn under Section 4 of the Enforcement Act of 1870. Of main interest are the Fifteenth Amendment counts, which failed because they did not allege a racial motive. Judge Bond stated that the victim must be "intimidated or hindered from voting because of his race, color, or previous condition of servitude."[96] Regarding the practical problem of punishing states, Bond stated, "As Congress cannot punish a state *qua* state, it is appropriate legislation within the meaning of the statute to attain its end, i.e., the protection of the citizen in his right to vote, by punishing the individuals who obstruct him in its exercise."[97] Again, this looks like an exemption from state action doctrine, but Bond never says clearly that the federal government can prosecute private individuals under the Fifteenth Amendment, irrespective of state behavior.

The historian Lou Faulkner Williams reads Bond as applying a state action/neglect rule.[98] If Williams is correct or if Bond is formulating an early version of the Fifteenth Amendment exemption, it is important to make three observations. The first pertains to the role of legalistic elements in these cases. Judge Bond was known as deeply sympathetic to federal prosecution of Klansmen, and he was "roundly distrusted by Southerners."[99] Yet he threw out indictments because they were not drawn correctly. As Williams notes, Bond exhibited "an honest concern that the indictment [in *Crosby*] exceeded constitutional authority."[100] A "policy preference" model of court decision making in which political ideology drives rulings cannot capture his behavior.

Bond's decisions also make clear that judicial partners of a political regime will not accept just any government theory or pleading. Bond limited coalition partners in the executive branch. "Regime" conceptions of court decision making that see judges as advancing coalition policies must take account of how judges influence and limit political partners in the other branches.

---

[95] *United States v. Petersburg Judges of Election*, 27 F. Cas. 506 (Case No. 16,036) (C. C. E. D. Virginia).

[96] See also the opinion of Judge Hughes, who heard the case with Bond: "By not charging that the [election officers'] refusal was on account of the race &c. of the injured persons, these indictments...do not come under the fifteenth amendment" (27 F. Cas. at 514–15). Both Bond and Hughes made clear that the indictment would have been good under Article 1, Section 4 of the Constitution (at 507, 510).

[97] 27 F. Cas. at 510. see also 25 F. Cas. at 704.

[98] As put by Williams, "state and local officials who failed to protect black rights were involved in a kind of state action that could be punished by the federal government. Bond was willing to go to the outside limit of the state-action concept but not one step beyond. Thus he decided that the federal government could stand in the place of a state when that state refused to protect a citizen's constitutional rights. If the state did not punish the individual conspirators of the Ku Klux Klan, the national government would do so." Williams, *The Great Klan Trials*, 72.

[99] Magrath 1963: 156.

[100] Williams, *The Great Klan Trials*, 71.

The Emergence of the Concept of State Neglect, 1867–1873

I want also to call attention to Judge Bond's combination of racial views, which look contradictory today: support for Reconstruction and rights-protective theories coupled with an embrace of racist sentiment. His private correspondence, notably, reveals opposition to social rights. "Equality before the law," he stated, did not require support for public accommodation rights. "To make a man equal before the law does not necessarily make it obligatory for me to eat, sleep, or drink with him."[101] But Bond's resistance to social equality did not entail or demand rejection of the efficacious enforcement of the Act of 1870.

A final example comes from *United States v. Given*, a Fifteenth Amendment case written by Supreme Court Justice William Strong. *Given* involved the federal prosecution of municipal election officials who neglected their duty on account of the race of the prospective voter. Stated Justice Strong:

> Suppose, as is largely the case in Delaware, the state passes no unfriendly act, but *neglects to impose penalties* upon its election officers for making discriminations on account of race or color, and provides *no remedy* for such wrongs, of what value is the constitutional provision unless it means that congress may interfere?...[W]hen state laws have imposed duties upon persons, whether officers or not, the *performance or non-performance* of which affects rights under the federal government.... I have no doubt that congress may make the non-performance of those duties an offence against the United States.... Undoubtedly, an act, or an omission to act, may be an offence both against the state law and the laws of the United States....[102]

Election officials thus had a duty to permit all voters, equally, to pay the prerequisite tax for voting. Dereliction of this duty – a refusal or omission to accept the tax – had to be on account of the race or color of the prospective voter in order to violate the amendment and incur federal penalty. Just as important: this race-based refusal was a rights violation.[103]

In this body of federal case law, then, we see a legal logic taking shape as judges explain why state neglect was a constitutional violation and why federal intervention was necessary. The fact of state neglect, the consequences that follow on it, and the principles of governance violated were designated by a specific vocabulary. These were the "normal possibilities"[104] of the language of state neglect.

---

[101] Williams, *The Great Klan Trials*, 51.

[102] *United States v. Given*, 25 F. Cas. at 1327–8, emphasis added. Justice Strong would later write the jury decisions of 1880. Strong, like Bradley, would also sit on the Electoral Commission that appointed Hayes president in 1876.

[103] The Supreme Court opinion in *United States v. Reese* tracked the reasoning in *Given*, in that race-based refusals to accept a black man's vote counted as a rights violation. I examine *Reese* in detail in Chapter 4, delineating the rights theory on which it was premised.

[104] The historian of political discourse must identify the "normal possibilities of the language" under investigation, "so that should we encounter the anomalies and innovations that accompany paradigmatic change, we will be able to recognize them, reiterate them, and begin to see how they came to be performed." Pocock, *Virtue, Commerce, and History*, 30.

When judges used this language, the terms "duty" and "protect" were typically present, and groups of words consistently appeared with them. References to the fact of neglect included "omission to protect, omission to pass laws for protection,"[105] "insufficient legislation,"[106] "prejudices affecting the administration of justice,"[107] "hostile...administ[ration of] justice,[108] "the mischief to be prevented would be flagrant, and yet...no remedy could be found,"[109] "state...neglects to impose penalties,"[110] and "no remedy [provided by states for] discriminations on account of race."[111]

A second group of words referred to the consequences of that neglect: "crimes of the deepest dye...committed by white men with impunity,"[112] society...is reduced to that condition of barbarism which compels those unprotected by other sanctions to rely upon physical force for the vindication of their natural rights,[113] the constitutional provision [loses] value,[114] and constitutional rights would be inadequately protected.[115]

A final group of words referred to ideas about the nature and proper organization of a republic. The prosecution of private individuals "remedies the existing evil...accomplish[ing] a purpose required by the constitution."[116] The "unseemly" character of interfering directly with state enactments and the inability to "compel the activity of state officials" made the prosecution of private individuals "the only appropriate legislation."[117] Congressmen debating the Ku Klux Klan bill had frequently invoked the purposes of government. "Governments are instituted among men principally for the purpose of protecting life, liberty and property," stated Rep. James H. Platt, "and when a Government fails to do this for its humblest citizen...it fails to perform its first and most important duty." Sen. George F. Edmunds pointed to the government duty, extending back to Magna Carta, to "execute justice and afford protection against all forms of wrong and oppression."[118]

---

[105] *United States v. Hall*, 26 F. Cas. at 81–2.
[106] Ibid.
[107] Ibid.
[108] *United States v. Rhodes*, 27 F. Cas. at 787.
[109] *United States v. Petersburg Judges of Elections*, 27 F. Cas. at 509.
[110] *United States v. Given*, 25 F. Cas. at 1327.
[111] Ibid.
[112] *United States v. Rhodes*, 27 F. Cas. at 787.
[113] Ibid. at 787–8.
[114] *United States v. Given*, 25 F. Cas. at 1327–28.
[115] *United States v. Hall*, 26 Fed. Cas. at 81–2.
[116] *United States v. Petersburg Judges of Elections*, 27 F. Cas. at 509.
[117] *United States v. Hall*, 26 F. Cas. at 81. "[A]s [Congress] cannot compel the activity of state officials, the only appropriate legislation it can make is that which will operate directly on offenders and offenses, and protect the rights which the amendment secures." *United States v. Given*, 25 F. Cas. at 1328: "Any other doctrine would place the national government entirely within the power of the states, and would leave constitutional rights guarded only by the protection which each state might choose to extend them."
[118] Platt and Edmunds are quoted in Calhoun, *Conceiving a New Republic*, 29.

The Emergence of the Concept of State Neglect, 1867–1873

Justice Samuel F. Miller used the vocabulary of state neglect in the infamous 1873 *Slaughter-House Cases*, widely regarded as hostile to Reconstruction. Southern states were not in their "proper" relation to the Union, Miller explained, when black lives "were at the mercy of bad men, either because the laws for their protection were insufficient or were *not enforced*."[119] This comment is routinely ignored in the Reconstruction legal literature. And while Justice Bradley dissented in *Slaughter-House*, he also identified the "delinquency" of state governments as a form of constitutional violation.[120] Both majority and dissenting justices, then, endorsed state neglect principles.

Why might the concept of state neglect – a conceptual innovation built into legislation – have seemed attractive to federal circuit judges as they began hearing cases relating to the recently passed amendments? We should look, first, at prevailing assumptions about the purposes of government. During the nineteenth century, the government's duty to protect its citizens stood in reciprocal relationship to the citizens' duty of allegiance.[121] The concept of state neglect, moreover, fit the master principle of the founding generation, which held that public power must be used disinterestedly. A preoccupation for nineteenth-century judges was public power corrupted by faction, and if government subjected "some to peculiar burdens" or granted "to others peculiar exemptions,"[122] this principle was violated.[123] It was not a stretch to interpret the failure to equally administer laws against murder as subjecting one class to special burdens while granting another special exemptions.

---

[119] 83 U.S. at 70, emphasis added. Miller made clear that the validity of state laws was not the only concern of Reconstruction: "As it is a State that is to be dealt with, and not alone the validity of its laws. . . ." (83 U.S. at 81).

[120] *Slaughter-House Cases*, 83 U.S. at 121. Discussing the situation prior to the passage of the Fourteenth Amendment, Bradley stated, "the protection of the citizen in the enjoyment of his fundamental privileges and immunities . . . was largely left to State laws and State courts, where they will still continue to be left unless actually invaded by the unconstitutional acts or delinquency of the State governments themselves."

[121] As we will see later, the reciprocal duties of protection and allegiance were explicitly referred to in *Cruikshank*, 92 U.S. at 549. ("We have in our political system a government of the United States and a government of each of the several States. Each one of these governments is distinct from the others, and each has citizens who owe it allegiance, and whose rights, within its jurisdiction, it must protect.") Republicans had long viewed citizen allegiance and government protection as reciprocal. See, e.g., the 1856 Republican Party platform, C. W. Johnson, ed., *Proceedings of the First Three Republican Conventions of 1856, 1860, and 1864* (1893), 27–8. See also Curtis, *John A. Bingham and the Story of American Liberty*, 660; Curtis, *No State Shall Abridge*, 53–4, 62, 142–5.

[122] Madison, "Memorial and Remonstrance," point 4, reprinted in Alley, *Supreme Court on Church and State*, 20. See also Alan Jones, "Thomas M. Cooley and Laissez-Faire Constitutionalism" (1967).

[123] This Jacksonian conception of illegitimate power was embedded in nineteenth-century police powers jurisprudence. See, e.g., Howard Gillman, *The Constitution Beseiged: The Rise and Demise of Lochner Era Polics Powers Jurisprudence* (Durham, NC: Duke University Press, 1993).

54   *Rethinking the Judicial Settlement of Reconstruction*

The equality of basic rights, moreover, was part of the natural law tradition.[124] The concept of state neglect can be seen as one of the last formulations of a God- or nature-centered model of human knowledge. When, in 1870, Christopher Langdell established the case, or "scientific," method of study at Harvard Law School, he rejected this natural theology, but it is a mistake to view the jurisprudence of the immediate postwar era through the lens of the "scientism" of the Gilded Age. Reconstruction-era judges came to maturity during the antebellum era when moral and political philosophy constituted the bases of educated thought. Recent research has shown that God- and nature-centered models remained widespread later than is commonly imagined.[125] The philosophical framework out of which centrist Republicans formulated the concept of state neglect was thus an antebellum framework. The key postbellum additions were (1) the recognition of blacks as members of the national collective and as political agents and (2) corrective federal power.

The Klan Trials of South Carolina were widely viewed as successful, and the number of federal prosecutions continued to climb, peaking in 1873, right before the economic Panic of 1873 triggered a long-running depression. In 1872, the *Christian Recorder* reported, "the Ku Klux have been awed and partially suppressed."[126] But even with the federal courts' approval of the concept of state neglect, political factors remained relevant to enforcement. Political obstacles had dogged agents of the Freedmen's Bureau in 1866[127] and these grew to massive proportions in the 1870s. Not only was caseload in the Carolinas enormous,[128] securing and protecting witnesses who were the targets of threats and intimidation were tremendous problems, as was jury nullification. An inadequate administrative structure also impeded effective prosecution, and the newly created Justice Department was strained severely. Without bureaucratic machinery to coordinate and vet the decisions of U.S. attorneys, poor prosecutorial decisions were made. As we will see, the mistakes of U.S. Attorney William A. Murray in *United States v. Harris*[129] generated a negative outcome: the invalidation of a section of the Klan Act. Finally, the high financial cost of prosecutions mattered greatly, especially after the economic Panic of 1873 constricted government spending and made spending in the South politically risky. Liberal Republican Thomas Tipton reprimanded his colleagues in the Senate: after the panic, voters who "were scarcely able to live

---

[124] Knud Haakonssen, "From Natural Law to the Rights of Man: A European Perspective on American Debates," in Michael J. Lacey and Knud Haakonssen, eds., *A Culture of Rights: The Bill of Rights in Philosophy, Politics, and Law* (1991), 51.

[125] See, e.g., Siegel, "Historism in Late Nineteenth Century Thought," and Grossman 2002.

[126] *Christian Recorder*, May 4, 1872.

[127] See e.g., Kaczorowski, *Politics of Judicial Interpretation*, 27, 43 (on the Bureau), and 58–9 (on the Klan). See also Robert M. Goldman, *A Free Ballot and a Fair Count* (2001).

[128] Williams, *The Great Klan Trials*, 123.

[129] 106 U.S. 629 (1883).

The Emergence of the Concept of State Neglect, 1867–1873

for want of bread" would reject "a party that proposed to live on blood."[130] Even before the Panic, however, Congress failed to provide money sufficient to cover prosecutorial costs. The massive problem of unpunished Klan violence overwhelmed resources.

THE STATE NEGLECT CONCEPT AND THE *SLAUGHTER-HOUSE CASES*

The *Slaughter-House Cases* (1873)[131] is taken to be the Supreme Court's opening blow against Reconstruction. In rejecting the claims of white butchers that they were being deprived of their right to pursue a trade, the Court upheld a Louisiana law mandating the centralization of slaughtering facilities in New Orleans. The majority opinion by Justice Samuel F. Miller narrowly defined the rights of national citizenship, significantly restricting the scope of the Fourteenth Amendment. Since the Second Reconstruction, Justice Miller's opinion has given rise to an enormous scholarship and inspired the derision of critics. A glance at the legal historiography of Reconstruction confirms the multiple charges against Miller's opinion: it upheld a monopoly established by a corrupt legislature; it defied original incorporation of the Bill of Rights; it embodied negligence if not malevolence toward the freedmen; and it began the judicial retreat from Reconstruction.

A pair of revisionist studies has built a new angle of vision on Justice Miller's infamous opinion by situating the case in its social, political, and economic contexts.[132] The Court's approval of an exclusive franchise that required butchers to do their slaughtering at a central facility looks reasonable in light of awful health conditions, prior regulation in New York and Chicago, and the state's dire financial circumstances.

As Michael Ross's work emphasizes, sanitary conditions in New Orleans had been abysmal. Slaughterhouses were located in the city's most populous areas, operating alongside crowded tenements, businesses, hospitals, and schools. As New Orleans had no public sewer system, butchers emptied waste and offal into the streets and the Mississippi River, the source of the city's drinking water. Outbreaks of cholera and yellow fever were routine. The establishment

---

[130] Quoted in Calhoun, *Conceiving a New Republic*, 68–9.

[131] 83 U.S. (16 Wall.) 36 (1873).

[132] Michael A. Ross, *Justice of Shattered Dreams: Samuel Freeman Miller and the Supreme Court during the Civil War Era* (2003); Ronald Labbe and Jonathan Lurie, *The Slaughterhouse Cases: Regulation, Reconstruction, and the Fourteenth Amendment* (2003). See also Pamela Brandwein, "Review of Labbé, Ronald M.; Lurie, Jonathan, *The Slaughterhouse Cases: Regulation, Reconstruction, and the Fourteenth Amendment* and Ross, Michael A., *Justice of Shattered Dreams: Samuel Freeman Miller and the Supreme Court during the Civil War Era*," H-Law, H-Net Reviews, May 2004, URL: http://www.h-net.org/reviews/showrev.php?id=9267. More recently, see Leslie Freidman Goldstein, "The Specter of the Second Amendment: Rereading *Slaughterhouse* and *Cruikshank*," *Studies in American Political Development* 21 (Fall 2007): 131–48.

of a central facility was a regulation of a noxious trade, and it brought these epidemics under control. Reconstruction was in part about modernization and northern-style public improvement projects, and the Louisiana effort to modernize sanitation was very much a feature of Reconstruction.

But the Louisiana law enflamed the butchers. The legislature was biracial, and while it imposed sanitary regulations on the "monopolistic" Crescent City Live-Stock Landing and Slaughtering Company, it also imposed fines if the company did not provide adequate facilities for all who desired them. The Gascon butchers, it turns out, had not only resisted health regulations for years, they had operated an informal monopoly, conspiring to inflate meat prices and driving off black competitors. The exclusive franchise undermined the butchers' control and lowered the capital requirements to enter the trade, thus opening it to blacks. Arch-racists, the butchers advanced charges of corruption and monopoly to delegitimize the action of the legislature.

In his majority opinion, Justice Miller rejected the butchers' claim, upholding the legislative grant as a health measure. In so doing, he narrowed the scope of the Fourteenth Amendment. The framers of the Fourteenth Amendment had advanced a robust conception of national citizenship,[133] identifying southern denials of Bill of Rights guarantees as part of the slavery problem. The Republican solution was to apply the Bill of Rights to the states.[134] Justice Miller, however, imposed an artificially narrow view of the war's issues, refusing to recognize this long-standing feature of antislavery criticism.[135] In narrowly defining the rights of national citizenship, the five-member majority refused to endorse a central feature of Republican constitutionalism.

There was an important exception. "The right to peaceably assemble and petition [the national government] for redress of grievances," Miller stated,

[133] In the secondary literature, see Michael Les Benedict, "The Slaughterhouse Cases," in Kermit L. Hall, ed., *The Oxford Companion to the Supreme Court* (1992), 789 ("the rhetoric of the debates suggested a vague but general belief that all Americans, white and black, had certain fundamental rights that had been violated in the interest of slavery and that should henceforth be secured against infringement"). See also Eric Foner, *Reconstruction: America's Unfinished Revolution* (1988), 258 ("In establishing the primacy of a national citizenship whose common rights the states could not abridge, Republicans carried forward the state-building process born of the Civil War"). In the primary literature, see, e.g., *Congressional Globe*, 39th Cong. 1st sess., 2542 ("There was a want hitherto, and there remains a want now, in the Constitution of our country, which the proposed [fourteenth] amendment will supply. What is that? It is the power...to protect by national law the privileges and immunities of all the citizens of the Republic and the inborn rights of every person within its jurisdiction" [Bingham]). See also the primary sources gathered by Foner, *Reconstruction*, 228–80.

[134] See *Cong. Glob.*, 39th Cong., 1st sess., 3 Feb 1866, 1088–95; 8 May 1866, 2542–3 (remarks of Rep. Bingham); and ibid., 23 May 1866, 2765–6 (remarks of Sen. Jacob Howard). See, generally, Michael Kent Curtis, *No State Shall Abridge: The Fourteenth Amendment and the Bill of Rights* (1986).

[135] On Justice Miller ignoring the congressional Republicans' broad understanding of "the problem" with slavery, which included southern denials of Bill of Rights freedoms to antislavery activists, see Brandwein, *Reconstructing Reconstruction*, 55–8, 61–2.

The Emergence of the Concept of State Neglect, 1867–1873   57

"are rights of the citizen guaranteed by the Federal Constitution."[136] The Court reiterated this the following year in *Cruikshank*: "The right of the people peaceably to assemble for the purpose of petitioning Congress for a redress of grievances, or for any thing else connected with the powers or the duties of the national government, is an attribute of national citizenship, and, as such, under the protection of, and guaranteed by, the United States."[137] This was an avenue for protecting expression rights and political meetings, and it was relevant for Republican party building.[138]

When Justice Miller refused to acknowledge incorporation of the Bill of Rights, he did two things: (1) he reduced federal rights enforcement to largely an equal protection formula,[139] and (2) he reduced the definition of *civil rights* to those listed in the Civil Rights Act of 1866.[140] The nonincorporation doctrine thus blocked a particular formulation of federal power to protect rights. Under it, the Bill of Rights would be among the rights of national citizenship, and states would be barred from denying Bill of Rights freedoms as well as the equal protection of the laws. (Even under the incorporation thesis, it must be remembered, states had to deny Bill of Rights freedoms before the federal government could intervene.) Federal punishment of private individuals would thus be permitted if there were specific intent to interfere, for any reason, with Bill of Rights freedoms and if these interferences went unpunished by states.

Compared with the broader formulation, the concept of state neglect that survives is considerably more narrow. Under the broader formulation, the federal government would have been empowered to prosecute Klan disruptions of Republicans' political meetings pertaining to state elections, attended by both blacks and white Republicans, that states left unpunished. There would have been no racial predicate for such prosecutions. Mob lynching of prisoners in state custody would also be clearly punishable by the federal government. Much was at stake, therefore, in the reduction.

But the impact of Miller's opinion should not be overdrawn. Assembly and petition rights regarding national elections remained protected against state violation and these rights were relevant for Republican party building in the South. Miller's opinion also did not block the concept of state neglect, or Justice Bradley's constructions of the Fifteenth Amendment and Article 1,

---

[136] 83 U.S. at 79.

[137] 92. U.S. at 552. The Supreme Court did not mobilize this until the twentieth century (see *Hague v. CIO*, 307 U.S. 496, 513 [1939], citing these passages in *Slaughter-House* and *Cruikshank*). Inquiries into why Republican administrations in the 1870s and 1880s did not use this legal tool would certainly be worthwhile, but doctrine did not tie their hands.

[138] See also Goldstein, "The Specter of the Second Amendment," 144.

[139] The Waite Court's federal elections jurisprudence, based on Article 1, Section 4, was not an equal protection jurisprudence. Interference in national elections, for any reason, could be directly punished by the federal government. For discussion, see Chapters 4 and 5.

[140] After the Court constricted the definition of national citizenship, Justice Bradley, who had dissented in *Slaughter-House* and endorsed original incorporation, could no longer include Bill of Rights freedoms as among the *civil rights* that were protected against state denial.

58   *Rethinking the Judicial Settlement of Reconstruction*

Section 4 of the Constitution, which provided broad federal power to enforce voting rights.[141]

And Miller himself gave expression to state neglect principles. Recall Miller's words in *Slaughter-House*, quoted earlier, that the South was not in "proper relation" to the Union where black lives "were at the mercy of bad men either because the laws for their protection were insufficient or were not enforced." The statement is a classic formulation of state neglect.[142] And it is less surprising in light of Miller's private correspondence, which condemned unpunished violence against blacks by intransigent whites. Responding strongly to William Pitt Ballinger (his frequent correspondent and brother-in-law), who had suggested that southerners opposed recent massacres in New Orleans and Memphis, Miller wrote:

> Show me a single white man that has been punished in a State court for murdering a negro or a Union man. Show me that any public meeting has been had to express indignation at such conduct. Show me that you or any of the best men of the South have gone ten steps to prevent the recurrence of such things. Show me the first public address or meeting of Southern men in which the massacres of New Orleans and Memphis have been condemned.[143]

Justice Miller did not trust southern whites to protect the safety of blacks.[144] In his intellectual biography of Miller, Michael Ross traces Miller's shifts on black rights. "Once a slaveholder, by the 1850s he favored gradual emancipation and the containment of slavery where it existed. By the end of the Civil War, he embraced immediate abolition and black civil rights."[145] Miller was a frontier Republican in Iowa, and "[t]he circumstances, processes, and strategies that won frontier Iowans to the civil equality of blacks remind us that there are egalitarian precedents as well as a racist tradition in America's past."[146] A few years after the war, Miller "advocated suffrage for African Americans. All black men, Miller believed, should be treated as citizens with full political and legal rights." But as Ross, quoting Robert Dykstra, observes, most Iowa Republicans did not embrace social equality between the races.[147] Like them, Miller came to support civil and political equality for blacks while simultaneously balking at social equality.

Ross's portrait of Miller is consistent with the latter's recognition of a concept of state neglect. Regarding federalism, Ross explains that "Miller believed

---

[141] While the federal government did not enforce voting rights vigorously after the economic Panic of 1873 and ensuing depression (political dynamics changed afterward, as we will see), voting rights enforcement persisted until the early 1890s.

[142] 83 U.S. at 70.

[143] Miller to W.P.B., February 6, 1867, quoted in Michael A. Ross, *Justice of Shattered Dreams: Samuel Freeman Miller and the Supreme Court during the Civil War Era* (2003), 147..

[144] Miller to W.P.B., August 29, 1869, cited in ibid. at 210.

[145] Ibid. at 165.

[146] Robert Dykstra, *Bright Radical Star: Black Freedom and White Supremacy on the Hawkeye Frontier* (1993), 270.

[147] Ross, *Justice of Shattered Dreams*, 165.

The Emergence of the Concept of State Neglect, 1867–1873

that African Americans should still look first" to their state governments. Miller likewise "sought a middle ground where the Fourteenth Amendment could be used to protect African Americans' rights, but without making the national government the primary defender of all the rights of all citizens." He believed in "the power of the Fourteenth Amendment's equal protection clause to achieve its object of protecting black rights."[148] The primacy but not exclusivity of state jurisdiction, a reluctance to expand federal power, and a belief in the juridical efficacy of the equal protection clause: each element of Miller's federalist commitments appears in centrist Republicans' development of the state neglect concept.

As I discuss in Chapter 6, Justice Miller wrote a key voting rights decision in 1884, *Ex parte Yarbrough*,[149] which accepted the Fifteenth Amendment exemption. The unanimous opinion is incompatible with a picture of Miller as out to bury Reconstruction, and the existence of this contradiction supports the reassessment of *Slaughter-House* prompted by Ross and others.

So why did Justice Miller narrowly constrict the meaning of national citizenship? The question is inescapable, but it cannot be addressed here. According to Michael A. Ross, Justice Miller had a pattern of siding with those who were burdened and thrown into debt by industrialization and his purpose in constricting the definition of national citizenship was to thwart economic conservatives like Justice Stephen Field, who were rising in power and searching for an instrument to invalidate all state regulation of business. An expansive conception of national citizenship would have provided this instrument.[150] (As it happened, Field eventually got what he wanted, but only through another route and only after substantial Court turnover.) Leslie Goldstein has proposed another answer: the desire to avoid Second Amendment incorporation. While scholars have associated the need for Second Amendment rights with blacks, Goldstein proposes that the Klan would have made much wider use of this amendment. Blocking Second Amendment incorporation, Goldstein suggests, actually facilitated state efforts to control the Klan.[151] My study supports the conclusion that Justice Miller's opinion was less of an expression of hostility to Reconstruction than conventionally imagined, but it does not provide direct support to either Ross or Goldstein.

In sum, despite *Slaughter-House*'s constriction of national citizenship, nothing in its language contradicts the logic of state neglect or impedes the ongoing development of the concept.

---

[148] Ibid. at 207, 208.
[149] 110 U.S. 651 (1884).
[150] Ross, *Justice of Shattered Dreams*, 174–5, 204–5, 210.
[151] Goldstein, "The Specter of the Second Amendment," 136–42.

3

The Civil/Social Distinction

An Intramural Republican Dispute

In the *Civil Rights Cases*, Justice Bradley cautioned against treating blacks as "the special favorite of the laws."[1] The comment appears in the majority opinion's invalidation of the public accommodation provisions and is regularly excerpted in textbooks to demonstrate Bradley's "ceremoniously washing his hands of the freedmen's problems."[2] From a contemporary perspective, in which equal access to public accommodations is taken to be an essential component of freedom and in which racist scorn for public accommodation rights entails a rejection of an efficacious Fourteenth Amendment, Bradley's derision appears to mark a categorical hostility to Reconstruction.

Meet Judge Emmons. Circuit Judge Halmer H. Emmons was a Grant appointee from Tennessee who wrote the first judicial opinion on the Civil Rights Act of 1875. In a case involving the denial of access to a theater, Judge Emmons advised the jury that the public accommodation provisions were unconstitutional.[3] He expressed disdain for these provisions, calling them "a grotesque exercise of national authority."[4] Declaring that no "civil right" was at issue in this case,[5] Judge Emmons left little doubt about his sentiments. "I have," he stated, "but small sympathy with the right of the negro to see the immodest and vulgar display in the ballet dance."[6]

It is not so easy, however, to peg Judge Emmons as antagonistic to Reconstruction. In the jury charge, he condemned "murder and cruel and shocking outrages" that were "perpetrated with impunity" and subject to

---

[1] 109 U.S. at 25. ("When a man has emerged from slavery, and by the aid of beneficent legislation has shaken off the inseparable concomitants of that state, there must be some stage in the progress of his elevation when he takes the rank of a mere citizen, and ceases to be the special favorite of the laws, and when his rights as a citizen, or as a man, are to be protected in the ordinary modes by which other men's rights are protected.")
[2] Williams, *The Great Klan Trials*, 143.
[3] *Charge to a Grand Jury–Civil Rights Act*, 30 F. Cas. 1005 (C. C. W. D. Tenn.) (1875).
[4] 30 F. Cas. 1007.
[5] 30 F. Cas. 1005.
[6] 30 F. Cas. 1007

The Civil/Social Distinction

"mock trials."[7] Calling these unpunished murders a disgrace to the nation, he denounced "courage-wanting murders of the innocent and the helpless" that were committed "without the slightest infliction of any legal penalty upon the offenders."[8] Protection from pillage and murder, he stated, was a "more precious and beneficent privilege" than access to the theater. Indeed, he added that he would "gladly stand upon" a recently expressed theory of federal civil rights enforcement by a "learned justice" that would exact justice on unpunished murderers. According to this theory, "violence upon the negro, simply because he is such, finding its sole animus in his race and color, may be made penal by congressional enactment."[9] Justice Bradley was that learned justice, and he had supplied this theory in his circuit opinion in *Cruikshank*.[10]

Judge Emmons's contempt for black access to the "ballet dance" is the touchstone for this chapter. Public accommodation rights, he claimed, were not civil rights. But the category of civil rights was not empty, as he made clear that rights enforcement included the federal punishment of individuals whose race-based violence went unremedied. I pursue the competing constructions of the civil rights category by recovering an intramural Republican debate over the distinction between civil rights and social rights.

The debate reveals both pragmatic and principled efforts to differentiate between a pre- or extrapolitical realm – that is, society – and one subject to legal regulation – that is, politics. While the former was ruled by nature or individual choice, the latter entailed state intervention, itself subject to the principles of federalism. Centrists' and radicals' competing conceptions of the society/politics distinction emerge in the debate over what was a civil as opposed to a social right. Only by revisiting the debate can we properly understand the Court opinion in *Civil Rights Cases*. Otherwise, anachronistic assumptions about what racism must look like will risk misapprehension of the case law and thus of the political and legal opportunities that remained.

CHARLES SUMNER'S SUPPLEMENTARY CIVIL RIGHTS BILL

What did it mean to move the nation from slavery to freedom? Intramural Republican debate over this question was a consistent feature of Reconstruction politics. By the war's end, centrist Republicans needed no convincing that the Civil Rights Act of 1866 protected the essential rights of freedom. Their support for the act of 1866 was principled and unshakeable. By 1867, centrists were willing to support black suffrage in the South. By 1870–71, they were willing to support the Fifteenth Amendment and strong voting rights enforcement legislation. But how much further would centrists go in expanding the meaning of freedom? Radical Republicans had a successful track record of

[7] 30 F. Cas. 1006–7.
[8] 30 F. Cas. 1007.
[9] Ibid.
[10] I focus on this 1874 opinion in the next chapter.

staking out unpopular positions among centrists (emancipation, suffrage) only to watch later as centrists embraced those positions.[11] Would policy on public accommodation rights fit this pattern?

Questions about public accommodation rights became more immediate to Republican Congressmen in 1870, as blacks became newly present among them. That year, Hiram Revels of Mississippi became the first black man elected to the U.S. Senate. That same year, Joseph Hayne Rainey became the first black member of the House of Representatives. In 1871, the forty-second Congress included five black members in the House of Representatives. The question of respecting blacks "as a social equal" seems to have been brought to the attention of Congress when blacks were admitted as senators and representatives and "seated...beside a white man." Black congressmen "objected to the inconsistency of sitting with white men in the Senate or the House and having to separate from them on the steamboat, railroad cars, or in the theaters."[12] The great abolitionist Sen. Charles Sumner took it upon himself to introduce a new bill in the Senate.

Sumner's bill, offered as a supplement to the Civil Rights Act of 1866, provided for "the full and equal enjoyment" of public accommodations as well as equal access to schools, cemeteries, and churches. The bill also prohibited race discrimination in jury service. The schools provision was most controversial, and it would eventually be stripped out along with the cemeteries and churches provisions. But the public accommodation provisions never had strong support.

The bill traveled a five-year odyssey. The journey began on May 13, 1870. After being introduced, it was promptly held up in the Senate Judiciary Committee, twice reported unfavorably, and bottled up until December of 1871.[13] Sumner maneuvered to get the bill attached as rider to an amnesty measure (which had wide support) and in January of 1872, extended discussion finally opened on his bill.

Charles Sumner defended his bill in a series of speeches between December 20, 1871, and May 21, 1872.[14] The "great principle of equality," he argued, was "the real issue of the war"[15] and the "irresistible logic of emancipation"[16] required passage of the bill. Sumner gave great weight to the Declaration

---

[11] Foner, *Reconstruction*, 238–9.

[12] L. E. Murphy, "The Civil Rights Act of 1875," *Journal of Negro History* 12 (1927): 113.

[13] According to John S. Ezell, "The lack of success of Sumner's early efforts probably is accounted for by the fact that the Republican majority either was not interested in them or feared them, and Lyman Trumbull of Illinois, chairman of the Senate Judiciary Committee, was in a position to kill them." Trumbull opposed the legislation. Ezell, "The Civil Rights Act of 1875," *Mid-America: An Historical Review* 50 (1968): 251, 253. On the role of Trumbull, see also Harris, *Quest for Equality*, 51.

[14] Charles Sumner, *The Works of Charles Sumner*, vol. 14 (1883), 533–73.

[15] Ibid. at 375–6.

[16] Ibid. at 370.

The Civil/Social Distinction

of Independence[17] and its first principle, the "equality of men."[18] "The Constitution is an earthly body, if you please; the Declaration is the soul.... Every word in the Constitution is subordinate to the Declaration."[19] But the Constitution was a source of power as well:

> Do you question the binding character of the Great Declaration? Then I invoke the Constitutional Amendments. But you cannot turn from either, as each establishes beyond question the boundaries of national power, making it coextensive with the National Unity and the Equal Rights of All, originally declared and subsequently assured. Whatever is announced in the Declaration is essentially National.... The Republican party must do its work, which is nothing less than regeneration of the Nation according to the promises of the Declaration of Independence."[20]

Sumner specifically cited the Thirteenth Amendment.[21] "Does it abolish slavery half, three-quarters, or wholly?"[22] Ejections from public places on account of color were "also a part of Slavery.... So long as it exists, slavery is still present among us."[23] Exclusions, just like separations, were the "essence of caste."[24] He also pointed to Section One of the Fourteenth Amendment,[25] as well as to its various clauses, such as the Citizenship Clause[26] and the Privileges or Immunities Clause.[27] Each clause was a "fountain of power.[28]

Sumner did not offer detailed interpretations of the clauses, and his imprecision drew a response from Sen. Lot M. Morrill from Maine, generally understood to be a "clear sighted lawyer."[29] "The question between the Senator and myself is precisely this: What is your authority?"[30] Morrill was no Democrat. He was a Maine Republican who strongly supported both the Civil Rights Act of 1866 and voting rights legislation. He called the Act of

[17] Ibid. at 362, 364, 375, 376, 377, 378, 401, 406, 412, 413, 415, 425, 426, 431, 436, 440, 443–7, 449, 451, 452, 455, 457, 460, 462, 465, 469.

[18] Ibid. at 220.

[19] *Cong. Globe*, 42nd Cong, 2nd sess., 825.

[20] Sumner, *Works*, 280–1. See also 425–6. ("I insist that the Declaration is of equal and coordinate authority with the Constitution itself.... The Constitution can never be interpreted in any way inconsistent with the Declaration.")

[21] Ibid. at 384 (speech of January 15), 426–30 (speech of January 17).

[22] Ibid. at 426.

[23] Ibid. at 384. See also 369 ("Some have thought Slavery is dead. This is a mistake.") and 370 ("the ancient criminal yet lingers among us, insisting upon the continued degradation of a race").

[24] Ibid. at 382, 450, 468.

[25] Ibid. at 385 (speech of January 15), 430–1 (speech of January 17).

[26] Ibid. at 384 (speech of January 15), 430 (speech of January 17).

[27] Ibid. at 386. Here he references Judge Washington's opinion in *Corfield v. Coryell*.

[28] Ibid.

[29] Edward L. Pierce, *Memoir and Letters of Charles Sumner*, vol. 4 (1893), 501. Ronald B. Jager, "Charles Sumner, the Constitution, and the Civil Rights Act of 1875," *New England Quarterly* 42 (1969): 365.

[30] Sumner, *Works*, 420.

1866 "absolutely revolutionary." Associating the act of 1866 with the "grand results of four years of war," Morrill asked, "Are we not in the midst of a civil and political revolution?"[31] It was possible, then, for enthusiastic supporters of Reconstruction like Morrill to argue that Sumner's bill was unconstitutional.

Responding to Morrill, Charles Sumner asserted a "new rule" of constitutional interpretation: "I say a new rule of interpretation for the National Constitution, according to which, in every clause and every line and every word, it is to be interpreted uniformly and thoroughly for human rights.... That, Sir, is the great victory of the war."[32] Sumner did not believe his bill hung on any one constitutional provision. "The National Constitution is bountiful of power; it is overrunning with power. Not in one place or two places or three places, but almost everywhere from the Preamble to the last line of the latest Amendment."[33]

All public institutions, Sumner maintained, were subject to law and maintained by law. "Show me...a legal institution, anything created or regulated by law, and I show you what must be opened equally to all without distinction of color."[34] An inn or hotel, he explained, "is a legal institution, originally established by the Common Law, subject to minute provisions and regulations."[35] Public conveyances are common carriers "subject to a law of their own."[36] Places of amusement are "duly licensed by law"[37] and "kindred to inns or public conveyances, though less noticed by jurisprudence."[38] Common schools are public institutions, "created by law, and supported by the taxation to which [all] have contributed."[39] Churches and cemeteries are also "public in character and organized by law."[40]

Sumner's "regulated by law" standard threatened to erase the boundary between state and private action, but his focus was on extending rights. The National Government, Sumner declared, is the "natural guardian of the citizen,"[41] and the right of equal access to public institutions was a right of national citizenship. Neither the Declaration nor the National Constitution, he explained, "knows anything of the word *white*."[42] Exclusions on account of color were "an indignity, an insult, and a wrong."[43]

Sumner's speeches were not met with enthusiasm, and only a handful of Republicans (for example, Oliver P. Morton of Indiana, John Sherman of Ohio,

---

[31] *Cong. Globe*, 39th Cong., 1st sess., 570 (February 1, 1866).

[32] Sumner, *Works*, 424.

[33] Ibid.

[34] Ibid. See also 371.

[35] Ibid. at 361. See also 388–90.

[36] Ibid. at 361. See also 390–2.

[37] Ibid. at 371.

[38] Ibid. at 392.

[39] Ibid. at 371. See also 393–7.

[40] Ibid. at 397.

[41] Ibid. at 407–9.

[42] Ibid. at 357. See also 384, 401.

[43] Ibid. at 361. See also 363, 364, 372, 408.

The Civil/Social Distinction

and Benjamin Butler of Massachusetts) defended the bill. Republicans opposing Sumner's bill included Carl Schurz, Sumner's closest friend in the Senate, and Senators Orris S. Ferry, John A. Logan, and Matthew H. Carpenter.[44] Carpenter specifically invoked the notion of *social equality*. "To undertake to force men into compliance with social and religious dogmas is to postpone the end desired."[45]

Social equality was a term of opprobrium[46] and all sides converged in opposing the legal imposition of social equality. The term connoted interracial sexual intimacy, which triggered profound identity-based anxieties among whites about the loss of racial "purity."

From the early days of Reconstruction, opposition to public accommodation rights for blacks was expressed in the language of social rights and social equality. In 1868, a radical coalition of activists in Louisiana proposed a state constitution that protected the public accommodation rights of blacks.[47] It was opposed on social equality grounds. Said William H. Cooley, a judge and a conservative Republican, "social equality is attempted to be enforced, and the right of citizens to control their own property is attempted to be taken from them for the benefit of the colored race."[48] Democrats, too, opposed public accommodation rights for blacks on social equality grounds. Sen. Eli Saulsbury of Delaware called Charles Sumner's Supplementary Civil Rights bill a bill for "social equality."[49] Crystallizing the point, Rep. James Brooks of New York stated, "the words civil rights should be changed to social rights."[50]

---

[44] Senator Ferry of Connecticut agreed that the measure lacked constitutional authority (Pierce, *Memoir and Letters*, 500). Carl Schurz, Sumner's friend, "did not sympathize with his friend's pressure.... He kept out of the debate, and his name rarely appeared in the votes" (Pierce, 501). In an early vote on Sumner's bill (when it was an amendment to the amnesty bill), the "no" votes included Carpenter, Ferry, Morrill, and Schurz. In a later vote (May 23, 1874), Carpenter and Schurz voted "no." Morrill and Ferry did not vote. See also Arthur R. Hogue, ed., *Charles Sumner, An Essay by Carl Schurz* (1951). Schurz voiced objections to the schools provision, but he still voted against the bill even after the schools provision was removed. His objections, then, must have been deeper. In 1883, Schurz refers to the bill as a "social equality" bill. In criticism of the bill, he also said the Fourteenth Amendment was "directed against State legislation, and not against the acts of individuals." Schurz states that support for "social rights" was "never strong enough to procure either the adoption of a constitutional amendment or the passage of an act, which anybody expected to be enforced." Quoted in the *Washington Post*, October 18, 1883, p. 2.

[45] Speech of February 27, 1875.

[46] Rebecca J. Scott, "Public Rights, Social Equality, and the Conceptual Roots of the Plessy Challenge," 106 *Michigan Law Review* 777, 787.

[47] Ibid. at 782–90.

[48] *Official Journal of the Proceedings of the Convention for Framing a Constitution for the State of Louisiana* (1867–68) at 290.

[49] *Cong. Globe*, 42d Cong., 2d sess., App. 9–11. Finck (D, Ohio) said Sumner's bill "sought to establish social equality" (*New York Times*, February 4, 1875, p. 6). The Democratic press characterized the bill in the same way. Readers of the *Chicago Tribune* got a sampling of the views of the southern press, and such characterizations abounded (*Chicago Daily Tribune*, May 29, 1874).

[50] *New York Times*, June 8, 1872, p. 5.

In facing charges that his bill protected "social rights" and was therefore outside the reach of the constitutional amendments, Sumner responded that the rights in his bill were *civil rights*. Pointing to *Bouvier's Law Dictionary*, Sumner stated, "A Law Dictionary, of constant use as a repertory of established rules and principles, defines a 'freeman' as 'one in the possession of the civil rights enjoyed by the people generally'."

> There is no colored person who does not resent the imputation that he is seeking to intrude himself socially anywhere. This is no question of society, no question of social life, no question of social equality.... As the law does not presume to create or regulate social relations, there are in no respect affected by the pending measure. Each person, whether Senator or citizen, is always free to choose who shall be his friend, his associate, his guest.[51]

This was not the first time Sumner had made this point. He had earlier defined "questions of society" to be limited to the choice of friends and dinner guests, and he agreed that law should have nothing to do with this. His bill was a matter of freedom and equality under law.

> There is no question of society. The Senator [Hill, who was objecting to the bill] may choose his associates as he pleases. They may be white or black, or between the two. That is simply a social question, and nobody would interfere with it. The taste which the Senator announces, he will have free liberty to exercise, selecting always his companions.[52]
>
> How often shall I say that this is no question of taste, – it is no question of society.... I may have whom I please as friend, acquaintance, associate, and so may the Senator; but I cannot deny any human being, the humblest, any right of equality.[53]

Rep. Benjamin F. Butler, who later managed the bill on the floor of the House, also denied that the public accommodation provisions were a grant of social equality. "The first objection stated on the other side is that it establishes social equality. By no means.... [S]ocial equality was not touched by it. It only allows men and women to come together in public, in the theatre, in the stage coach, in the public house." Social equality, Butler stated, "could only come from the voluntary will of each person."[54] *Harper's Weekly*, the rare white Republican newspaper to support Sumner's bill, called the bill "a moral obligation" of the Republican party.[55]

Republican resistance to the public accommodation provisions can be seen in an episode where the more controversial provisions were stripped. During a late-night session of Congress on May 21, 1872, Sen. Carpenter moved

---

[51] Ibid. at 379 (speech of January 15, 1872). See also 414 (speech of January 17).

[52] Ibid. at 361 (speech of December 20, 1871)

[53] Ibid. at 363–4 (speech of December 20, 1871).

[54] *New York Times*, February. 6, 1875.

[55] April 11, 1874, p. 310. See also *Harper's Weekly* 18 (November 14, December 19, 1874), 930, 1038.

The Civil/Social Distinction

aggressively to take control of Sumner's bill. As Edward Pierce told the story, Carpenter "resort[ed] to an artifice which most of his associates would have deemed unbecoming a senator, carr[ying] a motion to take up Sumner's bill in his absence, a bare majority of the senators being present."[56] Carpenter called up Sumner's bill, moved to strip the provisions pertaining to schools, churches, cemeteries, and juries. Over protest, he pushed the bill to an immediate vote, and it passed at 8 A.M. But despite its stripped-down nature, the measure still died in the Republican-controlled House.[57]

At this point the Court issued the *Slaughter-House Cases*. And based on the Court's constriction of the rights of national citizenship, a number of observers concluded that Sumner's bill was unconstitutional.[58] His bill was recommitted to the Judiciary Committee, where it again sat, as Sumner was absent at the time and in Europe for medical treatment.

The passage of Sumner's bill in 1875 suggests that unity finally emerged and that the party finally cohered on principle or pragmatism or some combination. But this appearance is easily punctured. Sumner died in March of 1874, and this was the major factor behind the bill's reemergence from the Judiciary Committee and its passage in the Senate. In an oft-told story at the time, Sumner made a last request to Judge E. R. Hoar, who was at his bedside: "Take care of my civil rights bill."[59] The day of April 27 was set aside for eulogies on Sumner. As reported by Pierce, all accorded him the foremost place in the history of his country as "the undoubted leader of the political opposition to slavery."[60] The *New York Tribune* noted of the eulogies, "One cannot fail to be impressed by the commanding presence of the dead senator in the midst of his late associates."[61] Only two days afterward, the Senate brought his original 1870 bill up for discussion and passed it on May 22. It is hard to imagine another explanation, other than Sumner's death, for the sudden reemergence of Sumner's bill. The Senate even restored the most controversial provision in the bill, the mixed schools provision. The *Chicago Tribune* viewed the Senate's action as "an act of posthumous glory to Charles Sumner."[62] Writing a history of the act in 1968, John Ezell calls passage "largely a memorial to the Massachusetts idealist."[63]

---

[56] Pierce, *Memoir and Letters*, 503. The Senate was holding the late-night session to consider a supplement to another bill (the enforcement bill of 1871). Sumner was ill, and he remained at home "not supposing any other bill would be taken up" (at 503).

[57] Ibid. at 467–8.

[58] See, e.g., the recounting of *The Nation*, 20 (March 4, 1875), 141.

[59] Ezell, "The Civil Rights Act of 1875," 257. "To Judge Hoar he said three times, varying the words somewhat, in the tone of earnest entreaty, 'You must take care of the civil-rights bill, – my bill, the civil-rights bill, – don't let it fail!' Pierce, *Memoir and Letters*, 598.

[60] Pierce, *Memoir and Letters*, 605.

[61] Quoted in Pierce, *Memoir and Letters*, 605.

[62] *Chicago Tribune*, November 3, 1874, p. 4.

[63] Ezell, "The Civil Rights Act of 1875," 258.

But even with Sumner's death, the House again balked. Republican members of the House faced the upcoming election of 1874, and the passage of Sumner's bill in the Senate was a liability for them as they campaigned in the South.[64] The economic Panic of 1873 was an even bigger problem. When the Philadelphia investment house of Jay Cooke went bankrupt on September 18, 1873, a major economic panic swept the nation.[65] Cooke's firm had been the government's chief financier of the Union military effort during the Civil War and it later became heavily invested in railroad construction. Many railroads had overbuilt, setting the stage for ruinous competition for freight traffic. Cooke's firm had overextended itself, and when it went bankrupt, the effects cascaded. Panicked banks demanded payment of loans; investors rushed to sell stocks to protect their capital; and businesses released workers. The New York Stock Exchange closed for ten days. Wages sunk, unemployment spiked, and an economic depression set in.

It is a political axiom that voters hold the party in power responsible for steep economic downturns. Republican Congressmen were worried. But the Senate's passage of Sumner's bill created another liability for them among white voters. No doubt, the economic downturn interacted with race politics in complicated ways. Perhaps new economic vulnerabilities deepened the intensity with which whites laid claim to a "social" realm where racial caste could be maintained. If lower wages, rising unemployment, and an ensuing depression threatened economic stability, at least the psychological and material "wages of whiteness"[66] could be cashed in. What was clear was that "lukewarmness is charged upon the Republican leaders in the House."[67] Sumner's bill stalled.

Republicans sustained heavy losses in the 1874 election, and the House (along with many governorships) returned to Democratic control.[68] But before House Republicans turned over the keys, they passed Sumner's bill on February 4, 1875, by a vote of 162–99, stripping out all provisions except the public accommodation and jury provisions. Fourteen Republicans voted against the bill, an unprecedented number. Significantly, 90 of the 162 Republicans who voted for the bill had lost their seats in the previous election. This was lame duck legislation. Grant signed it on March 1, 1875. Circumstances – Sumner's death and the loss of the House – conspired to permit the passage of Sumner's bill. Republicans were simply "not a unit"[69] on questions about the principles, political wisdom, or constitutionality of this bill.

---

[64] *New York Times*, September 17, 1874, p. 6, *New York Times*, September 25, 1874, *New York Times*, October 11, 1874, p. 12; *Chicago Tribune*, Nov. 3, 1874.

[65] Sources on the economic Panic of 1873: Henrietta Larson, *Jay Cooke: Private Banker* (1968).

[66] The phrase of course belongs to W. E. B. DuBois, though I am adapting it here.

[67] *Christian Recorder*, June 25, 1874.

[68] Murphy, "The Civil Rights Act of 1875." ("It is hard to estimate the influence of the civil rights legislation in the defeat of the Republican party in the congressional elections. It seems to have been a factor although not the principle one.")

[69] Ibid., 117.

The Civil/Social Distinction

The federalism principles embodied in the bill are also worth noting. In defending his bill, Sumner was using a radical Republican conception of congressional enforcement power. Like more radical Republicans, he held a vision of federal power that permitted the national government to directly enforce the rights of national citizenship, regardless of state behavior. Questioned about the need for such legislation, Sumner and others cited testimony from black professionals that the common law was not being enforced.[70] But his testimony did not occasion the insertion of a state action/neglect predicate. Under Sumner's theory of national power, the predicate was not necessary.

Debate over the Ku Klux Klan bill of 1871 provides a pointed contrast. As the previous chapter showed, centrists insisted that enforcement be limited to instances of state action/neglect. Rep. James A. Garfield was among those to insist on a state action/neglect predicate for federal enforcement of the Klan Act. But voting for Sumner's bill, Garfield made no similar insistence. Neither did centrists in the Senate who passed the stripped-down version on May 21, 1872. What might explain this? Did they suddenly, without explanation, abandon their vision of federalism? This is highly doubtful. It is more likely that they expected this stripped-down legislation to go unenforced.[71] A number of Republicans, including Matthew Carpenter, had also predicted that the Court would invalidate the bill. Then why pass it? Lukewarm support among some Republicans may have combined with the fact that the most advantaged and organized in the black community were loudly demanding the legislation. It may have been in part a political gesture in the Senate to maintain support among this key constituency. Once Republicans lost control of the House in 1874, it certainly became an easy one.

The five-year history of Sumner's bill highlights its difference from all other Reconstruction legislation. Unlike every other piece of legislation – advanced by vanguard radical Republicans and later gaining principled and pragmatic centrist support – the public accommodation provisions never achieved mainstream acceptance. Unity never emerged. If Sumner had not died and if the Democrats had not regained control of the House in 1874, the bill would have died in committee.

The *Civil Rights Cases*, which invalidated the public accommodation provisions in Sumner's bill, is commonly understood as a product of the Republican Party's jettisoning of its civil rights agenda. But if there was never solid support (principled or pragmatic) among Republicans for public accommodation rights, the *Civil Rights Cases* looks less like a result of the party's declining commitment to Reconstruction and rights. It looks more continuous with the situation of the early to mid 1870s: very few firm believers in public accommodation rights and a majority with neither principled nor pragmatic

---

[70] Sumner, *Works*, 372, 373, 422–3, 431–5, 437.

[71] Recall Schurz stating that support for "social rights" was "never strong enough to procure either the adoption of a constitutional amendment or the passage of an act, which anybody expected to be enforced." Quoted in the *Washington Post*, October 18, 1883, p. 2.

70 Rethinking the Judicial Settlement of Reconstruction

reasons for supporting these provisions. There are of course important ways in which the *Civil Rights Cases* reflected the changed political landscape of the early 1880s. But by telling the story of Sumner' bill in Congress, part of my goal has been to reveal a form of continuity between the early 1870s and the *Civil Rights Cases*. Most Republicans never supported public accommodation rights. While a handful of radical Republicans argued early and often that public accommodation rights were *civil rights* and necessary for freedom, more mainstream Republicans doubted or rejected Sumner's bill, calling it a bill for social equality.

THE CIVIL/POLITICAL/SOCIAL TYPOLOGY OF RIGHTS

As the above narration indicates, centrist and more radical Republicans staked out opposing positions on Sumner's bill using the categories of *civil rights* and *social rights*. These rights categories were part of a common typology that divided rights into three categories: civil, political, and social.[72] The typology had a history, though a genealogy has not yet been written.

The categories of civil rights and political rights appeared routinely in antebellum discourse.[73] The categories of social rights and social equality appeared during the Civil War era, when the possibility of ending chattel slavery became more immediate. In other words, as the question of what freedom meant became more pressing, the concept of a right to social equality gained currency. In 1858, for example, Abraham Lincoln stated, "I have no purpose to introduce political and social equality between the white and black races.... But in the right to eat the bread...which his own hand earns, [the Negro] is...the equal of every living man."[74] Expressing the free labor vision of the Republican Party, Lincoln insisted that blacks had the right to the fruits of their labor. These fundamental rights, which separated slave labor from free labor, were *civil rights*.

The civil/political/social typology was a feature of the postbellum era, as political actors of all stripes used it to debate the policies and reforms of Reconstruction. As Mark Tushnet has observed, "supporters and opponents

---

[72] See Tushnet (1987: 884–90), Hyman and Wiecek (1982: 395–6), and Belz (1976: xii–xiii).

[73] *Luther v. Borden*, 48 U.S. 1 (1849): "There are three classes of rights: natural, such as those recognized in the Declaration of Independence; civil, such as the rights of property; and political rights. Society had nothing to do with natural rights except to protect them. Civil rights belong equally to all. Every one has the right to acquire property, and even in infants the laws of all governments preserve this. But political rights are matters of practical utility. A right to vote comes under this class. If it was a natural right, it would appertain to every human being, females and minors. Even the Dorr men excluded all under twenty-one, and those who had not resided within the State during a year. But if the State has the power to affix any limit at all to the enjoyment of this right, then the State must be the sole judge of the extent of such restriction. It can confine the right of voting to freeholders, as well as adults or residents for a year."

[74] Paul M. Angle, ed., *Created Equal? The Complete Lincoln-Douglas Debates of 1858* (1958), 117.

The Civil/Social Distinction   71

of specific proposals shared a common vocabulary, describing three domains of equality."[75] *Civil rights* pertained to the economic sphere and were regarded as basic and fundamental. *Political rights* (or political privileges, as they were sometimes called) were granted by the political collective and were not seen (initially) as necessary for freedom. The *social rights* category designated a sphere in which "association" took place. There was a consensus that social equality could not be mandated by legislation.

The "core" of both the civil rights and political rights categories was well defined. The core civil rights were: the right to contract, to purchase, sell, inherit, hold and dispose of property, to sue in the courts, and to have redress for injuries the same as all others. Centrists and radicals agreed that these rights were necessary to being a "free laborer,"[76] and these were the rights enumerated in the Civil Rights Act of 1866. The idea that contract rights were necessary for freedom had a gendered component.[77] Contract rights, moreover, would soon be tied to the creation and maintenance of the white state.[78]

The core political right was the right to vote. Centrists did not initially see the right to vote as necessary for freedom, perceiving it as a privilege granted by the political community. But Southern violence convinced centrists, for both principled and pragmatic reasons, that black male suffrage was necessary for black freedom.[79] After the passage of the Fifteenth Amendment, the right to vote began a slow and uneven migration into the category of civil rights.[80]

---

[75] Tushnet, "Politics of Equality," 885.

[76] Foner, *Reconstruction*, 244.

[77] Amy Dru Stanley, *From Bondage to Contract: Wage Labor, Marriage, and the Market in the Age of Slave Emancipation* (1998). Women had incomplete access to contract rights. Prior to the Civil War, a number of states had passed Married Women's Property Acts, which provided that "the real and personal property" of any married woman "shall not be subject to the sole disposal of her husband." But contracting for labor was another matter, as made clear by an infamous concurrence in *Bradwell v. Illinois* (83 U.S. 130, 1873) by Justice Bradley. Women's "natural and proper" roles as wives and mothers were the source of this incapacity to contract for labor. This was in marked contrast to political and legal discourse on contract rights for blacks, where the right to contract was integral in demarcating the line separating slave labor from "free labor."

[78] See, generally, Julie Novkov, *Racial Union: Law, Intimacy, and the White State in Alabama, 1865-1954* (2008). While marriage was a contract, and while the Civil Rights Act of 1866 could be read as permitting racial intermarriage, it was established after a legal struggle that the marriage contract was not among the rights protected by the Civil Rights Act of 1866. Marriage was defined as a quasi-public institution, protecting the "purity" of the white family and state.

[79] Voting rights became essential for black freedom, but remained viewed as nonessential for women's freedom. See Garrett Epps, *Democracy Reborn: The Fourteenth Amendment and the Fight for Equal Rights in Post-Civil War America* (2006); Gretchen Ritter, *The Constitution as Social Design: Gender and Civic Membership in the American Constitutional Order* (2006).

[80] For example, Justice Bradley identified voting as a civil right in *Hornbuckle v. Toombs*, 85 U.S. 648, 656 (1874) and the *Civil Rights Cases*, 109 U.S. at 8. But voting continued to be classified as a political right in *Yick Wo v. Hopkins*, 118 U.S. 356, 370 (1886) and *Baldwin v. Franks*, 120 U.S. 678, 691 (1887).

72 · Rethinking the Judicial Settlement of Reconstruction

There was no consensus on a core social right.[81] Historians have identified access to public accommodations, education, and intermarriage as social rights,[82] but the category was misleading and incoherent. Centrist Republicans and Democrats conceived the possession of social rights to be a matter of social standing, and whites determined the social standing of blacks. They used the social rights category to delimit a sphere where racial caste was maintained. Possessing social rights really meant having a right to discriminate in these matters.

The question of public accommodation rights was highly charged, for in play were complex matters pertaining to the "protection" of white womanhood and the explosive issue of miscegenation. As Barbara Welke has explained, public travel, especially in railroads and steamboats, had long been structured by gender and class.[83] The ladies' car, always a first-class car, offered more amenities and safety, while being the cleanest car on the train (it was the last car and furthest from the engine). Unless accompanied by a woman, no man could sit in the ladies' car. The smoking car (the gentlemen's car) had hard seats and was filthy with smoke and soot, as well as spit. Drinking, too, was common in the smoking car. The refusal of black middle-class women's attempts to gain entry to the ladies' cars was a rejection of their claim to respectability. But it was also a policing of contact between white women and black men. Admitting black women to the ladies' car would also admit the black men who accompanied them.

With the end of chattel slavery, white racial anxiety about miscegenation proved the limit of centrist Republican movement to the left. Social equality connoted forced association for whites. More immediately, it connoted interracial sexual intimacy, which triggered profound identity-based anxieties about the loss of white "purity." For these reasons, social equality was generally used as a term of revilement or vituperation.[84]

Democrats expressed even more heated disapproval of public accommodation rights for blacks. They had raised the specter of "social equality" early,[85] strenuously resisting every step of Reconstruction and emphasizing repeatedly

---

[81] Tushnet identifies a "core" to the social rights category, but I do not. See Tushnet, "Politics of Equality," 886.

[82] Hyman and Wiecek, *Equal Justice Under Law*, 396.

[83] See Barbara Welke, "When All the Women Were White, and All the Blacks Were Men: Gender, Class, Race, and the Road to Plessy, 1855–1914," *Law & History Review* 13 (Fall 1995): 261–316.

[84] Rebecca Scott, "Public Rights, Social Equality," 787.

[85] Democratic concern that Republican legislation would extend social rights to blacks arose as early as 1866 during debate over the Civil Rights bill of 1866. Rep. George Shanklin (D) addressed Rep. James Wilson (R), who managed the bill on the floor of the House. Shanklin wanted to add this disclaimer to the bill: "Nothing in this act contained shall be so construed as to confer upon any negro, mulatto, or Indian the right to vote at any election, or to invest them with any other political or social right not expressly named herein." Wilson replied, "That would be only reasserting what is already in the bill." *New York Times*, March 2, 1866, p. 1.

The Civil/Social Distinction

that the United States was a "white man's country."[86] Democrats were committed to dismantling Reconstruction, and the political fighting that continued to take place between Democrats and centrist Republicans is evidence of a deep and continuing rift between them.

Supporters of public accommodation rights attempted to avoid or tamp down the explosive race-mixing dimensions that attached to the social rights category. They attempted to individualize the notion of social rights, defining it as "taste" and the right to choose one's dinner guests or friends. They narrowed "the social" so that is came to resemble what today might be called privacy.

Analytic difficulties attached to both centrist and radical conceptions of social rights. First of all, there was a notable difference between civil and political rights, on the one hand, and social rights, on the other. Rights are a form of individual freedom or liberty created by law, for example, the right to contract, property, and voting. Social rights, by contrast, were conceived by both sides as pre- or extralegal: assessments of social standing and personal taste exist outside the law.

Second, equality is a purely relational concept. If everybody gets contract, property, and voting rights, there is civil and political equality. This relational concept is applied incoherently to both centrist and radical notions of social rights. For centrists, social rights belonged to men *and races*.[87] Civil and political rights, of course, did not belong to races. And if social standing was something whites got to determine for blacks, the application of the equality concept was nonsensical; the prerogative to define the social standing of others could not be equally shared. For the radicals, there was also a troubled relationship between social rights and social equality: if social rights were the right to personal "taste," social equality was not the idea that everybody had the same tastes. The notion of social equality, then, was incoherent.

This general overview of the rights typology hints at an important feature: there was more philosophical and analytic coherence at the base of this hierarchy of rights, that is, at the core of the civil rights category, than there was at the tip. Before the Civil War, Chief Justice Roger Taney had famously declared that blacks "had no rights which the white man was bound to respect."[88] After the war, both centrist and radical Republicans decisively rejected that notion. Tying the meaning of the war to the Civil Rights bill of 1866, they agreed that the core civil rights protected in the bill were necessary in order for individuals to be "free laborers." These rights defined the essentials of freedom, a vision elaborated in Republican antislavery thought.

---

[86] See, e.g., the remarks of A. J. Rogers, 39th Cong., 1st sess., 2411. In general, see Brandwein, *Reconstructing Reconstruction*, 38–40.

[87] See, e.g., Justice Bradley's reference to "the social rights of men and races in the community" (109 U.S. at 22).

[88] *Dred Scott v. Sandford*, 60 U.S. 393, 407 (1857)

74 Rethinking the Judicial Settlement of Reconstruction

But the philosophical integrity of the typology must not be overstated. In addition to the incoherency of the social rights category, there was instability in the other categories. Jury rights were viewed alternately as a civil right and a political right[89] until settling firmly in the civil rights category by 1880. Voting rights, moreover, began migrating from the political rights category to the civil rights category after 1870, but the process was uneven. Once the migration was complete, the political rights category disappeared. The relationship between the civil and social realms, that is, the permeability of the boundary between these realms, was also uncertain.[90] Could blacks eventually gain equal access to the social sphere? Most centrist Republican statements evinced vagueness or ambiguity on the question.[91]

Scholars have referred to the use of the civil/political/social typology as a "shell game"[92] and as an "imagined taxonomy,"[93] characterizations that deny analytic or legal integrity to the categories. According to Richard Primus, "particular rights moved about the categories...depending on whether legislators or judges wanted to confer those rights on blacks.... [R]ights seen at any given time under one category might quickly be gone from that category and appear instead under another heading." Incoherence in the social rights category and the unstable status of jury and voting rights supply warrants for the assessment, but such characterizations are too simple. The core of the civil rights category, that is, the rights enumerated in the Civil Rights Act of 1866, possessed a stability and coherence rooted in Republican antislavery thought, which itself grew from Enlightenment traditions. Analytic and legal integrity thus attached to this region of the typology. Were radical Republicans being instrumental in categorizing public accommodation rights as civil rights? Yes. But the category had instrumental value only because of its legal and philosophical character. Were centrist Republicans being instrumental in categorizing public accommodation rights as social rights? Again, yes. But in both instances political instrumentalism rested on a philosophical foundation shared by centrists and radicals: unquestioned acceptance of property, contract, testifying, and so on as necessary for freedom, that is, as civil rights. Rule-of-law commitments to equal punishment of Klan intimidation and violence were a feature of that shared foundation.

---

[89] For example, in objecting to the jury rights provisions of Sumner's Supplementary Civil Rights bill, Sen. Matthew Carpenter argued that jury rights were political rights. Sumner replied that it did not matter whether it was a civil or political right. "I cannot bring myself to make any question whether it is a civil right or a political right. It is a right." Sumner, *Works*, 443. In the jury cases of 1880, the Supreme Court identifies jury rights as civil rights.

[90] Tushnet identifies the relationship among the three domains as a point of contestation during Reconstruction. ("Politics of Equality," 888–90).

[91] The *Chicago Tribune* posited permeability, but actual movement across the divide lay in the future. As blacks climb the ladder of social respect, the newspaper said, social prejudice will wear off gradually (March 8, 1875).

[92] Primus, *Language of Rights*, 128, 156–7.

[93] Scott, "Public Rights, Social Equality, and the Conceptual Root of the Plessy Challenge," 106 *Michigan Law Review* 777, 781.

The Civil/Social Distinction

REPUBLICAN OPPOSITION TO SUMNER'S BILL

Centrist Republicans blended a vision of black civil and political freedom with an antebellum sensibility about the unfitness of blacks for social assimilation. In his Second Inaugural in March of 1873, President Grant distanced himself from the idea of social equality. Having supported the Ku Klux Klan Act and endorsed the legal concept of state neglect, Grant stated, "Social equality is not a subject to be legislated upon, nor shall I ask that anything be done to advance the social status of the colored man, except to give him a fair chance to develop what there is good in him."[94]

Republican newspapers gave lively expression to this centrist viewpoint. The newspapers were active contributors to debate over Charles Sumner's Supplementary Civil Rights bill, and they closely followed the bill in Congress. They repeatedly referred to it as a social equality bill[95] and a "compulsory social equality measure."[96] "Social laws are laws of nature," declared *Scribner's Monthly*. "Power may destroy slavery but it cannot destroy the social inequality which attended slavery."[97]

When Sumner attempted to secure passage of the bill by attaching an amnesty bill, the *New York Times*, the leading Republican paper of the East,[98] reported that Sumner's objective was "to compel the Democrats to take amnesty, if at all, with social equality for the negro by law."[99] The *Times* stated, "the white people are unyielding in their determination to protect themselves from forced social equality."[100] The *New York Times'* opposition to the Civil Rights Act of 1875 did not mean it had become "conservative."[101] The newspaper would

---

[94] *New York Times*, March 5, 1873, p. 1; *Christian Advocate*, March 13, 1873; *New York Evangelist*, March 13, 1873.

[95] *New York Times*, January 1, 1872; *Zion's Herald*, January 18, 1872; *Chicago Tribune*, February 11, 1872; *New York Times*, June 8, 1872; *New York Times*, March 5, 1873; *Christian Advocate*, March 13, 1873; *New York Evangelist*, March 13, 1873; *New York Times*, December 20, 1873; *Christian Union*, January 14, 1874; *Chicago Tribune*, February 18, 1874; *Christian Union*, June 11, 1874; *New York Times*, August 3, 1874; *New York Times*, September 19, 1874; *New York Times*, September 25, 1874

[96] *Chicago Tribune*, January 24, 1872, p. 4.

[97] *Scribner's Monthly*, May 1874. Josiah Gilbert Holland, editor of the *Springfield Republican*, became the first editor of *Scribner's Monthy*, 1870–81.

[98] Elmer Davis, *History of the New York Times* (1921), 118.

[99] *New York Times*, January 1, 1872, p. 5. L. E. Murphy reports this strategy as well ("The Civil Rights Law of 1875," 114).

[100] *New York Times*, August 26, 1874, p. 5. The *Times* expressed post-passage hostility to the act. March 1, 1875; March 2, 1875; March 3, 1875.

[101] In a study of newspaper coverage given to the Civil Rights Act of 1875 by the *New York Times* and *Chicago Tribune*, A. N. Mohamed takes his bearings exclusively from the statements of Frederick Douglass. Mohamed includes in his sample none of the coverage given to other Reconstruction issues and projects the social Darwinism of the 1880s and 1890s backward onto the 1870s. Unaware, for example, of the *Times*'s coverage of Taft's circular, Mohamed incorrectly labels the *Times* as conservative. A. N. Mohamed, "Attitudes of Northern Papers toward the Egalitarian Laws of Reconstruction," *Newspaper Research Journal* 19.3 (Summer 1998): 47(1). See also note 106.

76   *Rethinking the Judicial Settlement of Reconstruction*

soon give extensive and admiring coverage to Attorney General Taft's 1876 circular concerning voting protections in the upcoming election, demonstrating the paper's support for key aspects of Reconstruction.

The *New York Times* was founded in 1851 by two journalists, Henry J. Raymond and George Jones.[102] Raymond was a centrist Republican and chairman of the Republican National Committee who directed the campaign that reelected Lincoln and strongly supported Ulysses S. Grant for president in 1868. Raymond's centrism was evident in his dislike of Thaddeus Stevens and the radical Republicans.[103] As Elmer Davis reports in a history of the *Times*, the paper opposed the impeachment of Johnson, although this was "not so much from love of Johnson as from an estimate of the motives, and a dislike of the methods, of his enemies." The *Times* was "whole-heartedly" for Ulysses S. Grant in the campaign of 1868, "for its editors had a great deal of confidence in General Grant and in the policies which the party in that year professed."[104] The Republican credentials of the *New York Times* were burnished, moreover, by a series of exposés in 1870–71 on William M. "Boss" Tweed and corruption in the Democratic political machine headquartered at Tammany Hall. The exposés in the *Times* helped lead to the downfall of Tweed (who went to prison in 1872), making the newspaper prosperous and powerful.[105]

The *Chicago Tribune*, the leading Republican paper of the West, consistently opposed Sumner's supplementary bill as it passed through Congress.[106] Calling it a "Civil Wrongs Bill"[107] and a "social equality bill,"[108] the *Tribune* declared early that "the social standing of men is whatever society chooses to give them."[109] The bill passed, the newspaper determined, only because of Sumner's death.[110]

---

[102] During the 1880s, the *Times* shifted its political allegiance and became an independent paper, endorsing Grover Cleveland, a Democrat, for president in 1884. Davis, *History of the New York Times*, 155.

[103] Davis, *History of the New York Times*, 67. Davis praises Raymond for "standing out against the vindictive punishment of the South" (71). Davis was a member of the editorial staff of the *New York Times* in 1921, when he published his history. His use of the word "vindictive" is a red flag, and it means his characterization should be regarded with caution. Davis was writing when "Lost Cause mythology" and Dunning School perspectives on Reconstruction were at their height. Stevens and the radicals were routinely painted as vindictive and vengeful, a characterization the now-standard history of Reconstruction has refuted. See, e.g., Blight, *Race and Reunion*; Klinkner and Smith, *The Unsteady March*.

[104] Davis, *History of the New York Times*, 73.

[105] Ibid., 118. Raymond died in 1869.

[106] Mohamed errs in stating that the *Tribune* was a "strong advocate of the Civil Rights Act of 1875 during the time that the bill was debated in Congress," a result of his method. Unaware of the long legislative history of the bill, Mohamed begins his coverage too late, in February 1875: "All items published during March 1875 (the bill became law on March 1) and February 1875 (presumed height of debate period) were included in the analysis." The error is the presumption. Mohamed, "Attitudes of Northern Papers."

[107] *Chicago Tribune*, May 31, 1874.

[108] *Chicago Tribune*, February 11, 1872.

[109] May 17, 1872.

[110] *Chicago Tribune*, November 3, 1874.

The Civil/Social Distinction

In an important indicator of brief instability in the *social rights* category among centrist Republicans, the *Tribune* expressed fleeting post-passage support for the act of 1875: "We hope that the bill may become a law...and that it will secure to the colored race the treatment they deserve."[111] On a single occasion, the *Tribune* referred to public accommodation rights as a "civic privilege" and "civil right."[112] But this never happened again, and the newspaper persisted in referring to public accommodation rights in terms of "social equality."[113] The *Tribune*'s tepid support is illustrated by its assessment of the act as a "comparatively insignificant measure."[114] It "did not much good, not much harm"[115] and the provisions would have little effect.[116] The paper noted without sorrow that Sen. Matthew Carpenter is "likely right" that the act is "unconstitutional."[117] The *Tribune* was also notably critical of Frederick Douglass and other black leaders who called for vigorous enforcement of public accommodation provisions.[118]

Like the *New York Times*, the *Chicago Tribune* had strongly supported Abraham Lincoln. Its founder, Joseph Medill, helped get Lincoln elected in 1860. The newspaper remained deeply involved in Republican politics throughout the Reconstruction and post-Reconstruction years.[119] Staking out positions that placed it in the Republican mainstream, the *Chicago Tribune* would remain there.

Politically independent journals balked at Sumner's bill. *The Nation*, founded in July 1865 as an independent journal of political opinion,[120] had supported all civil rights legislation until this point. But Sumner's bill put blacks "on a footing of complete social as well as political equality."[121] The bill was "so unconstitutional that probably not ten respectable lawyers in the

---

[111] February 7, 1875.

[112] Ibid.

[113] March 7, 1875. The *Tribune* continued to make frequent use of the language of social equality: "social claims" (February 7, 1875); "social relations" (February 7, 1875); "social prejudices" (March 1, 1875); "social progress lags" (March 1, 1875); "social affairs" (March 8, 1875); "social prejudice" will wear off gradually (March 8, 1875); exclusion from hotels and theatres is a "social prejudice" (March 26, 1875)

[114] March 1, 1875.

[115] February 7, 1875.

[116] March 1, 1875; March 8, 1875.

[117] March 1, 1875.

[118] February 7, 1875. Radical Republicans who pushed for enforcement were "idiots" (March 26, 1875) and "demagogues" (a headline: "Demagogues Disappointed in Making Political Capital").

[119] Lloyd Wendt, *Chicago Tribune: The Rise of a Great American Newspaper* (1979).

[120] The weekly was published out of New York by Joseph H. Richards (who had been editor of the *Independent* and selected Abraham Lincoln to speak at Cooper Union in 1860). The editor was E. L. Godkin, and under him *The Nation* "supported free trade, railed against political corruption and advocated liberal reforms." The literary editor was Wendell Phillips Garrison, son of William Lloyd Garrison. In 1881, Henry Villard, a newspaperman–railroad baron, acquired *The Nation*, but Godkin stayed on as editor until 1899.

[121] *The Nation*, vol. 37 (October 18, 1883).

country could be found who would be willing to father it."[122] But *The Nation* did not get angry. Instead, *The Nation* found the bill "amusing" and "teatable nonsense," stating that blacks traveled not on railroads but on foot or in wagons and did not often visit hotels. "The number of theaters and operahouses in the South is not so great as to warrant the expectation of a great advance of the race through the influence of the drama and music."[123] For *The Nation*, the act was a useful piece of party work that would not do any harm. *The Independent* condemned Sumner's bill more forcefully.[124]

Justice Bradley's personal writings from the time indicate that he distinguished between civil rights and social rights. Sometime between 1875 and 1876, he wrote in his copybook,

> Surely Congress cannot guarantee to the colored people admission to every place of gathering and amusement. To deprive white people of the right of choosing their own company would be to introduce another kind of slavery. The civil rights bill had already guaranteed to the blacks the right of buying, selling and holding property, and of equal protection of the laws. Are not these the essentials of freedom?[125]

In an undated essay, Bradley explained the concept of social equality this way:

> Such a state [social equality] would make all the classes (I do not say orders) of society commingle in their intercourse; would introduce the cobble into the most elegant drawing room to take a cup of tea with the gayest belle of the town, or else, perhaps, to debate with grave Senators on the affairs of State.... Men *will* choose their own company in whatever state of society you may choose to place them. This is the last vestige of liberty with which they are willing to part...."[126]

Bradley continued:

> We have *no orders* of society. No *privileged classes*. We have a plenty of classes, and this class [those who make laws and administer government] is one of them. It is made their business and their duty (they might have declined if they pleased) to attend to public matters. It all arises from the necessity of the division of labor. All cannot rule, nor can all be ruled. All cannot plow, nor can all sow, nor reap. No more can all neglect such employments, else the race would become extinct. Each has his business to perform, his part to act. It is a duty he owes to the rest as well as to himself. In this way, all are equally dependent, equally necessary, to the body politic.[127]

[122] *The Nation*, vol. 19 (December 3, 1874), 357. See also vol. 20 (March 4, 1875), 141.
[123] *The Nation*, vol. 20, March 4, 1875, 141. See also the *Chicago Tribune*, March 8, 1875 (the number of blacks that will avail themselves of the law is "as yet very small").
[124] *Independent*, January 29, 1874; February 5, 1874; February 26, 1874.
[125] Quoted in Lurie, "Mr. Justice Bradley," 367.
[126] Joseph P. Bradley, *Miscellaneous writings of the late Hon. Joseph P. Bradley, associate Justice of the Supreme Court of the United States : with a sketch of his life by his son, Charles Bradley, and a review of his "judicial record" by William Draper Lewis, and an account of his "dissenting opinions" by A. Q. Keasbey* (Newark, NJ: L. J. Hardham, 1901), 91–92 emphasis in original. No date is provided.
[127] Bradley, *Miscellaneous Writings*, 92–3, italics in original.

The Civil/Social Distinction

It is a shame the essay is not dated. Either it was written in the antebellum era and implicitly excluded slaves from society, or it was written after the passage of the Fifteenth Amendment when blacks were included in the polity (and the matter of slaves' exclusion was moot). Bradley expresses support for political equality,[128] so if blacks were members of the national collective but did not have political equality, he presumably would have thought a privileged class existed. Either way, the passage shows that Bradley ascribed duties to state officials. On the matter of racial hierarchy, the passage asserts directly what is implicit in Bradley's acceptance of public accommodation rights as social rights: once political equality is achieved, there are no orders or privileged classes. Applied to the situation at hand, whites, as a race, had the right to choose their "associates," even on common carriers, but whites were not deemed a privileged "class."

Jonathan Lurie is rare among legal historians in perceiving a hierarchy of rights in Bradley's writings: "[Bradley's] attitude toward racial matters involving social functions rather than political rights should be understood."[129] Bradley's rejection of the public accommodation provisions in the *Civil Rights Cases*, Lurie notes, is not inconsistent with his dissent in *Blyew v. United States* (1872), which expressed strong concern about the exposure to violence that resulted from exclusions of black testimony.[130] As Bradley stated in that earlier decision, it was

> an inestimable right, that of invoking the penalties of the law upon those who criminally or feloniously attack our persons or our property....To deprive a whole class...of this right, to refuse their evidence and their sworn complaints, is to brand them with a badge of slavery; is to expose them to wanton insults and fiendish assaults; is to leave their lives, their families, and their property unprotected by law.[131]

Later in 1883, Bradley explained that the Civil Rights Act of 1866 protected the rights that defined "the essential distinction between freedom and slavery." Recall his statement that the act "did not assume...to adjust what may be called the social rights of men and races in the community."[132]

The combination of Bradley's views should now look familiar. It was a hallmark of centrist Republican thought. It was possible to reject social equality for blacks and reject, in rather arresting ways, Democratic notions of state sovereignty that prohibited federal enforcement of civil rights. In a campaign speech during his run for Congress in 1862, Bradley called the war "a holy

---

[128] For Bradley, political equality meant "an equal right to govern the whole" (*Miscellaneous Writings*, 93). "In what, then, can this political equality consist? Does it consist in each man having an equal voice in the civil government of his country? This is what I conceive it to be" (*Miscellaneous Writings*, 92).

[129] Lurie, "Mr. Justice Bradley," 366.

[130] 80 U.S. 581 (1872).

[131] 80 U.S. at 598–9 (Bradley, J., dissenting).

[132] 109 U.S. at 22.

80   *Rethinking the Judicial Settlement of Reconstruction*

cause – the cause of civil freedom – the cause of human rights."[133] He expressed contempt for John Calhoun:

> This conspiracy has been ripening for thirty years among Southern politicians. They foresaw that power would depart from their grasp, and they concocted this rebellion. It was Calhoun and his compeers who were at the bottom of it. They are the guilty men whose lives ought to have paid the forfeit. General Jackson – God bless him – ought to have hung Calhoun, and then the seed would have been destroyed which has grown up and ripened to such a fearful harvest.[134]

As I show in the next two chapters, Bradley's judicial opinions in *Cruikshank* and *Siebold* and his origination of the Fifteenth Amendment exemption provide continued evidence of his commitment to black civil and political rights as warrants against state sovereignty.

The dominant conception of social equality came laden with tensions and contradictions that neither Bradley nor other centrist Republicans worked out. In addition to the analytic problems identified earlier, new problems were added. The realm of social equality was declared to be one of private association, yet racial intermarriage came to be framed as a quasi-public institution in order to justify anti-miscegenation laws. In addition, common law had long recognized common carriers and inns (though not places of public amusement) as public and duty-bound to accept patrons on an equal basis, a point emphasized by racial activists in New Orleans and by Charles Sumner. Indeed, Bradley, inspired the notion of a business "affected with a public interest."[135] So why didn't centrists confront these contradictions in the social equality concept? It's not as if jurists were incapable of constructing fine distinctions between public and private, or even theorizing a hybrid public-private category.

They were in the midst of doing precisely this in police powers doctrine. Jurists at the time agreed that states could regulate the contact between "businesses affected with a public interest" and the world (e.g., rates). But jurists also regarded such businesses as having a private inner core where the negotiations of labor and capital were not subject to regulation.[136] Even Justice Harlan agreed that a private core existed where labor and capital bargained "freely."[137] These distinctions between public and private ultimately proved

---

[133] Speech of October 28, 1862, reprinted in Bradley, *Miscellaneous Writings*, 137. See also his speech of October 22, 1862, reprinted in Bradley, *Miscellaneous Writings*, 133.

[134] Speech of October 28, 1862, reprinted in Bradley, *Miscellaneous Writings*, 144.

[135] *Munn v. Illinois*, 94 U.S. 113 (1877).

[136] Unless the business was hazardous. See *Holden v. Hardy*, 169 U.S. 366 (1898).

[137] Harlan authored the majority opinion in *Adair v. United States*, 208 U.S. 161 (1908). In this decision, the Court invalidated a federal statute, the Erdman Act, that banned yellow dog contracts. A yellow dog contract is an agreement between labor and capital in which labor agrees not to join a union. Harlan viewed yellow dog contracts to be the result of free bargaining.

The Civil/Social Distinction

81

unworkable as large-scale industrialization reconfigured social and economic relations.[138] But the point is that postbellum judges could work in careful ways with the relevent distinctions. Police powers doctrine demonstrated this. So why didn't the same thing happen in state action doctrine? They could certainly have built a more careful distinction between common carriers and inns, on the one hand, and places of public amusement on the other.

One answer, is that they could ignore the contradictions in their social equality concept because liberal and progressive forces were too weak to demand a coherent rationalization. But the existence of these inconsistencies should not be surprising. The cognitive structures that justify hierarchy are typically shot through with contradictions (e.g., slaves are helpless and childlike; slaves are capable of planning and executing a rebellion). "Social equality" appears to have emerged as a concept to express white anxiety about racial mixing. What mattered was preventing that mixing.

REPUBLICAN SUPPORT FOR SUMNER'S BILL

Supporters of public accommodation rights for blacks struggled against the dominant conception of social equality, and Republicans defending Sumner's bill were continually forced to address the social equality charge.

Rep. James A. Garfield sought to deflect the issue, stating, "God taught us early in that [antislavery] fight that the fate of our own race was indissolubly linked with the fate of the black race on this continent – not socially, for we are none of us linked by social ties except by own consent, but politically, in rights under the law." Sen. Frederick T. Frelinghuysen of New Jersey reported the bill from the Senate Judiciary Committee after Sumner's death.[139] Frelinghuysen denied that it was a social equality bill but also strongly rejected the mixed school and mixed cemetery provisions,[140] an indication that dispute on the civil/social boundary existed even among supporters of Sumner's bill. The Reverend Richard H. Cain of South Carolina, who spoke in the House on behalf of the public accommodation provisions, agreed with Frelinghuysen. As Ezell reports, "[Cain] did not believe that [blacks] wanted social equality; they were not concerned with mixed schools or graveyards."[141]

Radicals were forced to tack carefully on the subject of social equality as early as 1866. During debate over an 1866 bill that extended the vote to black men in Washington, D.C., Democratic Rep. Boyer argued that voting

---

[138] The Court acknowledged all businesses to be affected with a public interest in Nebbia (1935) and upheld the Norris-LaGuardia Act, which banned yellow dog contracts in *Jones & Laughlin* (1937).

[139] Frelinghuysen was a former New Jersey attorney general and would later serve on the 1876 Electoral Commission and in the Arthur administration as secretary of state (1881–85).

[140] 2 *Cong. Rec.* 487, 491.

[141] Ezell, "The Civil Rights Act of 1875," 261.

would mean "negro equality." Rep Glenni Scofield, who later voted in favor of Sumner's bill in 1875, queried Rep. Boyer about his notion of equality:

> Do you mean by equality personal friendship and social intercourse? Why, sir, if there is anything free in this country, or in any country, it is the right of each man to select his own associates. Companionship is free now, and will be then. It is your constitutional right to associate with men of color now, if you are so inclined, while you are not forced to associate with nor even speak to a white voter now, nor will you be with a black voter in the future. On the other hand, it is the constitutional right of the colored man to shun you now, and his right would neither be enlarged nor diminished by his enfranchisement.[142]

Like other more radical Republicans, Rep. Scofield reached for notions of companionship and association to define the social. Sensitive to the notion of "forced" association, he attempted to defuse it.

The negative connotations of *social equality* were so strong that in 1868 a radical activist coalition in New Orleans decided to avoid contesting it directly. Instead, the coalition built a notion of "public rights" centered on the equal dignity of citizens. They advanced a typology that distinguished among civil, political, and public rights.[143] "By framing their claims to equal access to public transportation and public accommodation within the rubric of public rights rather than social rights," Rebecca Scott explains, "Louisiana activists of the 1860s could both assert their status as honorable citizens and try to avoid the charge that they were claiming 'social equality' in matters of intimate or private life." These distinctions mattered, Scott explains. "To use the phrase public rights was to emphasize those forms of equality manifested in the public sphere." The goal of the radical activists was to distance their claims "from the overtones of enforced intimacy and intrusion into private space that the term social equality had come to connote."[144]

The radical coalition won early victories in Louisiana. The state constitution, in force between 1868 and 1879, guaranteed to all the state's citizens the same "civil, political, and public rights and privileges."[145] The radical coalition also had an impact at the national level. Planks in the 1872 and 1876 Republican Party platforms called for "civil, political, and public rights." Charles Sumner echoed the language of the activists, calling exclusions from public places "an indignity, an insult, and a wrong."[146]

In the House, John R. Lynch, a black congressman from Mississippi, spoke in favor of Sumner's bill, using the public rights concept. "It is not social rights

---

[142] *Cong. Globe*, 39th Cong., 1st sess., 179 (January 10, 1866).
[143] Scott, "Public Rights, Social Equality." See also Rebecca J. Scott, *Degrees of Freedom* (2005), 44–77.
[144] "The negative connotations of *social equality* led even quite radical thinkers to eschew the term. W. E. B.DuBois makes this point vividly in "On Being Crazy," 26 *Crisis* 55 (1923). Scott, "Public Rights, Social Equality," 787 n. 42.
[145] Louisiana Constitution, Title I, Article II (1868).
[146] See, e.g., Sumner, *Works*, 358–64.

The Civil/Social Distinction

that we desire. We have had enough of that already. What we ask is protection in the enjoyment of public rights."[147] This category of public rights also appeared in the *Christian Recorder*, a black newspaper: "Every sensible man knows that social equality is an impossibility," the *Recorder* stated, conceiving of social equality as a type of regard or respect. "Give us our public rights and social matters will take care of themselves."[148]

But the public rights concept never gained wide currency among radical Republicans.[149] After some early instability in references to Sumner's bill,[150] the *Christian Recorder* consistently referred to it as a civil rights measure[151] and included public accommodation rights in its frequent refrain for "equal civil and political rights."[152]

The struggle over miscegenation surely figures in any plausible explanation. During the process of negotiating a postbellum order, marriage was redefined as a quasi-public institution.[153] The important and widely reported Indiana case, *State v. Gibson*,[154] played an important role in this struggle. Marriage was more than a private civil contract, the court stated. The health and stability of the state depended on the capacity to regulate it. The move to define marriage as quasi-public was rendered necessary by creative interpreters of the Civil Rights Act of 1866, which prohibited racial discrimination in private contracts. If the marriage contract was defined as a private contract, anti-miscegenation laws were arguably invalid.[155] Radical activists in New Orleans had chosen the public rights notion to avoid any association with sexual and marital intimacy, but *State v. Gibson* conjured precisely this association.

Avoiding the subject of racial intermarriage, the *Recorder* gave extensive coverage to the exclusions of black preachers, lawyers, and other professionals

---

[147] Lynch was probably referring to the rape of slaves. Rep. Benjamin Butler, defending Sumner's bill, used the social equality concept in the same way: "This bill does not touch the worst – the most terrible, the most awful – question of social equality that grew up under the slavery system, when men traded in the results of their lust." *New York Times*, February 6, 1875.

[148] *Christian Recorder*, March 20, 1873.

[149] But it did not disappear, appearing in the *Plessy* challenge to the Louisiana segregation statute in *Plessy v. Ferguson* (1896). See Scott, "Public Rights, Social Equality, and the Conceptual Roots of the Plessy Challenge," 106 *Michigan Law Review* 777 (2008).

[150] There was early variation in the way the *Christian Recorder* referred to Sumner's bill. See, e.g., an early reference to the bill as protecting "civil and social rights" (February 10, 1872) and a reference to the bill as protecting "public privileges" (May 1, 1873).

[151] *Christian Recorder*, February 10, 1872; April 20, 1872; June 29, 1872; December 21, 1872; May 1, 1873.

[152] *Christian Recorder*, September 25, 1873; February 6, 1873; March 26, 1874; June 25, 1874; September 30, 1875; May 12, 1881; January 26, 1882; March 9, 1882; April 26, 1883; May 17, 1883.

[153] Julie Novkov, "*Pace v. Alabama*: Interracial Love, the Marriage Contract, and Postbellum Foundations of the Family," in Ronald Kahn and Ken Kersch, eds., *The Supreme Court and American Political Development* (2006), 329–65. See also Novkov, *Racial Union* (2007).

[154] 36 Ind. 389 (1871).

[155] See *Burns v. State*, 48 Ala. 195 (1872) and the discussion in Novkov, *Racial Union*, 144–8.

84 *Rethinking the Judicial Settlement of Reconstruction*

from inns and railroad cars.[156] Reports consistently referenced the humiliations and insults experienced by the men.[157] There were also numerous reports of the affronts to dignity suffered by black women during failed attempts to gain entry to the ladies' car.

In covering Sumner's bill, the *Recorder* made references to social equality. There was a report, for example, on the views of Mr. J. Sella Martin: "He was no advocate of social equality, because there were plenty of white people whom he wouldn't have in his house."[158] A lecture by Miss F. M. Jackson was also discussed. "[T]he cry of social equality," she stated, "shows deficiency of common sense. Money, influence or congeniality is the law of social intercourse."[159]

The *Chicago Tribune* transmitted a view of civil rights broadly conceived to its readers even as it remained opposed to Sumner's bill. Reporting on a lecture by County Commissioner John Jones, who called for passage of the bill, the *Tribune* quoted Jones: "We must have our civil rights [as] they are essential to our complete freedom.... We are not demanding what is known as social rights. These social relations lie entirely outside the domain of legislation and politics. They are simply matters of taste, and thus I leave them."[160] One Thomas E. Younger agreed, stating that the question of social equality was outside the province of legislation.[161]

An 1872 exchange between the Colored Men's National Convention and the *Tribune* captures the intramural Republican disagreement over the definition of social equality. Meeting in New Orleans, the convention declared its support for Sumner's bill and issued a resolution declaring "a difference between civil rights and social rights, and recogniz[ing] the fact that the social standing of men can only be determined by personal merit and individual achievement."[162] The *Chicago Tribune* responded, "This is not true. The social standing of men is whatever standing society chooses to give them."[163]

---

[156] *Christian Recorder*, June 29, 1872; May 1, 1873; September 25, 1873; January 3, 1884; May 15, 1884; May 22, 1884; June 26, 1884; October 16, 1884. "It was said," noted L. E. Murphy (1927:118), "that it was the professional class of colored people that were concerned by having equal rights such as were included in the bill."

[157] On December 4, 1873, Sumner introduced a petition in the Senate with 10,000 signatures in support of his bill. From December 1873 to May 1874, the *Congressional Record* listed twenty-nine pleas, mainly from blacks and from across the nation, asking for his bill. *Congressional Record*, 43rd Cong., 1st sess. (1873–74), 50, 76, 100–1, 139, 187, 217, 325, 353, 388, 568, 1032, 1135–6, 1346, 1579, 1883, 1920, 1976, 1977, 3564, 3827, 4000.

[158] *Christian Recorder*, August 19, 1875.

[159] *Christian Recorder*, January 16, 1873.

[160] *Chicago Tribune*, January 2, 1874, p. 5.

[161] *New York Times*, August 21, 1873, p. 1.

[162] *Chicago Tribune*, April 16, 1872, p. 1. The same plank was issued, nearly verbatim, over a decade later at the Louisville Colored Convention, *Washington Post*, December 21, 1883, p. 2.

[163] *Chicago Tribune*, April 17, 1872, p. 4.

The Civil/Social Distinction

Radical Republicans continued to forward their version of the civil/social distinction into the 1880s. In 1884, T. Thomas Fortune, editor of a black newspaper, the *New York Globe*, contrasted "civil rights and social privileges."[164] Civil rights, he continued to assert, belong to every citizen in a republic, while social privileges are enacted "according to tastes and conveniences." Likewise, the *Virginia Star*, insisted, "The colored people...do not desire social rights as our enemies are pleased to define them." Invoking the personal friendship/ companionship definition of "association," the *Virginia Star* declared, "We understand social rights and social equality to be the right and privilege of associating and refusing to associate with whomsoever we choose."[165]

The radicals' definition of social rights brought a host of analytic difficulties. The first problem was that personal choice in house guests or friends could take place alongside the denial of social standing to blacks. A white man could invite a black man to dinner (personal taste), even while the laws permitted owners of theaters or railroads to ascribe him a lower social standing and deny him access. A white man's personal choice to have a black man as a friend, in other words, was not logically separate from a system of social standing based on race. There was a second problem. Because radicals conceived social rights as the right to one's taste in friends and companions, social equality cannot be the result of all individuals possessing social rights. Social equality becomes, in this formulation, the right to belong to withdraw from society. Why this realm would be called "social" is not explained.

In the *Civil Rights Cases*, Justice John Marshall Harlan constructed the civil/social distinction as radical Republicans had been constructing it for the previous decade. Born into a prominent Kentucky slaveholding family, Harlan wrote a famous and forceful lone dissent in the *Civil Rights Cases*. Like Sumner and the *Christian Recorder*, Harlan viewed the public accommodation provisions as protecting the "equality of civil rights."[166] Social equality, he stated, was outside the reach of government:

> I agree that government has nothing to do with social, as distinguished from technically legal, rights of individuals. No government ever has brought, or ever can bring, its people into social intercourse against their wishes. Whether one person will permit or maintain social relations with another is a matter with which government has no concern. I agree that if one citizen chooses not to hold social intercourse with another, he is not and cannot be made amenable to the law for his conduct in that regard; for even upon grounds of race, no legal right of a citizen is violated by the refusal of others to maintain merely social relations with him.[167]

---

[164] T. Thomas Fortune, Esq., "Civil Rights and Social Privileges," *A.M.E. Church Review* (January 1884). See also a summary of Fortune's article in the *Christian Recorder*, January 21, 1884. See also letter of Leo Nance to General W. S. Rosencrans, *Washington Post*, October 20, 1883, p. 2.

[165] Quoted in the *Christian Recorder*, April 10, 1884.

[166] *Civil Rights Cases*, 109 U.S. at 48 (Harlan, J., dissenting).

[167] 109 U.S. at 59.

86   *Rethinking the Judicial Settlement of Reconstruction*

In the *Civil Rights Cases*, as in *Plessy v. Ferguson*, Justice Harlan used the civil/social distinction as radical Republicans had used it for the previous decade.[168] But the broad conception of civil rights and the conception of social rights as "taste" never gained institutional traction, proving the limit of centrist Republican commitments.

Early in the 1870s, the *Christian Recorder* scorned what it called the "bugbear of social equality," invoking the imaginary goblin or creature that excited fear in folklore.[169] Late in the nineteenth century, the African-American author and abolitionist Frances E. W. Harper invoked the term in a novel about a slave who is rescued by the Union army and later returns to the postwar South.

> "But, Doctor, what kind of society would we have if we put down the bars and admitted everybody to social equality?"
>
> "This idea of social equality," said Dr. Latimer, "is only a bugbear which frightens well-meaning people from dealing justly with the Negro. I know of no place on earth where there is perfect social equality, and I doubt if there is such a thing in heaven."[170]

The bugbear of social equality existed not only for Democrats but also for centrist Republicans who supported the Civil Rights Act of 1866. Republican Senator Lot Morrill supported that act but also questioned Charles Sumner about the constitutional authority for his supplementary bill. Sumner was partly right when he said that Morrill "makes the system of interpretation, born of Slavery his melancholy guide. With such a Mentor, how can he arrive at any conclusion other than alien to Human Rights?"[171] Some of Sen. Morrill's conclusions, but not all of them, had their source in slavery. The same can be said of Judge Emmons, who derided black access to the "ballet dance" but pointed to Justice Bradley's circuit opinion in *Cruikshank* as providing for federal civil rights enforcement when states left racial violence unpunished. I now turn to that opinion.

[168] According to Rebecca Scott, Harlan articulated the public rights tradition in his *Plessy* dissent. She acknowledges that Harlan "did not use the words 'public rights'" but asserts that "his claim that the Constitution *neither knows nor tolerates classes among citizens* and thus *there is no caste here* echoes the underlying logic of the equal public rights tradition." Scott, "Public Rights, Social Equality, and the Conceptual Roots of the Plessy Challenge," 803. However, in *Plessy* Harlan used *civil rights* twelve times and *civil freedom* four times in referring to public accommodation rights (163 U.S. 554–63). The claim that the Constitution does not tolerate classes among citizens is also part of the radical Republican tradition that advanced a broad conception of civil rights.

[169] *Christian Recorder*, March 20, 1873. The *New York Times* also once called "negro social equality" a "bugbear," using the expression to condemn Democrats who invoked the idea of social equality to stir up violence. *New York Times*, September 7, 1874, p. 4. A supporter of Sumner's bill used the "bugbear" expression, stating, "[s]ocial equality seems to be the bugbear at which American justice is frightened, and the colored man denied many public privileges accorded to other American citizens." Patrick O. Gudridge, "Privileges and Permissions: The Civil Rights Act of 1875," 8 *Law & Philosophy* 83, 125 (1989).

[170] Frances Ellen Watkins Harper, *Iola Leroy; or Shadows Uplifted* (1893), 228.

[171] Sumner, *Works*, 425.

4

The Birth of State Action Doctrine, 1874–1876

It was an act of horrific violence and the worst massacre in all of Reconstruction.[1] After a contested election for governor in Colfax, Louisiana, the Ku Klux Klan and its allies in the White League stormed a courthouse occupied by a contending black faction killing an estimated sixty-two to eight-one men.[2] Some in the faction initially fought back, but most of those murdered had been unarmed or had surrendered.

The case *United States v. Cruikshank* grew from this voting-related massacre. After seeking indictments against ninety-seven men, the federal government brought nine of them to trial and won convictions against three of them. Those three men – William J. Cruikshank, John P. Hadnot, and William B. Irwin – challenged their convictions. And they won, first at the circuit court and then at the Supreme Court. The case is commonly understood as leaving black voters "defenseless"[3] against the Klan and bringing an end to black voting. According to numerous scholars, the Supreme Court decision was devastating because it closed off a state-failure conception of state action. As Lou Faulkner Williams characterizes the decision, "a state's failure to protect its citizens could not be construed as a reason for the federal government to intervene."[4]

---

[1] Foner, *Reconstruction*, 530, 437. For an account of the massacre, see Goldman, *Free Ballot and a Fair Count*, 42–51. The most detailed account is Charles Lane, *The Day Freedom Died* (2008).

[2] Charles Lane has authoritatively estimated the death toll as between sixty-two and eighty-one. *The Day Freedom Died* (2008), 265–6.

[3] Loren Miller, *The Petitioners* (1966), 158.

[4] Williams, *The Great Klan Trials*, 141. See also Kaczorowski, *The Politics of Judicial Interpretation*, xiii (the decision "relegated Southern blacks...to the protection of local law and law enforcement agencies"); Foner, *Reconstruction*, 530. See also Leonard W. Levy, "United States v. Cruikshank," in Leonard W. Levy and Kenneth L. Karst, eds., *Encyclopedia of the American Constitution* (2000), 733; Kermit L. Hall, ed., *The Oxford Companion to the Supreme Court* (1992), 209; Michael Kent Curtis, *No State Shall Abridge* (1986), 179 ("Republican judges were abandoning a commitment to enforcement of...the rights of blacks").

88   *Rethinking the Judicial Settlement of Reconstruction*

Over the course of the next two chapters I argue that *Cruikshank* has been misunderstood. One of its legacies was the succor it provided to mobs that wanted Cruikshank and his confederates freed. The decision also made clear that the Bill of Rights (with First Amendment exceptions) would not be applied to the states, thus blocking an objective of the framers of the Fourteenth Amendment. But its legacies are more complex. The Court opinion made sense within a doctrinal framework that government lawyers and federal courts understood and that became the basis for later successful prosecutions brought by the federal government. Federal civil rights enforcement was no longer vigorous and remained grossly inadequate. But federal rights enforcement remained alive after *Cruikshank*. Acting on their understanding of the Court opinion, the Grant Administration deployed federal marshals in the 1876 election, and the Hayes, Garfield, and Arthur administrations brought cases that resulted in rights victories, putting election officials and Klansmen in jail. The voting rights theories that justified these later federal efforts trace back to Justice Bradley's 1874 circuit opinion in *Cruikshank*.

The complex legacy of *Cruikshank* thus includes both the release of savage murderers and the communication of rules for federal rights enforcement – in a shorthand made possible by the wide circulation and authority of Justice Bradley's circuit opinion – that Republican administrations perceived and later successfully acted upon. These later prosecutions do not mean that *Cruikshank* was a victory for black rights or for Reconstruction in general. But they do indicate that the decision is far more complicated than modern observers have recognized. *Cruikshank* is a key part of a developmental process that culminates in the successful *Siebold* (1880) and *Yarbrough* (1884) decisions, which took place during a period of political transition.

These next two chapters, then, contextualize *United States v. Cruikshank*. I begin with some brief biographical information on Justice Bradley and move on to provide a close reading of Bradley's 1874 circuit opinion, which has never received full scholarly attention. I then examine the briefs for Cruikshank and the arguments before the Supreme Court for the light they shed on Bradley's opinion. Finally, I arrive at Chief Justice Waite's 1876 opinion for the Court. I identify his shorthand – a truncated but legible form of communication that signaled the rights theories elaborated by Bradley in his circuit opinion – and sink Waite's opinion into its political context: the unstable run-up to the 1876 presidential election, when it looked as if the Republican Party might lose the White House. I explain this shorthand as a strategic move, enabled by Bradley's circuit opinion, to both help the party and protect the Court's influence. I leave for the next chapter the reception of *Cruikshank*, which shows clearly that Republican administrations understood Waite's shorthand communication.

JOSEPH BRADLEY: A BRIEF BIOGRAPHICAL DETOUR

Law professor Charles Fairman published a series of articles on Bradley in the 1940s and 1950s and had intended to write a biography, but was unable to

The Birth of State Action Doctrine, 1874–1876

complete the project.[5] Fairman's articles remain the starting point for anyone seeking an understanding of the justice, but a handful of other sources are relevant as well, including a collection of his personal writings.[6]

Fairman's work is devoted to dismantling one of the central myths about Bradley, namely, that he was a "railroad lawyer"[7] and servant of the interests of the great corporate clients. The myth took hold during the Progressive era and was part of the materialist story line about *Lochner v. New York* (1905), which attributed "laissez-faire" policy preferences to the Court.[8] Fairman shows that Bradley's role in cases such as *Munn v. Illinois* (1877)[9] and *Chicago & St. P. Railway. Co v. Minnesota* (1890)[10] run counter to the myth.

The legal historian Jonathan Lurie agrees that he had an "independent attitude toward railroads." Given Bradley's thirty-year association with the Camden & Amboy Railroad in New Jersey,[11] a state-granted transportation monopoly with enormous political and economic power in the state, this is "noteworthy and...very unexpected."[12] Explains Fairman, "Bradley believed that the economic clout of railroad corporations should not permit them to "abdicate their essential duties."[13] Fairman's conclusion was shared by Justice

---

[5] Charles Fairman, "Mr. Justice Bradley's Appointment to the Supreme Court and the Legal Tender Cases" (pts. 1 and 2), 54 *Harvard Law Review* 977 (1941); Fairman, "The Education of a Justice: Justice Bradley and Some of His Colleagues," 1 *Stanford Law Review* 217 (1949); Fairman, "What Makes a Great Justice? Mr. Justice Bradley and the Supreme Court, 1870–1892," 30 *Boston University Law Review* 46 (1950).

[6] Jonathan Lurie, "Mr. Justice Bradley: A Reassessment," 16 *Seton Hall Law Review* 343, 345 (1986); "Joseph P. Bradley" in Leon Friedman and Fred Israel, eds., *The Justices of the United States Supreme Court 1789–1969: Their Lives and Major Opinions* (1969), vol. 2, pp. 1182–94; Cortlandt Parker, "Mr. Justice Bradley of the United States Supreme Court," 11 *Proceedings of the New Jersey Historical Society* 158 (2d ser. 1892); *Miscellaneous Writings of the Late Hon. Joseph P. Bradley*, Preface by Charles Bradley (Newark, NJ: L. J. Hardham, 1902). See also Ruth Ann Whiteside, *Justice Joseph Bradley and the Reconstruction Amendments* (1981).

[7] Gustavus Myers, *History of the Supreme Court of the United States* (Chicago: C. H. Kerr, 1912), 537; Benjamin F. Wright, *Growth of American Constitutional Law* (1942), 95–107; Robert G. McCloskey, *American Conservatism in the Age of Enterprise* (1951), 79–80, 181; Hyman and Wiecek, *Equal Justice Under Law*, 480.

[8] A line of scholarship beginning in 1967 has challenged this narrative. See Alan Jones, "Thomas Cooley and Laissez-Faire Constitutionalism: A Reconsideration," *Journal of American History* 53 (1967) 751–71; Charles McCurdy, "Justice Field and the Jurisprudence of Government-Business Relations: Some Parameters of Laissez-Faire Constitutionalism," *Journal of American History* 61 (1975): 970–1005; Michael Les Benedict, "Laissez-Faire and Liberty: A Re-Evaluation of the Meaning and Origins of Laissez-Faire Constitutionalism," *Law and History Review* 3 (1985): 293–331; Howard Gillman, *The Constitution Beseiged* (1993).

[9] Bradley's role in formulating the doctrine in *Munn* has been well documented. See Charles Fairman, "The So-Called Granger Cases, Lord Hale and Justice Bradley," 5 *Stanford Law Review* 587 (1953).

[10] Fairman, "Joseph P. Bradley," 79.

[11] Bradley was chief counsel, spokesman, and lobbyist.

[12] Lurie, "Mr. Justice Bradley," 368

[13] Fairman, "Mr. Justice Bradley's Appointment," 85.

Felix Frankfurter, who concluded that "Bradley was a striking disproof of the theory of economic determinism, because he, who by his previous experience would supposedly reflect the bias of financial power, was as free from it as any judge and indeed much more radical."[14] Bradley also used his power and influence with the Camden & Amboy Railroad to support the war. "As counsel and director of the New Jersey railroad companies, he assisted very materially in forwarding troops and military supplies. On several occasions he accompanied new regiments to the field, and addressed them on the pending issues."[15]

Waite's biographer C. Peter Magrath notes that "[a]fter the 1850s, no business lawyer worth his salt could avoid involvement in railroad cases."[16] Bradley of course served in a central and enduring capacity for Camden & Amboy, but he also specialized in patent law and had a variety of clients. In short, Bradley remained politically independent from the railroads. His deep commitment to the Union is the probable reason.[17]

As a Whig turned Republican, Bradley became an outspoken supporter of Lincoln. Located squarely in the middle of the party, Bradley firmly opposed the extension of slavery into the western territories, was willing to permit slavery in the southern states, and initially sought compromise to avoid war. He had belonged to the New Jersey colonization society,[18] though it is unclear whether this reflected the interests of his mentors or his own views. Like many of his generation, however, Bradley came to see slavery as "a great evil."[19]

He stepped reluctantly into the political arena in 1862, accepting the Republican nomination for Congress in the sixth district of New Jersey. It was a heavily Democratic district and Bradley lost. His campaign speeches provide a window on his political views. Bradley called the civil war "a holy cause – the cause of civil freedom – the cause of human rights."[20] Recall his statements quoted earlier about the Civil Rights Act of 1866 protecting the "essential rights of freedom." On the stump, Bradley condemned John C. Calhoun. The South Carolinian's doctrine of states' rights was the "seed" that had "grown up and ripened to such a fearful harvest."[21] General Andrew Jackson, Bradley declared, "ought to have hung Calhoun."[22] While details of

---

[14] Joseph P. Lash, *From the Diaries of Felix Frankfurter* (1975), 312.

[15] James Grant Wilson and John Fiske, eds., *Appleton's Cyclopaedia of American Biography*, Vol. 1 (New York: D. Appleton and Co., 1891), 353.

[16] Magrath, *Morrison R. Waite*, 48–53. Magrath suggests that the label "railroad lawyer" is properly applied to Republican justices of the Fuller Court, who specialized in serving large railroad interests.

[17] Whiteside describes this "enduring passion" as overshadowing his professional/career relationships. (*Justice Joseph P. Bradley*, 68).

[18] Ibid., 41.

[19] Ibid., 90.

[20] Bradley, *Miscellaneous Writings*, 137. Bradley was the Republican candidate for Congress. Speech of October 22, 1862.

[21] Bradley, speech of October 28, 1862, reprinted in Bradley, *Miscellaneous Writings*, 144.

[22] Ibid.

The Birth of State Action Doctrine, 1874–1876

his views on war-related issues in the postbellum years are scarce,[23] he made no secret of his contempt for President Andrew Johnson. Referring to the "wretched sophistries" and "detestable heresy" of Johnson,[24] Bradley repeatedly condemned the "recent states rights heresies"[25] of the Democratic Party.

For Bradley, as for Republicans generally, antislavery existed side by side with a belief in white superiority: "of all races of people none has ever appeared better fitted and calculated in all its essential characteristics for advancing the case of human freedom and political liberty than the Anglo-Saxon, Anglo-American race."[26] Whiteside paints Bradley's position as conservative,[27] but in fact it put Bradley squarely in the mainstream of the party. His opposition to black suffrage in 1866[28] also put him at the party's center.

President Ulysses S. Grant appointed Bradley to the Court in 1870.[29] Bradley, as his son Charles put it, was "by belief, by association, by past history" a "staunch Republican."[30] Indeed, a body of evidence regarding Bradley's political views connects him to the political coalition or "regime" that brought us Reconstruction. Eric Foner's portrait of mainstream Republicanism is our lodestar. Clearly, Bradley was no abolitionist or radical Republican. But as Foner traces the contours of mainstream Republicanism and charts the leftward movement of the party's center, Bradley fits that story rather well.

So, too, Bradley had an important political connection: Radical Republican Sen. Frederick Frelinghuysen, with whom he studied law. Frelinghuysen, whom Bradley describes as one of a handful of individuals who "exercised a permanent influence over my life,"[31] played an instrumental role in obtaining Bradley's Court appointment.[32] Frelinghuysen placed Sen. Lot Morrill in special charge of Bradley's nomination, and Morrill, along with Senators Edmunds and Howe, looked after Bradley's case in executive session. Bradley also had the support of Charles Sumner. As an indicator of Bradley's thoroughgoing Republicanism, he earned the "No" votes of eight Democratic Senators.

[23] Whiteside, *Justice Joseph P. Bradley*, 98.
[24] Ibid., 102.
[25] Ibid.
[26] Ibid., 73. The millennial project of republicanism was a racialist project, and Bradley's views were conventional. On this millennial project, See Dorothy Ross, "Historical Consciousness in Nineteenth Century America," *American Historical Review* 89 (1984): 909–28. Bradley left no specific record of his attitudes on race before 1860. That he was capable of changing his views on groups of people is evidenced in his reflections on whether to vote for a Roman Catholic. His personal writings show that in 1870, he answered in the negative. An 1876 notation states that he had lived to learn "that Roman Catholics are as good patriots as any."
[27] Whiteside, *Justice Joseph P. Bradley*, 48.
[28] Ibid., 98.
[29] Bradley's appointment came after the Senate rejected Grant's first choice, Attorney General E. Rockwood Hoar, and after Grant's second choice, President Lincoln's secretary of war, Edwin Stanton, died. Both were more widely known at the national level than Bradley.
[30] Charles Bradley, *Miscellaneous Writings*, 9.
[31] Quoted in Whiteside, *Justice Joseph P. Bradley*, 19.
[32] Ibid., 127–8.

Scholars have made consistent note of Justice Bradley's intellectual discipline. Harold Hyman and William Wiecek call Bradley "one of the most systematic analysts ever to serve as an associate justice."[33] "In terms of legal intellect and learning," states Jonathan Lurie, "Bradley was the most distinguished and able of Grant's four appointments to the Court."[34] Referring to Bradley's "penchant for thoroughness" and "scholarly attitude,"[35] Whiteside describes "precision in method and language" as "the leitmotif of Bradley's lawyering style."[36]

Bradley had graduated from Rutgers with honors, "unusually distinguished as a mathematician." He had a lifelong interest in mathematics[37] and was constantly engaged in solving mathematical and engineering problems.[38] Translating from Latin, Greek, and German was also an intellectual pastime.[39] Charles Fairman recounts Bradley as a "desperately serious" man with an enduring commitment to learning.[40] Over the course of his life he amassed a personal library of over 16,000 books.

Joseph Bradley's blend of characteristics is perhaps captured best by the *Chicago Tribune* as it summed up the worries triggered by Justice Bradley's selection to the Electoral Commission, which Congress set up to resolve the disputed presidential election of 1876:[41] "The fear that the Republicans have is that Bradley is an intensely legal man ... even more legal than Republican ... the Democrats fear that he is more Republican than lawyer."[42] The statement captures succinctly the need to refuse the choice between a "legal" and a "political" interpretation of Bradley's circuit opinion, to which I now turn.

[33] Hyman and Wiecek, *Equal Justice Under Law*, 414.
[34] Lurie, "Mr. Justice Bradley," 351. As an example Lurie points to a civil liberties case, *Boyd v. United States*, 116 U.S. 616 (1886). "Replete with scholarly footnotes, this opinion is a good example of Bradley's deep interest in legal/historical research." Lurie, "Mr. Justice Bradley," 368.
[35] Whiteside, *Justice Joseph P. Bradley*, 66.
[36] Ibid., 137. See also p. 30 ("inquiring mind and Calvinist sense of duty").
[37] As noted by his son Charles, "Much, probably three-quarters, of the time occupied in studies distinct from those incident to the prosecution of his profession, was devoted to mathematics, his favorite subject, and the results of his thoughts and work in that department of science are found recorded in many places, whole blank books being filled and reams of paper covered with solutions and discussions of various problems, indicating profound knowledge of and familiarity with the principles of astronomical, geometrical and physical mathematics." Charles Bradley, Preface to *Miscellaneous Writings*, viii.
[38] See, e.g., his letter to Secretary of the Treasury George S. Boutwell regarding a solution to the problem of exploding steam boilers (April 15, 1872) and his essay on weights and measures (July, 3, 1880). Bradley, *Miscellaneous Writings*, 341–5, 347–9. See also the Preface, ix.
[39] Whiteside, *Justice Joseph P. Bradley*, 67.
[40] Charles Fairman, "The Education of a Justice: Justice Bradley and Some of His Colleagues," 1 *Stanford Law Review* 217, 229 (1949).
[41] Justice David Davis, appointed by President Lincoln, was to have been the fifth justice, but he was elected to the Senate by the Illinois legislature before the commission began its work, and so he withdrew.
[42] *Chicago Tribune*, Feb 14, 1877.

THE CIRCUIT OPINION IN *CRUIKSHANK*

The significance of Justice Bradley's circuit opinion cannot be overstated. It was here that Justice Bradley – a disciplined and systematic thinker – attempted to theorize all three Reconstruction amendments. There was nothing in particular about the legal dimensions of the case that required this effort. Justice Bradley had charge of the Fifth Circuit, the region that encompasses the six states from Florida to Texas, and so the case fell to him. He made an opportunity for himself to attempt a coordinated treatment of the three amendments.

One result was the emergence of state action doctrine in its fullest articulation: the doctrine of state action/neglect applied only to the Fourteenth Amendment. The fullest development of state action doctrine exempted the Fifteenth Amendment from state action neglect rules.

Justice Bradley also indicated in his circuit opinion that Article 1, Section 4 – the "times, places and manner" clause[43] – was the source of federal power to protect national elections.[44] In the South Carolina Klan trials, Judge Hugh L. Bond had similarly indicated that Congress had "power...to interfere in the protection of voters at federal elections."[45] In his 1874 opinion, Bradley fleshed out a theory of rights that linked the Fifteenth Amendment exemption to federal election jurisprudence.

As noted earlier, Justice Bradley attached significant importance to this opinion. In a move that was "uncharacteristic of the reticent justice,"[46] he sent it immediately upon completion to prominent cabinet members and senators, the attorney general, all the justices, federal district judges throughout the South, the editors of three legal periodicals, and newspapers.[47] The opinion, had the imprimatur of the Court, for Bradley had returned to Washington for two weeks to consult with his brethren.[48] Remarkably, later Supreme Court and lower court decisions, cited Bradley's opinion as the authoritative statement in *Cruikshank*.[49]

---

[43] U.S. Constitution, Article 1, Section 4: "The times, places and manner of holding elections for Senators and Representatives, shall be prescribed in each state by the legislature thereof; but the Congress may at any time by law make or alter such regulations, except as to the places of choosing Senators."

[44] "Before the [fifteenth] amendment congress had the power to regulate elections and the right of voting in the District of Columbia and in the territories, and to regulate (by altering any regulations made by the state) the time, place and manner of holding elections for senators and representatives in the several states." 25 F. Cas. 712.

[45] *United States v. Crosby*, 25 F. Cas. 701, 704.

[46] Whiteside, *Justice Joseph P. Bradley*, 55.

[47] Diary, June 12–July 1, 1874, Bradley Papers.

[48] Kaczorowski, *The Politics of Judicial Interpretation*, 184.

[49] Recall the cited cases: *LeGrand v. United States*, 12 F. 577 (1882) (written by Justice William B. Woods on circuit); *United States v. Harris*, 106 U.S. 629 (1883); *Presser v. Illinois*, 116 U.S. 252 (1886); *United States v. Sanges*, 48 F. 78 (1891); *Green v. Elbert*, 63 F. 308 (1894); *Lackey v. United States*, 99 F. 952 (1900); *United States v. Morris*, 125 F. 322 (1903); *Karem v. United States*, 121 F. 250 (1903); *Ex parte Riggins*, 134 F. 404 (1904); *United States v. Powell*, 151 F. 648 (1907).

The Question

After a long and fitful process, the Justice Department secured convictions of three men (among the ninety-seven originally indicted) under Section 6 of the Enforcement Act of 1870.[50] William Cruikshank and his confederates argued that the federal government lacked the authority to prosecute them. They claimed that Section 6 was an unconstitutional intrusion into state matters. "The main ground of objection," as reported by Justice Bradley, "is that the act is municipal in its character, operating directly on the conduct of individuals, and taking the place of ordinary state legislation; and that there is no constitutional authority for such an act, inasmuch as the state laws furnish adequate remedy for the alleged wrongs committed."[51] The Enforcement Act of 1870 was passed under the Fourteenth and Fifteenth Amendments, and so the power of Congress to protect rights under both amendments was at issue.

The Hybrid Constitution

He began by pointing to *Prigg v. Pennsylvania*.[52] The antebellum decision invalidated the personal liberty laws of Pennsylvania that required slave catchers to produce proof of identity for runaway slaves. The Court invalidated the laws, holding that the Fugitive Slave Clause in the Constitution and the Fugitive Slave Law of 1793 created the right to the return of fugitive slaves. The personal liberty laws interfered with this right. However, the decision was not as pro-slavery as it appeared: states could pass laws that prohibited their officers from administering the rendition process. The federal government could provide for rendition, but it would have to do so itself.[53]

Bradley cited *Prigg* for the contention that "congress has power to enforce, by appropriate legislation, every right and privilege given or guarantied by

---

[50] Recall that Section 6 was a conspiracy statute that made it a felony for two or more persons to "band or conspire together" to "injure, oppress, threaten, or intimidate any citizen with intent to prevent or hinder his free exercise and enjoyment of any right or privilege granted or secured to him by the Constitution or laws of the United States."

[51] 25 F. Cas. 708–9.

[52] 41 U.S. 618 (1842).

[53] "As to the authority so conferred upon state magistrates [to deal with runaway slaves], while a difference of opinion has existed, and may exist still on the point, in different states, whether state magistrates are bound to act under it; none is entertained by this Court that state magistrates may, if they choose, exercise that authority, unless prohibited by state legislation" *Prigg v. Pennsylvania*, 41 U.S. at 622. The inability of the federal government to compel the actions of state officials was a problem that drew the intellectual energy of Judge Bond (see *United States v. Petersburg*, 27 F. Cas. at 510) and Justice Bradley/Judge Woods in *United States v. Hall*, 26 F. Cas. at 81 ("as it would be unseemly for congress to interfere directly with state enactments, and as it cannot compel the activity of state officials, the only appropriate legislation it can make is that which will operate directly on offenders and offenses, and protect the rights which the amendment secures").

The Birth of State Action Doctrine, 1874–1876

the constitution."[54] Note the distinction between *given* and *guaranteed* rights. The distinction might easily slip by modern readers who regard the words as synonymous. But in fact they designated two types of rights. The distinction proves central inasmuch as it was from it that Justice Bradley generated both state action doctrine, which included state neglect as a form of state action, and the Fifteenth Amendment exemption.

During the nineteenth century, the Constitution was conceived as a hybrid document. However alien to our own understanding, it was taken for granted that the Constitution protected both natural rights secured by the document and positive rights created by it. A handful of terms designated each type of right. Natural rights *secured* by the Constitution were also termed *recognized*, *declared*, or *guaranteed*. Positive rights *created* by the Constitution were also termed *granted*, *given*, or *conferred*. Section 6, notably, protected rights "granted or secured" by the Consitution.

Granted rights, Bradley explained, had their source in the Constitution or federal law.[55] The Constitution or federal law "gives" or "creates" a right when it "confers a positive right which did not exist before."[56] Recall the discussion of the *Prigg* analogy in Chapter 2 and Justice Story's identification of the right to rendition as a created right, which follows on the consensus view that slavery violated natural law and could be created only by positive law. Congressional authority to enforce created/granted rights, Bradley explained, arose either "from the correlative duty of government to protect" or from the general power "to make all laws necessary and proper for carrying into execution the foregoing powers."[57]

In contrast, rights guaranteed by the Constitution were "not created or conferred"[58] by the document. Rather, these rights were derived "from those inherited privileges which belong to every citizen, as his birthright, or from that body of natural rights, which are recognized and regarded as sacred in all free governments."[59] Guaranteed rights were part of the "political inheritance derived from the mother country." These natural rights were "challenged and vindicated by centuries of stubborn resistance to arbitrary power."[60] If such

---

[54] 25 F. Cas. 710. Republicans during the thirty-ninth Reconstruction Congress, such as James Wilson, pointed to *Prigg* as a source of authority for Reconstruction legislation. My discussion of the *Prigg* analogy in Chapter 2 sets the stage here.

[55] 25 F. Cas. 714.

[56] 25 F. Cas. 712.

[57] Bradley cited *Prigg v. Pennsylvania* as the source of this doctrine (25 F. Cas. at 709).

[58] 25 F. Cas. 710

[59] 25 F. Cas. 714.

[60] 25 F. Cas. 710. See also *Boyd v. United States* (1884: 630) (Bradley, J.). Bradley here is appealing to the Whig view of history as the story of Teutonic liberty. Dorothy Ross describes the Whig view of history as a static form of early modern historical consciousness: "Born among the Teutonic tribes that vanquished Rome, the seeds of democratic and federal self-government were thought to have been carried by the Saxons to England, preserved in the Magna Carta and Glorious Revolution, and then planted in the colonies, particularly New England, where they reached their most perfect form in the American Revolution and the

rights were denied, there was tyranny. Bradley had spoken of these rights before. In his dissenting opinion in the *Slaughter-House Cases*, he had written that the rights to "personal security, personal liberty and private property" were "wrested from English sovereigns."[61]

The idea of natural rights was a familiar one and had long been used to justify the American Revolution. As Haakonssen explains, "If certain basic rights were to be the moral touchstone by means of which the conduct of all instituted authority was to be checked, such rights must exist on a basis that made them transcend all institutions of authority. They must somehow be inherent to the human species.... Furthermore, the institutions of civil society must be seen primarily as safeguards for such rights."[62] Some body of, inalienable rights – never conceived with exactitude – remained a basic minimum.

> The contract supporting civil government was between individuals who retained an identifiable core of rights, for the sake of whose protection other [natural] rights were alienated to create government. At the same time, by limiting the natural rights proper to the well-known three (life, liberty, the pursuit of happiness), it underlined the alienable [or acquired] character of the rest and so allowed wide scope for the assimilation of the historically contingent.[63]

Civil rights, as Hyman and Wiecek have explained, was "a natural law concept."[64] An equality of basic rights was also part of natural law thinking.[65] When the Civil Rights Act of 1866 (or the Thirteenth Amendment, by some accounts) extended *civil rights* to blacks, it was not conceived as a *creation* of rights. Rather, the legislation extended natural rights to a new class of persons. An equality of rights had always been part of the natural law tradition.[66]

The category of *declared* rights may look familiar to experts on the antislavery origins of the Fourteenth Amendment.[67] Howard Jay Graham, one of the first legal historians to view Republican legal thought from an antislavery perspective, published an article in 1954 titled "Our 'Declaratory' Fourteenth Amendment." Offering a partial recovery of this nineteenth-century notion,

---

Constitution." Dorothy Ross, "Historical Consciousness in Nineteenth Century America," *American Historical Review* 89 (1984): 917.

[61] 83 U.S. at 115.

[62] Knud Haakonssen, "From Natural Law to the Rights of Man: A European Perspective on American Debates," in Michael J. Lacey and Knud Haakonssen, eds., *A Culture of Rights: The Bill of Rights in Philosophy, Politics, and Law* (1991), 48.

[63] Ibid., 50.

[64] Hyman and Wiecek, *Equal Justice Under Law*, 406.

[65] Haakonson, "From Natural Law," 51.

[66] This is in part why framers of the Fourteenth Amendment identified it as revolutionary and corrective at the same time. See Brandwein, *Reconstructing Reconstruction*, 6–7.

[67] See Akhil Reed Amar, *The Bill of Rights: Creation and Reconstruction* (1998), 148; Howard Jay Graham, "Our 'Declaratory' Fourteenth Amendment," 7 *Stanford Law Review* 3, 3–4 (1954); Jacobus tenBroek, *Equal Under Law* (1951), 90–1.

Graham described the concept of a declaratory constitutional amendment as "baffling" to a modern audience.[68] It was necessary to recover the concept, Graham argued, in order to perceive the original incorporation of the Bill of Rights by the Fourteenth Amendment. Justice Bradley, along with the other *Slaughter-House* dissenters, lost the battle to gain Court recognition for original incorporation, but natural rights concepts and the notion of a *declared* right did not disappear from post–Civil War jurisprudence.[69] Court decisions as late as 1892 (*Logan*) map the declared/created distinction.

Justice Bradley worked this legal distinction to build a coordinated view of the Reconstruction amendments. He tried to generate rules for congressional enforcement, first, from the type of right protected and, second, from the wording of the amendment. The nature of the three amendments, however, resisted theorization.

The Emergence of State Action Doctrine

Bradley explained that the manner in which Congress could enforce rights under the Reconstruction amendments depended on the type of right at issue.[70] Thus, different rules pertained to the federal enforcement of declared and created rights.

When natural rights were declared or secured through prohibitory language, Congress could provide only corrective remedies. Federal remedies were contingent on state rights denials.

> With regard to those acknowledged rights and privileges of the citizen, which form a part of his political inheritance derived from the mother country, and which were challenged and vindicated by centuries of stubborn resistance to arbitrary power, they belong to him as his birthright, and it is the duty of the particular state of which he is a citizen to protect and enforce them, and to do naught to deprive him of their full enjoyment. When any of these rights and privileges are secured in the constitution of the United States only by a declaration that the state or the United States shall not violate or abridge them, it is at once understood that they are not created or conferred by the constitution, but that the constitution only guaranties that they shall not be impaired by the state, or the United States, as the case may be.[71]

Here is state action doctrine, theorized: the state action rule pertained to congressional enforcement of natural rights secured or declared by the Constitution.

---

[68] Howard Jay Graham, "Our 'Declaratory' Fourteenth Amendment," 7 *Stanford Law Review* 3 (1954).

[69] Both Miller and Waite invoked "natural rights" in their opinions. See, e.g., *United States v. Cruikshank* (1876: 555) (Waite), *Campbell v. Holt* (1885: 629) (Miller), and *In re Brosnahan* (1883: 67) (Miller). See also *Yick Wo v. Hopkins* (1884: 370) (Matthews).

[70] 25 F. Cas. 710. ("The method of enforcement, or the legislation appropriate to that end, will depend upon the character of the right" at issue.)

[71] Ibid.

98 *Rethinking the Judicial Settlement of Reconstruction*

Congress's power to enforce these rights did not extend, Bradley explained, to "ordinary crime." The effect of such an extension, "would be to clothe congress with power to pass laws for the general preservation of social order in every state." Congressional enforcement power was thus limited to oversight.

> The enforcement of the guaranty does not require or authorize congress to perform the duty which the guaranty itself supposes it to be the duty of the state to perform, and which it requires the state to perform. The duty and power of enforcement *take their inception from the moment that the state fails to comply with the duty enjoined, or violates the prohibition imposed.*[72]

This is state action doctrine. A state's failure to comply with duties thus counts as a state denial of rights, that is, state action, triggering federal enforcement power. Bradley summed up the state action rule on the next page of the opinion. And again he included the concept of state neglect as a form of state action.

> [W]ith regard to mere constitutional prohibitions of state interference with established or acknowledged privileges and immunities, the appropriate legislation to enforce such prohibitions is that which may be necessary or proper *for furnishing suitable redress when such prohibitions are disregarded or violated.* Where no violation is attempted, the interference of congress would be officious, unnecessary, and inappropriate.[73]

Bradley is thus being consistent with his articulation of state action doctrine, identifying state neglect as a form of state action several times.

The *Chicago Tribune* clearly perceived the concept of state neglect, offering this paraphrase of Bradley's state action rule:

> The moment the State fails to comply with the duties enforced upon it, the United States is called on to interfere, and the interference of Congress, when a State is ready to punish a violation of these rights, is unnecessary, injudicious and illegal.... When a State refuses this right, Congress has the power to pass laws to enforce the amendment. Congress has also the power to secure these rights against individuals.[74]

The New Orleans *Picayune* had a similar understanding. In conveying this sense of the decision, neither newspaper expressed shock or horror, which the norms of the time certainly permitted.

The Fifteenth Amendment Exemption

To understand Justice Bradley's rule for Fifteenth Amendment enforcement, we must track the legal distinction between *secured* and *created* rights previously noted. We have just seen that the Fourteenth Amendment had prohibitory language and protected *declared* rights, and it was from this combination

---

[72] Ibid., emphasis added.
[73] 25 F. Cas. 711, emphasis added.
[74] *Chicago Tribune*, June 28, 1874, p. 16.

The Birth of State Action Doctrine, 1874–1876

that Bradley derived the state action/neglect rule. The Fifteenth Amendment had prohibitory language but *created* a new right: the right to exemption from racial interference in voting. This put Bradley in a bind, as the amendment's prohibitory text and its creation of a right pointed to different rules for federal enforcement.

He took note of the prohibitory language: "negative in form, and therefore, at first view, apparently to be governed by the rule that congress has no duty to perform until the state has violated its provisions." But "nevertheless in substance, *it confers a positive right which did not exist before*. The language is peculiar. It is composed of two negatives. The right shall not be denied. That is, the right shall be enjoyed; the right, namely, to be exempt from the disability of race, color, or previous condition of servitude, as respects the right to vote."[75]

> The manner in which the prohibition (or the equal right to vote) may be enforced is, of course, the question of principal interest in this inquiry. When the right of citizens of the United States to vote is denied or abridged by a state on account of their race, color, or previous condition of servitude, *either by withholding the right itself or the remedies which are given to other citizens to enforce it*, then, undoubtedly, congress has the power to pass laws to directly enforce the right and punish individuals for its violation, because that would be the only appropriate and efficient mode of enforcing the amendment.[76]

At a minimum, then, a state neglect rule applied. But the creation of the new right made it clear "that the only practical way in which congress can enforce the amendment is by itself giving a remedy and giving redress."[77]

> The real difficulty in the present case is to determine whether the amendment has given to congress any power to legislate except to furnish redress in cases where the states violate the amendment. Considering, as before intimated, that the amendment, notwithstanding its negative form, substantially guaranties the equal right to vote to citizens of every race and color, I am inclined to the opinion that congress has the power to secure that right not only as against the unfriendly operation of state laws, but against outrage, violence, and combinations on the part of individuals, irrespective of the state laws.[78]

Bradley thus dispensed with the text. The creation of a right to vote free from racial interference gave the federal government plenary control over enforcement. Congress had the power to punish private race-based interference in voting without predicating such intervention on state behavior, which is to say that federal enforcement of the Fifteenth Amendment was

---

[75] 25 F. Cas. 712, emphasis added.

[76] 25 F. Cas. 713.

[77] Ibid. Judge Hugh Bond appeared to say the same thing in an 1874 decision, *U.S. v. Petersburg Judges of Elections*, 27 F. Cas. 506 (1874).

[78] 25 F. Cas. 713.

exempt from the state action/neglect rule.[79] The only requirement for federal enforcement was that interference in voting (by officials or private individuals) be "on account of race, color, or previous condition of servitude."

> No interference with a person's right to vote, unless made on account of his race, color or previous condition of servitude, is subject to congressional animadversion. There may be a conspiracy to prevent persons from voting having no reference to this discrimination. It may include whites as well as blacks, or may be confined altogether to the latter. It may have reference to the particular politics of the parties. All such conspiracies are amenable to the state laws alone. To bring them within the scope of the amendment and of the powers of congress they must have for motive the race, color or previous condition of servitude of the party whose right is assailed.[80]

Thus we have the Fifteenth Amendment exemption: the federal government could punish private race-based interference in voting regardless of state behavior. As we will see, Republican administrations did not take vigorous advantage of the exemption, but they did use it, winning some important cases. The Fifteenth Amendment exemption was also identified, employed, and cited as late as 1903 in case law and 1909 in scholarship.

There was, in sum, a rationale for different enforcement rules under the Fourteenth and Fifteenth Amendments, though the presence of "no state" language in both amendments meant that the different rules were not fully principled. But the declared/created rights distinction had integrity and was used in a consistent manner across different cases. The Waite Court's subsequent attribution to the federal government of plenary power to enforce all created rights confirms this. The consistent recognition of plenary power to protect the right to vote in national elections (another created right) is just one example.

Bradley's choice to ignore the text of the Fifteenth Amendment and give priority to the type of right it protected also worked to the benefit of the Republican Party. This lends a political dimension to that choice. Bradley could have given priority to its prohibitory language, an alternative legal move, which more narrowly restricted federal enforcement power (keep in mind that the state neglect rule is, here, the more narrow of the two choices). Therefore, the Fifteenth Amendment exemption was not necessary. He had to prioritize text or type-of-right – they could not be reconciled in deriving a rule for federal rights enforcement – and in giving precedence to the latter Bradley helped Republican administrations. Federal voting rights enforcement was easier under the Fifteenth

---

[79] The case summary provided by Lexis.com misses all of this, completely misidentifying Bradley's Fifteenth Amendment rule. Here is the Lexis case summary: "Congress only had the power under the Fifteenth Amendment to interfere with the state's regulation of the right to vote when state laws made a distinction as to race, color, or previous condition of servitude." Lexis misses both the state neglect formulation and his final statement, substituting a Democratic state action rule, which Bradley never came close to articulating.

[80] 25 F. Cas. 713–14.

The Birth of State Action Doctrine, 1874–1876

Amendment exemption than it would have been under the state neglect rule, and so party efforts to build southern Republicanism were buttressed.

Racializing the Thirteenth Amendment

Justice Bradley also elaborated a rule for federal enforcement of the Thirteenth Amendment. He worked a distinction between "ordinary crimes" and race-based interferences in "liberty," which would later be central in his construction of the equal protection clause of the Fourteenth Amendment.

The Thirteenth Amendment declares that "Neither slavery nor involuntary servitude...shall exist in the United States," and so it was incumbent upon Bradley to supply a legal definition of freedom. For this he turned to the Civil Rights Act of 1866. Under the Thirteenth Amendment, he explained, Congress "acquired the power not only to legislate for the eradication of slavery, but the power to give full effect to this bestowment of liberty on these millions of people. All this it essayed to do by the civil rights bill, passed April 9, 1866."[81] The act of 1866 provided in part for the equal protection of *civil rights*, that core group of rights that centrist and radical Republicans agreed were necessary for freedom. The federal government could thus punish race-based interference in *civil rights* under the Thirteenth Amendment.

But Congress was not authorized under the Thirteenth Amendment "to pass laws for the punishment of ordinary crimes...against persons of the colored race or any other race. That belongs to the state government alone."[82] By "ordinary felonious or criminal intent,"[83] Bradley meant "malice, revenge, hatred, or gain," without any design to interfere with the rights of citizenship or the equal protection of the law on a racial basis.[84] "All ordinary murders, robberies, assaults, thefts, and offenses whatsoever are cognizable only in the state courts, unless, indeed, the state should deny to the class of persons referred to the equal protection of the laws."[85] Charges drawn up under the Thirteenth Amendment, therefore, had to specify a racial motive:

> To constitute an offense, therefore, of which congress and the courts of the United States have a right to take cognizance under this amendment, there must be a design to injure a person, or deprive him of his equal right of enjoying the protection of the laws, by reason of his race, color, or previous condition of servitude. Otherwise it is a case exclusively within the jurisdiction of the state and its courts.[86]

---

[81] 25 F. Cas. 711. Later in the *Civil Rights Cases*, Justice Bradley was noncommittal about whether the act of 1866 was authorized under the Thirteenth Amendment. He explicitly identified the act of 1866 (which was re-enacted in the Act of 1870) as Fourteenth Amendment legislation. There was instability on this subject for Bradley.

[82] 25 F. Cas. 712.

[83] 25 F. Cas. at 714.

[84] 25 F. Cas. at 712.

[85] 25 F. Cas. at 711–12.

[86] Ibid.

Justice Bradley thus racialized the Thirteenth Amendment. He imposed a racial limitation that was not present in the text. A commitment to protecting the civil freedom of blacks is evident in Bradley's conclusion, where he declares that the national government was permitted to intervene in the "war of race." His language was forceful:

> The war of race, whether carried on in a guerrilla or predatory form, or by private combinations, or even by private outrage or intimidation, is subject to the jurisdiction of the government of the United States; and when any atrocity is committed which may be assigned to this cause it may be punished by the laws and in the courts of the United States.[87]

In generating a rule for federal enforcement of the Thirteenth Amendment, Bradley was confronted with the opposite version of the problem generated by the Fifteenth Amendment, though he did not walk through this problem in similar fashion. The Thirteenth Amendment's text and the type of right it protected could not be reconciled, but here it was the text that supported the broader view of federal authority. The Thirteenth Amendment had no prohibitory language, suggesting that no state action/neglect rule applied. The amendment "is not merely a prohibition against the passage or enforcement of any law inflicting or establishing slavery or involuntary servitude, but it is a positive declaration that slavery shall not exist. It prohibits the thing."[88] But it did not create a right. It was the consensus position that natural law protected freedom (the right to enslave was a created right), and so the Amendment's recognition of the natural right suggested that state infringement was a necessary predicate for federal intervention.

In presenting the "war of race" rule, Bradley appeared to prioritize the language of the Thirteenth Amendment (even as he ignored the absence of a racial limitation). The federal government had jurisdiction of the "war of race" under the Thirteenth Amendment regardless of state behavior. In the *Civil Rights Cases*, Bradley explicitly treats the Civil Rights Act of 1866 as Fourteenth Amendment legislation, insisting on a state action/neglect predicate for the federal enforcement of the act of 1866. This appears to reflect a prioritization of the type-of-right, though Bradley does not say so explicitly. This instability is a feature of Bradley's jurisprudence.

Both prioritizations, however, bespeak a commitment to black civil freedom and to federalism. As Justice Bradley explained in *Cruikshank* when he distinguished between ordinary and race-based crimes and when he identified state neglect as a form of state action: unless both moves are made, "we are driven to one of two extremes – either that congress can never interfere where the state laws are unobjectionable, *however remiss the state authorities may be in executing them*, and however much a proscribed race may be oppressed; or that congress may pass an entire body of municipal law for the

---

[87] 25 F. Cas. 714.
[88] 25 F. Cas. 711.

The Birth of State Action Doctrine, 1874–1876   103

protection of person and property within the states, to operate concurrently with the state laws, for the protection and benefit of a particular class of the community."[89] Together the two moves protected blacks' civil freedom and preserved federalism.

Later in the *Civil Rights Cases*, Bradley stated that Section 5 did not authorize Congress to pass a "code of municipal law for the regulation of private rights."[90] The canonical interpretation of this language insists that it definitively prohibits the federal government from punishing private individuals. Bradley's *Cruikshank* opinion, however, used the no-code-of-municipal-law language not to reject congressional regulation of private individuals in all instances but rather to steer between the radical Republican position, which would permit congressional enforcement regardless of state behavior, and the Democratic position, which would bar federal intervention unless state laws discriminated on their face. In steering between these poles, Bradley affirmed the federal prosecution of unpunished private individuals under the Civil Rights bill of 1866. That bill "was intended to give to the colored race the rights of citizenship, and to protect them, as a race, or class, from unfriendly state legislation and from lawless combinations."[91] In both his *Cruikshank* opinion and the *Civil Rights Cases*, we see commitments to both race-based protections and federalism.

Bradley's middle path between Democratic and Radical Republican positions was different in a key respect from the middle path carved out by centrist Republicans in the forty-second Reconstruction Congress, which passed the Klan Act of 1871. In specifying that a racial motive must be alleged in the indictment, Bradley blocked the effort of centrist Republicans in Congress to include political violence against white Republicans in the ambit of the equal protection clause. Just as there was no textual basis for racializing the Thirteenth Amendment, there was no textual basis for limiting the concept of state neglect to race-based interference. (Keep in mind, there is no textual basis for the twentieth-century practice of applying "strict scrutiny" to racial classifications and "intermediate scrutiny" to gender classifications. These practices emerge from history and from general understandings about group-based subordination.) But as we will see, Bradley and the Court would not leave white Republicans entirely unprotected; they were covered in the Court's federal elections jurisprudence.

A side point: there are scholars today who have taken note of Bradley's "war of race" language and have concluded from it that he abandoned the view in 1883 when he ruled that race-based exclusion from public accommodations was not a violation of the Thirteenth Amendment. John Anthony Scott, for example, sees a contradiction between Bradley's 1874 statement that private race-based intimidation and outrages were part of the "war of race,"

---

[89] Ibid., emphasis added.
[90] 109 U.S. at 11.
[91] 25 F. Cas. 708.

104   *Rethinking the Judicial Settlement of Reconstruction*

which could be punished by the federal government under the Thirteenth Amendment, and Bradley's 1883 view that private race-based exclusions from public accommodations were not part of the "war of race," and so could not be punished. Scott concludes that Bradley's 1883 rejection of the Civil Rights Act of 1875 was a reversal of his support in 1874 for the Civil Rights Act of 1866.[92]

But there was no contradiction or reversal. Scott misses the critical significance of the civil/social distinction used by Justice Bradley. For Bradley, the "war of race" pertained to the *civil rights* category, which now included voting. Centrist Republicans, as we have seen, put public accommodation rights into the *social rights* category.[93] The recovery and translation of the civil/social distinction in centrist Republican thought is thus essential for understanding the scope of Bradley's "war of race" language. It never encompassed race-based exclusions from public accommodations.

Throwing Out the Indictment

With his *Cruikshank* opinion, Justice Bradley thus puts into place rules for congressional enforcement of the Fourteenth and Fifteenth Amendments. He proceeds to make short order of the indictment, throwing out all counts. Of particular importance here are the counts drawn under the equal protection clause[94] and the Fifteenth Amendment.

Let's start with the equal protection counts. What was wrong with them? The first headnote gives the answer: "An indictment under the enforcement act [of 1870] or civil rights bill [of 1866] for violating civil rights, should state that the offense charged was committed against the person injured by reason of his race, color, or previous condition of servitude."[95] The opinion contains an elaboration:

> The [fourth] count manifestly refers to the rights secured by the civil rights bill.... But the count does not contain any allegation that the defendants committed the acts complained of with a design to deprive the injured persons of their rights on account of their race, color or previous condition of servitude. This... is an essential ingredient in the crime to bring it within the cognizance of the United States authorities.[96]

---

[92] John A. Scott, "Justice Bradley's Evolving Concept of the Fourteenth Amendment," 25 *Rutgers Law Review* 552, 564 (1971). Scott asserts that Bradley once held Justice John Marshall Harlan's view and supported the public accommodation provisions of the Civil Rights Act of 1875 (at 563).

[93] In the *Civil Rights Cases*, Bradley rejects Thirteenth Amendment grounds for the public accommodation provisions: Congress, in passing the Civil Rights Act of 1866, "did not assume, under the authority given by the Thirteenth Amendment, to adjust what may be called the *social rights* of men and races in the community" (109 U.S. at 22, emphasis added).

[94] These counts, the fourth and the twelfth, charged the intent to interfere with "the full and equal benefit of all laws and proceedings" enacted by Louisiana and the United States.

[95] 25 F. Cas. at 707, emphasis added. This language is from headnote 1.

[96] 25 F. Cas. at 715.

The Birth of State Action Doctrine, 1874–1876

> [The Act of 1866] was intended to give to the colored race the rights of citizenship, and to protect them, as a race, or class, from unfriendly state legislation and from lawless combinations. An injury to a colored person, therefore, is not cognizable by the United States courts under that act, unless inflicted by reason of his race, color, or previous condition of servitude. An ordinary crime against a colored person, without having that characteristic, is cognizable only in the state courts.[97]

The equal protection counts failed because no racial motive was alleged. Justice Bradley is clear that an injury to a black person *is* cognizable under the act of 1866 if it is inflicted on account of race, color or previous condition of servitude. Bradley invalidated the Fifteenth Amendment counts because they, too, did not allege a racial motive.[98]

> The fifteenth amendment does not confer upon congress the power to regulate the right to vote generally; but only to provide against discrimination on account of race, color, or previous condition of servitude. Congress, therefore, cannot legislate in reference to any interference with the right to vote, which does not proceed from that cause, unless in elections of senators or representatives. A conspiracy to prevent a colored person from voting is no more a United States offense than a conspiracy to prevent a white person from voting, unless entered into by reason of the voter's race, color, or previous condition of servitude.[99]

Bradley concluded his Fifteenth Amendment discussion by identifying the flaw with Section 6: "The law on which this count is founded is not confined to cases of discrimination above referred to. It is general and universal in its application. Such a law is not supported by the constitution."[100] In his opinion for the Court, Chief Justice Waite treated Section 6 as constitutional, even as he never explained why.

---

[97] 25 F. Cas. at 708. This language is from headnote 5. For language in the opinion on the distinction between "ordinary" crimes and federally cognizable crimes, see 25 F. Cas. at 711–12. ("All ordinary murders, robberies, assaults, thefts, and offenses whatsoever are cognizable only in the state courts....To constitute an offense...of which congress and the courts of the United States have a right to take cognizance...there must be a design to injure a person, or deprive him of his equal right of enjoying the protection of the laws, by reason of his race, color or previous condition of servitude.")

[98] 25 F. Cas. 713–14. Waite followed his reasoning (92 U.S. at 555).

[99] 25 F. Cas. at 708. This language is from headnote 6. For language in the opinion, see 25 F. Cas at 713–14. ("Congress, so far as the fifteenth amendment is concerned, is limited to the one subject of discrimination – on account of race, color or previous condition of servitude. It can regulate as to nothing else. No interference with a person's right to vote, unless made on account of his race, color or previous condition if servitude, is subject to congressional animadversion. There may be a conspiracy to prevent persons from voting having no reference to this discrimination. It may include whites as well as blacks, or may be confined altogether to the latter. It may have reference to the particular politics of the parties. All such conspiracies are amenable to the state laws alone. To bring them within the scope of the amendment and of the power of congress, they must have for motive the race, color or previous condition of servitude of the party whose right is assailed.")

[100] 25 F. Cas. 715.

Commenting on Bradley's opinion, the *New York Times* identified the problem with the indictment to be the missing racial allegation.[101] So did the *Chicago Tribune* and the New Orleans *Times-Picayune*.[102] James Beckwith, the U.S. attorney who wrote the indictment, reacted bitterly in the months following the publication of Bradley's decision. Beckwith wrote a series of letters to Attorney General George Williams in which he complained that Bradley "has not shed upon us any light or disclosed any rule by which a good indictment can be formed. If the demolished indictment is not good, I am incompetent to form a good one."[103] Beckwith further claimed that the White Leagues received their "only vitality" from Bradley and "never would have existed but for" Bradley's opinion.[104] Ruth Ann Whiteside has suggested that Beckwith's reaction had more to do with "Bradley's judgment on the way the District Attorney had shaped the case."[105] Given Bradley's clear instructions for drawing future indictments, the many sections of the enforcement acts still standing, the alarm Bradley's opinion evoked for Democratic lawyers, and the multiple causes of White League violence, Whiteside's interpretation is compelling.[106]

And yet it can be argued that a race-based motive was obviously present in William Cruikshank's behavior, even if not formally alleged. Was this bad faith on Bradley's part and a retreat into formalism intended to subvert judicial protection for blacks? To answer this question, we would need to know how much of the violence directed at blacks during Reconstruction could be captured (and hence remedied) by his requirement for a racial motive. As violence against blacks was politically as well as racially motivated, would the racial requirement operate to put the violence beyond reach? We need to know his evidentiary threshold for establishing action "on account of race." One can imagine standards either easy or difficult to meet.

In an 1874 district court case, *United States v. Blackburn*, Judge Arnold Krekel of Missouri (a colonel in the Civil War and a Lincoln appointee) set a very low threshold for determining race-based action. Instructing the jury, Judge Krekel stated:

---

[101] *New York Times*, June 19, 1874.

[102] "To constitute an offense of which the United States has jurisdiction it must be shown that a conspiracy was formed to take away certain rights from a person on account of his race, color or previous condition of servitude...Not a word is said that this was done because of race, color, or previous condition. This is vitally necessary." *Chicago Tribune*, printing a story from the New Orleans *Times-Picayune*, June 28, 1874, p. 16.

[103] Quoted in Whiteside, *Justice Joseph P. Bradley*, 211.

[104] Beckwith stated, "The white league as an armed organization never would have existed but for [Bradley's] action and the immunity supposed to be found in his opinion of the law in that case" (quoted in Whiteside, *Justice Joseph P. Bradley*, 213). Beckwith also claimed that the White Leagues "received their only vitality from the action of Justice Bradley" (quoted in Whiteside, *Justice Joseph P. Bradley*, 212).

[105] Ibid., 213.

[106] Compare Whiteside's more skeptical treatment of Beckwith's claims with that of Charles Lane, who presents Beckwith's assessments as credible (Lane, *The Day Freedom Died*).

The Birth of State Action Doctrine, 1874–1876

> It is not necessary that there should be direct proof of a conspiracy, but such as may be inferred from acts of the parties, such as going together, in disguise, in the nighttime, the doing of illegal acts, in which two or more unite, using language in the hearing of each other indicating a common purpose; in fine, anything satisfying your mind that they acted in harmony, with a common design, and for a common illegal purpose.[107]

He elaborated on the nature of the acts relevant for assessing motive. "Acts such as entering the houses of colored persons only, while on their nightly, illegal, and criminal errands; talk such as, 'We will give you a touch of the civil rights bill'; notices such as indicate hostility to colored schools, – more or less tend to lead you to proper conclusion in reference to their object, design and intention."[108] In setting the evidentiary threshold, Judge Krekel considered the words of the Enforcement Act, the same legal materials interpreted in *Cruikshank*.

Of course, this example does not speak directly to Bradley's definition of race-based crime. But it does indicate that very low thresholds were possible. Even more important was Chief Justice Waite's 1877 circuit opinion in a Fifteenth Amendment case, *United States v. Butler*. Waite, who had a practice of relying on Bradley,[109] set a requirement that does not appear onerous:

> To convict under this [Fifteenth Amendment] indictment, it is not necessary to find that the conspiracy charged was formed against Bush [the victim] alone. It is sufficient if it is made to appear to your satisfaction that he was included among persons actually conspired against. Neither is it necessary that he should have been mentioned by name in the agreement or mutual understanding of the conspirators. It is sufficient if you find that the conspiracy was formed against a class which included him, and that in the execution of the common purpose it was actually carried into effect against him.[110]

The federal government later brought a successful prosecution under the Fifteenth Amendment, though it was unclear whether the Court was applying Waite's 1877 standard (it didn't say).[111] While Krekel's and Waite's decisions are significant, they do not allow us to reach a firm conclusion about the Court's evidentiary standard. For that we would need a larger body of case law.

It was only in 1976 that the Court imposed a standard of intentional discrimination under the equal protection clause that was difficult to meet.[112] In

---

[107] 24 F. Cas. 1158, 1159 (1874).

[108] Ibid.

[109] Waite's comment to Bradley, which is quoted in the literature on *Munn v. Illinois* (as it was Bradley who was the architect of the *Munn* doctrine and Waite who wrote the opinion): "I will take the credit and you will do the work as usual." Quoted in Whiteside, *Justice Joseph P. Bradley*, 242.

[110] *United States v. Butler*, 25 F. Cas. 213 (C. C. D. S.C.) (1877).

[111] See, e.g., *Ex parte Yarbrough* (1884).

[112] *Washington v. Davis*, 426 U.S. 229 (1976). A large body of case law confirms that the evidentiary threshold was difficult to meet.

108   *Rethinking the Judicial Settlement of Reconstruction*

originating the Fifteenth Amendment exemption, Bradley chose the rule that imposed a lower evidentiary threshold. His choice seems incompatible with a bad faith explanation.

THREE CONTEMPORANEOUS JURY CHARGES: CONTINUOUS INTERPRETATIONS

Justice Bradley's constructions were not idiosyncratic. Three federal judges used the concept of state neglect in jury instructions. Such usage alone makes the opinions noteworthy, but each has other important features worth considering. Judge Krekel's jury charge is of special interest because the indictment at issue was properly drawn (it contained a racial allegation) and because it specified that the neglect of the state officers also had to be on account of race. Judge Ballard's jury charge is of special interest because it previews the reasoning we will encounter in *United States v. Harris.*[113] Judge Emmons's jury charge is noteworthy because, as we have seen previously, he pointed to Bradley's circuit opinion as providing an equal protection remedy for unpunished race-based murder.

The jury instructions by Judge Krekel appear in the previously mentioned *United States v. Blackburn.*[114] In this October 1874 case, the U.S. attorney drew the indictment properly, implementing the rules laid down by Justice Bradley. The indictment was drawn under the equal protection clause, and it contained the allegation of a racial motive:

> The defendants are indicted for conspiring together and going in disguise on the highway, and on the premises of Lucas and others, for the purpose of depriving them, as a class of persons, *and because of their being colored citizens of the United States of African descent*, of the equal protection of the laws.[115]

Judge Krekel made clear an element of the concept of state neglect that Justice Bradley did not explicitly address. Did the failure or refusal of state officers to remedy racial violence also have to be motivated by race? One might assume from the general structure of the legal concept of state neglect that the answer is *yes*, but Bradley did not say so. Judge Krekel did. In the course of articulating and endorsing the concept of state neglect, Judge Krekel explained:

> By the equal protection of the laws, spoken of in the indictment, is meant that the ordinary means and appliances which the law has provided shall be used and put in operation alike in all cases of violation of law. Hence, if the outrages and crimes shown to have been committed in the case before you

---

[113] Judge Ballard's charge to the grand jury cannot be found in Lexis.com. I rely on extended excerpts provided in newspaper articles to be cited later.

[114] 24 F. Cas. 1158 (1874) (District Court, W. D. Missouri).

[115] Ibid., emphasis added.

The Birth of State Action Doctrine, 1874–1876

were well known to the community at large, and that community and the officers of the law willfully failed to employ the means provided by law to ferret out and bring to trial the offenders, because of the victims being colored, it is a depriving them of the equal protection of the law.[116]

District Judge Bland Ballard of Louisville, Kentucky was also a Lincoln appointee. In his grand jury charge, he indicated that Section 2 of the Ku Klux Klan Act was invalid. Among other things, Section 2 made it a crime for two or more persons to conspire to deprive "any person or any class of persons of the equal protection of the laws, or of equal privileges or immunities under the laws."[117] According to Judge Ballard, Section 2 was unconstitutional because it was "too general."[118] Fortunately, he provided extensive discussion regarding proper legislation under the Fourteenth and Fifteenth Amendments. This discussion made clear that the federal government was not handcuffed. Doors to future prosecutions of private individuals remained open. In 1883, the Supreme Court invalidated this section (now Rev. Stat. 5519) in *United States v. Harris*,[119] a decision that is traditionally read to close the door on federal enforcement. Ballard's jury charge, which parallels the Court's reasoning but is more extensive, opens other ways of reading *Harris*.

Ballard responded to six questions put to him by the jury, for example, "Is it an offense against the United States for two or more persons to conspire together to deprive any citizen of the right to vote on account of his race?" and "Is it an offense against the United States to assault a citizen because he has exercised the right to vote, provided the violence was on account of race"? Ballard answered "yes."[120] He clearly acknowledged the federal power to punish private individuals under the Fifteenth Amendment, and he did so in terms that tracked Bradley's Fifteenth Amendment exemption. The United States had jurisdiction over voting but "only when committed from motives of depriving some person, on account of his race or color, of his right to vote."[121] The United States, Ballard stated, had no power to punish ordinary crimes. Invoking Bradley's distinction between "ordinary" and race-based crimes, Ballard explained that the problem with Section 2 was that it covered ordinary crimes.[122]

But there was another problem with Section 2. According to Ballard, federal jurisdiction under the equal protection clause existed only when states denied equal protection. When a state "denies to some persons within its

---

[116] Ibid.
[117] Section 2 also outlawed other types of conspiracies, including those to levy war against the United States, to overthrow or destroy by force the government of the United States, and to prevent anyone from testifying truthfully as a witness, serving as a juror or grand juror, or in any other role in the court system.
[118] *New York Times*, October 26, 1874, p. 4.
[119] 106 U.S. 629 (1883).
[120] *New York Times*, October 24, 1874, p. 1; *Chicago Tribune*, October 24, 1874, p. 7.
[121] *New York Times*, October 24, 1874, p. 1; *Chicago Tribune*, October. 24, 1874, p. 7.
[122] *New York Times*, October 26, 1874, p. 4.

jurisdiction protection which it accords to others," the federal government may step in "to give all of its inhabitants equal protection; that is, to afford to those inhabitants to which the States gives the least protection the same protection it gives to those whom it protects the most." To give *the least protection* is to withhold or refuse protection. Again we see a court's acceptance of the concept of state neglect. Section 2, however, did not "meet the contingency of a State denying to any person within its jurisdiction the equal protection of the its laws."[123] In other words, the law was not predicated on state denial of equal protection, which could take the form of providing lesser protection.

Ballard, finally, affirmed the constitutionality of the reenacted Civil Rights Act of 1866 because it did both things right: it limited coverage to crimes against property and contract on account of race, color, or alienage, and it predicated federal jurisdiction on state denial of equal protection, that is, on crimes having the "color of law...or custom."[124] In answering one of the questions put to him from the jury, Ballard explained that it was an offense against the United States to threaten to deprive a person of employment or occupation or to eject a person from rented houses, lands, or other properties *if* such threat was on account of race and so on and *if* such threat had the "color of law...or custom."[125] His explanation follows the structure of the concept of state neglect.

If all one knows about Judge Ballard's charge is the outcome (that Section 2 of the Klan Act is unconstitutional), and if all one reads is the *Tribune*'s summary statement of the court's doctrine ("the Fourteenth Amendment itself affects the States, not individuals"),[126] it is easy to jump to a modern abandonment interpretation of Judge Ballard's charge. Indeed, Democrats gave their "enthusiastic endorsement" to Ballard's decision. But Judge Ballard's charge did not support "home rule"[127] as the Democratic press asserted. Of course, it was in the interest of Democrats to ignore Judge Ballard's actual rules.[128] Unless we recover Ballard's reasoning on the amendments, the Democratic perspective will look simply accurate rather than politically interested.

---

[123] *New York Times*, October 24, 1874, p. 1; See also *Chicago Tribune*, Oct. 24, 1874.

[124] *New York Times*, October 24, 1874, p. 1. Congress added "alienage" when it reenacted the Civil Rights bill of 1866 in the Enforcement Act of 1870.

[125] *New York Times*, October 24, 1874. See also *Chicago Tribune*, October 24, 1874.

[126] *Chicago Tribune*, October 19, 1874, p. 4.

[127] *New York Times*, October 15, 1874, p. 2, quoting the Democratic *Courier-Journal*.

[128] Michael Les Benedict has made a similar observation about the Waite Court's Fifteenth Amendment cases. "Neither black Americans nor radical Republicans felt much like thanking the Waite Court for sustaining congressional power while they released southern killers." Democrats, furthermore, praised the decisions for "it was in their interests politically to ignore the fact that these decisions were based on technicalities of statutory construction, [and] that beneath the surface most of Congress's power to protect rights remained unimpaired." Benedict directs these comments at the Waite Court's Thirteenth and Fifteenth Amendment rules ("Preserving Federalism," 79). I apply them to the Fourteenth Amendment rules developing during this time, as well.

The Birth of State Action Doctrine, 1874–1876

Finally, recall Judge Halmer H. Emmons's statement that he would "gladly" approve a remedy for the murders "perpetrated with impunity." Judge Emmons pointed to Bradley's interpretation of the Thirteenth and Fourteenth Amendment as supplying that remedy.

> A recent judgment of one of the learned justices of the supreme court, after enjoying the benefits of the elaborate arguments, and participating in the dissenting opinions in the Slaughterhouse Cases, still affirms that violence upon the negro, simply because he is such, finding its sole animus in his race and color, may be made penal by congressional enactment. This utterance suggests, what otherwise we should have deemed impossible, that *the supreme court may still find in the thirteenth amendment, which abolishes slavery, or the first clause in the fourteenth, which creates citizenship*, so much incidental power to protect what they create, as will sustain a national law punishing the crime, where life, liberty, and property are violently taken, solely on account of the race and color of the party injured. Our sympathies are in that direction.[129]

Emmons's reference to the Fourteenth Amendment's citizenship clause is ambiguous: does he perceive the concept of neglect, which was an equal protection notion that made federal enforcement contingent on state rights denials/state neglect? Emmons appears to find in the citizenship clause a plenary enforcement (Thirteenth Amendment) rule, in which federal enforcement was not so contingent. But Emmons's emphasis on unpunished racial murder, noted in Chapter 3, might well indicate that he took for granted an equal protection and hence state neglect rule under the citizenship clause.

Justice Bradley's invalidation of Section 6 created legal uncertainty about its fate. Would the Supreme Court rule it unconstitutional as well? The invalidation hampered federal rights enforcement, though it is difficult to estimate the extent to which this occurred. In the aftermath of Bradley's April 1874 opinion, Attorney General Williams told U.S. attorneys that "criminal prosecutions...ought to be suspended until it is known whether the Supreme Court will hold them constitutional, or otherwise."[130] But federal prosecutions under the Enforcement Acts continued. The Annual Report of the Attorney General shows that the national government brought 216 prosecutions in the South in 1875.[131] Bradley's opinion had provided multiple theories for prosecution, and even without Section 6, twenty-eight of the thirty sections of the Enforcement Acts of 1870–71 still stood. Bradley's opinion was clearly not an evisceration of enforcement power.

---

[129] *Charge to Grand Jury–Civil Rights Act*, 30 F. Cas. 1005, 1007 (1875), emphasis added.
[130] Quoted in Lane, *The Day Freedom Died*, 242.
[131] Wang, *Trial of Democracy*, 300. The Government brought 890 prosecutions in 1874. As the number peaked in 1873 at 1,148, it is unlikely that all 890 occurred before April. The number of post-Bradley prosecutions is therefore likely to be higher than 216.

112   *Rethinking the Judicial Settlement of Reconstruction*

In March of 1876, the Supreme Court made clear that Section 6 was constitutional, but extensive violence marked the interim between Bradley's opinion and that of the Court, and some twentieth-century observers attribute this violence to Bradley's opinion.[132] The Panic of 1873, however, had already spurred the growth of White Leagues and altered the politics of rights enforcement. And though the Justice Department dropped 179 pending enforcement act cases in northern Mississippi during the twelve-month period following Bradley's opinion, Grant had already begun the practice of dropping all but the worst cases. In August of 1873, the Justice Department sent instructions to U.S. attorneys in the Carolinas to *nolle prosequi* (Latin for "we shall no longer prosecute") all but the most horrific crimes.[133] Republican losses in the 1874 election convinced Grant to renew enforcement efforts, and he ordered prosecutions for cases arising out of the election. This renewal occurred after the issuance of Bradley's opinion, as did the six convictions the federal government managed to secure in ravaged northern Mississippi.

ARGUING BEFORE THE SUPREME COURT

The Briefs for Cruikshank

An all-star cast of Democratic lawyers represented William Cruikshank and his fellow Klansmen before the Supreme Court,[134] and they were well aware that Justice Bradley's reasoning in his circuit opinion did not support "home rule" and did not (*contra* Beckwith) give immunity to the White Leagues. The roster included John A. Campbell, the former Supreme Court justice who joined the *Dred Scott* majority and resigned his seat to join the Confederacy. (Justice Samuel Miller despised Campbell.[135] Miller wrote privately, "He has made himself an active leader of the worst branch of the New Orleans democracy.... [H]e deserves all the punishment he...can receive."[136]) David Dudley Field, brother of Supreme Court Justice Stephen J. Field, was also among Cruikshank's lawyers. David Dudley Field had defended William "Boss" Tweed, leader of the New York Democratic political machine, against corruption charges (Tweed went to jail). Field was also a major figure in New York's revision of its code of civil procedure, which became a model throughout the nation. Field took

---

[132] See, e.g., Lane, *The Day Freedom Died*, 242–4.

[133] Kaczorowski, *Politics of Judicial Interpretation*, 110–13. See also Goldstein, "Specter of the Second Amendment," 133.

[134] Philip B. Kurland and Gerhard Casper, eds., *Landmark Briefs and Arguments of the Supreme Court of the United States: Constitutional Law* (1975), vol. 7, pp. 285–417. Filed by David Bryon (hereinafter the "Bryon Brief"), R. H. Marr (hereinafter the "Marr Brief"), John A. Campbell (hereinafter the "Campbell Brief"), and David Dudley Field (hereinafter the "Field Brief"). Field was the brother of Associate Justice Stephen J. Field. See also the oral presentation of David Dudley Field (hereinafter the "Field Oral Presentation").

[135] Ross, *Justice of Shattered Dreams*, 200 (quoting letters from Miller to William Pitt Ballinger, March 18 and October 15, 1877).

[136] Ibid.

The Birth of State Action Doctrine, 1874–1876

the lead and defended William Cruikshank in oral argument before the Court. Robert H. Marr, a New Orleans–based attorney, participated as well. He had been the lead attorney at the original 1874 trials.

The briefs reveal Democratic alarm at Bradley's circuit opinion, a significant indicator of the rights-friendly content of that opinion despite its outcome. Read in chronological sequence, the briefs show that a methodological focus on judicial outcomes will lead to a distorted understanding of Bradley's circuit opinion. Bradley of course had thrown out every count of the indictment, but in this the Democratic lawyers did not take solace. They understood that Bradley had handed a blueprint for writing future indictments and laws to federal prosecutors and Congress. Field and his co-counsel sought to slam the doors that Bradley had left open. In a drama that played out before the readers of the *Chicago Tribune*,[137] the Democratic lawyers all but ignored the issue of the indictment and Bradley's reasons for invalidating Section 6. Instead, they devoted their presentation to a conservative theory of enforcement legislation. A chasm separated their theory from that articulated by Bradley in his circuit opinion, as well as in contemporaneous opinions by Judges Krekel, Ballard, and Emmons. An examination of the Democratic arguments reveals the extent to which the Supreme Court rejected their entreaties.

Field and his co-counsel advocated an extremely narrow definition of state action. For Field and others, a state acted only through its legislature, not through its executive or judicial branches.[138] The sole condition on which Congress could pass legislation under the Fourteenth or Fifteenth Amendment was the existence of state laws that violated federally guaranteed rights. If a State "makes no law" abridging equality of rights, "the condition on which alone Congress can act has not arrived."[139]

Field's extraordinarily narrow definition of state action was at odds with Justice Miller's opinion in *Slaughter-House*, which had explicitly stated that the validity of state laws was "not alone" the concern of the Fourteenth Amendment.[140]

---

[137] The *Tribune* reported nearly verbatim the Democratic arguments (*Chicago Tribune*, April 1, 1875, p 5).

[138] Bryon Brief at 20, 25 (a state acts "solely through its legally constituted legislature, or its people in general convention, legally assembled"); Campbell Brief at 24–6 (Fourteenth Amendment "only afforded an additional guarantee to existing rights and liberties, but authorizing an appeal by the citizens against an exorbitant law of the State") at 26; Field Brief at 4–5; Field Oral Presentation at 20, 33.

[139] Field Oral Presentation at 20, emphasis mine. See also 30 ("Congress cannot act until the States have legislated in violation of the prohibition, and then only by way of nullifying their action through the Courts"). At one point, Field included the acts of corporate officers, though he argued that the *abuse* of official position was not "state action." This was simple trespass and hence not within reach of the Amendments. "The State can act only by its corporate officers, and then only in pursuance of State legislation. If a State Governor despoils a citizen, he is a simple trespasser, unless there be a State law to justify him." Field Oral Presentation at 24.

[140] "But as it is a State that is to be dealt with, and not alone the validity of its laws, we may safely leave that matter until Congress shall have exercised its power, or some case of State

Rethinking the Judicial Settlement of Reconstruction

At the heart of the Democratic briefs was a rejection of the legal concept of state neglect. Bradley's use of the state neglect concept had alarmed them.

> Will it be said...that the equal protection of the laws presupposes the existence and enforcement of laws, and that if the States do not make the laws, or, being made, *do not enforce them*, then Congress may interfere?...Let the question be put in this form: Suppose a State *not to provide adequate remedies* for the protection of life, liberty and property, what may Congress do?... The answer must be, Congress may do nothing whatever, beyond providing judicial remedies in Federal Courts for parties aggrieved by deprivation of their rights. Beyond this there is no alternative between doing nothing or doing everything.[141]

Recall that Bradley's circuit opinion, using almost identical language, had clearly identified a middle ground between "doing nothing" and "doing everything." Field ignored this, boiling down his main point: "State inaction...is no cause for Federal action. There must be affirmative action by a State tending to deprive a citizen of his rights before Congress can interfere....Failure to provide a remedy for a wrong is not the same thing as depriving of a right."[142]

The lawyers tried to buttress their rejection of the state neglect conception of state action by pointing to Justice Miller's language in *Slaughter-House*. Citing Miller's language, they argued that if the Court were to let Section 6 stand and permit the punishment of private individuals as a remedy for the practice of state neglect, this would "completely revolutionize" government and destroy the states.[143]

> All the serious, far reaching and pervading consequences, so forcibly depicted in the *SlaughterHouse Cases*, will be realized; and we shall have taken a fatal departure from the structure and spirit of our institutions. The State governments will be fettered and degraded, by subjecting them to the control of

---

[141] oppression, by denial of equal justice in the courts, shall have claimed a decision at our hands. We find no such case in the one before us...." 83 U.S. at 81. (The brief of R. H. Marr quotes this sentence but leaves out the crucial fragment "and not alone the validity of its laws" without including an ellipsis. Marr Brief at 17.)

[141] Field Oral Presentation at 22.

[142] Field Oral Presentation at 18. See also Field Brief at 4–5. Marr's brief acknowledged that "faithless" state officials or a "corrupt" judiciary might impair rights. Laws might be maladministered, leading to the deprivation of rights. But, according to Marr, Congress could not provide remedies for such wrongs. "The enforcement [of rights] devolves upon the officers of the State charged with the administration and execution of the laws; and it is difficult to perceive how individuals could hinder or prevent the free exercise and enjoyment, by any citizen, of the equal benefit of all the laws of the State or of the United States. *It might be done by an incompetent or corrupt Judiciary, possibly by other faithless officials*; but the redress of any such wrong is not within the legislative power of Congress. It would depend, in last resort, on this Court." Marr Brief at 28, emphasis added.

[143] Bryon Brief at 23, 24, 26, 30; Marr Brief at 13, 15–17, 30–1; Campbell Brief at 12, 13, 26, 28; Field Oral Presentation at 10, 26–32.

The Birth of State Action Doctrine, 1874–1876

> Congress in the exercise of powers, heretofore universally conceded to them, of the most ordinary and fundamental character.[144]

The Democratic lawyers thus urged the Court to rule Section 6 unconstitutional[145] and disclaim the state neglect conception of state action in order to preserve the "whole theory of the relations of the State and Federal governments to each other, and of both these governments to the people." The Supreme Court must have understood *Slaughter-House* and state sovereignty in a different way, because the Court left Section 6 standing.

Scholars have scarcely noticed these elements of the Democratic briefs, which reveal anxiety about Bradley's opinion and the extent to which the Court refused to follow the Democrats.

The Government Brief

Attorney General George H. Williams and Solicitor General Samuel F. Phillips had charge of the government's case. Justice Bradley's circuit opinion left them little room to argue, unless they wanted to challenge him head on and argue a case based on legislative history of the Enforcement Act of 1870. As we have seen, there was plenty of evidence that Congress sought to bring both political violence and racial violence under the cover of the equal protection clause. So Williams and Phillips could have argued that Bradley erred in requiring a racial motive for the counts drawn under the equal protection clause. But the brief did not do this, attempting an end-around Bradley's opinion. The government lawyers tried to justify both Section 6 and the indictment based on an entirely new argument.

The brief began by restricting the government's case to essentially two counts, the fourteenth and sixteenth counts.[146] The fourteenth count charged conspiracy to interfere in voting rights. The sixteenth count charged conspiracy to interfere in the "free exercise and enjoyment of each, every, all, and singular the several rights and privileges granted or secured" by the Constitution and laws of the United States. The government's case hinged on their defense of the fourteenth count, for it was here that the lawyers had to establish that the case involved a specific right under the Constitution or federal law. If they could not establish this, then the sixteenth count did no

---

[144] Marr Brief at 31. See also Campbell Brief at 28. Field's oral presentation suggested that if Section 6 were left standing, the government would become "consolidated" (at 26) and the Court would be turned into a "perpetual censor" (at 30).

[145] Bryon Brief at 27–8; Campbell Brief at 12, 13, 20; Field Oral Presentation at 1, 15.

[146] Technically, it was four counts (the fourteenth and sixteenth, and the sixth and eighth). There were two series of counts against the defendants. The first series charged that the defendants "banded together" etc. The second series charged that the defendants "conspired" etc. The government brief acknowledged that "counts 6 and 8 of the first series...are in effect the same" as counts 14 and 16 of the second series. *Landmark Briefs*, vol. 7, pp. 287–325. Filed by the United States (hereinafter the "Brief for the Government"), 290.

good, for this was a catchall count that referred generally to rights under the Constitution and federal law.

The fourteenth count charged the defendants with attempting to prevent and hinder Levi Nelson and Alexander Tillman (the named victims) in their "right and privilege to vote at any election." Justice Bradley had treated the count as drawn under the Fifteenth Amendment and found it insufficient because it did not contain the allegation that interference was on account of race. The government lawyers offered a wholly different reading of the count, arguing that it had nothing to do with the Fifteenth Amendment. They argued that the conspiracy to deprive Nelson and Tillman of the "right...to vote at any election" pertained not to the election that gave rise to the case at hand (which was a state election) but referred to all elections including federal ones. More specifically, they argued that the conspiracy to prevent Nelson and Tillman from voting was a conspiracy to prevent them from voting in *any future* election, and those included federal elections.[147] The government argued, in effect, that the conspiracy to kill Nelson and Tillman was the equivalent of trying to prevent them from voting in an unnamed future federal election.

The argument was tenuous, as killing Nelson and Tillman could be seen as retribution for voting, for organizing politically, or for simply being free. The list easily multiplies, as does any claim about the prospective exercise of rights. The government's maneuver was an attempt to bring the case under the protective cover of a doctrine that Judge Hugh Bond and Justice Bradley had articulated: that congress had the power to protect federal elections. But it was a weak attempt.

The next step in their argument was to argue that voting in federal elections was among those few privileges or immunities of national citizenship.[148] Citing the *Slaughter-House Cases* for support, the brief argued, "The right to vote in Federal elections is entirely a Federal right, and cases affecting it must be cases under the Federal Constitution."[149] The right did not spring from the Reconstruction amendments. Rather, the right to vote in federal elections "is coeval with the earliest adoption of the Constitution."[150] Congress had the power to legislate so as to protect the right to vote in federal elections against criminal conspiracy and assault, including "political murder."[151] As the government presented it, Section 6 was constitutional and it reached private political violence because it protected the right to vote in federal elections, which was a right of national citizenship that Congress could protect.

Here is where the sixteenth count, the general conspiracy charge, comes into play. Count 16, the government argued, tracked the words of Section 6.

---

[147] Brief for the Government, 291, emphasis in original. (The expression "voting at *any* election in the State of Louisiana" included "of course...all Federal elections in such States.")

[148] Ibid. at 293.

[149] Ibid. at 294.

[150] Ibid. at 297.

[151] Ibid. at 302.

The Birth of State Action Doctrine, 1874–1876

This was in accordance with rules of pleading in statutory cases[152] and so it could not be found vague. "As to statutory offenses, the only general rule...is to allege the offense in the very terms of the statute."[153] The remainder of the brief gathered a storehouse of citations on this point.

The argument about indictments for statutory conspiracies, however, was for naught if the Court refused to accept the foundational claim of the government's brief, namely, that the conspiracy to deprive Nelson and Tillman of the "right...to vote at any election" pertained to future federal elections. In other words, there had to be a constitutional right before the statute could protect it. If there was no constitutional right at issue, the rules for pleading in statutory cases did not matter.

The effort to pull the case under the protective cover of a federal elections argument seemed intended to justify the prosecution without challenging a word of Bradley's circuit opinion. Williams and Phillips would certainly have known that the opinion carried weight. The much more obvious legislative history argument was available, after all, but that would have confronted Bradley directly. In any event, the Court ignored the government's brief entirely.

THE OPINION FOR THE COURT

Political Instability in the Run-up to the 1876 Election

The economic Panic of 1873 had a major impact on politics and the Republican Party.[154] The downturn fueled the fragmentation of the party as it struggled unsuccessfully to repair the nation's economy. The fragmentation was also related to the party's oscillating southern policy, that is, the party's efforts to find a strategy to build southern Republicanism.

The bankruptcy of Jay Cooke's Philadelphia investment house on September 18, 1873, precipitated what was at the time called the Great Depression. As previously noted, Cooke's firm had been the chief financier of the Union military effort during the Civil War, and after the war ended Cooke and Company became heavily invested in booming railroad construction. The bankruptcy had a cascading effect. Panicked banks demanded payment of loans. Investors rushed to sell stocks in order to protect their capital. As stocks on the New York exchanges sunk lower, borrowers had no money with which to pay their debts. The New York Stock Exchange closed for ten days. Businessmen, many of whom had borrowed money to expand their operations during boom times, released workers. Of the country's 364 railroads, 89 went bankrupt. A total of 18,000 businesses failed between 1873 and 1875. By 1876, unemployment had risen to 14 percent. Falling farm prices, wage cuts, and unemployment

---

[152] Ibid. at 299.
[153] Ibid. at 305.
[154] On the panic of 1873, see Wang, *Trial of Democracy*, 110–12; Foner, *Reconstruction*, 512–24; Calhoun, *Conceiving a New Republic*, 59, 80, 102, 110. See also Henrietta Larson, *Jay Cooke: Private Banker* (1968).

118 Rethinking the Judicial Settlement of Reconstruction

generated deep labor unrest, and labor strikes ensued, including the well-known Great Railroad Strike of 1877.

As Chief Justice Waite prepared his *Cruikshank* and *Reese* opinions for the Court, the 1876 presidential election was approaching[155] and it was reasonable to think the Republicans might lose. The previous election boded ill for the party. The economic Panic of 1873 had been a major factor in the 1874 election: the Democrats had crushed the Republicans and taken control of the House of Representatives.[156] The nation's economy was still reeling. "The greatest obstacle to Republican victory in 1876, as in 1874, was the depressed state of the economy."[157] Adding to Republican worry was the spring 1875 election in Connecticut, the most important northern bellwether, which returned large victories for Democrats. With money scarce and with rights enforcement expensive (in terms of both cash and political capital), federal prosecutions under the enforcement acts continued to decline in 1875, contributing to the "redemption" of Mississippi in 1875. Writing to Edward Pierrepont in September 1875, Grant condemned the press for making military intervention seem "despotic."[158]

Imagine the situation that confronted the justices in early 1876: if the Democratic candidate, Samuel Tilden, should win the 1876 election, his administration would certainly ignore an explicit restatement of Bradley's theory of federal rights enforcement. The Court would then appear weak, and this would damage its influence. But if the Republicans should win and if they continued the struggle to build southern Republicanism, it would be important to keep available the rules and rights theories that Bradley had articulated in his 1874 opinion, which the Court presumably approved (recall that Bradley consulted with the justices and gave that opinion wide circulation).

The evidence suggests that the Court hedged its bets. Chief Justice Waite communicated in truncated ways about rules for federal rights enforcement, in effect using a shorthand style that the wide circulation of Justice Bradley's opinion made comprehensible. In so doing Waite made available the tools that the Republican Party needed to continue the project of party building in the South if it so chose. The shorthand style also protected the influence of the Court in case Tilden won.

---

[155] The *Cruikshank* decision was rendered on March 27, 1876, and the election took place on November 7, 1876.

[156] "[O]nly the depression can explain the electoral tidal wave that swept over the North in 1874." Foner, *Reconstruction*, 523. The Republican Party's 110-seat margin in the House was transformed into a 60-seat majority for Democrats. In the previous 1872 election, Grant had won by a large margin: 56% of the popular vote and a 4:1 margin in the electoral college. Calhoun, *Conceiving a New Rebublic*, 45.

[157] Calhoun, *Conceiving a New Republic*, 102.

[158] Grant to Edward Pierrepont, September 13, 1875. Quoted in Brooks D. Simpson, *The Reconstruction Presidents* (1998), 186. Grant also had to contend with press reports that reinforced negative, corrupt images of southern Republicans. The telegraph wires in the South were controlled by Democrats.

The Birth of State Action Doctrine, 1874–1876

As I show in the next chapter, courts and government officials at the time understood Waite's shorthand, using theories of federal voting rights enforcement that trace back to Bradley's circuit opinion. The Hayes, Garfield, and Arthur administrations all won cases using these theories.

Chief Justice Waite's Shorthand

Chief Justice Morrison R. Waite followed Bradley and threw out the indictment, leaving no one legally accountable for the massacre. William Cruikshank and his fellow Klansmen walked free. But the cadre of Democratic lawyers who defended Cruikshank walked away with much less than they came for. Recall that these lawyers urged the Court to invalidate Section 6 and disclaim the concept of state neglect. The Court did neither. Chief Justice Waite treated Section 6 as constitutional. He did not, however, explain why. But while Waite did not disclaim the state neglect concept, he did not explicitly repudiate David Dudley Field's assertions about state inaction. He also said nothing of the horrific violence. This combination seems confusing.

Of chief concern here is Waite's handling of the counts of the indictment drawn under the equal protection clause and the Fifteenth Amendment. Except for treating Section 6 as constitutional, Waite's handling of the indictment tracked Bradley's in every respect.

Waite repeated Bradley's diagnosis of the flaw in the equal protection counts: "There is no allegation that this was done because of the race or color of the persons conspired against.[159] On the next page of the opinion, Waite said the same thing with regard to the Civil Rights Act of 1866.

> No question arises under the Civil Rights Act of April 9, 1866, which is intended for the protection of citizens of the United States in the enjoyment of certain rights, without discrimination on account of race, color, or previous condition of servitude, because, as has already been stated, it is nowhere alleged in these counts that the wrong contemplated against the right of these citizens was on account of their race or color.[160]

There are two different ways of making sense of Waite's identification of the missing racial allegation as the flaw in the indictment: (1) it is comprehensible within a doctrinal framework, which was laid out by Justice Bradley's circuit opinion and which observers would have understood, and

---

[159] 92 U.S. at 554.

[160] 92 U.S. at 555. The Fifteenth Amendment counts failed for the same reason: the allegation of a racial motive was missing. Stated Waite, "Inasmuch, therefore, as it does not appear in these counts that the intent of the defendants was to prevent these parties from exercising their right to vote on account of their race, &c., it does not appear that it was their intent to interfere with any right granted or secured by the constitution or laws of the United States. We may suspect that race was the cause of the hostility, but it is not so averred. This is material to a description of the substance of the offence, and it cannot be supplied by implication. Every thing essential must be charged positively, and not inferentially. The defect here is not in form, but in substance."

(2) it is a way of disallowing punishment for a massacre, which reveals a disinterest in federal intervention while offering a sop to a declining political movement. Deciding between the two competing interpretations requires an investigation of *Cruikshank*'s reception: what did Republicans do with the decision?

The next chapter provides a historically contextual analysis that supports the former interpretation. Here I want to underscore that even if the evidence sustained the latter interpretation, we would have a *political* account of *Cruikshank* that identifies the case as part of the retreat from Reconstruction. But that "sop" (treating Section 6 as constitutional; using technicalities) introduced ambiguity into the *legal* definition of state action. The conventional view that the decision closed off a state neglect conception of state action is logically inconsistent with Waite's emphasis on the missing racial motive.

Relevant to the problem of refereeing between these interpretations is the fact that the Court went out of its way to consider the equal protection counts: they were not technically before the Court. If the Court were hostile to federal intervention in general, it is unclear why it would choose to consider these counts. The choice suggests purposeful communication about two things: to provide direction on drawing up future indictments and to pointedly refuse the effort of Republicans in the forty-second Congress to cover political violence under the equal protection clause. Chief Justice Waite, like Bradley and the circuit judges before him, put political violence outside the reach of the Fourteenth Amendment, racializing the equal protection clause. Indictments drawn under the equal protection clause had to state that the offense was on account of "the race or color of the *persons conspired against*."

In this significant feature of *Cruikshank*, the Court filtered political violence out of the concept of state neglect. There was no textual warrant for racializing the equal protection clause, and the Court blocked a clear legislative intention. The blow to white Republicans in the South was heavy. The Court would later provide a measure of protection for white Republicans in its federal elections jurisprudence. But this would be done under Article 1, Section 4, not the Fourteenth Amendment. Justice Bradley had racialized the Thirteenth Amendment in his circuit opinion; the Court was now racializing the equal protection clause as well.

An oft-quoted statement from *Cruikshank* – "the fourteenth amendment... adds nothing to the rights of one citizen as against another. It simply furnishes an additional guaranty against any encroachment by the States"[161] – is taken to mean that the amendment precludes federal punishment of private individuals, even if states fail to punish them. But the statement is consistent with state neglect principles, as are Waite's statements about the missing

---

[161] 92 U.S. at 542, 543.

The Birth of State Action Doctrine, 1874–1876

racial allegations. Why would the missing allegations be relevant if there were no circumstances under which the federal government could prosecute men like William Cruikshank?[162]

There is scant historical evidence suggesting that Waite was personally hostile to the Civil Rights Act of 1866 or to black voting rights. The radical Republican Senator Charles Sumner investigated Morrison R. Waite when President Grant nominated him. So did Senators Sherman and Edwards, two radical Republicans strongly in favor of Sumner's Civil Rights bill. Indeed, Sherman, Edwards, and Sumner were the only Senators to speak during the executive session considering Waite, which concluded with his unanimous confirmation.[163] And Sumner was not hesitant about criticizing Republicans. He had unleashed a torrent on President Grant.[164] Sumner and his colleagues' willingness to go along with Waite suggests that they uncovered nothing pointing to any such hostility.

A question remains here about why the Court treated Section 6 as constitutional, without ever explaining why.[165] Michael Les Benedict, one of the few scholars to notice the reversal, also observed that the Court was "unclear on the grounds."[166]

One possible explanation for the lack of clarity concerns the revision of statutes that occurred in 1874. The revision chopped up the Enforcement Acts and reorganized their many sections. Section 6 of the Enforcement Act of 1870 – the section at issue in *Cruikshank* and originally passed under the Fourteenth and Fifteenth Amendments – now appeared as Rev. Stat. 5508. In other words, the revision severed Section 6 – now Section 5508 – from the amendments. Recall that Bradley had treated Section 6 as Fifteenth Amendment legislation, saying that Section 6 was flawed because it lacked a racial restriction. When the statute revision of 1874 severed Section 6 from the amendment, it no longer needed to be so confined. Section 5508 could now cover rights in addition to black voting rights.

---

[162] Frantz makes this point. Laurent B. Frantz, "Congressional Power to Enforce the Fourteenth Amendment Against Private Acts," *Yale Law Journal* 73 (1964): 1353–84.

[163] Pierce, *Memoir and Letters*, 587. Pierce reports, "It was incorrectly stated at the time of Chief Justice Waite's death that Sumner spoke and voted against his confirmation. He did neither. The correspondents of the New York Tribune and Boston Journal, who were in personal relations with him, gave in those journals, Jan. 22, 1874, an entirely different impression." Pierce, *Memoir and Letters*, 588.

[164] Ronald B. Jager, "Charles Summer, the Constitution, and the Civil Righs Act of 1875," *New England Quarterly* 42 (1969): 369. Pierce, *Memoirs and Letters*, 587.

[165] Waite said, for example, that the counts of the indictment "do not present a case within the sixth section of the Enforcement Act" (92 U.S. at 543, 544). He also stated, "To bring this case under the operation of the statute ... it must appear that the right ... was one granted or secured by the constitution...." (92 U.S. at 549).

[166] Benedict, "Preserving Federalism," 74. Benedict does not discuss the Democratic briefs or juxtapose Waite's treatment of Section 6 as constitutional with Democratic arguments.

Indeed, after *United States v. Cruikshank* the Court interpreted Section 5508 to protect the right to vote,[167] the right to protection while claiming rights under federal homestead laws,[168] and the right to protection from violence while in custody of a federal marshal, all created rights (though in a twist, Section 5508 now referred only to "secured" rights, something the Court ignored).[169] These cases suggest that the statute revision of 1874 provided an opportunity for the Court to save Section 6, and save it they did. (And they did not have to.)

THE COMPANION CASE: *UNITED STATES V. REESE*

United States v. Reese, the companion case to *Cruikshank*, is traditionally understood as hostile to Reconstruction. I want to turn briefly to the decision and destabilize that view. In *Reese*, the Supreme Court threw out Sections 3 and 4 of the Enforcement Act of 1870. Two municipal election officials in Lexington, Kentucky, were charged with refusing to receive and count the vote of William Garner, a black citizen, on account of race. The officials, Hiram Reese and Matthew Foushee, argued that the two sections were invalid Fifteenth Amendment legislation, and the Court agreed.

Writing for the Court, Chief Justice Waite discussed the power of Congress to regulate elections under the Fifteenth Amendment.[170] "The Fifteenth Amendment," he began, "does not confer the right to suffrage upon anyone."[171] However, the amendment does confer a new constitutional right. "[T]he amendment has invested the citizens of the United States with a new constitutional right which is within the protecting power of Congress. That right is exemption from discrimination in the exercise of the elective franchise on account of race, color, or previous condition of servitude." Fifteenth Amendment legislation, therefore, had to be limited to interferences based on race &c.

---

[167] In *Ex parte Yarbrough*, 110 U.S. 651 (1884), the Court sustained an indictment of a private individual under Section 5508, citing the Fifteenth Amendment.

[168] In *United States v. Waddell*, 112 U.S. 76 (1884), the Court sustained an indictment of a private individual under Section 5508: "The particular right held in that case to be dependent on and secured by the laws of the United States, and to be protected by section 5508 of the Revised Statutes, against interference by individuals, was the right of a citizen, having made a homestead entry on public land, to continue to reside on the land for five years". Dependent and secured are here treated as synonyms.

[169] In *Logan v. United States*, 144 U.S. 263 (1892), the Court sustained an indictment of a private individual under Section 5508. It was held that a citizen of the United States, in the custody of a marshal of the United States under a lawful commitment to answer an offense against the United States, has the right to be protected by the United States against lawless violence. "Every right created by, arising under, or dependent upon the Constitution of the United States may be protected and enforced by Congress by such means and in such manner as Congress, in the exercise of the correlative duty of protection, or of the legislative powers conferred upon it by the Constitution, may, in its discretion, deem most eligible and best adapted to attain the object."

[170] 92 U.S. at 218, later quoted in *Cruikshank*, 92 U.S. at 555.

[171] 92 U.S. at 217.

The Birth of State Action Doctrine, 1874–1876

> It has not been contended, nor can it be, that the amendment confers authority to impose penalties for every wrongful refusal to receive the vote of a qualified elector at State elections. It is only when the wrongful refusal at such an election is because of race, color, or previous condition of servitude that Congress can interfere, and provide for its punishment.

The problem with Sections 3 and 4 was that they did not "in express terms" limit the offence to refusals "on account of race, color, or previous condition of servitude."[172] While Sections 1 and 2 were confined to interferences "on account of race &c.," Sections 3 and 4 used the phrase "as aforesaid" to refer to the prohibited interferences. The phrase introduced a problem, Waite explained, because the Fifteenth Amendment accomplished a "radical change," and the statute "should be explicit in its terms. Nothing should be left to construction, if it can be avoided.[173]

Justice Hunt, writing in dissent, argued strongly that the racial limitation was in fact present through the words "as aforesaid." Stated Hunt, "By the words 'as aforesaid,' the provisions respecting race and color of the first and second sections of the are incorporated into and made a part of the third and fourth sections.... No other meaning can possibly be given to them."[174] The point was indeed compelling and the main reason scholars have regarded *Reese* as hostile to Reconstruction.

But there is an alternative interpretation. As Leslie Goldstein has explained, Hiram Reese was indicted under the statute as it was written in 1870, and so the Court was obligated to deal with that statute. In the 1874 codification of statutes, however, Congress had *omitted* the words "as aforesaid."[175] The relevant sections of the Revised Statutes, then, were not currently in any way limited to interferences on account of race. The current and revised versions of Sections 3 and 4, the would-be sources of authority for future prosecutions, were now indisputably overbroad, in no way containing the racial limitation. Even Justice Hunt's logic could not have saved the revised Sections 3 and 4. So it is a mistake to imagine that, but for the *Reese* decision, the original Sections 3 and 4 would have been in place.

By "perversely interpreting" the original statute, Goldstein suggests, the majority "could act to force Congress to reinsert the original sense [i.e., limitation] into the statute with the inclusion of the phrase, on account of race &c."[176] The current Congress would not likely have acted, but it was not clear that Reconstruction was over. And it was clear that the current versions of Section 3 and 4 would have been inoperative as Fifteenth Amendment legislation because they were missing the "as aforesaid" limitation. The

---

[172] 92 U.S. at 218.
[173] 92 U.S. at 219.
[174] 92 U.S. at 242.
[175] Leslie Friedman Goldstein, "The Specter of the Second Amendment: Rereading Slaughterhouse and Cruikshank," *Studies in American Political Development* 21 (Fall 2007): 131–48.
[176] Ibid. at 142.

conventional reading of *Reese* as hostile to Reconstruction, in sum, presumes that Sections 3 and 4 would have been available and operative, but for the decision. But this was not in fact the case. The statutory revision – perhaps an attempt to direct the statutes at federal elections – removed the "as aforesaid" limitation rendering them unconstitutional even under Justice Hunt's argument. Knowledge about *Reese*'s legislative context is thus essential for interpreting the opinions.

The wording of Sections 3 and 4 is relevant to another seemingly hostile element of the opinion, specifically, the fact that the race-based refusal to receive Garner's vote was within reach of the Fifteenth Amendment. In other words, even though Sections 3 and 4 were written in only general terms, they were applied properly in this instance. The Court, however, did not use as-applied reasoning. Rather, Chief Justice Waite stated that the sections were too broad and that the Court could not do the narrowing: "[A] penal statute enacted by Congress," explained Waite, "with its limited powers, which is in general language broad enough to cover wrongful acts without as well as within the constitutional jurisdiction [cannot] be limited by judicial construction so as to make it operate only on that which Congress may rightfully prohibit and punish."[177] Waite continued:

> [I]t would certainly be dangerous if the legislature could set a net large enough to catch all possible offenders, and leave it to the courts to step inside and say who could be rightfully detained, and who should be set at large. This would, to some extent, substitute the judicial for the legislative department of the government.... To limit this statute in the manner now asked for would be to make a new law, not to enforce an old one. This is no part of our duty. We must, therefore, decide that Congress has not as yet provided by 'appropriate legislation' for the punishment of the offence charged in the indictment.[178]

The Court's mode of statutory construction was conventional and Laurent Frantz has called it the "*Reese* approach to statutory construction."[179] It was not until *United States v. Raines*[180] that the Court finally threw off this approach, embracing the as-applied mode of statutory construction.[181] It is therefore anachronistic to assume that the as-applied mode was established and available to the Waite Court but lay unused.

---

[177] 92 U.S. at 221.
[178] Ibid.
[179] Frantz, "Congressional Power to Enforce the Fourteenth Amendment,"1360.
[180] 362 U.S. 17 (1960).
[181] "To the extent that *United States* v. *Reese*, 92 U.S. 214, depended on an approach inconsistent with what this Court considers the better one and the one established by the weightiest of the subsequent cases, it cannot be followed here." 362 U.S. at 24. Frantz identifies *United States v. Raines*, 362 U.S. 17 (1960), as the point of appearance of the modern approach to overbroad statutes. Frantz, "Congressional Power to Enforce the Fourteenth Amendment," 1360.

The Birth of State Action Doctrine, 1874–1876

One more element of *Reese* has escaped analysis by modern commentators, most likely because it is an anomaly in the conventional abandonment narrative. Recall the Court's statement, "It is only when the wrongful refusal at such an election is because of race, color, or previous condition of servitude that Congress can interfere, and provide for its punishment." The Court accepts that wrongful official refusals and omissions on account of race count as a state violation. Indeed, the Court uses "wrongful refusal,"[182] "discrimination,"[183] and "wrongful acts"[184] as synonyms. This language goes unremarked in the legal literature on Reconstruction, but it is not anomalous in this period: it fits seamlessly into the discourse on state rights denials. Even Democratic Supreme Court Justice Clifford used the language of omission and refusal without any objection.

Notice, finally, Waite's statement quoted at the beginning of this section that the Fifteenth Amendment created a new constitutional right. Modern observers have understood *Reese* as a state action decision,[185] likely because state election officials were prosecuted. But it was not. The Court did not apply state action doctrine. Rather, the Court's theory of federal power to prosecute the election officials was rooted in the notion of a *created right*, which Justice Bradley had articulated in his 1874 circuit opinion in *Cruikshank*. Recall that the creation of a right by the Constitution gave the federal government plenary power to enforce that right. The creation of a right by the Fifteenth Amendment gave the federal government power to punish race-based interference in voting whether committed by officials or private individuals. The only limit on this enforcement power – which the Court judged to be absent in Sections 3 and 4 – was that interferences be "on account of race, color, or previous condition of servitude."

The notion of a created right was again in play in Waite's brief reference to Article 1, Section 4 as a source of federal power to protect national elections. Waite stated: "The effect of art. 1, sect. 4 of the Constitution, in respect to elections for senators and representatives, is not now under consideration."[186] As we shall see in the next chapter, Attorney General Taft seized upon Waite's signal to justify the deployment of a large contingent of federal marshals in the 1876 election. The right to vote in national elections,

---

[182] "It is only when the wrongful refusal at such an election is because of race, color, or previous condition of servitude that Congress can interfere, and provide for its punishment" (92 U.S. at 218).

[183] "[T]he language of the third and fourth sections does not confine their operation to unlawful discriminations on account of race, &c." (92 U.S. at 220).

[184] "We are, therefore, directly called upon to decide whether a penal statute enacted by Congress, with its limited powers, which is in general language broad enough to cover wrongful acts without as well as within the constitutional jurisdiction, can be limited by judicial construction so as to make it operate only on that which Congress may rightfully prohibit and punish" (92 U.S. at 221).

[185] See, e.g., Laurence H. Tribe, *American Constitutional Law*, 3rd ed. (2000), 931. See also Chin 2004 and Metzger 2005.

[186] 92 U.S. at 218.

126   *Rethinking the Judicial Settlement of Reconstruction*

like the right to vote free from racial interference, was a created right, and so the federal government possessed plenary enforcement power. The Grant, Hayes, Garfield, and Arthur administrations all attempted to take advantage of this power.

IMMEDIATE RECEPTION

After the *Reese* decision, the Senate moved immediately to insert the necessary language, "on account of race, color, or previous condition of servitude" into the relevant statutes. Sen. Oliver P. Morton of Indiana introduced a bill "to bring the statutes of the United States up to a 'concert pitch' with the decisions of the Supreme Court on the subject of civil rights and the right of suffrage."[187] The Senate passed the bill. The House, under Democratic control since the 1874 election, let it die. But the Justice Department was not without resources. With many statutes still at their disposal, Republican administrations shifted enforcement efforts onto other statutes, bringing more than 1,200 voting rights prosecutions between 1877 and 1893 in the ex-Confederate states.[188] *Cruikshank* and *Reese* did not handcuff the federal government.

Not that Democrats did not try to spin the decisions as doing precisely that. Democratic efforts to control the meaning of *Cruikshank* and *Reese* began within months of the decisions.[189] But as I show in the next chapter, Republican and independent newspapers gave careful and detailed attention to the cases, refuting Democratic assertions that the decisions rendered unconstitutional the entire edifice of Reconstruction voting rights law.

Newspapers and legal periodicals at the time understood *Cruikshank* as decided on the basis of an improperly drawn indictment, that is, on the basis of technicalities. As reported in the *Chicago Tribune*, "It had been expected that the Court would fully consider the main question, but the decision [was]

---

[187] 4 *Cong. Rec.* 3098 (Edmunds) (May 16, 1876). This new Fifteenth Amendment bill was a substitute for Sections 5506 and 5507 of the Revised Statutes (originally Sections 3 and 4 of the Enforcement Act of 1870). Morton's bill "to conform to the decision of the Supreme Court" (4 *Cong. Rec.* 3721) was passed by the Senate on June 23, 1876. See 4 *Cong. Rec.* 4057–75. See also comments of Sen. Frelinghuysen, 4 *Cong. Rec.* 2112 (noting the need to add simply the phrase "on account of race or color").

[188] Goldman, *A Free Ballot and a Fair Count*, xxix, 23, 200.

[189] Other Democrats gave similar interpretations of *Cruikshank*: "[T]he fifteenth amendment [does] not operate on individuals, but on the United States and on the States only. I beg now, although I am not going into a re-argument of that matter, to read a short paragraph from the decision of the Supreme Court in the case of the United States vs. Cruikshank which supports the view I have submitted. The clause reads as follows: Every republican government is in duty bound to protect all its citizens in the enjoyment of this principle, if within its power. That duty was originally assumed by the States and it still remains there. The only obligation resting upon the United States is to see that the States do not deny the right. This the amendment guarantees, but no more. The power of the national Government is limited to the enforcement of this guarantee." 4 *Cong. Rec.* 4073 (June 13, 1876) (remarks of Sen. Merrimon).

The Birth of State Action Doctrine, 1874–1876

rendered, for the most part, on questions of pleadings and the case dismissed on a technicality."[190] The *New York Times* identified the missing allegation of racial motive as the basis for the decision,[191] as did the *Selected Digest of State Reports*.[192] The *Independent*, too, saw little meat on the bones of the decision. *Cruikshank* contained only "general observations" and left much to be determined.[193] Later that year, the Republican and independent press offered a highly detailed analysis of *Cruikshank*, reiterating these points and emphasizing that the Court treated Section 6 as constitutional.[194] (Today, a small group of scholars argues that *Cruikshank* was decided on the basis of technicalities,[195] although they appear unaware that the view aligns with perspectives from the time.)

At least some Republican congressmen perceived ambiguity in *Cruikshank* regarding the concept of state neglect. Sen. Oliver P. Morton got into the following exchange with Democratic Senator Thomas F. Bayard, who insisted that the Court had clearly repudiated the state neglect concept:

> Mr. MORTON. What is it for a State to deny the equal protection of the laws? When a State by her legislation expressly withholds from part of her people the equal protection of the laws, that is one thing; but when a State government utterly fails to protect a large class of her people, that is denying to them the equal protection of the laws. It is the duty of the State to protect every class of her population; and when a State fails to do it, I do not care whether that failure is intentional on the part of the officers or the result of the weakness or imbecility of the State government, it is denying the equal protection of the laws, and Congress can come in and furnish that protection. This was the understanding with which both those amendments were passed. I know it, and we all know it.
>
> Mr. BAYARD. The Supreme Court of the United States does not recognize your understanding.
>
> Mr. MORTON. The Supreme Court of the United States uses some general phrases. I do not know exactly what they mean; I shall not stop to consider; but what I am speaking of now is what was understood, and this whole country knows it; and if the Supreme Court does not know it, it is the only body of men in this country that does not.[196]

---

[190] *Chicago Tribune*, March 28, 1876, p. 1.

[191] *New York Times*, March 28, 1876, p. 2.

[192] *Selected Digest of State Reports*, April 1877, vol. 11, iss. 3, p. 518.

[193] *Independent*, October 12, 1876. "The alleged violation was not so stated as to make the indictment good."

[194] The *Independent*, October 12, 1876. See also *New York Times*, October 26, 1876, p. 1.

[195] Magrath, *Morrison R. Waite*, 124–5; Frantz, "Congressional Power to Enforce the Fourteenth Amendment"; Benedict, "Preserving Federalism"; Michael Collins, "Justice Bradley's Civil Rights Odyssey Revisited," *Tulane Law Review* 70 (1996): 1994–5; Kennedy, *Race, Crime and the Law*, 50–1; Wang, *Trial of Democracy*; Goldman, *Free Ballot and a Fair Count*, 14–17; Valelly, *The Two Reconstructions*.

[196] 4 *Cong. Rec.* 2071 (March 30, 1876).

I am suggesting, of course, that the justices did know it. Bradley's articulation of the state neglect concept in 1874 and again in 1883 is evidence of this.

The Grant administration deployed troops and federal marshals for the 1876 election, and with troops in Colfax blacks voted in high numbers: "the Republican ticket in Grant Parish polled nearly as high a percentage...as the percentage of African-American males of voting age in the parish."[197] At the 1879 Louisiana constitutional conventional, moreover, "[m]ost delegates...resisted moves to limit the vote because they feared federal intervention."[198] Why would these delegates fear federal intervention if *Cruikshank*, *Reese*, and the settlement of the 1876 election marked the end of Reconstruction? And then too, how can the rebound in federal rights enforcement between 1880 and 1885 be explained?

---

[197] J. Morgan Kousser (2003), "Review of Robert Goldman, Reconstruction and Black Suffrage: Losing the Vote in Reese and Cruikshank," H-Pol, H-Net Reviews, January, http://www.hnet.org/reviews/showrev.cgi?path=179141046324369.

[198] Kousser, *The Shaping of Southern Politics: Suffrage Restriction and the Establishment of the One-Party South, 1880–1910* (1974), 152. In the 1880 election, an estimated 56 percent of blacks in Louisiana still voted (Kousser 1974: 15).

5

A Surviving Sectional Context, 1876–1891

A half-century ago, the classic work of C. Vann Woodward established a view of the Compromise of 1877 as a demarcation line – a falling curtain – marking the death of Reconstruction. Contemporaneous indicators appeared to confirm Woodward's view. In a well-known proclamation, *The Nation* declared: "The Negro will disappear from the field of national politics. Henceforth the nation, as a nation, will have nothing more to do with him."[1] A line between the election of 1876 and its aftermath, however, cannot be so sharply drawn. "If the Republican Party had deserted blacks in 1877," stated Stanley Hirshson, "that abandonment was short-lived. By 1878, sectionalism was once again the official policy of a Republican administration. For fifteen years after that, the race problem played a key role in party affairs."[2] Charles Calhoun explains that the Southern question remained "central…to the party's sense of itself and its mission, even in the years after 1877"[3] and Republican administrations "still embraced the threat of intervention."[4] Indeed, federal voting rights enforcement rebounded in the 1880s.[5]

The *Cruikshank* and *Reese* decisions took place in a political context marked by enduring North-South sectional antipathies and a surviving Republican investment in black civil and political inclusion. A period of political transition and fluctuation had already set in; the Panic of 1873 and election of 1874 had altered the politics of rights enforcement. But even while the Reconstruction coalition was weakened, it was not powerless or defeated.

---

[1] The Nation 24 (April 5, 1877), 202.

[2] Hirshson, *Farewell to the Bloody Shirt*, 251.

[3] Calhoun, *Conceiving a New Republic*, 1.

[4] Ibid., 91.

[5] The number of enforcement act cases brought in the South: 16 (1870), 206 (1871), 603 (1872), 1,148 (1873), 890 (1874), 216 (1875), 108 (1876), 133 (1877), 23 (1878), 93 (1879), 53 (1880), 177 (1881), 154 (1882), 201 (1883), 160 (1884), 107 (1885), 8 (1886), 2 (1887), 14 (1888), 22 (1889), 42 (1890), 19 (1891), 12 (1892). Wang, *Trial of Democracy*, 300 (Appendix 7). These numbers disprove Kaczorowski's assertion that "[d]uring the spring and summer of 1873 the Justice Department completely abandoned civil rights enforcement" (Kaczorowski, *Politics of Judicial Interpretation*, 110).

Cruikshank and *Reese* held the door open to party building in the South, and the Justice Department persisted in walking through it, though never vigorously. Intractable Southern resistance to Reconstruction had rendered the question of federal intervention in the South enormously complex. "By 1876, notions about how to sustain the republican project of Reconstruction no longer rested primarily on upholding individual state regimes against the implacable opposition of Southern white conservatives."[6] Dismayed, Republicans turned their attention to "prevent[ing] the Democrats from regaining control of the national government."[7]

In this chapter, I focus on the reception of *Cruikshank* and *Reese*. The story of Attorney General Taft's 1876 circular to federal marshals, which has not yet been told, is part of the reception history. I also identify the voting rights theory used not only by Taft but also by the federal government in their important victories, *Ex parte Siebold* (1880) and *Ex parte Yarbrough* (1884). This theory traces back to Justice Bradley's circuit opinion in *Cruikshank*. Even as the Reconstruction coalition was unwinding, it remained strong enough to permit the continuation of jurisprudence building.

ATTORNEY GENERAL TAFT'S CIRCULAR

On September 4, 1876, Attorney General Alphonso Taft, father of future president and chief justice William Howard Taft, issued a set of instructions to federal marshals for the upcoming presidential election. In his circular, Taft explained that the power of the United States to protect voters and the voting process varied according to whether state or national elections were at issue. Federal marshals possessed full power to protect "the peace of the United States."

> In elections at which members of the House of Representatives are chosen, which by law included elections at which the Electors for President and Vice President are appointed, the United States secure voters against whatever in general hinders or prevents them from a free exercise of the elective franchise, extending that care alike to the registration lists, the act of voting, and the personal freedom and security of the voter, as well as against violence on account of any vote he may intend to give as against conspiracy because of any that he may have already given.[8]

The reference to whatever *in general* hinders voting is significant: political as well as racial violence was covered and so white Republicans came under federal legal protection.

[6] Calhoun, *Conceiving a New Republic*, 90.
[7] Ibid.
[8] There was a *posse comitatus* provision in the circular, which permitted federal marshals to conscript individuals for law enforcement. In his Cooper Union speech, Taft stated, "This was done when a master in pursuit of his fugitive slave resorted to the civil process of the United States and the Marshal, meeting resistance, called on United States soldiers, and they came and assisted to arrest and return the slave to his owner. The present application of the principle is quite as legal and a good deal more humane." *New York Times*, October 26, 1876, p. 1.

A Surviving Sectional Context, 1876–1891

Political assemblies were also to be protected by the marshals, which was crucial for Republican party building. As reported by the *New York Times*,

> The Attorney General maintains that the holding of meetings in a peaceable and orderly manner to discuss the issues of an election...is a preliminary part of the election itself, necessary to its fulfillment, and any violent or unauthorized interference with such meetings is a malicious intimidation, which the United States authorities have full power under the statutes to suppress and punish.[9]

Taft's theory of national elections was thus one way to authorize federal protection of assembly rights.

Taft's circular targeted a number of states, including South Carolina and Louisiana. In South Carolina, state officials had failed utterly to control the White Leagues and the "rifle clubs" that had resurged after the 1873 economic panic. The White Leagues spread terror across the state, targeting political meetings in particular. South Carolina (Republican) Governor David H. Chamberlain, who had appealed to President Grant for help, was assured that "sufficient force will be placed within the call of Marshals of that State to secure the arrest and punishment of this class of offenders."[10] Instructions to federal marshals were also circulated through General Rugger, who had command of the Department of the Gulf. Indeed, federal marshals were stationed throughout the region for the 1876 election: 338 in South Carolina, 166 in North Carolina, 745 in Florida, and 840 in Louisiana. Richard Valelly calls this a "truly massive federal presence."[11]

Taft viewed the deployment of federal marshals as a response to the incapacity of states to control Klan violence and intimidation. In his October speech at Cooper Union, Taft declared that the questions of Reconstruction – "great, difficult, original" – remained before the country.

In that speech, he pointed a finger directly at the Democratic Party. That party was "seiz[ing] by force the political power of South Carolina...and possess[ing] all the machinery of the State Government."[12] The circular to federal marshals, he explained, was "intended only to counteract that malice, wrong-headedness, or inconsideration which sometimes triumphs at critical moments."[13] Violence in South Carolina "has been insurrectionary, because it has been utterly uncontrolled, and uncontrollable, by any authority of the State Government."[14] Making extensive use of the language of state neglect, Taft declared that the state government "is wholly unable to restrain [the rifle clubs]....No one has ever been held to any accountability in any court. It has never been known that any man in any of these States has been held

---

[9] *New York Times*, September 5, 1876, p. 2.
[10] Ibid.
[11] Valelly, *The Two Reconstructions*, 120.
[12] Taft Speech at Cooper Union, *New York Times*, October 26, 1876, p. 1
[13] Circular of Attorney General Taft, reprinted in the *New York Times*, September 5, 1876, p. 2.
[14] Taft Speech at Cooper Union, *New York Times*, October 26, 1876, p. 1.

132 *Rethinking the Judicial Settlement of Reconstruction*

responsible or convicted for killing a Negro." The state courts, he emphasized, had failed completely. "The State Judiciary was found entirely inadequate to protect the colored people against the outrages and murders committed by that organization."[15]

Taft's assertion that he was enforcing the "peace of the United States" was more momentous than it might appear today. Taft was using this concept to create and demarcate a national police power that did not exist before the Civil War. In a letter dated August 1868, Attorney General William M. Evarts used the distinction between the "statutory peace of the United States" and ordinary peace (that broken by common law offences, and so on).[16] But it was under Taft, who had a brief stint as secretary of war,[17] that the concept "peace of the United States" was accompanied by an effort to make a national police power effective, that is, to arrest people who disrupted it.

Attorney General Taft's theory of federal voting rights enforcement was rooted in Article 1, Section 4, of the Constitution, the "times, places, and manners" clause.[18] The theory contained no "state neglect" predicate. That is, the power of the federal government to protect voters in national elections was plenary because voting in national elections was a *created* right. But while federal enforcement was not contingent on the practice of state neglect, Taft made it clear during a speech at Cooper Union that the practice of state neglect was motivating the deployment of the federal marshals.

In his circular, Taft pointed to *Reese* and *Cruikshank* as authority for the circular:

> It is proper to advise you that, in preparing this circular, I have considered recent important judgments given by the Supreme Court of the United States upon the acts of Congress that regulate this general topic.... I need, in this place, add no more than that these judgments do not concern Federal elections.[19]

Taft later spoke in detail about the *Reese* decision. That case "arose upon an election of State officers, only, and this order relates to the election of Federal officers, only. He provided an accurate summary of the case:

> The Fifteenth Amendment provided that no citizen should be denied the right to vote "on account of race, color, or previous condition of servitude," and that "Congress should have power to enforce this article by appropriate

---

[15] Ibid.

[16] The *New York Times* reprints the letter, which "has never been published officially among the opinions of the Attorney Generals," and reports the letter as "bearing on the recent circular of Attorney General Taft." *New York Times*, September 8, 1876, p. 5.

[17] March 8, 1876 to May 22, 1876.

[18] Recall the text: U.S. Constitution, Article 1, Section 4: "The times, places and manner of holding elections for Senators and Representatives, shall be prescribed in each state by the legislature thereof; but the Congress may at any time by law make or alter such regulations, except as to the places of choosing Senators."

[19] Circular of Attorney General Taft, reprinted in the *New York Times*, September 5, 1876, p. 2.

A Surviving Sectional Context, 1876–1891

legislation." Congress passed an act which it was supposed would enforce this amendment. A case arose in Kentucky at an election of State officers, only, for denying the right to vote to a negro. The Court held that the act of Congress as passed was not "appropriate legislation" for the promises of that suit.... The act should have been confined to the denial of the right of voting on account of race, etc.

Taft then turned his attention to a statement in Chief Justice Waite's opinion:

> But the Court said that they were not considering the effect of the fourth section of the first article of the Constitution.... The effect of that section is to enable Congress to make or alter any or all "regulations" as "to the times, places, and manner of holding elections for Senators and Representatives in Congress."[20]

Taft's use of Article 1, Section 4 rather than the Fifteenth Amendment or the state neglect concept made eminent sense given the context in which he was working: a national election was approaching, and Article 1, Section 4 provided him with plenary power to protect national elections. Waite had signaled its availability. So had Bradley.[21] Taft was not "flouting the Court."[22] He was taking its cue.

Democrats denounced Taft and the circular in vehement and violent terms. They charged that federal marshals had been deployed to intimidate Democratic voters. They also claimed the Klan was a fiction. Taft's Cooper Union speech responded directly to these charges. Recounting unpunished Klan violence, he asserted, "Nothing in history was ever better proved. Nothing is more unquestionable."[23] He also made a pointed observation about northern disbelief about the extent of Klan violence: "It is to be borne in mind," he stated, that Democrats "control the telegraph service of that part of the country." Initial accounts over the wires were not accurate. The "final and authentic accounts... are almost entirely different from the first statements which appear by the telegrams."[24] President Grant had long complained about the Democratic press as an obstacle to securing northern support for rights enforcement. Taft was making a similar point.

---

[20] Cooper Union speech, quoted in the *New York Times*, October 26, 1876, p. 1; *Chicago Tribune*, Oct. 26, p. 1. Chief Justice Waite's exact language: "The effect of art. 1, sect. 4, of the Constitution, in respect to elections for senators and representatives, is not now under consideration." *United States v. Reese*, 92 U.S. 214, 218.

[21] Justice Bradley had previously identified Article 1, Section 4 as a source of congressional power over federal elections in his circuit opinion in *Cruikshank*. "Before the [fifteenth] amendment congress had the power to regulate elections and the right of voting in the District of Columbia and in the territories, and to regulate (by altering any regulations made by the state) the time, place and manner of holding elections for senators and representatives in the several states." 25 F. Cas. 712.

[22] Valelly describes Taft as flouting the Court (*The Two Reconstructions*, 120).

[23] *New York Times*, October 26, 1876, p. 1.

[24] Ibid.

The Democrats' claim that the Klan did not exist was not new. But the long-standing Democratic effort to evade federal suppression of the Klan now had a new dimension: attempts to seize control of the meaning of *Cruikshank* and *Reese*. Democratic Senator Thomas F. Bayard (who later became U.S. secretary of state under Grover Cleveland) and the lawyer-scholar George Ticknor Curtis (a Cotton-Whig who joined the Democratic Party in 1856) advanced views of *Cruikshank* and *Reese* that track the modern account in important ways, minus their praise for the decisions. Ticknor Curtis published his views in the Democratic New York *Sun*, which Charles Bradley, son of Justice Joseph Bradley, later called "that scorpion of journalism."[25]

More specifically, Bayard and Curtis asserted that Taft was putting into force a law the Supreme Court had declared null and void in *Reese* and *Cruikshank*. They asserted, in other words, that the decisions dismantled federal power to enforce voting rights As we saw in the last chapter, Bayard had already claimed in 1876 that *Cruikshank* rejected a state neglect conception of state action. Now he claimed that the Court had voided the entire Enforcement Act of 1870.

Republican and independent newspapers responded to Bayard and Curtis in a swift and forceful manner. The coverage in these newspapers, which demonstrated a high level of facility with case law, shows (again) that alternative understandings of the Court's decisions were available at the time. The *Independent* charged Bayard and Curtis with "lying"[26] not once but twice. "[N]either rendered truthful and exact justice to the subject which he professed to be considering."[27] The *Independent* undertook a sustained effort to survey "the state of the law." It also published a lengthy article focusing on the "Election of National Officers."[28]

The *Independent* shrugged off *Reese* as invalidating only two of the twenty-three sections of the Enforcement Act of 1870.[29] The journal also pointed to *Reese* as supporting Taft's circular. "That part of the Constitution which relates 'to elections for senators and representatives,' as the Court expressly said, was not 'under consideration' at all, and, hence, not involved in the case."[30] Demonstrating a high level of legal knowledge, the journal cited sections 2011–2020 of the Revised Statutes, as well as sections 5507, 5508, and 5522, as provisions to secure voters in national elections "the full and

---

[25] The *Independent* refers to "a long and labored article, published in the New York *Sun*." Charles Bradley was discussing the vilification of Justice Bradley for his vote on the Electoral Commission that decided the disputed election of 1876. *Miscellaneous Writings of the Late Hon. Joseph P. Bradley*, 9 ("As the proceedings of the commission advanced and the probable outcome was seen, the fury of the Democratic press, led by that scorpion of journalism, the New York Sun, knew no bounds").

[26] *Independent*, October 19, 1876.

[27] *Independent*, October 12, 1876.

[28] *Independent*, October 19, 1876.

[29] The Enforcement Act of May 31, 1870, contained twenty-three sections. The supplement of February 28, 1871, contained nineteen sections.

[30] *Independent*, October 12, 1876.

A Surviving Sectional Context, 1876–1891

free enjoyment of the elective franchise and to punish those who interfere with their exercise of this right."[31] The specific statutory references were notable: the sections cited would later provide enforcement machinery for Justice Department officials, which the Supreme Court would approve.

The *Independent* also offered a highly detailed assessment of *Cruikshank*. The newspaper referred to the Court's remarks about dual federalism as a "series of general observations upon the separate and distinct functions of our two systems of government, neither new nor different from repeated previous utterances by the same tribunal. All these observations are general, and do not in a solitary instance mark out the precise line which separates these two classes of governmental functions." The problem in *Cruikshank* was the indictment. The "alleged violation was not so stated as to make the indictment good." The *Independent* emphasized that Section 6 of the Enforcement Act still stood and that the decision invalidated no part of the act. "No opinion was expressed adversely to the sixth section of the Enforcement Act." There was "not the slightest intimation" that Section 6 was unconstitutional.[32] And indeed there was not. Section 6 (as noted) became the basis for later successful prosecutions.

The *Independent* also commented on language in *Cruikshank* – the Fourteenth Amendment "adds nothing to the rights of one citizen as against another" – that has since become a canonical expression of state action doctrine. According to the *Independent*, "these principles of construction" are "very broad in their application, and how they would affect other parts of the enforcement legislation can be authoritatively determined only when the Supreme Court itself shall make the application; and this will not be until a case arises calling for it."[33] Concluding its detailed examination, the *Independent* pointed to the "sum of the whole."

> [The] Court has declared two sections of the original Enforcement Act to be unwarranted by the Fifteenth Amendment, because so drawn they are applicable to other offenses other than the specific one which Congress is by the amendment authorized to punish. All the other sections of the Act and of its amendments remain untouched by any decision...and are today a part of "the supreme law of the land." The pretense of Democrats, including Senator Bayard and Mr. George Ticknor Curtis, that the whole Act has been declared null and void, and that, therefore, the Government proposes to put in force legislation which the Supreme Court has condemned, is either founded in sheer ignorance or is a willful attempt to deceive and mislead the public mind. There is not a particle of truth in the pretense and no justice in the furious denunciation which has been poured upon Attorney-General Taft....What the Supreme Court has actually done is to condemn two sections of the enforcement legislation, and that is all. All the rest stands.[34]

---

[31] *Independent*, October 19, 1876.
[32] *Independent*, October 12, 1876.
[33] Ibid.
[34] Ibid.

The *New York Times* also gave especially strong support to Taft's circular. Reporting on the circular under the headline "Fair Elections Provided For,"[35] the *Times* devoted substantial space to the topic, printing both the circular in its entirety and the full text of his nearly two-hour speech at Cooper Union.[36] The newspaper editorialized, "The outrageous interference with peaceable assemblies of the people now practiced in South Carolina will be stopped under this circular."[37] The purpose of the federal troops was "to secure the arrest and punishment of this class of offenders."[38]

The *New York Times* also ran a number of stories identifying the failure or refusal of state governments to put down political violence as evidence of a need for Taft's circular. Under the headline "Political Murders in Texas," the *Times* printed a letter by U.S. Attorney D. J. Baldwin to Attorney General Taft reporting that "the present State Government in Texas is totally inadequate to the protection of life and property.... Every one of the [not less than nine, not more than fifteen] murdered men were Republicans.... Death, swift and sudden, awaits any person testifying in respect to the matter."[39]

The same day in the *Times*, another article appeared under the headline "The Mississippi Plan: The Governor Reminded of Some Recent Outrages and of His Utter Failure to See that Justice Was Done." H. R. Ware, chairman of the Republican State Executive Committee in Mississippi, expressed "astonishment" at the claim of Mississippi Governor Stone that he was able and determined to execute the laws. Recounting just a few of many wrongs, Ware identified the failure to punish, or even to arrest, offenders. "Public prejudice and feeling are such that the courts are powerless to enforce the law against offenders who violate it in the interest of the Democratic Party."[40]

The *Chicago Tribune* supported Taft's circular as well. The *Tribune* did not run a story on Taft's circular until two weeks after it was issued.[41] It made earlier mention of the circular, but only to note that resolutions at Democratic conventions in Delaware[42] and Maryland[43] had denounced it. The *Tribune* also printed a story (as did the *New York Times* and the *Independent*) condemning the Baltimore *Gazette*, which had called for armed resistance to federal marshals in the upcoming election.[44] The *Gazette* "is at work firing the

---

[35] *New York Times*, September 5, 1876, p. 2.
[36] *New York Times*, October 26, 1876, p. 1.
[37] *New York Time*, September 5, 1876, p. 2.
[38] Ibid.
[39] *New York Times*, October 22, 1876, p. 5.
[40] Ibid.
[41] *Chicago Tribune*, September 19, 1876, p. 4.
[42] *Chicago Tribune*, September 13, 1876, p. 1.
[43] *Chicago Tribune*, September 14, 1876, p. 2.
[44] Stated the Baltimore *Gazette*, "Now that this infamous order of Judge Taft has given to their bloodthirsty purposes the color of law, we shall see the ballot-box violated and the streets reddened with blood. The only way to prevent it is to meet force with force. We must have the State Militia and 10,000 Minute men, led by the most elevated men in the State." The *Independent* reported the *Gazette* "swelling into a furious rage.... It was the old pro-slavery,

A Surviving Sectional Context, 1876–1891

Southern heart," the *Tribune* declared. "Attorney General Taft's letter...has inflamed that sheet to the verge of madness."[45] Responding directly to the Gazette, the *Tribune* retorted, "The troops in the South have nothing to do with the election, except in case the civil authorities should be overcome by the White-Liners and Ku-Klux." Only "if the civil power is insufficient, then by the military power of the United States" fair elections will be secured.[46]

A point worth mentioning about the *Tribune*'s coverage of the episode is its misstatement of the history of the enforcement acts in a way that turned attention from the South to the North:

> The history of the election laws show that they were not suggested by any necessities of reconstruction, nor framed with any reference to the negro vote. They were the outgrowth of the outrageous and confessed frauds in New York State in 1868 when Seymour was running for President, and when the chief management of the Democratic campaign was in the hands of Samuel J. Tilden, the present Democratic candidate for President.[47]

In fact, only the second of the four enforcement acts was framed in response to Democratic fraud in New York.[48] The *Tribune* had covered the passage of the Ku Klux Klan Act, so one would presume that it knew better. Perhaps the *Tribune*'s position on the Klan Act is relevant here, as the newspaper had vigorously opposed the sections of the act that provided the president with authority to send troops into the South. This was precisely what was happening now, as Taft's circular, along with Grant's proclamation supplying federal troops, made the Union army available for federal marshals.

The *Tribune*'s false statement was not a reflection of the views of its well-known Liberal Republican editor, Horace White, who sought to turn the party away from Reconstruction. In 1874, White lost the editorship after his association with the Liberal Republicans damaged the paper.[49] Joseph Medill, who concluded that federal intervention was not helping the Republican Party – he supported Hayes' reconciliation policy – had regained control. The framing of the enforcement act as a response to Democratic fraud distanced Taft's circular from Reconstruction policies

---

states rights, secession threat over again." *Independent*, September 14, 1876; the *New York Times* also reprinted a *Gazette* excerpt, commenting, "That kind of talk is at least eleven years too late" (September 8, 1876, p. 4).

[45] *Chicago Tribune*, September 9, 1876, p. 4.

[46] Ibid.

[47] *Chicago Tribune*, September 19, 1874, p. 4.

[48] See Wang, *Trial of Democracy*, 68–78. The second enforcement act was the Naturalization Act of 1870, and it has generally been overlooked in the study of enforcement legislation. Several of the twenty-three sections of the Enforcement Act of 1870 also dealt with fraud in northern elections. Wang mentions that the Republican "loss in New York in the 1868 presidential election ... remained a fresh memory" (Wang, *Trial of Democracy*, 68).

[49] Horace White was a principal supporter of Horace Greeley and the Liberal Republican presidential ticket in 1872. After the loss of the Liberal Republicans, the status of the *Tribune* dropped, and the paper lost money. White was replaced by Medill in 1874 (Medill, who helped found the paper, was the Chicago mayor, 1871–73), and the paper regained its position.

138 *Rethinking the Judicial Settlement of Reconstruction*

while also highlighting abuses by Samuel Tilden, the Democratic candidate for President whom the *Tribune* opposed.

But during the weeks that followed the issuance of the circular, the tone and character of the *Tribune*'s reporting shifted, coming into line with that of the *Independent* and the *New York Times*.

It is likely that the increasing number of calls for armed resistance to Taft's circular by Democratic newspapers in Maryland, Virginia, Georgia, South Carolina, and Alabama generated more support for Taft at the *Tribune*.[50] The pattern is familiar at this transitional time in American politics: it is only after Democratic violence and threat levels rise precipitously that sectional ire among a significant chunk of the Republican Party revives. Under the headline "South Carolina Ku-Klux to be Put Down," the *Tribune* now lined up squarely behind the use of federal troops.

> It was demonstrated to the entire satisfaction of the Cabinet that the life of Republicans is unsafe in several counties in South Carolina, that Gov. Chamberlain is powerless to preserve the peace, and that the purity of the ballot cannot be preserved or the rights of citizens to vote be protected, except by a compliance with Gov. Chamberlain's request. It is furthermore the opinion of Judge Taft that Gov. Chamberlain's application is entirely constitutional, and that the President has no other alternative than to issue the proclamation, which he does tonight.[51]

There was not a word in Taft's circular, the *Tribune* declared, "which conflicts with the law or exaggerates the rights and privileges of Marshals or other officers of the Court." The paper gave admiring page one coverage to Taft's speech at Cooper Union. Praising Taft's dispassion, the paper used language that was also a coded expression of contempt for radicals like Benjamin Butler. Taft, the *Tribune* declared,

> made no attempt to lead his hearers into enthusiasm for fiery denunciation, but hearty applause frequently interrupted his argument, and the attention of the audience was complete and sympathetic. The subject of Southern outrages was treated dispassionately, and in a way to convey information without arousing prejudice. His discussion of the question of Federal interference in the Southern States was listened to with the utmost interest, and the conclusions of the speaker were accepted and approved.[52]

But the *Tribune* had amped up its rhetoric, despite its (typical) sideswipes at the radicals. Now referring to "unreconstructed Rebels," the paper stated:

> The only purpose of Judge Taft's order was to secure a fair election by preventing the murder and intimidation of voters, leaving every man free to

---

[50] See also the Petersburg (Va.) *Index-Appeal*, reprinted in the *New York Times*, September 11, 1876, p. 2 ("let the carpet-bag scoundrels who bring this trouble upon innocent men beware of the consequences to their own infamous heads").

[51] *Chicago Tribune*, October 18, 1876, p. 2.

[52] *Chicago Tribune*, October 26, 1876, p. 1.

A Surviving Sectional Context, 1876–1891

vote as he pleases, but this the [Alabama] Mobile *Register* says shall not be done. "The people shall not submit."... This is the same paper that recently asserted that the negro shall be disfranchised and thrust out of politics. Such assertions as these plainly show the animus of the Southern people.... There is but one course for the United States Marshals in the South to pursue. They must enforce the laws of the country. If they are resisted, the responsibility rests upon the Southern Democracy.[53]

The *Tribune* was now firmly in the camp of the *Independent* and the *New York Times*.

The fires of the Civil War had not gone out for centrist Republicans. The *Independent* reported and commented on a report by a federal marshal who had been instructed by Attorney General Taft to investigate an episode of violence near Charleston, South Carolina. In this instance, Wade Hampton Democrats initiated a fight with black Republicans, but ended up with more extensive injuries than those they had attacked. The *Independent* was not sorry:

> Generally, the "shot-gun" policy has resulted in the slaughter of Negroes, without any harm to the Hampton Democrats; but this time the tables were turned, and these gentlemen got more than they bargained for. It would not be a bad order of things if rioters were always their own victims. Such an order would make them more peaceful, and this in South Carolina would be a great public benefit.[54]

The large federal presence deployed by Grant and Taft was not large enough to stave off disputed election results in Florida and Louisiana. But without the federal marshals it is quite possible that the Democrats might have won the White House in 1876, an outcome that would surely have accelerated disfranchisement and the establishment of Jim Crow. It is worth considering, too, that Grant and Taft might never have deployed such numbers without the cue from the Court. The same can be said for President Hayes, who might never have pursued voting rights enforcement in the wake of the disastrous 1878 election without Waite's cue.

THE NEW POLITICAL HISTORY, 1876–1891

In his classic 1951 work, C. Vann Woodward coined the phrase *Compromise of 1877* to describe a "sectional truce"[55] between Republicans and Democrats that settled the disputed presidential election of 1876. Among the terms of the so-called agreement reached at the Wormley Hotel on February 26, 1877, the Republican Party "abandon[ed] the Negro to his former master"[56] in exchange for the peaceful possession of the presidency. Historians have

---

[53] *Chicago Tribune*, October 28, 1876, p. 4.
[54] *Independent*, October 26, 1876.
[55] Woodward, *Reunion and Reaction*, 3.
[56] Woodward, *Reunion and Reaction*, 211.

challenged Woodward's thesis,[57] but it was transported intact into the legal literature on Reconstruction. The seminal work of Harold Hyman and William Wiecek explained that the price of southern acquiescence to the installment of Rutherford B. Hayes as president included "the Republicans' commitment to end Reconstruction...and to cease enforcing civil rights laws."[58] Along with many others, Hyman and Wiecek attribute political and racial stability to the years between the textbook "end" of Reconstruction in 1877 and *Plessy v. Ferguson*,[59] the infamous Supreme Court decision that ratified legal segregation.

Woodward thus treated the Compromise as the end of sectionalism. The Compromise "marked the abandonment of principles"[60] and "the close of one era and the beginning of another."[61] Some observers in 1877 said much the same thing. Decrying Hayes's reconciliation policy, Republican critics minced no words. "Hayes has sold us all out," charged John A. Logan of Illinois. His attacks were joined by Benjamin Wade, James A. Garfield, Wendell Phillips, and Roscoe Conkling, all of whom accused Hayes of abandoning the freedmen.[62] William E. Chandler's bitter denunciations of Hayes were the most comprehensive,[63] and Woodward's account of the Compromise tracks Chandler's denunciations.

But Woodward stopped his account of the 1876 election too soon.[64] Had he kept going – had he focused on the elections of 1878 and 1880 – he would have found that the aftermath of the 1876 election was complex and uncertain. President Hayes was initially optimistic about his internal improvements strategy. "The pacification policy still gains," Hayes wrote in May 1878. "I am confident it will secure North Carolina, with a fair chance in Maryland, Virginia, Tennessee, and Arkansas."[65] The off-year election of 1878, however, broke his confidence. The election was marred by Democratic violence,

---

[57] See Allan Peskin, "Was There a Compromise?" *Journal of American History*, (1973), 63–75; Keith Ian Polakoff, *The Politics of Inertia: The Election of 1876 and the End of Reconstruction* (Louisiana State University Press, 1973).

[58] Hyman and Wiecek, *Equal Justice Under Law*, 493. There are echoes of Woodward in Kaczorowski's argument that the Waite Court's civil rights rulings "facilitated the healing of the breaches caused by the Civil War and accelerated the return to normality" (Kaczorowski, *Politics of Judicial Interpretation*, 225) .

[59] 163 U.S. 537 (1896).

[60] Woodward, *Reunion and Reactiion*, 3.

[61] Ibid., 207. The term "abandonment" appears throughout Woodward's account of the Compromise. See, e.g., pp. 3, 4, 8, 211, 214.

[62] Hirshson, *Farewell to the Bloody Shirt*, 33–41.

[63] *Letters of Mr. William E. Chandler Relative to the So-Called Southern Policy of President Hayes* (Washington, DC: Gibson Brothers, 1878).

[64] Robert Goldman takes Kaczorowski and Gillette to task for their premature announcements of the "the ending" or "the elimination" of federal enforcement of civil rights (Kaczorowski 1985: 113, 226; Gillette 1979: 45–54). While Kaczorowski stops his account with Grant, Gillette (like Vann Woodward) stops his in 1877.

[65] Hayes to W. D. Bickham, May 3, 1877, in Williams, ed., *Diary and Letters of Hayes*, vol. 3, p. 432.

A Surviving Sectional Context, 1876–1891

atrocities, and fraud. Hayes conceded in an interview, "I am reluctantly forced to admit that the experiment was a failure."[66]

The 1878 election gave Democrats control of both the House and the Senate, and they tried strenuously to rescind voting rights laws. The Republican attitude "stiffened considerably"[67] and Hayes vetoed no less than seven repealer bills.[68] His annual message of December 2, 1878, was a "far cry" from his inaugural.[69] Requesting larger appropriations to enforce voting rights laws and vowing to protect the ballot, Hayes condemned the violence and fraud that had been widespread in Louisiana and South Carolina during the recent election. In a report to Congress, Attorney General Charles Devens strongly condemned Bourbon Democrats. He pointed at ballot box stuffing and asked Congress for increased appropriations to prosecute offenses against federal election laws.[70] On December 7, Senator James G. Blaine introduced a resolution calling for investigation of events in Louisiana and South Carolina, which the lame duck Senate passed on December 17 by a party vote.[71] Robert Goldman explains that the most important prosecutions arising from the congressional elections of 1878 were in those two states. Investigations in Baltimore, Maryland, led to the prosecution of election officials in *Ex parte Siebold* (1880), an important win for the federal government.

The 1880 presidential election made clear that race remained a "central issue"[72] for the Republican Party. With Democrats threatening to take the presidency in addition to Congress, "the political calendar of the Republican party...seemed to have been turned back to 1872."[73] The electoral map looked familiar as the Republican candidate James A. Garfield, a compromise candidate between the party's major factions, won a very close election. (Like other national elections between 1874 and 1892, the margin of victory was razor thin.)[74] As New York Governor Alonzo B. Cornell observed, it was "a square division of the old free States against the Slave States."[75] The Republicans also

---

[66] Hirshson, *Farewell to the Bloody Shirt*, 49. See also Wang, *Trial of Democracy*, 182.

[67] Hirshson, *Farewell to the Bloody Shirt*, 46. On the radical differences between the first and second halves of the Hayes administration, see also pp. 45–62

[68] Hayes's vetoes are the basis for Klarman's conclusion that Hayes "did not abandon southern blacks" (2004: 14).

[69] Hirshson, *Farewell to the Bloody Shirt*, 50; see also Goldman, *Free Ballot and a Fair Count*, 61

[70] Goldman, *Free Ballot and a Fair Count*, 69. In response to Democratic efforts in 1879 to block rights enforcement by denying appropriations for federal marshals, Devens instructed the marshals to continue performing their duties until they could be paid. Calhoun, *Conceiving a New Republic*, 164.

[71] Hirshson, *Farewell to the Bloody Shirt*, 51–2. On the final report of the special Senate committee investigating violence and fraud in Louisiana and South Carolina, see Goldman, *Free Ballot and a Fair Count*, 73–4. See also Calhoun, *Conceiving a New Republic*, 171.

[72] Wang, *Trial of Democracy*, 182.

[73] Ibid., 180.

[74] Joel H. Silbey, *The American Political Nation, 1838–1893* (1991).

[75] Cornell to Andrew White, November 1, 1880 (quoted in Wang 1997: 188).

regained the House in the 1880 election (but not the Senate), which gave them greater control over the budget for rights enforcement. It also permitted them to use contested election cases to help police voting. As Richard Bensel has explained, "Through the power of the House to rule on the qualifications of its members in these cases, [Republicans] attempted to impose standards of election conduct that the party was unwilling or unable to enforce through a resort to arms."[76] While it was not the equivalent of sending troops, now a political impossibility, the Garfield and Arthur administrations increased voting rights prosecutions noticeably.

For newly elected President James A. Garfield, the South was "rooted and grounded in feudalism based on slavery."[77] As a congressman, Garfield had given vocal support to state neglect principles during House debate over the Ku Klux Klan Act, and he had a strong record of supporting black rights.[78] Almost half of his inaugural address was devoted to issues concerning black rights in the South, and not just voting rights. Once he took office, the rate of voting rights enforcement in the South jumped.[79]

During the same period, the Republican Party remained divided on major economic issues such as the tariff and the revenue system. The party remained faction-ridden as different blocs jockeyed for control over the party's economic and financial policy.[80] The tariff was one of the proposed strategies to gain southern Republican support: workers in the growing southern textile sector would benefit by the tariff and perhaps could be persuaded to vote Republican. "It is through the tariff that Sen. Sherman calculates to break into the Solid South," commented the Kansas City *Times*.[81] But unity on the tariff was still something for the future as was the use of the tariff exclusively to support large corporations. Unity on any subject was at this point beyond the reach of the party. This lack of united economic policy must be emphasized given the tendency to project the characteristics of the Republican Party of the 1890s backward onto the party during the transitional era.[82]

When Republican Chester Arthur assumed the presidency after the assassination of Garfield, the northern press once again predicted that Republicans would end their policy of rights enforcement in the South.[83] Arthur was a

---

[76] Bensel, *Sectionalism and American Political Development*, 87.
[77] Quoted in Wang, *Trial of Democracy*, 193.
[78] See, e.g., James A. Garfield, "Ought the Negro to Be Disenfranchised? Ought He To Have Been Enfranchised?" *North American Review* 268 (March 1879): 244–50.
[79] Recall the number of cases brought under the enforcement acts in the South, from a low of 23 in 1878: 53 (1880), 177 (1881), 154 (1882), 201 (1883), 160 (1884), 107 (1885), 8 (1886).
[80] The "stalwart" faction of the party, led by William Chandler, pushed for the enforcement of black rights, believing that relentless law enforcement in the South was the only way to build southern Republicanism.
[81] Hirshson, *Farewell to the Bloody Shirt*, 149.
[82] Hyman and Wiecek, *Equal Justice Under Law*, 511–15; Richard F. Bensel, *The Political Economy of American Industrialization, 1877–1900* (2000) and *Sectionalism and American Political Development, 1880–1980* (1984).
[83] *Atlantic Monthly* 49 (March 1882), 393–9.

A Surviving Sectional Context, 1876–1891

machine politician and an active and efficient party worker. Unlike Garfield, Arthur had no record on black rights. But once again, the press was premature. In 1882, the *Atlantic Monthly* announced that "new questions" had taken over the country, "chiefly economic in character."[84] But President Arthur's attorney general instructed U.S. attorneys to pursue voting rights cases. Under Arthur, the rate of voting rights enforcement in the South remained steady, that is, at the (elevated) levels of the Garfield administration.

President Arthur, like Hayes and Garfield before him, searched for new ways to build southern Republicanism. Arthur's strategy was to build alliances with independents in key Southern states. Toward this end, Justice Department officials enforced federal election statutes in Texas, Alabama, and Louisiana, where independent movements took the form of Greenback parties.[85]

Republicans could not afford to renounce protection for black suffrage, for a number of northern states (New York, Connecticut, Ohio, Indiana) were not yet reliably Republican. And so Arthur did not give up on southern prosecutions. He, too, returned to fiery denunciations of the South.[86] The vitally important *Yarbrough* prosecution, which sent Klansmen to jail under both the Fifteenth Amendment and Article 1, Section 4, was an Arthur administration case. Federal District Attorney Emory Speer pushed "with great earnestness" the prosecution of the Banks County, Georgia Klan.[87] The administration knew Banks County to be a center of Klan activity and the *Yarbrough* prosecution was a major doctrinal victory for them.

Amid all of this, and despite campaigns of violence in Louisiana, Alabama, Mississippi, and South Carolina, blacks still voted at high enough rates after 1876 to make a difference in local and state elections. Blacks were elected to southern state legislatures in significant numbers through the 1880s, though none were elected to the Virginia legislature after 1891, the Mississippi legislature after 1895, or the South Carolina legislature after 1902. Black office holding also persisted past 1877, in some states not peaking until the 1880s. A major theme of North Carolina's white supremacy campaign of 1898 was the necessity of ending black office holding. (It was not until then that federal patronage appointments of southern blacks became significantly more controversial, leading to mass protests by whites and the lynching of a black South Carolina postmaster in 1898.)[88] Blacks also continued to serve on southern juries, at least through the 1880s and in some states into the 1890s.[89] In general, the south was not reliably "solid," except in Georgia.[90]

---

[84] Quoted in Wang, *Trial of Democracy*, 202.

[85] Goldman, *Free Ballot and a Fair Count*, 110–17.

[86] Hirshson, *Farewell to the Bloody Shirt*, 151.

[87] Goldman, *Free Ballot and a Fair Count*, 109. Speer was the leader of the Independent Party in Georgia. In response to the Independent movement, which had the support of Republicans and blacks, the Klan became reinvigorated, and the center of this activity was Banks County. On Speer's work in the *Yarbrough* case, see Goldman, *Free Ballot and a Fair Count*, 108–10.

[88] Michael J. Klarman, "The Plessy Era," 1998 *Supreme Court Review* 303, 374.

[89] Klarman, "The Plessy Era," 374, 307–8. See also Foner, *Reconstruction*, 590.

[90] Kousser, *Shaping of Southern Politics* (1974).

144 *Rethinking the Judicial Settlement of Reconstruction*

The transitional character of the 1880s is indicated as well by contests over Civil War memory. Northern expressions about who was right and who was wrong in the Civil War continued to surface. During the diehard era of Lost Cause mythology[91] (1865–late 1880s), magazines still published narratives of Union soldiers' prison experiences, which generated resentment in the South.[92] In 1887, a dispute erupted over the return of captured battle flags to ex-Confederates.[93] In 1888, the silver anniversary of Gettysburg, the "everyone was right" mantra of Lost Cause mythology still evoked dissent. From 1886 to 1892, the editor of *Harper's*, William Dean Howells, kept up a critical assault on the sentimentalist rendering of the war.[94] By the 1890s, such expressions had disappeared [95]

ELECTORAL FEDERALISM: *BUTLER* (1877), *SIEBOLD* (1880), AND *YARBROUGH* (1884)

Changes in the distribution of national and state power over elections were vital if Republican party building was going to succeed after the Civil War.[96] Southern Republicans were under siege, and they needed the Court to build a jurisprudence that permitted the national government to protect elections. *Cruikshank* and *Reese* did not spell doom, as Attorney General Taft's circular made clear.

The executive branch was a partner in building the voting rights jurisprudence that emerged in the wake of the decisions. When the Grant administration prosecuted 1876 election violence, when President Hayes vetoed repealer bills, when Attorney General Devens ordered federal marshals to keep working without pay until funds could be appropriated, when President Garfield increased the number of voting rights prosecutions, and when President Arthur targeted enforcement efforts in states where Republicans sought alliances with independents, Republican administrations provided the federal courts with opportunities to elaborate voting rights doctrine.

The courts took up these opportunities and fleshed out cues they had themselves provided in 1874 and 1876. The two-pronged voting rights jurisprudence

---

[91] Lost Cause mythology removed slavery as the cause of the war and repudiated Reconstruction as a mistake. This mythology portrayed the union as "saved" from Reconstruction and blacks. The antebellum South was sentimentalized; states' rights was presented as an honorable cause; soldierly devotion on both sides was exalted; and Klansmen were cast as saviors.

[92] David Blight, *Race and Reunion: The Civil War in American Memory* (2001), 242–3.

[93] Ibid. at 202, 203.

[94] Ibid. at 238.

[95] According to David Blight, two major events signaled the shift from the "diehard era" to the "reconciliation era": the 1899 death of Jefferson Davis, who had rejected reconciliation, and the 1890 unveiling of a giant statue of Robert E. Lee in Richmond (Blight, *Race and Reunion*, 266–7). By the late 1880s and beyond, the reconcilationist phase saw American culture awash in sentimental reconciliationist literature and happy soldiers' reunions.

[96] Valelly, *The Two Reconstructions*, 15.

A Surviving Sectional Context, 1876–1891

elaborated between 1877 and 1884 rested on the Fifteenth Amendment and Article 1, Section 4. State action limitations did not apply.

In *United States v. Butler*,[97] an 1877 circuit opinion that is largely unknown among scholars, Chief Justice Waite (on circuit) embraced the Fifteenth Amendment exemption. Recall that this rule permitted the federal government to prosecute individuals under the Fifteenth Amendment, regardless of state behavior, if their interference in voting was on account of race or color.

The case stemmed from the Ellenton riot in South Carolina, and it was the first important black rights case to be tried after *Cruikshank* and *Reese*. Until 1871, Ellenton had been a part of the notoriously violent Edgefield County, and the riot "manifested some of the most barbarous treatment of African Americans of the entire Reconstruction era."[98] During the election campaign in September 1876, white mobs in Aiken County (in which Ellenton now sat) and Edgefield County marauded across a thirty-mile radius for over a week.[99] "All is not quiet in our hellish county," reported Republican probate judge H. N. Boney to South Carolina Governor Chamberlain. The state militia was in disarray, and Republicans appealed to Grant for help. (Democrats insisted that the region was characterized by "profound peace.")

While some blacks were armed and shot back in self-defense, most were killed in cold blood. Estimates range from 15 to 125 dead. The raging violence drew national attention, and President Grant sent troops, saving one group of besieged blacks from certain massacre.[100] A congressional investigation ensued.

Ellenton was a major Republican stronghold as blacks outnumbered whites about three to two in the area. According to a Senate investigating committee, local whites circulated "dead lists" of Republican leaders. The aim was to "kill out" educated blacks and break up the local Republican clubs so that "there would be no one to lead the others." According to black testimony before Congress, the white men of Edgefield and Aiken had sworn they "were not going to be governed by Lincoln law no longer."[101]

The federal government charged Andrew Pickens Butler (a former colonel in the Confederate army and soon-to-be-elected state senator), a leader of the rifle clubs that instigated the violence, along with Capt. George W. Croft, chairman of the Democratic Party in Aiken County, another leader of

---

[97] *United States v. Butler*, 25 Fed. Cas. 213 (#14,700) (C. C. D. S.C. 1877).

[98] Lou Faulkner Williams, "Federal Enforcement of Black Rights in the Post-Redemption South: The Ellenton Riot Case," in C. Waldrep and D. Nieman, eds., *Local Matters: Race, Crime, and Justice in the Nineteenth-Century South* (Athens: University of Georgia Press, 2001), 173. See also p. 172: "the most vicious demonstration of racial violence in Reconstruction South Carolina." In typical southern style, there was a pretext for the violence: the claimed rape of a white woman.

[99] Edgefield County had thirty-nine rifle companies and Aiken had twenty-nine. Together, the counties fielded an army of 3,400 men. Williams, "Federal Enforcement of Black Rights," 173.

[100] Ibid., 178, 179.

[101] Ibid., 177.

146 *Rethinking the Judicial Settlement of Reconstruction*

the violence, and ten others.[102] The national attention drawn by the violence ensured that the trial and C. J. Waite's opinion would be closely observed.

The federal government brought a five-count indictment, and the court sustained four of the five counts, "good news for civil rights enforcement efforts in the post-Reconstruction era."[103] Waite's jury charge was also published with an extended recounting of the horror of the massacre. The recitation of facts preceded his opinion, but it is highly implausible that this narration appeared without Waite's approval.[104] Descriptions of racial violence were politically charged. Indeed, the absence of such a description in *Cruikshank* is evidence of their political nature. The court's approval of four of five counts in *Butler* prefaced by a long recounting of the brutality would have sent a clear message to the Hayes administration. The court's action would also have signaled the White Leagues that the threat of federal intervention remained real. Waite also expressed private dismay. He could hardly "comprehend such a state of society. Negroes...shot down in cold blood without any cause or provocation." Writing to his wife during the trials, he said with discouragement, "The people here are further from reconstruction than they have been since the war."[105]

Federal prosecutors advanced theories of enforcement based on both Article 1, Section 4 and the Fifteenth Amendment. Counts 1–3 were framed under Section 5520 and Article 1, Section 4. There was no allegation of a racial motive, as all prior case law made clear that no such allegation was necessary. Counts 4–5 were Fifteenth Amendment charges, framed under Section 5508 (formerly Section 6 of the Act of 1870, under which William Cruikshank had been charged). U.S. attorneys alleged a racial motive as *Cruikshank* and *Reese* required.

The court endorsed the federal government's theory of prosecution. As Williams observes, "*Butler* demonstrated that it was still possible to frame an indictment that would stand up in court.... *The law was sufficient to convict.*"[106] Chief Justice Waite's jury instructions explicitly endorsed the Fifteenth Amendment exemption. The "controlling element" in counts 4 and 5, he explained, was "the race or color" of the victim, David Bush. In order to find the defendants guilty under the Fifteenth Amendment, the jury had to find that the conspiracy was motivated by Bush's race. It was not enough that

---

[102] The state of South Carolina charged about 100 *blacks* with assault and murder, advancing a dramatically different version of events than that presented in the U.S. Justice Department records. Williams, "Federal Enforcement of Black Rights," 182

[103] Ibid., 186.

[104] Judge Hugh L. Bond joined Waite on the bench for the trial, and the recitation of facts was possibly written by him or by District Judge Robert William Hughes, a postwar Republican and Grant appointee. Hughes reported the *Butler* case and other cases from the Fourth Circuit at the time. (Thanks to Chuck Lane for information on Hughes.)

[105] Waite wrote to his wife during the trials. Quoted in Williams, "Federal Enforcement of Black Rights," 189, 183.

[106] Ibid., 193, emphasis added.

A Surviving Sectional Context, 1876–1891

the "defendants may have conspired against him on account of his political opinions, or on account of his support advocacy of any political party."[107] Waite then added: "Equally unimportant to you or to us is whether the state or its officers have been unable or unwilling to punish offences against its own laws, or to bring to judgment in its own courts the violators of its own peace."[108] Clearly, there was no state neglect predicate for federal prosecution under the Fifteenth Amendment.

The *Butler* case also made manifest that the social and political – not legal – obstacles to federal enforcement were profound. Against all the evidence, the jury refused to convict. Made up of six white and six black men,[109] the jury deadlocked along racial lines. There was no retrial.

The 1880 decision, *Ex parte Siebold*, grew out of the 1878 congressional election. Written by Justice Bradley, the case was a major step in the development of electoral federalism, as it established the federal government's power under Article 1, Section 4 to punish state officials who committed fraud in national elections. Albert Siebold and four other election officials in Baltimore, Maryland, stuffed ballot boxes, failed to deliver ballot boxes for counting, and allowed ballot boxes to be opened and the ballots destroyed. They also interfered with and resisted federal marshals, who arrested them. They were indicted and convicted under election statutes (Sections 5515 and 5522), which provide the federal government with power to prosecute an official at a national election "who neglects or refuses to perform any duty in regard to such election required of him by any law of the United States" or who "interferes with or prevents" national election supervisors or federal marshals from performing their duties."[110] Siebold and the other officials applied to the Supreme Court for a writ of habeas corpus to be freed from imprisonment. The Court turned down the petition.

Siebold and the other officials rested their challenge to the statutes on a notion of state sovereignty: the federal arrest of state election officers violated state autonomy and threatened the existence of states. They denied the power of federal marshals to arrest state officials; keeping the peace was a duty that belonged to the state authorities alone. The Court divided 7–2 along partisan lines. Democratic Justices Field and Clifford dissented.

In his majority opinion, Justice Bradley vigorously rebutted the claim that keeping the peace was a duty that belonged to state authorities alone:

> It is argued that the preservation of peace and good order in society is not within the powers confided to the government of the United States, but belongs exclusively to the States. Here again we are met with the theory that

---

[107] 25 F. Cas. 223–4.

[108] 25 F. Cas. 224.

[109] During the voir dire process, Waite rejected several attempts by the Democratic defense attorney to remove prospective black jurors. See Williams, "Federal Enforcement of Black Rights," 188.

[110] 100 U.S. at 381.

148   *Rethinking the Judicial Settlement of Reconstruction*

> the government of the United States does not rest upon the soil and territory
> of the country. We think that this theory is based on an entire misconception
> of the nature and powers of that government. We hold it to be an incontro-
> vertible principle, that the government of the United States may, by means
> of physical force, exercised through its official agents, execute on every foot
> of American soil the powers and functions that belong to it. This necessarily
> involves the power to command obedience to its laws, and hence the power
> to keep the peace to that extent.[111]

Bradley thus insisted on a national police power. "The questions involved
have respect not more to the autonomy and existence of the States, than to
the continued existence of the United States."[112] The nation and the states,
he explained, had "concurrent authority" over the same subject matter
(national elections), but the nation's power trumped state power, that is, "is
paramount."[113] The election statutes at issue "created additional sanctions"[114]
for the performance of the ordinary duties of state election officials and were
valid under Article 1, Section 4.[115]

The Supreme Court decision, *Ex parte Yarbrough* (1884), involved
charges against private individuals – a Klan mob – drawn under the Fifteenth
Amendment (§5508) and Article 1, Section 4 (§5520). Jasper Yarbrough, his
three brothers, and five other men were indicted and convicted for the brutal
beating of Berry Saunders, a black voter. The Fifteenth Amendment count
included a racial allegation, as *Cruikshank* required. The other charged interference in a congressional election.[116]

Writing for a unanimous Court, Justice Miller approved both charges. The
Yarbrough brothers had challenged the Fifteenth Amendment count on state
action grounds, arguing that that congressional power to enforce the Fifteenth
Amendment was contingent upon state violations. The Court turned away
this state action challenge, invoking the concept of a *conferred* right.[117]

---

[111] 100 U.S. at 394–5

[112] 100 U.S. at 399.

[113] 100 U.S. 385.

[114] 100 U.S. at 388.

[115] 100 U.S. at 372, 382–4. See also *United States v. Munford*, 16 F. 223 (C.C. E. D. Va.) (1883),
applying *Siebold*. (Robert Munford, a Democratic tax commissioner, was charged with
violating Section 5506 of the Revised Statutes for conspiracy to fail to assess and collect a
poll tax.)

[116] 110 U.S. at 656. "Stripped of its technical verbiage, the offense charged in this indictment as
that the defendants conspired to intimidate Berry Saunders, a citizen of African descent, in
the exercise of his right to vote for a member of the congress of the United States, and in the
execution of that conspiracy they beat, bruised, wounded, and otherwise maltreated him;
and in the second count that they did this on account of his race, color, and previous condition of servitude, by going in disguise and assaulting him on the public highway and on his
own premises" (at 657). One count rested on Article 1, Section 4. The other count rested on
the Fifteenth Amendment. Both were upheld.

[117] Recall that Justice Bradley distinguished between natural rights that preexisted the
Constitution but were "secured" by the Constitution (these rights could be protected
by Congress, but only if states violated these rights) and rights conferred/granted by the

A Surviving Sectional Context, 1876–1891

> The reference to cases in this court in which the power of congress under the first section of the fourteenth amendment has been held to relate alone to acts done under state authority can afford petitioners no aid in the present case; for, while it may be true that acts which are mere invasions of private rights, which acts have no sanction in the statutes of a state, or which are not committed by any one exercising its authority, are not within the scope of that amendment, it is quite a different matter when congress undertakes to protect the citizen in the exercise of rights *conferred* by the constitution of the United States, essential to the healthy organization of the government itself.[118]

Justice Miller thus invoked the created/conferred rights category to distinguish between Fifteenth and Fourteenth Amendment enforcement. He also cited *Reese* for the proposition that the Fifteenth Amendment created a new right: to vote free from racial interference:

> While it is quite true, as was said by this court in *United States v. Reese* that [the Fifteenth Amendment] gives no affirmative right to the colored man to vote, and is designed primarily to prevent discrimination against him whenever the right to vote may be granted to others, it is easy to see that under some circumstances it may operate as the immediate source of a right to vote....In such cases this fifteenth article of amendment does, *proprio vigore*, substantially confer on the negro the right to vote, and Congress has the power to protect and enforce that right.[119]

Even in the now-growing literature that emphasizes *Yarbrough*,[120] the Court's theory of the Fifteenth Amendment has been missed. The Fifteenth Amendment exemption – now approved by a unanimous Court – can be traced directly to Justice Bradley's 1874 *Cruikshank* opinion.

As noted, the Court never confronted an analytic hitch in its use of Section 5508: while the original Section 6 referred to "granted or secured" rights, the revised Section 5508 referred only to "secured" rights. But in a long line of cases from *Butler* to *Logan v. United States*,[121] the Court approved federal enforcement of created rights under Section 5508, explicitly using the theory of created rights to authorize the federal prosecutions.

Yarbrough is also important as a federal elections case. Under Section 5520, U.S. attorneys charged the Klansmen with interfering in Saunders's right to vote in a congressional election. Yarbrough's lawyers argued that the right to vote for a member of Congress "is not dependent upon the Constitution or laws of the United States, but is governed by the law of each State respectively."[122] Turning away this objection, Miller again used the notion of a created right

---

Constitution or by federal laws. Congress could protect these rights directly, irrespective of state behavior.

[118] 110 U.S. at 667, emphasis added.

[119] 110 U.S. at 665.

[120] Wang, *Trial of Democracy*; Goldman, *Free Ballot and a Fair Count*; Valelly, *The Two Reconstructions*. See also Lane, *The Day Freedom Died* (2008), 252–3.

[121] See the line of precedent cited in *Logan*, 144 U.S. 263 (1892).

[122] 110 U.S. at 662–3.

to uphold the charges. He stated that "it is not correct to say that the right to vote for a member of Congress does not depend on the Constitution of the United States. The office [of Congressman], if it be properly called an office, is *created* by the Constitution and by that alone. It also declares how it shall be filled, namely, by election."[123]

The theory that the federal government had plenary power over created rights had already been accepted in the lower federal courts. In *United States v. Goldman*, Circuit Judge (soon Supreme Court Justice) William B. Woods upheld the federal prosecution of private individuals under Section 5520 of the Revised Statutes, stating: "rights and immunities created by, or dependent upon, the Constitution of the United States, can be protected by Congress." For this doctrine, Woods cited *Reese* and *Cruikshank*.[124]

Yarbrough completed the ten-year developmental process that began with Bradley's 1874 circuit opinion in *Cruikshank*. As we have seen, Bradley used the notion of a created right to theorize the Fifteenth Amendment exemption. The right to vote in congressional elections was a created right, and so the federal government had plenary power to enforce that right as well. Working in tandem, the federal courts and the Republican Party developed both prongs of the Court's voting rights jurisprudence.

At the conclusion of his *Yarbrough* opinion (and in the context of the stepped-up voting rights enforcement that had been occurring for the previous years), Justice Miller offered the following commentary:

> If the recurrence of such acts as these prisoners stand convicted of are too common in one quarter of the country, and give omen of danger from lawless violence, the free use of money in elections, arising from the vast growth of recent wealth in other quarters, presents equal cause for anxiety. If the government of the United States has within its constitutional domain no authority to provide against these evils, – if the very sources of power may be poisoned by corruption or controlled by violence and outrage, without legal restraint, – then, indeed, is the country in danger, and its best powers, its highest purposes, the hopes which it inspires, and the love which enshrines it, are at the mercy of the combinations of those who respect no right but brute force on the one hand, and unprincipled corruptionists on the other.[125]

This does not sound like a justice (or a Court) that has abandoned blacks and turned to support big money and large corporations.

Valelly gives a prominent place to *Yarbrough* in his account of the struggle for black enfranchisement during Reconstruction.[126] The decision, he explains, "laid a key foundation for federal correction of private electoral fraud and voter intimidation."[127] The Democrats launched an effort to repeal voting

---

[123] 110 U.S. at 663, emphasis added.
[124] 25 F. Cas. 1350, 1353 (1879).
[125] *Ex parte Yarbrough*, 110 U.S. 651, 666–7 (1884).
[126] Valelly, *The Two Reconstructions*, 69–70, 245–6.
[127] Ibid., 245.

A Surviving Sectional Context, 1876–1891

legislation during the second Cleveland administration (succeeding in 1894) because they too understood that Republican administrations and the Waite Court had kept these statutes alive.

I offer one final word about *Yarbrough*, or rather about the new political history of Wang, Goldman, and Valelly, which highlights the case. There is an internal tension in this literature. While contributors perceive a strong Court commitment to black rights in *Yarbrough* (though mainly the Article 1, Section 4, dimension), they also accept the conventional abandonment reading of the *Civil Rights Cases*. As Robert Goldman himself recognizes, "*Yarbrough* is not easily explained."[128] But his inability to account for *Yarbrough* is a function of his acceptance of the conventional wisdom about state action doctrine and the *Civil Rights Cases*.

THE FEDERAL PURSUIT OF VOTING RIGHTS CASES

Can we conclude that the federal enforcement of voting rights in the late 1870s and 1880s transitional period meant that this was the only route available to the federal Government? In other words, can we conclude that the government's reliance on the Fifteenth Amendment and Article 1, Section 4 meant that the Court rejected the state neglect conception of state action? No. Politics affects the way Supreme Court decisions are received, characterized, and acted upon. The reception of a Court decision is an important source of information about its legal content. But while reception is related to the legal content of that decision, reception is still a distinct question. That legal content, moreover, can take a variety of forms. It can be quite specific – for example, barring a federal income tax. It can also be open to a range of interpretations, applied and "lived" in a multitude of ways.[129]

A combination of legal doctrine, politics, and resources can explain the prioritization of voting rights cases in Republican administrations during this time. In 1876, the Grant administration faced a tight national election. An economic depression gripped the country; the Republican Party was fracturing; and the Democrats were putting themselves forward as the

---

[128] Goldman, *Free Ballot and a Fair Count*, 129.

[129] Regarding the complex relationship between reception and legal content, we have seen Democrats receive *Cruikshank* as shutting the door on civil rights enforcement, though Republicans hotly contested this, and later rights enforcement refuted it. Negative receptions, therefore, should not necessarily be taken at face value. Another example: the hostile reception to *Lochner v. New York* among Progressives does not tell us whether Justice Holmes's characterization of the decision as a product of "laissez-faire" policy preferences is actually right. One has to examine the construction of police powers doctrine over time to see if there was any legal pedigree to Justice Peckham's majority opinion. The reception of a case is contextual, shaped by a variety of factors. Even positive receptions of a case do not tell us all we need to know about its legal content. The embrace of *Brown v. Board of Education* by liberals does not tell us whether the Court used a color-blind or an anti-caste legal principle (or was ambiguous on the matter). One has to examine the Court opinion to answer this question about the legal meaning of the decision.

party of reform. Chief Justice Waite's cue must have seemed a godsend, and Attorney General Taft seized the opportunity. The Republicans got early convictions under Article 1, Section 4, and so they pursued that path. Justice Bradley, moreover, had supplied the national government with a theory of the Fifteenth Amendment that permitted federal prosecutions of private, race-based interference in black voting in state elections, regardless of state action/neglect. Waite's opinion in *Butler* assured Republicans, in Williams's words, that "the law was sufficient to convict." So they continued to prosecute under Sections 5508 (the Fifteenth Amendment) and 5520 (Article 1, Section 4).

But it was not just early wins that made these paths sensible. The proof thresholds in voting rights cases were lower than those in state neglect cases and so U.S. attorneys were more likely to win them. Proof thresholds were lowest under Article 1, Section 4 (it was necessary only to show interference in voting); higher under the Fifteenth Amendment (it was necessary to show interference "on account of race," and Waite's standard in *Butler* did not appear onerous); and higher still under the Fourteenth Amendment (it was necessary to show both the practice of state neglect and interference "on account of race"). These U.S. attorneys would hardly be unusual if they preferred bringing cases they were more likely to win. The scarce economic resources available to the U.S. attorneys, moreover, heightened the investment in each and every case.

Political factors, also, mattered greatly in the party's prioritization of voting-related cases. Senator William E. Chandler and the "regular Republicans" urged the party to protect black rights.[130] In 1870–71, it was clear that "the protection of the black electorate and the success of the Republican Party were so dependent on each other that it is impossible to separate them."[131] Chandler remained convinced that the protection of blacks and of southern Republicanism were inseparable. But after the economic Panic of 1873 made rights enforcement politically tricky, different factions in the party urged different policies to build the southern wing of the party.

All of the factions remained invested in building southern Republicanism, but recall that national elections were being decided by close margins, and the resurgence of the Democratic Party meant Republican rule was not secure. Democratic violence was widespread, but the economic downturn was also exacting a tremendous toll, and white voters demanded attention to their growing misery. Unemployment was high, farm prices were low, and labor strikes were becoming more and more common (and violent). At the same time, the pro-business faction continued to grow. In this unstable political world in which no faction dominated, Republican leaders "quarreled continually," advocating numerous approaches to party building in the South.[132]

---

[130] Hirshson, *Farewell to the Bloody Shirt*, 25, 41–2.
[131] Williams, *The Great Klan Trials*, 23.
[132] Hirshson, *Farewell to the Bloody Shirt*, 253.

A Surviving Sectional Context, 1876–1891

Presidents Grant, Hayes, Garfield, Arthur, and Harrison were all disdainful of the southern administration of justice.[133] But in their efforts to build southern Republicanism without agitating northern white voters who demanded the party's energy, they each tried fresh strategies for building the southern wing of the party. As Hirshson explains,

> Every Republican president between 1877 and 1893...adopted a scheme which he hoped would attract Southern white men to Republicanism. Hayes appealed to former Southern Whigs on a platform stressing internal improvements; Garfield was drawing up plans to foster Southern education [when he was assassinated]; Arthur allied with the Independents; and Harrison tried to form a white, high tariff organization in Louisiana, Alabama, and Virginia.[134]

After each of these strategies failed in the face of Democratic violence and fraud, each president returned to sectionalism, stiffened rhetoric about voting rights, and voting rights enforcement. In such an environment the (intermittent) protection of black voting rights was the most that regular Republicans like Chandler could achieve. So it was efficient to invest in more easily winnable cases with lower evidentiary thresholds, and not just because economic resources were scarce. Political capital was waning.

To summarize, the fact that federal prosecutors persisted in bringing voting-related prosecutions between 1877 and the early 1890s is significant for several reasons. First, it indicates that these federal lawyers did not see a definitive or wholesale abandonment of black rights by the Waite Court. Second, it indicates that black voters remained significant players in various southern locations (and that one-party rule had not yet been established across the South) despite the fact that voting rates among blacks declined substantially after 1877. Third, the Court's clear and strong language in *Butler*, *Siebold*, and *Yarbrough* contrasts with its coded language in *Cruikshank* and *Reese*. The Court would not lead, but it would cue and it would reinforce. The federal government did not bring state neglect cases – prosecutions that imposed higher proof thresholds than voting rights cases – but not because legal doctrine had closed off the option. As we will see, contemporaneous political and legal observers perceived the concept of state neglect in the *Civil Rights Cases*.

UNITED STATES V. HARRIS (1883)

The state action pantheon has an additional case, *United State v. Harris*, and buried beneath the customary account of this case is a twisting, turning drama complete with bad lawyering, mysteries, and still unanswered questions.

---

[133] Brooks Simpson, *The Reconstruction Presidents* (1998). It is perhaps not a coincidence that every Republican president during the transitional period (Grant, Hayes, Garfield, Arthur, Harrison) was a Union general, a rank that connoted generational commitments.

[134] Hirshson, *Farewell to the Bloody Shirt*, 253.

154   *Rethinking the Judicial Settlement of Reconstruction*

The historian Lou Faulkner Williams offers the customary view of *Harris* as putting "sins of omission" outside the purview of the Fourteenth Amendment.[135] The standard view is that *Harris*, like *Cruikshank* before it and the *Civil Rights Cases* after it, rejected a state neglect conception of state action. But Justice Harlan, from whom one might expect a ringing and elaborated dissent if the standard view is correct, "expressed no opinion on the merits."[136]

In *Harris*, twenty men were indicted under Section 5519 (originally Section 2 of the Klan Act), which punished conspiracies to deprive individuals of the equal protection of the law or to prevent or hinder state authorities from securing the equal protection of the law. Four men, Robert R. Smith, William J. Overton, George W. Wells, Jr., and P. M. Wells, were under lawful arrest and in the custody of Deputy Sheriff William A. Tucker when a mob led by R. G. Harris attacked them. One of them, P. M. Wells, died as a result of the beating. The indictment charged Harris and the others with conspiring "for the purpose of preventing and hindering the constituted authorities of the State of Tennessee, to wit, the said William A. Tucker from giving and securing the due and equal protection of the law." The defendants challenged the constitutionality of Section 5519, arguing that the offenses created by the statute were not within the jurisdiction of the United States and were state matters only. Writing for the Court, Justice William B. Woods held Section 5519 unconstitutional, unsupported by either the Thirteenth or Fourteenth Amendment.

And there the familiar information about *Harris* ends. My own research has uncovered an abundance of oddities and mysteries unknown to or unaddressed by Reconstruction scholars that make the interpretation of the opinion by Justice Woods especially challenging.

The oddities begin with the fact that the victims were white. Scholars have universally assumed that the victims were black.[137] The assumption no doubt took hold because the defendants were charged under the Ku Klux Klan Act. But George W. Wells, Jr.,[138] Robert R. Smith,[139] William J. Overton,[140] and

---

[135] Williams, *The Great Klan Trials*, 142. She cites Loren Miller at 113–14.

[136] 106 U.S. at 644. Harlan dissented on the question of jurisdiction.

[137] Wikipedia gets it right thanks to Joe Wells, who is related to the P. M. Wells in the case. I discovered this after stumbling upon the unexpected assertion on Wiki that the victims were white. I was suspicious of this assertion, but its specificity lent credibility. Finding a post on another site by a "Joe Wells" that repeated the claim with even greater specificity and with a corroborating post by the independent scholar Melanie Adams, I began an e-mail exchange with Joe Wells. An exchange with Chris Waldrep also helped bring this aspect of the case into view.

[138] http://www.rootsweb.ancestry.com/~tncrocke/1870census/pg0515a.txt. See also http://tn-roots.com/tncrockett/1870census/515a-520b.html#517A.

[139] An "R. R. Smith," thirty, a farmer, is listed as white in the 1880 census. He has a one-year-old son named Robert. 1880 census for Crockett County, Tennessee, http://ftp.rootsweb.ancestry.com/pub/usgenweb/tn/crockett/census/census/1880/pg0279d.txt. A "Robert Smith," twenty one, white, a farmhand, is listed in the 1870 census. See also http://tn-roots.com/tncrockett/1870census/496a-501b.html#501B.

[140] There are two "W. J. Overtons" in the 1870 Crockett County census. One is twenty-five years old. The other is thirty years old. Both are white. http://www.rootsweb.

A Surviving Sectional Context, 1876–1891

Perry McDonald (P. M.) Wells[141] all lived in Crockett County, Tennessee and census records identify all of them as white.

U.S. Attorney William A. Murray brought the charges against Harris and the others, arguing that Tennessee had a duty to provide "equal protection" to prisoners in lawful custody. In a letter to Attorney General Taft, who wanted a copy of the indictment, Murray explained his theory of prosecution.

> [W]henever a citizen had committed an offence against the laws of the State in which he lived, and for which offence he had been placed in the custody of the proper officer of the Executive Department of such state, that it then became the duty of such officer to see that such citizen had the equal protection of the laws of such state, and in as much as this duty was thrown upon such officer, by the provision of [the Fourteenth Amendment], that Congress must have the power to punish a conspiracy, the object of which was to prevent such State officer from securing to such citizen the rights guaranteed to him by the laws of the state.[142]

In other words, the state had a duty to (equally) protect prisoners in lawful custody. If the state failed to (equally) protect prisoners from conspiracies to harm them, the federal government could punish the conspirators. This theory of state action might explain why U.S. Attorney Murray did not identify R. G. Harris as a sheriff (or A. J. Collinsworth and James W. Harris, also charged, as deputy sheriffs). Murray was arguing that prisoners have a right to the equal protection of their lives and safety while in state custody. The "state action" is the failure to provide equal protection to prisoners in lawful custody, it did not arise with the participation of a sheriff and deputy sheriffs in the conspiracy.[143]

But there was an obstacle in Murray's way. He was making an equal protection argument, and *United States v. Cruikshank* had just limited equal protection to race. As both Bradley and Waite had said in their *Cruikshank* opinions, indictments brought under the equal protection clause had to allege that violations were "on account of the race, color, or previous condition of servitude" of the victim. It mattered, then, that the victims were white and that

---

ancestry.com/~tncrocke/1870census/pg0482a.txt. See also http://tn-roots.com/tncrockett/1870census/482a-487b.html#482A.

[141] "Perry Wells" listed as white and living with his father, G. W. Wells, in the 1870 Haywood, Tennessee, census. "Perry McDonald Wells" is buried in the Lebanon Methodist Church Cemetery. http://www.rootsweb.ancestry.com/~tncrocke/1870census/pg0515a.txt. http://tn-roots.com/tncrockett/1870census/515a-520b.html#518A. http://tn-roots.com/tncrockett/cemetery/lebs-w.html.

[142] Letter from William A. Murray to Alphonso Taft, September 25, 1876. RG 60, General Records of the Department of Justice, Source Chronological Files, Western Tennessee, Box 998.

[143] Murray's theory of prosecution should not be confused with the theory in *United States v. Price*, 383 U.S. 787 (1966). In that later case, the Court ruled that private individuals could be punished under a federal conspiracy statute if state officers were involved in that conspiracy. Murray's theory of prosecution did not rest on the participation or involvement of state officials.

the violence was not race-based. Murray seemed unaware that *Cruikshank* blocked his theory of prosecution.

Murray chose badly in prosecuting the men under Section 5519, an equal protection statue.[144] He needed to use a more general statute (like Section 5508) that protected rights "secured by the Constitution." This would have permitted him to forward a *due process* argument (namely, that prisoners in lawful custody have a due process right to trial, court determinations of guilt and punishment, etc.). A due process theory remained unchartered and hence open for development.

So the story of *Harris* begins with white victims and the U.S. attorney using the wrong statute. But the story continues, for it is quite likely that Justice Woods knew neither that the victims were white nor that Harris was a sheriff. There was a large time gap between the incident in 1876 and argument before the Court (in 1882) because the case was held over due to vacancies on the Court. And when it came time for oral argument, no counsel for the defendants appeared. The record was scanty, and the indictment as written by Murray did not identify the race of the victims. The indictment also did not identify four of the defendants as sheriff/deputy sheriffs. The *New York Times*, which reported the *Harris* decision, laid out "the facts out of which this litigation arises so far as they are disclosed by the record and the pleadings."[145] The *Times* assumed that the victims were black: they were "supposed" black. But the *Times* took care to note that they were "not so described in the record."[146] The *Times* identified "R. G. Harris and others" as defendants but did not identify Harris as a sheriff.

Justice Woods appears to have assumed that the victims were black, though he never identified them as such, which one notices only after one has reason to check. (Perhaps scholars should have noticed the missing "colored" or "African descent" identifier as an oddity warranting further investigation, as the Waite Court habitually identified black individuals as "colored" or of "African descent.")[147] Likewise Woods seemed unaware that Harris was a sheriff. The indictment did not identify him as such. Woods stated, "In the indictment in this case...there is no intimation that the State of Tennessee has passed any law or done any act forbidden by the Fourteenth Amendment."[148]

---

[144] Poor case selection can have damaging effects on reform movements. For a twentieth-century example, see Barry Cushman's discussion of the incompetence of Attorney General Homer Cummings. This produced bad precedents like *Schecter Poultry*. In contrast, the superior skills of Charles Fahy during the Second New Deal generated positive precedents (Cushman 1998: 36–40). There are differences, however, between this example and that of U.S. Attorney Murray. The direction of transition was favorable for New Deal lawyers, so that Charles Fahy got the chance to correct Cummings's mistakes.

[145] *New York Times*, January 23, 1883, p. 2.

[146] Ibid.

[147] See, e.g., *United States v. Cruikshank*, 92 U.S. at 542; *United States v. Reese*, 92 U.S. at 215; *Virginia v. Rives*, 100 U.S. at 314; *Strauder v. West Virginia*, 100 U.S. at 304; *Civil Rights Cases*, 109 U.S. at 3; *Ex parte Yarbrough*, 110 U.S. at 656.

[148] 106 U.S. at 639–40.

A Surviving Sectional Context, 1876–1891 157

Presuming, then, that Justice Woods thought the victims were black and that there were no state actors involved in the conspiracy, what did he have to say?

He began by considering whether the Thirteenth Amendment could authorize Section 5519 and concluded it could not. The section was overly broad, "cover[ing] cases both within and without the provisions of the amendment."

> The provisions of that section are broader than the Thirteenth Amendment would justify. Under that section [5519] it would be an offence for two or more white persons to conspire, &c., for the purpose of depriving another white person of the equal protection of the laws. It would be an offence for two or more colored persons, enfranchised slaves, to conspire with the same purpose against a white citizen or against another colored citizen who had never been a slave. It covers any conspiracy between two free white men against another free white man to deprive him of any right accorded him by the laws of the State or of the United States.[149]

In order to be valid Thirteenth Amendment legislation, in other words, Section 5519 had to be limited to race. And provisions of the law, Woods explained, "which are broader than is warranted by the article of the Constitution...cannot be sustained." *United States v. Reese* was "in point."

The reasoning did not gut the Thirteenth Amendment, just as *Reese* did not gut the Fifteenth Amendment. For both amendments, enforcement legislation had to be limited to deprivations on account of race, color, or previous condition of servitude. Recall that Judge Ballard had said the same thing in his 1874 charge to the grand jury.

Justice Woods moved on to consider whether Section 5519 could be sustained under the Fourteenth Amendment. Again, his answer was no. Much as in *Cruikshank*, two very different theories of federal rights enforcement could generate his finding. One theory slammed the door on future legislation (Congress could never reach private individuals under Section 5; "sins of omission" were outside the scope of the Fourteenth Amendment). Another theory did not (Congress could write Section 5 legislation reaching private individuals, but legislation had to be predicated on state action/neglect). In his 1874 jury charge, Judge Ballard rested his opinion on the second theory explaining that Section 5519 was not properly predicated. Justice Woods also used the second theory:

> Section 5519 of the Revised Statutes is not limited to take effect only in case the State shall abridge the privileges or immunities of citizens of the United States, or deprive any person of life, liberty, or property without due process of law, or deny to any person the equal protection of the laws. It applies, *no matter how well the State may have performed its duty....* When the State has been guilty of no violation of its provisions...when, on the contrary, the laws of the State, as enacted by its legislative, and construed by its judicial, and *administered by its executive departments*, recognize and protect the

---

[149] Woods previews this reasoning in *LeGrand*, 12 F. at 581.

158   *Rethinking the Judicial Settlement of Reconstruction*

rights of all persons, the amendment imposes no duty and confers no power upon Congress.[150]

On the next page, Woods made the point again:

> As, therefore, the section of the law under consideration is directed exclusively against the action of private persons, without reference to the laws of the State *or their administration by her officers*, we are clear in the opinion that it is not warranted by any clause in the Fourteenth Amendment to the Constitution.[151]

Justice Woods had written an opinion the previous year that was almost a boilerplate copy of *Harris*.[152] There was nothing new now, except that this time he was writing for the Court. His references to maladministration, moreover, were part of a constellation of terms that federal courts had been using since 1867 to identify the non-enforcement of neutral laws protecting black *civil rights* as a rights violation. The constellation of terms, as I argued in Chapter 2, helped make up the idiom of state neglect (e.g., "prejudices affecting the administration of justice,"[153] the "hostile...administ[ration of] justice").[154] When Justice Woods explained that Section 5519 was directed exclusively against individuals without reference to the laws or their administration, he was tapping into the established language of state neglect, of which he himself had made use in the past.[155]

Was a rights theory that would have permitted him to find state action available to Woods? Did Murray offer him an equal protection theory that he declined to use?

Murray offered no theory of the "equal" part of the protection he was claiming for the prisoners. His argument about the right to safety while in lawful state custody reads like a modern due process argument. No comparison is necessary in due process arguments, and Murray offered no comparison. Such a comparison, however, is necessary for an equal protection argument. Murray had to explain what was "unequal" about the state's failure to provide safety. The mere fact that safety was not provided is insufficient. Murray, then, provided no theory of equal protection for Woods to accept.

Could Woods have generated his own equal protection theory? Possibly. But it is important to remember that his ruling left the door open to such a theory. If one does want to think along these lines, the difficulties are daunting. Does one compare the treatment of black prisoners and white prisoners? What if white prisoners, too, were kidnapped, as in fact was the situation in

---

[150] 106 U.S. at 639, emphasis added.

[151] 106 U.S. at 640, emphasis added. Frantz focuses on these two passages in challenging the conventional reading of *Harris*. "Congressional Power" (1964).

[152] *LeGrand v. United States*, 12 F. 577 (July 6, 1882) (C. C. E. D. Tx.). Woods ruled Section 5519 unconstitutional under both the Thirteenth and Fourteenth Amendments.

[153] *United States v. Hall* (1871: 81–2).

[154] *United States v. Rhodes* (1867: 787).

[155] Recall that Woods authored *United States v. Hall* (1871).

A Surviving Sectional Context, 1876–1891   159

Harris? The need for comparison poses stiff evidentiary hurdles. In this light, the turn to a due process argument makes eminent sense.

Later that year in the *Civil Rights Cases*, Justice Bradley provided just this due process cue. As an example of a Fourteenth Amendment violation, Justice Bradley identified state officials "allowing persons who have committed certain crimes (horse stealing, for example) to be seized and hung by the posse comitatus without regular trial."[156] Bradley pointed directly at a fault-based due process argument.

A contemporaneous interpreter saw the absence of state fault to be the problem. As Judge Thomas Goode Jones explained, the necessary predicate (fault by the state) was missing:

> In United States v. Harris, the indictment, *which charged no fault on the part of the state or officers*, was for conspiracy to deprive the prisoners "of the due and equal protection of the laws of the state of Tennessee" – a right of the enjoyment of which the prisoner cannot be deprived, in the constitutional sense, by the acts of private individuals, and of which he has the enjoyment, in the constitutional sense, *if the state laws and its officers be without fault*, although a mob may work its will upon the prisoner.[157]

The convergence of understandings in the opinions of Judge Jones, Justice Woods, and Judge Ballard supports a state neglect reading of *Harris*.

There is one final dimension of *Harris* that warrants discussion, and it pertains to the question of state fault. How did state officials (the guard[s]) behave in this instance? Did Justice Woods know the answer, or should he have known the answer?

We encounter at this point an abiding mystery, and it pertains to one William A. Tucker. The indictment stated repeatedly that the defendants conspired to "prevent and hinder" William A. Tucker, deputy sheriff, from providing protection. Modern accounts of the facts in *Harris* state that, "the deputy sheriff attempted to protect the prisoners."[158] Was this William A. Tucker? That would seem to be the logical conclusion. But a "W. A. Tucker" is named as a defendant in the indictment. Why would he attempt to protect the prisoners if he was part of the conspiracy? In fact, there is strong evidence that the "Tucker" who resisted the attack was W. E. Tucker, the father of the deputy sheriff.[159] The indictment never linked "William A. Tucker, deputy sheriff,"

---

[156] 109 U.S. at 23.

[157] 151 F. 648, 650, emphasis added. Judge Jones, it should be noted, did not read the indictment to charge fault on the part of William A. Tucker, deputy sheriff. In other words, Jones did not connect "W. A. Tucker," defendant, and William A. Tucker, deputy sheriff.

[158] http://www.oyez.org/cases/1851–1900/1882/1882_0. See also Robert A. Divine, *The American Story* (2005), 413.

[159] According to Crockett County Court minutes dated September 5, 1876 W. A. Tucker, constable elect of the fourteenth Civil District, entered bond. W. F. Tucker, P. M. Neal, and W. W. Wray provided security. W. E. Tucker was W. A. Tucker's father, so in all likelihood "WF" was a typo or transcription error. The day before, George Wells (it is unclear if it is Jr. or Sr.) filed a bill with the county court charging R. G. Harris with neglect of duty and

and "W. A. Tucker," defendant, but Murray may not have felt it necessary to do so. He might have presumed that the status of the victims as state prisoners automatically meant that state action, within the meaning of the amendment, had occurred. (It would have been a poor presumption to make given that he was in unchartered territory and that it was incumbent upon him to define the scope of state responsibility.)[160]

Should Justice Woods have connected "William A. Tucker, deputy sheriff," and "W. A. Tucker," listed as one of twenty defendants? Can we conclude that Woods knew, or should have known, that a state actor was involved in the conspiracy? The indictment reads as though Deputy Sheriff Tucker was not involved. Census records at the time indicate, as well, that fathers and sons could be listed with the same initials.

The uncertainties aside, we return to the matter of cueing. State prisoners were involved. Whether or not the guard(s) were derelict in their duty, a due process argument seemed available. It is reasonable to think that Justice Woods should have provided this cue in *Harris*. Perhaps this is why Justice Bradley provided it in the *Civil Rights Cases*.

In the 1880s, the jurisprudence building of the Waite Court advanced even as the Republican coalition that brought us Reconstruction declined in strength. During this transitional period, dynamics of jurisprudence building and party unwinding occurred simultaneously. A weakened coalition remained strong enough to support the Court's jurisprudence building in *Butler*, *Siebold*, and *Yarbrough* but not strong enough to institutionalize its rights-friendly theories.

---

asking that Harris not be bonded and qualified as sheriff. Wells lost his case. Perhaps this last piece of information has something to do with the feud at the center of this incident. Thanks to Joe Wells for this information.

[160] If Murray meant to charge fault on the part of the deputy sheriff, simply by listing "W. A. Tucker" as a defendant, then he is open to the charge of incompetence.

6

The *Civil Rights Cases* and the Language of State Neglect

By the time Justice Bradley and Justice Harlan argued over the constitutionality of the public accommodation provisions in the *Civil Rights Cases*, the Supreme Court had not yet offered a deep analysis of equality. That did not change with Justice Bradley's majority opinion. But Bradley's combination of support for the Civil Rights Act of 1866 and rejection of the public accommodation provisions would have been recognizable to contemporaries. The instability in centrist Republican use of the *social rights* category[1] was short-lived, and the civil/social distinction Bradley advanced had been established in political and legal realms for over a decade.

According to conventional wisdom, the *Civil Rights Cases* struck down the public accommodation provisions of the Civil Rights Act of 1875 because these provisions regulated private individuals (e.g., owners of inns, theaters, railroads, and steamboats), and private individuals were beyond the reach of the Fourteenth Amendment. It did not matter if states applied neutral laws unevenly and failed to punish crimes against blacks. The conventional view holds that individual perpetrators of those crimes were beyond the reach of the Fourteenth Amendment.

There is an obstacle to this understanding of the *Civil Rights Cases*: Justice Bradley's construction of the legal phrase "under color of law...or custom."

THE "COLOR OF LAW...OR CUSTOM"

The "color of law...or custom" language appeared in Section 2 (the enforcement provision) of the Civil Rights Act of 1866.[2] The *Civil Rights Cases* involved the act of 1875, but Bradley provided a discussion of the 1866 act

---

[1] Recall the instance of the *Chicago Tribune*'s momentary and tepid support for the Civil Rights Act of 1875, discussed in Chapter 3.

[2] Act of April 9, 1866, 14 Stat. 27. Reenacted in the Enforcement Act of 1870.

162 *Rethinking the Judicial Settlement of Reconstruction*

in order to identify the requirements for valid Section 5 legislation under the Fourteenth Amendment.[3] The "color of law" discussion was part of the articulation of state action doctrine and not merely *dicta*.

Justice Bradley explained that the Civil Rights Act of 1866 was "clearly corrective in its character."[4] Because it was "intended to counteract and furnish redress against State laws and proceedings, and customs having the force of law, which sanction the wrongful acts specified."[5] The act was valid Section 5 legislation.[6] The act aimed at state laws, notably the infamous Black Codes of 1865–66, but not only at such discriminatory laws. It provided penalties for "persons" who "should subject parties to a deprivation of their rights under color of any statute, ordinance, custom, etc., of any State or Territory."[7] It was not the first time Bradley had explained that federal remedies might reach individual wrongs having the "color of law...or custom." In an 1878 case, he stated that the act of 1866 "vindicated" the right to "the equal benefit of the laws" against "individual aggression; but only when committed under color of some law, statute, ordinance, regulation or custom."[8]

The "color of law...or custom" phrase survives today in federal civil rights law,[9] but both scholars and jurists interpret this phrase narrowly, holding that individual wrongs cannot have the "color of law...or custom" unless state agents jointly and actively participate in the wrongdoing.[10] Bradley offered a more expansive construction in which he indicated that *individual* race-based wrongs against *civil rights* gain the color of law or custom if laws are

---

[3] U.S. Constitution, Amend. XIV, Section 5: "The Congress shall have power to enforce, by appropriate legislation, the provisions of this article."

[4] 109 U.S. at 16. Bradley cited with approval Sections 1977, 1978, 1979, and 5510 of the Revised Statutes, all of which derived from the act of 1866. Today, key civil rights statutes derive from these sections: 42 U.S.C. 1981 derives from §1977; 42 U.S.C. 1982 derives from §1978; 42 U.S.C. 1983 derives from §1979; 18 U.S.C. 242 derives from §§5510.

[5] 109 U.S. at 22.

[6] The Civil Rights Act of 1866 was originally passed to enforce the Thirteenth Amendment, but Rep. John A. Bingham expressed concerns about the constitutionality of the act. Deeming the act fundamental to the establishment of freedom, Congress erased all doubt about its constitutionality and passed the Fourteenth Amendment. The Civil Rights Act of 1866 was also later reenacted in the Enforcement Act of 1870, a measure passed to enforce the Fourteenth and Fifteenth Amendments. Justice Bradley, notably, stayed uncommitted about whether the act of 1866 was authorized under the Thirteenth Amendment. "Whether [the Civil Rights Act of 1866] was fully authorized by the Thirteenth Amendment alone, without the support which it afterward received from the Fourteenth Amendment, after the adoption of which it was re-enacted with some additions, it is not necessary to inquire" (109 U.S. at 22).

[7] 109 U.S. at 16–17.

[8] *Ex parte Wells*, 29 F. Cas. 633 (1878).

[9] The "color of law...or custom" phrase survives today in 18 U.S.C 242 of the Federal Criminal Code and its civil counterpart 42 U.S.C. 1983.

[10] For the Court's constructions of §242, see *Screws v. United States*, 325 U.S. 91 (1945) and *United States v. Price* (1966). For constructions of §1983, see *Monroe v. Pape*, 365 U.S. 167 (1961). See also Eisenberg 2000: 444–5.

The Civil Rights Cases *and the Language of State Neglect*

not in "full force" and state authorities "protect," "shield," or "excuse" these wrongs, that is, if state authorities systematically fail to punish them.

Consider the following extended passage, in which Justice Bradley defined a "rights denial." The crucial passage followed his endorsement of statutes (§1977, §1978, §1979, §5510) derived from the Civil Rights Act of 1866:

> In this connection it is proper to state that civil rights, such as are guaranteed by the Constitution against State aggression, cannot be impaired by the wrongful acts of individuals, unsupported by State authority in the shape of laws, customs, or judicial or executive proceedings. The wrongful act of an individual, unsupported by any such authority, is simply a private wrong, or a crime of that individual; an invasion of the rights of the injured party, it is true, whether they affect his person, his property, or his reputation; but if not sanctioned in some way by the State, or not done under State authority, [the] rights [of the injured party] remain in full force, and may presumably be vindicated by resort to the laws of the State for redress. An individual cannot deprive a man of his right to vote, to hold property, to buy and sell, to sue in the courts, or to be a witness or a juror; he may, by force or fraud, interfere with the enjoyment of the right in a particular case; he may commit an assault against the person, or commit murder, or use ruffian violence at the polls, or slander the good name of a fellow citizen; but, unless protected in these wrongful acts by some shield of State law or State authority, he cannot destroy or injure the right; he will only render himself amenable to satisfaction or punishment; and amenable therefore to the laws of the State where the wrongful acts are committed.[11]

To understand the passage we must consider that Bradley was using the recognizable legal concept of *civil rights*. Bradley's list of civil rights referenced physical assault, property, and contract. As noted earlier, a Republican consensus in 1866 regarded these rights as fundamental. Voting was included on the list, having begun its migration into the civil rights category after the passage of the Fifteenth Amendment in 1870.[12] Bradley left out public accommodations, marriage, and education. Their absence was just as significant as the enumeration of the civil rights category. In rejecting Thirteenth Amendment grounds for the public accommodation provisions, Bradley explained that in passing the Civil Rights Act of 1866, Congress "did not assume, under the authority given by the Thirteenth Amendment, to adjust what may be called the social rights of men and races in the community."[13] This civil/social distinction had been in use by centrist Republicans since 1872 when the Senate opened debate on Charles Sumner's Supplementary bill.

The passage also identified the circumstances under which Section 5 regulation of individuals became permissible. Some form of state "support" or

---

[11] 109 U.S at 17.

[12] The migration of voting rights (a created right) into the catagory deemed "fundamental" posed conceptual problems for Bradley's theorization of only "secured" rights as fundamental. He did not confront the issue.

[13] 109 U.S. at 22.

164   *Rethinking the Judicial Settlement of Reconstruction*

"sanction"[14] had to be given to the race-based wrongs. State authorities had to "protect" these wrongs "by some shield." The wrong had to "rest upon" some state authority "for its excuse and perpetration."[15] If this occurred, individual invasions of civil rights gained the "color of law...or custom."

The phrase "color of law" is thus clearly associated with state action of some kind. As the passage makes apparent, individuals cannot deprive other individuals of rights; a state can, however, deny rights. And a state can deny rights by shielding, excusing, or protecting individual race-based wrongs. Rights remain in "full force" unless such shielding, excusing, or protecting occurs. This last statement requires pause, for it means that in the circumstances under discussion, state laws are neutral on their face.

In what ways might state authorities shield, protect, or excuse Klan violence if state laws are facially neutral? The practice of refusing to punish it is one obvious answer. Indeed, recall Bradley's statement that an individual wrongdoer "will only render himself amenable to satisfaction or punishment" unless that wrong is protected "by some shield of State authority." Active participation in Klan violence by state officials might also support or protect such wrongdoing. But Bradley's language does not require the active participation of state agents in order for that wrongdoing to have the color of law.

The conclusion is indicated by Bradley's use of the term *individual*. Hundreds of federal court opinions before and after the *Civil Rights Cases* used a distinction between individuals and officers,[16] and there is overwhelming intertextual agreement on usage. While "officials" might sometimes fall into the category of individuals, the category of individuals cannot be limited to officials. Thus, individual wrongs can gain the "color of law or custom" even when laws are facially neutral and even without the active participation of state agents in that wrongdoing. What else could "shield" the wrongs but the failure to remedy them?[17]

Such an understanding of *shield*, *protect*, and *excuse* is consistent with Bradley's 1874 statement that when a right is

> denied or abridged by a state on account of race, color, or previous condition of servitude, either by withholding the right itself or *the remedies which are given to other citizens to enforce it*, then undoubtedly, congress has the power to pass laws to directly enforce the right and punish individuals for its violation, because that would be the only appropriate and efficient mode of enforcing the amendment.[18]

[14] 109 U.S. at 16. Sanction here means permission or approval.
[15] 109 U.S. at 18.
[16] A Lexis-Nexis search for Supreme Court cases between 1874 and 1888 using both the words "individuals" and "officers" produced 525 hits. I was unable to locate a case among them in which "individual" did not mean either person or human being.
[17] Letter from Joseph Bradley to George S. Boutwell, secretary of the treasury (April 15, 1872), reprinted in Bradley, *Miscellaneous Writings*, 342. In this letter, Bradley explained that the cause of such explosions was not, in fact, mysterious. Bradley, well versed in mathematical and engineering sciences, was deeply engaged in such matters outside the Court.
[18] *United States v. Cruikshank*, 25 F. Cas. at 713, emphasis added.

The Civil Rights Cases *and the Language of State Neglect*

We are now in a position to see that the passage from the *Civil Rights Cases* quoted above divides the race-based wrongs of private individuals into two categories: (1) "merely private" wrongs, and (2) private wrongs that state authorities shield, excuse, sanction, support, or protect. The Fourteenth Amendment does not authorize Congress to reach the first category. As the Court stated, "Individual invasion of individual rights is not the subject matter of the Amendment."[19] But the amendment does reach the second category, permitting federal punishment of private persons whose race-based wrongs against *civil rights* gain the imprimatur of the state through the state's failure to remedy them. The status of individual race-based wrongs – as "merely private" or having the "color of law...or custom" – thus depends on how state authorities respond to them.

Three years prior to the *Civil Rights Cases*, the Court used a conception of state action that included a state's failure to redress a race-based wrong against a civil right. The case, *Neal v. Delaware* (1880), involved an unremedied wrong committed by a state actor, not by a private individual.[20] So *Neal* is not direct evidence of the Court's support for state neglect principles. The case remains significant because it provided a legal framework for conceptualizing state neglect as a form of state action.

In this little-studied but revealing jury case, a black man was charged with raping a white woman. Defendant William Neal argued that black men had been excluded from the jury that indicted him and that the trial court had violated his rights by failing to quash the indictment. The Waite Court agreed, stating that the trial court had a duty to correct the wrong. The Court stated that the trial court was "bound to redress"[21] this exclusion and its refusal to do so was a rights denial: "The refusal of the State court to redress the wrong by them [the jury officers] committed was a denial of a right secured to the prisoner by the Constitution and laws of the United States. Speaking by Mr. Justice Strong, in *Ex parte Virginia*, we said, and now repeat, that 'a State acts by its legislative, its executive, or its judicial authorities.'"[22] The state's refusal to redress the racially motivated wrong was "state action." Bradley joined the *Neal* decision.

Neal involved a jury right, which the Court referred to as a *civil right*,[23] and relied mainly on *Virginia v. Rives*, another jury case that laid out rules for removing cases to federal court under Section 641, which derived from the act of 1866. The *Civil Rights Cases* also cited *Rives* as among those cases containing a "quite full" discussion of the rules for proper Section 5 legislation.[24] But this initially seems puzzling. Why would rules for applying a removal statute be relevant to an exposition of state action doctrine?

---

[19] 109 U.S. at 11.
[20] 103 U.S. 370 (1880).
[21] 103 U.S. at 394.
[22] 103 U.S. at 397.
[23] 103 U.S. at 386, 387.
[24] 109 U.S. at 12.

In *Virginia v. Rives*,[25] the Court turned down a petition to remove a case to federal court, explaining that the defendant's expectation that he would not get a fair trial was insufficient to establish a cause for removal. Justice Strong stated: "It is during the trial or final hearing that the defendant is denied equality of legal protection, and not until then. Nor can he know till then that the equal protection of the laws will not be extended to him. Certainly not until then can he affirm that it is denied."[26] The removal statute, the Court explained, could be used before a trial begins when a defendant can affirmatively know – from a state's unequal laws – that equal protection will be denied. If state laws are neutral on their face, a defendant cannot say ahead of time that equal protection will be denied. The defendant in *Rives* was thus denied a removal petition, keeping the matter under state authority, because it had to be presumed that the state would enforce its neutral law; no denial of equal protection had yet occurred.

The rule in *Rives* – that it must be presumed that states will enforce neutral laws and that only a factual contradiction of the presumption legitimated a federal remedy – makes sense of Bradley's reference to *Rives* in the *Civil Rights Cases*. The rule also aligns with Bradley's construction of "under color of law . . . or custom." Recall his statement that rights "remain in full force and may presumably be vindicated by resort to the laws of the state for redress" unless state authorities maladminister those laws by shielding or excusing certain wrongdoing. Thus, according to *Rives* and the *Civil Rights Cases*, a federal remedy becomes legitimate only after state practices have defeated the presumption that the state will equally enforce its neutral laws. The refusal of the state court to redress the wrong in *Neal* was a rights denial because the refusal defeated this presumption.[27]

In an introductory lecture to law students at the University of Pennsylvania in 1884, Justice Bradley explained that in order to study law, "[i]t is not only necessary to know the rule, but to know how to express it in the appropriate language." One had to master "language and forms of expression."

> There is no science in which the words and forms of expression are more important than in law. Precision of definition and statement is a *sine qua non*. Possessing it, you possess the law; not possessing it, you do not possess the law, but only the power of vainly beating the air with uncertain words which impress nobody, instruct nobody, convince nobody.[28]

Twentieth-century observers have not mastered the forms of expression for the state action rule in the *Civil Rights Cases*. Appropriate language for the

---

[25] 100 U.S. 313 (1880).

[26] 100 U.S. at 319, summarized in Headnote 4. The quoted text is the headnote.

[27] For the conventional view of *Rives*, see Magrath 1963: 146–7 ("the Negro's right to freedom in the selection of juries became meaningless").

[28] Joseph P. Bradley, "Law: It's Nature and Office as the Bond and Basis of Civil Society: Introductory Lecture to the Law Department of the University of Pennsylvania (1884)," in *Miscellaneous Writings*, 256–7.

The Civil Rights Cases *and the Language of State Neglect*

precise expression of the state action rule was to be found in the "color of law...or custom" phrase. Twentieth-century jurists and scholars have missed the extent to which the Court viewed the non-enforcement of neutral laws as a rights denial and preserved federal power to reach private individuals as a remedy.

The recovery of these historical constructions means, too, that any constitutional limitation on the scope of and justification for remedies that reach private individuals remains to be established, as do any requirements concerning the connection between remedies and the underlying violations. A more historically attuned reading of the *Civil Rights Cases* can give us a better account of constitutional development and provide a window on the nature of Supreme Court decision making. But it cannot answer these questions.

Let me conclude this discussion by returning to classic quotes from the *Civil Rights Cases*, which are routinely cited as expressions of state action doctrine:

> The first section of the Fourteenth Amendment...is prohibitory in its character, and prohibitory upon the States.... That Amendment erects no shield against merely private conduct, however discriminatory or wrongful....
> Individual invasion of individual rights is not the subject-matter of the amendment.

> [The Fourteenth Amendment] does not authorize Congress to create a code of municipal law for the regulation of private rights; but to provide modes of redress against the operation of State laws, and the action of State officers, executive or judicial, when these are subversive of the fundamental rights specified in the amendment.[29]

These passages are fully consistent with the legal concept of state neglect, which in sum holds that private race-based interferences in *civil rights* are "merely private" wrongs unless the state fails to punish them, a failure that is itself "subversive of...fundamental rights." In such situations of state neglect, Congress has the power to correct the maladministration under Section 5 by providing for the federal prosecution of the offenders.

Bradley's construction of the phrase "under color of law" was the Waite Court's only direct response to the cadre of Democratic lawyers who urged the Court to reject the state neglect concept. Recall that David Dudley Field, Cruikshank's lawyer, argued that "state inaction...is no cause for federal action." Bradley had clearly endorsed the concept of state neglect in his 1874 circuit opinion in *Cruikshank*. In the *Civil Rights Cases*, he reaffirmed that acceptance.

The *Chicago Tribune* perceived the state neglect concept in the *Civil Rights Cases*. Reporting on the case the day after it was decided, the newspaper explained the Fourteenth Amendment's prohibition against the states:

> The negro citizen enjoys everywhere the same political and civil rights under the law which the white citizen enjoys. Any person who interferes with these

---

[29] 109 U.S. at 11.

168 *Rethinking the Judicial Settlement of Reconstruction*

rights is subject to the same penalties as if he had interfered with the rights of a white citizen. If there are State or local laws anywhere which decree otherwise, *or if there are State or local officers who refuse to extend to black citizens the protection to which they are entitled as citizens*, it is the function of the United States courts and authorities to defend their citizenship and their rights....[30]

As noted in the Introduction, it is hard to overstate the importance of this evidence. The *Tribune* had been closely following judicial responses to Reconstruction legislation. Its detailed coverage encompassed both Supreme Court and circuit opinions, including Bradley's 1874 *Cruikshank* opinion, in which it also identified the concept of state neglect.

Likewise, consider the understanding of state action doctrine by Edward L. Pierce in his 1893 retrospective on Charles Sumner. The *Civil Rights Cases* was a relevant topic for Pierce, as the Court there invalidated two sections of Sumner's legislation. Pierce stated:

> The opinion of the court was to this effect.... The fourteenth amendment... is directed only against State laws and proceedings, and not against individual acts which are not done under their authority. It does not extend the power of Congress to the domain of private rights, which still remains with the States; it authorizes legislation corrective of state action, but not primary and direct legislation.[31]

In contemporary constructions of state action doctrine, the private status of a criminal perpetrator renders that wrong *private*. The status is fixed, that is, it does not change if state authorities systematically withhold punishment for that type of crime. Pierce is working with a distinction absent in contemporary times. Explaining that the Fourteenth Amendment is not directed against "individual acts which are not done under [state] authority," he implies that there are individual wrongs that *are* done under state authority. Bradley, too, articulated the understanding that individual wrongs may or may not have state authority. For Bradley, the status of a race-based wrong transforms from "merely private" to having the "color of law...or custom" if states fail to provide remedies.

Notice, finally, that Justice Bradley did not use the same words in his 1883 opinion as those used in his 1874 *Cruikshank* opinion, his 1873 *Slaughter-House* dissent, or his 1871 letter to Judge Woods.[32] But Bradley did not need

---

[30] *Chicago Tribune*, October 17, 1883, p. 4 (emphasis added). The *Tribune* continued to emphasize that the Fourteenth Amendment reached not just state laws. State authorities could deny rights, as well. "The officers and agents of the State have always been held amenable to the authority of United States law....the constitutional provision must mean that no agency of the State, or of the officers or agents by whom its powers are exercised, shall deny to any person within its jurisdiction the equal protection of the laws." *Chicago Tribune*, November 22, 1883, p. 4.

[31] Pierce, *Memoir and Letters of Charles Sumner*, 582.

[32] Recall his 1874 language: "The duty and power of enforcement take their inception from the moment that the state fails to comply with the duty enjoined....When the right of citizens of

The Civil Rights Cases *and the Language of State Neglect*

to use the same words in order to deploy the concept of state neglect. The vocabulary of state neglect was extensive, and it could be used in various ways. Of course, on any account, Bradley's expression of state neglect principles was not vigorously articulated. Had it been, the misreadings of the past century would not have occurred. Yet it remains critical that actors at the time perceived state neglect principles, as well as the Fifteenth Amendment exemption, where later interpreters have not. While twentieth- and twenty-first-century observers may need a forceful and assertive endorsement of black rights to "see" these concepts, actors at the time did not.

Bradley might have chosen against a more forceful expression in 1883 because his commitment to the state neglect concept was slipping. It had not slipped entirely, of course. If it had, he never would have added the "color of law...or custom" discussion. Another possibility pertains to interaction between the judicial and executive branches. Recall that the Court had produced a cautiously written pair of 1876 decisions in the context of political uncertainty and Republican decline, cueing the executive branch but not leading with a vigorous expression of support for black rights. The Court forcefully expressed support for voting rights in 1880 in *Siebold*, as it would in 1884 in *Yarbrough*. But this was only after the political branches had stepped up voting rights prosecutions and used the cues and theories the Court supplied. The joint judicial-executive development of voting rights doctrine demonstrated that the Court would supply and cue, but it would not lead. In short, the Court's vigorous expressions in *Siebold* and *Yarbrough* came only after the Republican Party's resurgent efforts.

As I suggested earlier, if the Court led and if the executive branch did not follow, the Court would look ineffectual.[33] And leading might well have been considered a violation of the judicial role. Justice Bradley's presentation of the state neglect concept in the *Civil Rights Cases* kept the concept available to the Arthur administration – which still showed life on rights enforcement – without putting the Court out in front of the political branches and thus without risking the Court's influence.

Bradley's "unheroic" expression of the state neglect concept in the *Civil Rights Cases* might be usefully apprehended by drawing a comparison to recent revisionism on *Brown v. Board of Education*.[34] While early work on *Brown* advanced a heroic view of the Court, casting it as independent and

---

the United States to vote is denied or abridged by a state on account of their race, color, or previous condition of servitude, either by withholding the right itself or the remedies which are given to other citizens to enforce it...." His 1873 language: "... delinquency of the state governments..." His 1871 language: "Denying includes inaction as well as action. And denying the equal protection of the laws includes the omission to protect as well as the omission to pass laws for protection."

[33] Scholars have identified institutional legitimacy as an implicit decision calculus in other contexts, such as civil liberties cases in times of war. See Rossiter 1957: 1–10.

[34] 347 U.S. 483 (1954).

able to buck the retrograde practices of the 1950s, *Brown* revisionists have argued that the Court was not so independent and followed historical and institutional trends.[35] The Holocaust affected the way liberals thought about Jim Crow, making it morally untenable.[36] Cold War politics made Jim Crow a liability to the United States's influence abroad.[37] The military had been desegregated. Jackie Robinson was already playing baseball with the Brooklyn Dodgers. The South had become a national outlier.[38]

The insights of *Brown* revisionism shed light on Bradley's muted expression. If it now seems unrealistic to hold the "heroic" and independent model of *Brown*, it is similarly unrealistic to expect a vigorous expression of state neglect principles from Bradley in 1883. By that time, institutional trends were going in the opposite direction. Indeed, it was when the wind was at the Court's back that Bradley gave his most vigorous expression of the state neglect concept. In 1871, 1873, and early 1874, Congress had just passed powerful new legislation, the Klan trials had just occurred, and federal enforcement rates were still rising (peaking in 1873). Bradley published his circuit opinion in *Cruikshank* in April of 1874. The midterm election of 1874, which gave the House to the Democrats and changed the politics of rights enforcement, had not yet occurred. The 1874 election thus marked a turning point in institutional trends.

If my explanation for Justice Bradley's modulated expression of the concept of state neglect is accurate – if he/the Court was keeping the concept available to the Arthur administration, which had pursued voting rights enforcement but had not used the state neglect concept – there is a lesson here about the vulnerability to "loss" of newly established rights-friendly legal concepts during periods of political retrenchment.

RECEPTION: THE CIVIL/SOCIAL DISTINCTION, REDUX

Frederick Douglass had harsh words for the *Civil Rights Cases*. Speaking at a mass meeting at Lincoln Hall in Washington, D.C., Douglass stated, "We have been grievously wounded in the house of our friends.... The enemies of liberty rejoice; the friends of freedom mourn today.... The humiliation of the negro is the humiliation of the Nation itself." Several days earlier, Douglass averred, "I regard the decision... as a part of the general reaction naturally following the increased friendship between the North and the South which comes of the dying out of the old controversy on the subject of slavery. The decision is in the direction and interest of the old Calhoun doctrine of State

---

[35] Jack M. Balkin summarizes this scholarship in his Introduction to *What Brown v. Board of Education Should Have Said* (2001), 3–28.

[36] Richard A. Primus, *The American Language of Rights* (1999).

[37] Mary Dudziak, *Cold War Civil Rights: Race and the Image of American Democracy* (2000).

[38] Lucas A. Powe, Jr., *The Warren Court and American Politics* (2000).

The Civil Rights Cases *and the Language of State Neglect*

rights as against Federal authority."[39] The noted political orator Col. Robert G. Ingersoll said the decision was the worst since *Dred Scott.*[40]

An exchange between Frederick Douglass and the *Chicago Tribune* reprised the intramural Republican debate over civil rights and social rights and exemplified the reactions of (what was left of) the radical wing of the Republican Party and the centrist/stalwart Republicans. Stated Douglass, "I think the decision has resulted largely from confounding social with civil rights."[41] Responded the *Tribune*: "Mr. Douglass is right when he says that social and civil rights have been confounded, but this was the fault of the law and not of the decision."[42] The *Chicago Tribune* consistently referred to the *Civil Rights Cases* as "The Social Rights Decision."[43] Publishing a number of articles with the headline "Civil vs. Social Rights," the *Tribune* reiterated the centrist Republican distinction between civil rights and social rights.[44] The *New York Times* said the same thing.[45]

The *Tribune*, never fond of radicals, castigated Douglass and Ingersoll for leaving

> the false impression that the decision amounts to a judicial sanction of any discrimination which may be practiced against the black man. There is not the slightest warrant for that construction of the decision.... The real civil rights of the blacks – the right to make contracts, to serve on juries, to give testimony in court, etc. – are secured to them in a separate law which has been sustained by the United States courts. These are not brought into question by the recent decision on social rights.[46]

Identifying *civil rights* with the Civil Rights Act of 1866, the *Tribune* stated:

> Civil Rights are the rights to make and enforce contracts; to sue, be parties to suits in court, give evidence, serve on juries; to inherit, purchase, hold, and convey property; and to be protected from pains, penalties, taxes, and exactions not imposed upon other citizens.[47]

"The civil rights of blacks," the *Tribune* emphasized, "may be and ought to be enforced by the National Government wherever there is a local effort to abridge them." But access to public accommodations was a different matter.

---

[39] *Chicago Tribune*, October 20, 1883, p. 4.

[40] Speeches of Douglass and Ingersoll reported in the *Chicago Tribune*, October 23, 1883, p. 1.

[41] Reported by the Washington correspondent of the *Tribune*. *Chicago Tribune*, October 20, 1883, p. 4. See also the comments of Robert Ingersoll on the civil/social distinction – *Washington Post*, November 3, 1883, p. 1.

[42] *Chicago Tribune*, October 20, 1883, p. 4.

[43] *Chicago Tribune*, October 17, 1883, p. 4; October 20, 1883, p. 4; October 20. 1883, p. 11; October 24, 1883, p. 4; October 26, 1883, p. 4.

[44] *Chicago Tribune*, November 6, 1883, p. 4; November 7, 1883, p. 11; November 22, 1883, p. 4. The *Washington Post* used the same "Civil vs. Social Rights" headline, November 3, 1883, p. 1.

[45] *New York Times*, October 16, 1883, p. 4; October 18, 1883, p. 4.

[46] *Chicago Tribune*, October 24, 1883, p. 4.

[47] *Chicago Tribune*, November 6, 1883, p. 4. See also October 20, 1883, p. 4.

172 Rethinking the Judicial Settlement of Reconstruction

"[T]he right to occupy a berth on a sleeping-car, to sit at a hotel-table, or to secure a certain place at a theatrical or operatic performance is of a social character, because it involves the personal comfort or preference of those occupying adjoining seats or berths.[48] The paper also asserted that Douglass's invocation of Calhoun was misplaced. "The late Senator Carpenter was certainly never suspected of leaning to the Calhoun doctrine of State sovereignty, and yet he opposed the Social Rights bill as unconstitutional."[49]

In a demonstration that social Darwinist principles (or, more, precisely, Herbert Spencer's spin on Darwin) had not yet taken hold, the *Tribune* did not appeal to nature as a permanent block to social equality. "To emerge from slavery to full social equality is necessarily an evolution requiring time and favorable conditions." The *Tribune* identified "prejudice" on the part of whites as the problem, but made black demonstration of worth the solution:

> The social separation of blacks and whites is due to prejudice on the part of the latter, and it is a prejudice which can only be conquered by time and the demonstration of the negro's personal claims to equality and uniformity of association with the whites. It is a prejudice which the negroes must overcome without the aid of laws, which can always be evaded when such evasion does not entail civil injury or personal injustice.[50]

As in earlier years, the *Tribune*'s combination of views – its support for the Civil Rights Act of 1866, its perception of the state neglect concept in Bradley's opinion, its reference to the "characteristic African disregard of logic," its paternalism, and its perception of the civil/social boundary as ultimately permeable – placed the newspaper in the mainstream of the Republican Party. The mix, which clearly contained racist elements, was nevertheless distinct from the view articulated more than a dozen years later in *Plessy v. Ferguson*. In that decision, the Court presented the boundary between the civil and social spheres as impermeable. That was the "nature of things." In 1896 we find social Darwinism and unalloyed reaction.[51]

The *Tribune*'s language is also usefully contrasted with that of the *New York Times*. The language of disengagement is clear in the paper's commentary on the *Civil Rights Cases*: "As early as December 1873, we remarked: Law has done all that it can for the negroes, and the sooner they set about securing their future for themselves the better it will be for them and their descendants."[52]

---

[48] *Chicago Tribune*, November 6, 1883, p. 4. See also October 20, 1883, p. 4.

[49] *Chicago Tribune*, October 20, 1883, p. 4. The *Tribune* noted on multiple occasions that "many of the most learned lawyers in the country" questioned the constitutionality of the Civil Rights Act of 1875 when it was passed (October 17, 1883, p. 4; October 16, 1883, p. 1).

[50] *Chicago Tribune*, November 6, 1883, p. 4. See also *Chicago Tribune*, October 20, 1883 ("Time and better education will wear away the existing social prejudices between whites and blacks").

[51] 163 U.S. at 544 ("[I]n the nature of things [the Fourteenth Amendment] could not have been intended to abolish distinctions based upon color, or to enforce social, as distinguished from political equality").

[52] *New York Times*, October 18, 1883, p. 4.

The Civil Rights Cases *and the Language of State Neglect*

Reporting on the *Civil Rights Cases*, the Democratic *Washington Post* expressed strong approval for the result: "It will not be surprising," the *Post* stated, "if the relations of the races are made more friendly by the removal of a source of irritation and annoyance."[53] Black voters would split off from the Republican Party, the newspaper predicted, which would be a welcome result: "The independent movement on the part of the colored voters cannot but be strengthened by the civil rights decision."[54]

The southern Democratic newspapers were even more satisfied. The *Atlanta Constitution* did not hope "to compass with words the feeling of deep and perfect satisfaction" with which the *Civil Rights Cases* would be received in the South. It referred to the public accommodations provisions as an "infamous and malignant bill" for "social equality."[55] Reaction from most Southern presses was generally calm, an indication that the public accommodations provisions had been a dead letter.[56]

Reaction among blacks was not uniform. Reporting on the decision, the *Chicago Tribune* cited a "Division of Opinion Among Colored Leaders."[57] Mass protest meetings were organized across the United States (e.g., in New York City, Washington, D.C., San Francisco, Denver, and Indianapolis), and these meetings were always reported by the *Christian Recorder*. The Hon. J. M. Langston, an envoy to Haiti, expressed a different view. He did not see the case as a disaster and urged the use of the common law as a remedy for exclusions from public accommodations.[58] The Rev. Dr. Law stated, "I am satisfied with the decision so far as I am concerned, and I know one thing – that it is a useless law. It has never done any good in any case." John F. Cooke, a tax collector in Washington, D.C., gave a similar assessment.

SPECIAL LEGISLATION?

Were the public accommodations provisions "special legislation"? While *special* might refer to the targeting of a particular or singular need, the term also connotes favoritism. Mainstream Republican newspapers perceived a flaw in the provisions that Bradley did not explicitly identify: blacks were favored over Jews and the Irish, who were also excluded from public accommodations on the basis of their status but were outside the protection of the new law. The public accommodations provisions were, on this reading, "special legislation."

---

[53] *Washington Post*, October 17, 1883, p. 2.
[54] *Washington Post*, October 20, 1883, p. 2.
[55] Quoted in the *Chicago Tribune*, October 20, 1883, p. 11.
[56] Ezell 1968: 266, 269. See also *Chicago Tribune*, October 25, 1883, p. 3; Franklin 1964; Lofgren 1988.
[57] October 18, 1883, p. 1.
[58] Langston's views were picked up and repeated by the Democratic *Washington Post*, October 20, 1883, p. 2. In 1877 the black newpaper the *Christian Recorder* reported that Langston opposed Sumner's Civil Rights bill and urged reliance on the common law. *Christian Recorder*, June 28, 1877.

174 *Rethinking the Judicial Settlement of Reconstruction*

We should be immediately suspicious of any claim that Reconstruction legislation advantaged blacks. In his message vetoing the Civil Rights Act of 1866, President Johnson made precisely that claim. "[T]he distinction of race and color is by the bill made to operate in favor of the colored and against the white race."[59] Republicans found this preposterous, as whites enjoyed the rights to property, contract, and physical security as a matter of law. Justice Bradley referred to the act of 1866 as "beneficent legislation" that enabled the freedmen to "shake off the inseparable concomitants" of slavery.[60] In the very same sentence, however, Bradley cautioned against treating freedmen as the "special favorite of the laws."

> When a man has emerged from slavery, and by the aid of beneficent legislation has shaken off the inseparable concomitants of that state, there must be some stage in the progress of his elevation when he takes the rank of a mere citizen, and ceases to be the special favorite of the laws, and when his rights as a citizen, or as a man, are to be protected in the ordinary modes by which other men's rights are protected.[61]

Justice Harlan rebuked Bradley for this language:

> It is, I submit, scarcely just to say that the colored race has been the special favorite of the laws. The statute of 1875, now adjudged to be unconstitutional, is for the benefit of citizens of every race and color. What the nation through Congress, has sought to accomplish in reference to that race, is – what had already been done in every State of the Union for the white race – to secure and protect rights belonging to them as freemen and citizens; nothing more. It was not deemed enough "to help the feeble up, but to support him after." The one underlying purpose of congressional legislation has been to enable the black race to take the rank of mere citizens.[62]

This looks like a villain-hero exchange. A righteous Harlan reproaches a hostile Bradley. But there is a context for the exchange that makes it more complicated.

Harlan asserted that the public accommodation provisions gave blacks "nothing more" than what "had already been done...for the white race." The *Chicago Tribune* challenged this assertion. The *Tribune* agreed with the Court's decision to invalidate the public accommodation provisions because those provisions gave blacks "exceptional privileges": the public accommodation provisions gave blacks special advantages that others did not enjoy.

> The American hotelkeeper or restauranteur can prevent an Irishman or a German – or indeed a Kentuckian – from eating at the same table with any other class of guests. If in any State this is contrary to law, the negroes in that State who may be aggrieved can appeal to the courts for redress just as the Irishman, or the Jew or the Kentuckian may appeal. A few years ago a

[59] Richardson, ed., *Messages and Papers*, vol. 6, pp. 405ff.
[60] 109 U.S. at 25.
[61] Ibid.
[62] 109 U.S. at 61.

The Civil Rights Cases *and the Language of State Neglect*

> New York hotelkeeper refused to accommodate Jews... but there was no law under which they could obtain material redress.... The negroes of New York claimed under the Civil Rights bill a right and privilege which was denied to the Jews.[63]

A few days later, the *Tribune* pointed again to the New York hotelkeeper's exclusion of Jews. "That was an instance in which a certain class or race of white citizens were denied privileges which the negroes maintain the General Government ought to enforce in their behalf. This of course would involve the use of Government powers to secure to the blacks higher privileges than the whites can assert under the same protection."[64] The *Tribune* concluded, "The decision thus places the negro upon the same plane of equality in the exercise of his personal privileges as that upon which the white citizen stands, and the former has the same remedy in law which the latter has for any infringement of his social rights."[65]

Jews and the Irish were culturally regarded as a lower order of whites and were the targets of exclusion and discrimination.[66] The *Tribune* described Jews as "a certain class or race of white citizens."[67] Jews and Irishmen however, were "white" under the law of naturalization.[68] They were white by law. So while the public accommodations law would cover the exclusion of blacks from the Palmer House Hotel in Chicago, the law would not cover the exclusion of Jews from the Saratoga Hotel in New York. According to the *Tribune*, this is favoritism in social privileges. Either all status-based discrimination in public accommodations must be banned, or none at all.

From this perspective – when the "racial" inferiority of Jews and Irishmen coexists with their legal status as white – Justice Harlan's claim that the public accommodation provisions gave nothing more to blacks than was given to Jews or the Irish is open to challenge.

The Preamble to the Civil Rights Act of 1875, which references religious discrimination, is irrelevant to the matter. Not typically quoted in the Reconstruction legal literature it reads:

> Whereas, it is essential to just government we recognize the equality of all men before the law, and hold that it is the duty of government in its dealings with the people to mete out equal and exact justice to all, of whatever nativity, race, color, or persuasion, religious or political; and it being the appropriate object of legislation to enact these great fundamental principles into law.[69]

---

[63] *Chicago Tribune*, October 18, 1883, p. 4.

[64] *Chicago Tribune*, October 20, 1883, p. 4.

[65] *Chicago Tribune*, October 24, 1883, p. 4.

[66] David Roediger, *The Wages of Whiteness: Race and the Making of the American Working Class* (1999); Matthew Pratt Guterl, *The Color of Race in America, 1900–1940* (2001).

[67] This sounds odd to the modern ear. Today, whites are regarded as a single race with no racial subdivisions. As Guterl explains, this development occurred in the twentieth century.

[68] Under the immigration act of 1792, naturalization was limited to "free white persons." See Ian Haney Lopez, *White by Law: The Legal Construction of Race* (1996).

[69] 18 Stat. 335

The Preamble is in fact taken from a plank in the Democratic platform of 1872. At the final stages of passage in the House, Rep. Shanks mischievously proposed its inclusion. The proposal by Shanks irritated Democrats, who promptly repudiated the plank.[70] One might wonder why the plank was included in their platform in the first place. In 1872, the Democrats were so weak at the national level that they did not nominate their own slate of candidates, instead nominating the Liberal-Republican Greeley/Brown ticket. The Liberal Republicans had bolted from the Republican Party, nominating for president Horace Greeley, editor of the *New York Tribune*. But in nominating the Liberal Republican ticket, the Democrats had to take the Liberal Republican platform, the first plank of which read: "We recognize the equality of all men before the law, and hold that it is the duty of government in its dealings with the people to mete out equal and exact justice to all, of whatever nativity, race, color, or persuasion, religious or political."[71] The lack of enthusiasm among Democrats for Liberal Republicans was evident in the fact that the convention lasted only nine hours, the shortest major political party convention in U.S. history. The repudiation of the plank by Democrats in 1874 as the political tide turned is easily understandable. Republicans happily voted in favor of the Preamble.

Disregarding the inoperative Preamble, the *Chicago Tribune* described the public accommodation provisions as special legislation. In 1875, the *New York Daily Tribune* referred to the Civil Rights Act of 1875 as class legislation. "The closing hours of the debate in the Senate yesterday on the Civil Rights bill were marked by no enthusiasm or excitement of any kind, and only the large preponderance of colored people in the galleries showed that any class legislation was being enacted."[72] The *New York Times* also indicated that the act was class legislation.[73] During the period, references to class legislation connoted legislative favoritism and advantages gained by faction.[74]

What is perhaps more surprising is that the *Christian Recorder* referred to civil rights legislation as special legislation and class legislation. Indeed, the *Christian Recorder* made numerous references to civil rights laws – not just the Civil Rights Act of 1875 but civil rights laws in general – as special legislation: "With the present election of President Grant, the questions at issue underlying the three last amendments of the Constitution will be permanently secured and settled; we shall therefore never again be the subjects of any special acts of Congress save the pending supplementary Civil Rights bill."[75] Or later: "We get nothing of civil rights save by special legislation."[76] On multiple occasions, the *Recorder* called the Civil Rights Act of 1875 special

---

[70] *New York Times*, February 6, 1875, p. 8. The Preamble was approved by a vote of 219–26.
[71] Kirk H. Porter, ed., *National Party Platforms, 1840–1956* (1956), 41, 44.
[72] *New York Daily Tribune*, March 1, 1875.
[73] *New York Times*, October 18, 1883, p. 4.
[74] See Howard Gillman, *The Constitution Beseiged* (1993).
[75] *Christian Recorder*, November 30, 1872.
[76] *Christian Recorder*, August 6, 1874.

The Civil Rights Cases *and the Language of State Neglect* 177

legislation.[77] In 1884, the newspaper called for "special legislation or another civil rights bill."[78] The *Recorder* also used the term "class legislation," referring to anti-Klan legislation as class legislation.[79] Likewise, the preacher Rev. Dr. Laws called the Civil Rights Act of 1875 class legislation.[80]

The connotations of favoritism that attach to "special legislation" emerge in the *Recorder*'s response to critics of such legislation. In a bitter holding forth, the newspaper contrasted blacks with the "almost worthless" class of "Indian savages."

> To this objection we answer that it is nothing new for the Government to be so employed. Witness the Indians. There is an Indian Bureau established by our government, supported not by States by the expenditure of millions of dollars annually in the payment of officers and sub-agents; besides still larger amounts for the furnishing and distribution of material and aid to the savages, to all of which the black man is compelled to pay his proportion, and that too, for a people savage, indolent and almost worthless as a class – a people who respect neither Christianity nor our civilization, rearing the walls of their tribal economy against everything but material aid. This ought to be an effective estoppel to all protests against us because we may demand special legislation and special aid.[81]

The obvious accusation of favoritism in the *Recorder*'s contempt for the Indian Bureau did not preclude a position establishing blacks' own need for special legislation which was not associated with unfair favoritism.

The newspaper continued to refer to civil rights laws as special or class legislation into the 1880s, even as it stopped demanding new civil rights laws. "We do not ask for any more class legislation. We have had enough of this. But we do believe that many of the laws intended to secure us our rights as citizens are nothing more than dead letters."[82] Or later: "I plead no special legislation, I seek no favors of grace, I ask no preferment."[83] Or later still: "I want no civil rights bill, no special legislation, no special appropriation. I only want now to work out my own salvation."[84] Experiences had become demoralizing, and the enforcement context had changed, even if the understanding of civil rights laws as special legislation had not.

The term *special legislation* thus had a wider set of meanings and uses than a twentieth-century observer might imagine. Arguments about the exclusion of Jews and Irishmen from the coverage of the public accommodations provisions and the *Recorder*'s frequent reference to civil rights laws as special

---

[77] *Christian Recorder*, March 26, 1874; February 18, 1875; November 1, 1883, November 15, 1883.
[78] *Christian Recorder*, October 30, 1884.
[79] *Christian Recorder*, May 4, 1893.
[80] *Chicago Tribune*, October 18, 1883, p. 1.
[81] *Christian Recorder*, June 6, 1878.
[82] *Christian Recorder*, October 4, 1883.
[83] *Christian Recorder*, April 16, 1885.
[84] *Christian Recorder*, June 6, 1889. See also February 6, 1890.

178   *Rethinking the Judicial Settlement of Reconstruction*

legislation provide a context for Bradley's "special favorite" comment, thus adding uncertainty to its twentieth-century interpretation.

WOULD A STATE NEGLECT PREDICATE HAVE SAVED THE STATUTE?

A final question pertaining to the *Civil Rights Cases* must be addressed: if Congress had written the public accommodation provisions differently – if Congress had made the punishment of innkeepers, theater owners, and so on, contingent on the failure of states to punish them – would the provisions have passed constitutional muster? As they stood, the provisions made no reference to state action of any kind. As the *Chicago Tribune* put it, "The law passed by Congress... was not aimed at any State, nor called out by State effort to violate its terms." But *if* the public accommodation provisions had made regulation of private individuals and corporations a remedy for state violations – for example, the maladministration of state laws – would the penalties against private innkeepers, theater owners, and common carriers have been constitutional? The question is important, and a number of twentieth-century interpreters have said *yes*.

Among the first were Justices Goldberg, Douglas, and Warren in the sit-in case, *Bell v. Maryland* (1964).[85] That same year, the lawyer Laurent B. Frantz argued in the *Yale Law Journal* that the *Civil Rights Cases* did not block Section 5 legislation punishing private individuals.[86] He focused on the following passage from Justice Bradley's opinion:

> An inspection of the law shows that it makes no reference whatever to any supposed or apprehended violation of the Fourteenth Amendment on the part of the States. It is not predicated on any such view. It proceeds ex directo to declare that certain acts committed by individuals shall be deemed offences, and shall be prosecuted and punished by proceedings in the courts of the United States. It does not profess to be corrective of any constitutional wrong committed by the States; it does not make its operation to depend upon any such wrong committed.[87]

Bradley's discussion would have been "entirely superfluous," asserted Frantz, if the owners of inns, railroads, and theaters were wholly beyond congressional power.[88] But Frantz was distorting Bradley's stated purpose in providing this discussion. Bradley had provided it in order to lay down "principles of interpretation."[89] As Bradley explained:

---

[85] 378 U.S. at 306–7.
[86] Laurent B. Frantz, "Congressional Power to Enforce the Fourteenth Amendment Against Private Acts," 73 *Yale Law Journal* 1353 (1964).
[87] *Civil Rights Cases*, 109 U.S. at 14.
[88] Frantz, "Congressional Power to Enforce the Fourteenth Amendment," 1380.
[89] 109 U.S. at 18.

The Civil Rights Cases *and the Language of State Neglect*

We have discussed the question presented by the law on the assumption that a right to enjoy equal accommodation and privileges in all inns, public conveyances, and places of public amusement, is one of the essential rights of the citizen which no State can abridge or interfere with. Whether it is such a right, or not, is a different question which, in the view we have taken of the validity of the law on the ground already stated, it is not necessary to examine.[90]

The Court put aside a series of other questions, as well, carefully delineating the questions that it did not address.[91] Of central relevance is the fourth headnote of the decision: "Whether the accommodations and privileges sought to be protected by the 1st and 2d sections of the Civil Rights Act [of 1875], are, or are not, rights constitutionally demandable; and if they are, in what form they are to be protected, is not now decided."[92] The point was hard to miss. So Frantz made precisely the assumption that Bradley said should not be made, reading the decision as support for public accommodation provisions that were predicated on state behavior. In later years, a handful of law professors endorsed Frantz's thesis in ways that range from strong to oblique.[93]

---

[90] 109 U.S. at 19.

[91] Bradley continued, "We have also discussed the validity of the law in reference to cases arising in the States only; and not in reference to cases arising in the Territories or the District of Columbia, which are subject to the plenary legislation of Congress in every branch of municipal regulation. Whether the law would be a valid one as applied to the Territories and the District is not a question for consideration in the cases before us: they all being cases arising within the limits of States. And whether Congress, in the exercise of its power to regulate commerce amongst the several States, might or might not pass a law regulating rights in public conveyances passing from one State to another, is also a question which is not now before us, as the sections in question are not conceived in any such view" (109 U.S. at 19). This last comment was seized upon by supporters of the Civil Rights Act of 1964, who, perceiving the state action cases as an obstacle to Fourteenth Amendment authorization of the act, turned to the Commerce Clause. See Richard C. Cortner, *Civil Rights and Public Accommodations: The Heart of Atlanta Motel and McClung Cases* (2001).

[92] 109 U.S. 3.

[93] See Frank I. Michelman, "Conceptions of Democracy in American Constitutional Argument: The Case of Pornography Regulation," 56 *Tennessee Law Review* 291, 307 n.54 (1989); Michael W. McConnell, "Originalism and the Desegregation Decision," 81 *Virginia Law Review* 947, 1090 (1995); Robert C. Post and Reva Siegel, "Equal Protection of the Law: Federal Antidiscrimination Legislation After Morrison and Kimel," 110 *Yale Law Journal* 441, 475–6 (2000). See the more oblique comments by Gerald Gunther and Kathleen Sullivan in *Constitutional Law* (1997: 122, Teaching Supplement) ("Note Justice Bradley's crucial assumption that state-law redress was available for common law injuries and that the right to nondiscriminatory treatment was an aspect of common law liberty. Thus the holding was essentially that Congress lacked the power under Section 5 of the Fourteenth Amendment to create common law rights....Could Congress act if it had evidence that the states had failed to enforce their common law against private racial discrimination?"). See also Geoffrey Stone, Louis Seidman, Cass Sunstein, and Mark Tushnet, *Constitutional Law* (1996), 1597–8 ("Might it count as a state invasion of individual rights for a state to fail to remedy acts of racial discrimination undertaken by owners of public accommodations who are required by state law to serve the public? Do the *Civil Rights Cases* hold that a state can constitutionally leave such discrimination unremedied?").

180 *Rethinking the Judicial Settlement of Reconstruction*

It is not an accident that every one of the challenges to the conventional reading of the *Civil Rights Cases* comes from lawyers. "Thinking like a lawyer" is an analytical exercise that involves interrogating the fit between specific facts and a legal principle. The goal is to identify what a case "stands for." As Elizabeth Mertz explains, "whether or not a legal claim can be established in [a] new case...will depend in part on whether these facts are arguably similar to those in previous cases where legal claims were upheld."[94] When the fit between the facts and the legal rule (state action) is interrogated in the *Civil Rights Cases*, it is possible to generate alternatives to the conventional view of what the decision "stands for." Bradley's fourth headnote made explicit the Court's refusal to address potentially valid constitutional claims on public accommodation rights, but the Court's refusal does not preclude Frantz or anybody else from pursuing and elaborating such possibilities.

That such elaborations entail the use of analytic reason rather than historical precedent is a point I am making throughout this study. A more historically attuned reading of the state action cases is necessary for understanding constitutional development and the Court's relationship to the political branches. But originalist assumptions are misplaced. Frantz's use of analytic reason to extend the state neglect principle to public accommodations is perfectly defensible, even if the Court refused to do it and even if Frantz provides no way of understanding Justice Bradley's categorization of public accommodation rights as *social rights*. As a historian, Frantz does poorly. As a lawyer, he offers a good argument indeed.

LOGAN V. UNITED STATES (1892): THE HYBRID CONSTITUTION, REDUX

In the little-known case *Logan v. United States* (1892),[95] the federal government charged private individuals with conspiring against and murdering a person in lawful federal custody. Upholding the prosecution of Eugene Logan and three others under Section 5508, Justice Horace Gray, appointed in 1882 by Republican President Chester Arthur, explained that the right to be protected from conspiracies and violence while in lawful federal custody was a right *created* or *conferred* by federal law and that Congress had the power to affirmatively enforce such rights. Citing Justice Bradley's 1874 circuit opinion in *Cruikshank* as providing "the main principles on which that decision was based,"[96] Justice Gray cleanly mapped the declared/created rights distinction that structured and organized the rights enforcement jurisprudence of the Waite Court. Gray canvassed a series of cases that included *Cruikshank*,

---

[94] Mertz, *The Language of Law School: Learning to Think Like a Lawyer* (2007), 71. See, e.g., the exchange between "Prof." and "Ms. S." in which Prof. probes the connection between the facts and the rule for which the case stands.
[95] 144 U.S. 263 (1892).
[96] 144 U.S. at 288.

The Civil Rights Cases *and the Language of State Neglect*

Ex parte Siebold, Ex parte Virginia, United States v. Harris, the *Civil Rights Cases,* and *Ex parte Yarbrough,* summing up their organizing principle:

> The whole scope and effect of this series of decisions is that, while certain fundamental rights, *recognized* and *declared,* but not *granted* or *created,* in some of the Amendments to the Constitution, are thereby guaranteed only against violation or abridgment by the United States, or by the States, as the case may be, and cannot therefore be affirmatively enforced by Congress against unlawful acts of individuals; yet that every right, created by, arising under or dependent upon, the Constitution of the United States, may be protected and enforced by Congress by such means and in such manner as Congress, in the exercise of the correlative duty of protection, or of the legislative powers conferred upon it by the Constitution, may in its discretion deem most eligible and best adapted to attain the object.[97]

Turning away Logan's challenge, Gray situated the Court's ruling in a line of precedent that included *United States v. Waddell* (1884),[98] which affirmed the federal prosecution of private individuals under Section 5508 for interfering in a person's right to protection while meeting occupancy requirements set by a federal homestead law, another right created by federal law.

Logan provides additional evidence of contemporaneous understandings of Waite Court cases. Justice Gray, who served with Justice Bradley, gave this understanding of the flaw in the *Cruikshank* indictments: *Cruikshank,* he stated, "held...that counts for conspiracy to prevent and hinder citizens of the African race in the free exercise and enjoyment of the right to vote at state elections, or to injure and oppress them for having voted at such elections, *not alleging that this was on account of their race, or color, or previous condition of servitude, could not be maintained.*"[99] As we have seen, this understanding of the problem with the indictments was repeated throughout the period.

Similarly worth noting is the characterization of state action doctrine made by Logan's lawyer in an attempt to challenge the federal prosecution. Counsel cited the whole line of state action cases, including *Cruikshank, Harris,* and the *Civil Rights Cases,* for the argument that the federal government could not punish Logan because no state action had taken place. According to Logan's counsel, these cases stood for the rule that "constitutional amendments are restrictive upon the power of the general government and the action of the States.... [T]here is nothing in their language or spirit which indicates that they are to be enforced by Congressional enactments, authorizing the trial, conviction and punishment of individuals for individual invasions of individual rights, *unless committed under state authority.*"[100] This is the same language that appears in Edward Pierce's description of the *Civil Rights Cases*

---

[97] 144 U.S. at 293, emphasis added.
[98] 112 U.S. 76.
[99] 144 U.S. at 288, emphasis added, citing *Cruikshank* at 556.
[100] 144 U.S. at 280.

182 — Rethinking the Judicial Settlement of Reconstruction

in his 1893 retrospective of Sumner.[101] As I explained earlier, this language implies a distinction – between wrongs committed by private individuals that are done under state authority and those that are not – that is consistent with Bradley's construction of the concept of state neglect.

THE LAST GASP OF RECONSTRUCTION

The election of 1888 demonstrated that Reconstruction was still not dead. A "policy window" opened for the Republican Party when it gained control of both the presidency and Congress for the first time since Reconstruction.[102] President Benjamin Harrison, still trying to build southern Republicanism, turned first to the tariff. Matthew Quay, the political boss and powerful chairman of the Republican National Committee, pushed the high tariff policy. But many Republican leaders who initially urged Harrison to adopt it, such as Grenville Dodge and James S. Clarkson, continued to embrace sectionalism and voting rights enforcement when it became clear in the midterm election that the tariff was an ineffective party builder.

The policy window created the chance for the Republican Party to pass a new elections bill. Massachusetts Rep. Henry Cabot Lodge was the House manager of the bill, which permitted federal supervisors to observe the registration of voters and guard against fraud at the polls. The bill passed the House on July 2, 1890, but in the Senate Democrats and western "silver" Republicans joined forces to hold it over until the next session. In the reconvened Congress, the bill was still alive, and George F. Hoar, the Senate sponsor, moved to reconsider it. After a 33–33 tie was broken by Vice President Levi P. Morton in favor of reconsidering, Democrats filibustered. On January 20, Republicans attempted to close debate, but the Democrats walked out of the Senate chamber, preventing a quorum. Two days later, Democrats and silver Republicans again allied to sidetrack the Lodge-Hoar bill and take up an apportionment measure. The bill was now dead.[103]

Having constantly searched for methods to build up the party in the South, Republicans "abandon[ed] the quest in 1891."[104] The scholarship that I

---

[101] Recall Pierce's statement: "The opinion of the court was to this effect.... The fourteenth amendment... is directed only against State laws and proceedings, and not against individual acts which are not done under their authority. It does not extend the power of Congress to the domain of private rights, which still remains with the States; it authorizes legislation corrective of state action, but not primary and direct legislation." Pierce, *Memoir and Letters of Charles Sumner*, 582.

[102] Richard M. Valelly, "Partisan Entrepreneurship and Policy Windows: George Frisbie Hoar and the 1890 Federal Elections Bill," in S. Skowronek and M. Glassman, eds., *Formative Acts: American Politics in the Making* (2007); Richard M. Valelly, "The Reed Rules and Republican Party Building: A New Look," *Studies in American Political Development* 23 (October 2009): 115–42. For an earlier account of the Lodge bill, see Hirshson, *Farewell to the Bloody Shirt*, 215–35.

[103] Hirshson, *Farewell to the Bloody Shirt*, 233.

[104] Ibid.

The Civil Rights Cases *and the Language of State Neglect*

described earlier as the new political history identifies the Lodge bill as the last attempt to reconstruct the South, the failure of which marked the Republican party's abdication of rights enforcement.[105]

The transitional years between 1876 and 1891 were marked by numerous congressional investigations of southern atrocities, persistent though inadequate voting rights enforcement, an oscillating southern policy in the Republican Party, and a steady stream of Republican speeches in favor of equal civil and political (but not social) rights for blacks. All of this ended with the failure of the Lodge bill. The complete disenfranchisement of black voters that occurred in the wake of this failure was due to a confluence of factors that included southern intransigence, northern popular apathy, a deep economic depression, an inadequate administrative structure, and the changing character of the Republican Party. A "closed" doctrine of state action, one that shut the door on federal efforts to protect black rights, was not among them.

In the years following the Republican Party's definitive political abandonment of blacks in 1891, the Court under Chief Justice Melville Fuller issued a series of decisions that shut down or closed off the rights-friendly elements of Waite Court jurisprudence. It is to these decisions that I now turn.

---

[105] See Calhoun, *Conceiving a New Republic*, 226–59; Wang, *Trial of Democracy*, 232–52; Kousser, *Shaping of Southern Politics*, 29–33. See also Richard E. Welch, Jr., *George Frisbie Hoar and the Half-Breed Republicans* (1971).

7

Definitive Judicial Abandonment, 1896–1906

Like scholars of Reconstruction, I argue that the definitive judicial abandonment of blacks followed and consolidated the Republican Party's definitive political abandonment of them. Unlike them, I offer an importantly different periodization of definitive judicial abandonment and its vehicles. My alternative account points to the Fuller Court (1888–1910), which definitively abandoned blacks in a series of decisions starting in 1896 with *Plessy v. Ferguson* and culminating in *Hodges v. United States* in 1906. It was during the Fuller era that district judges also offered the last, residual expressions of the concept of state neglect and the Fifteenth Amendment exemption.

DEFINITIVE POLITICAL ABANDONMENT

The party's definitive abandonment of blacks had a signal moment: the failure of the Lodge-Hoar elections bill in 1891. But generational change was also a factor. Many Republican leaders who had participated, if not always vigorously, in the party's campaigns for black civil and political equality died or were defeated (by overwhelming margins) in 1890 and 1892.[1] They were replaced by a generation of "younger men to whom abolition and Reconstruction seemed irrelevant, merely picturesque, or even evil."[2] As J. Morgan Kousser has explained, "to the new generation of Republican leaders, domestic politics consisted almost entirely of the promotion and/or regulation of business."[3]

The Republican coalition that had oscillated on a southern policy for almost two decades was now gone. Giant corporations, made possible by

---

[1] Kousser, *Shaping of Southern Politics*, 31. Kousser names James G. Blaine, John Sherman, Benjamin Harrison, John J. Ingalls, Henry W. Blair, George F. Edmunds, William E. Chandler, and Thomas B. Reed.
[2] Ibid.
[3] Ibid. See also Klarman, *From Jim Crow to Civil Rights*, 15; Wang, *Trial of Democracy*, 224–7, 242–2, 263.

184

Definitive Judicial Abandonment, 1896–1906

completion of national railroad and telegraph lines,[4] established full control of the Republican Party. In 1894, when the Democrats tried yet again to repeal most of the voting rights laws enacted during Reconstruction, they finally succeeded. Republicans no longer cared to stop them. In the midterm elections of 1894, which followed the depression of 1893 (the Democrat Grover Cleveland was in office), Republicans won one of the largest victories in congressional history. In 1896, they won the largest presidential victory in a quarter-century. *The Nation* observed a "striking" shift from just four years earlier in "the entire absence of any allusion" to black political rights in Republican Party state conventions.[5]

The defeat of the Lodge bill was a very close call for Democrats, and they did not let the lesson go unheeded. The disfranchisement movement, which began in Mississippi in 1890, took off across the Deep South and then the border states.[6] The results were devastating. Crushing the black vote, populism, and coalition movements, the purveyors of disfranchisement established one-party rule in the South, enabling whites to take full control of local offices and so easily to exclude blacks from juries and to easily pass segregation measures. Lynching rates soared in the early 1890s, and violence took unprecedented forms. Atrocities and torture became familiar features of the American landscape.

Patterns in black migration confirm the devastating effects of disenfranchisement. Black migration northward and westward had tapered off in the 1870s and 1880s but increased appreciably in the 1890s.[7] Federal patronage appointments of southern blacks also became significantly more controversial, leading to mass protests by whites and the lynching of a black South Carolina postmaster in 1898. The political fights in the South became intramural fights among Democrats, that is, between those who sought to establish white supremacy violently and those who sought to establish it in a more "civilized" – that is, legal – way.

Disfranchisement had rippling effects that made it impossible, for example, for blacks to preserve their fair share of public moneys for schools, leading to enormous disparities in educational spending.[8] New peonage statutes

---

[4] Bensel, *The Political Economy of American Industrialization*, 314. See also Naomi R. Lamoreaux, *The Great Merger Movement in American Business, 1895–1904* (1985).

[5] Quoted in Klarman, "Plessy Era," 319.

[6] On the disfranchisement movement, see J. Morgan Kousser, *The Shaping of Southern Politics: Suffrage Restriction and the Establishment of the One-Party South, 1888–1910* (1974); Michael Perman, *Struggle for Mastery: Disfranchisement in the South, 1888–1908* (2001). The instruments of disfranchisement were literacy and understanding tests, eight-box laws, grandfather clauses, secret ballots, complex registration requirements, etc.

[7] Klarman notes that migration appreciably increased in the 1890s and 1910s. "Plessy Era," 309–12, 374. See also James R. Grossman, *Land of Hope: Chicago, Black Southerners, and the Great Migration* (1989). Southern black migration to northern and western states had been about 49,000 in the 1870s and 62,000 in the 1880s. It rose to roughly 132,000 in the 1890s and to 143,000 in the 1900s.

[8] Klarman, "Plessy Era," 358.

186   *Rethinking the Judicial Settlement of Reconstruction*

aimed at coercing black labor were also passed. In short, the racial-economic regime of Jim Crow was put into place. Racial demagogues campaigning for white supremacy like Ben Tillman and James Vardaman replaced the Wade Hamptons of South Carolina and L. Q. C. Lamars of Mississippi, who accepted limited aspects of Reconstruction.

These changes took place in a cultural context shaped by the rise of social Darwinism, which strengthened enormously the intellectual prestige of white supremacist doctrines.[9] It was also the age of empire, which itself drew on and elaborated racialist doctrines. Full-blown "Lost Cause" constructions of Civil War memory now cemented reunion and reconciliation.[10]

DEFINITIVE JUDICIAL ABANDONMENT, 1896–1906

A new generation of justices accompanied the new generation of Republican politicians. In 1896, the only justices left who had served during the Waite era were Field, Harlan, and Gray.[11] Now under Chief Justice Melville Fuller, the Court issued a series of decisions that closed off options left open by the Waite Court. These decisions began with *Plessy v. Ferguson* (1896), continued with *Giles v. Harris* (1903) and *James v. Bowman* (1903), and culminated with *United States v. Hodges* (1906). This new periodization repositions *Plessy*: it is no longer the capstone of definitive abandonment, but rather the beginning.

The succession of these cases is also notable. Recall the hierarchy of rights (envisioned as a pyramid) that Harold Hyman and William Wiecek used to describe the mid-nineteenth-century civil/political/social rights typology. Definitive abandonment began at the top of the pyramid with social/public accommodation rights, worked its way down to political/voting rights, and then finally reached civil/contract rights. The succession follows the "logic" of the pyramid: it was easiest to restrict rights in the social sphere, where Republican support had always been weak, and hardest to renege on basic protections supplied by the Civil Rights Act of 1866, which had genuine and principled Republican support from the beginning of Reconstruction.

There are key discontinuities between these Fuller Court decisions and earlier Waite Court decisions. In summarizing them, I end my story about state action/neglect doctrine and the Fifteenth Amendment exemption. I also begin a new story, allusive only, about the process by which early understandings of

---

[9] See Rogers M. Smith, "Beyond Toqueville, Myrdal, and Hartz: The Multiple Traditions in America," *American Political Science Review* 87:3 (1993): 559.

[10] Recall that Lost Cause mythology removed slavery as the cause of the war and repudiated Reconstruction as a mistake. This mythology portrayed the union as "saved" from Reconstruction and blacks. The antebellum South was sentimentalized, states' rights was presented as an honorable cause, soldierly devotion on both sides was exalted, and Klansmen were cast as saviors.

[11] The Fuller Court in 1896: Melville Fuller, Stephen Field, John M. Harlan, Horace Gray, David Brewer, Henry B. Brown, George Shiras, Edward D. White, Rufus Peckham.

Definitive Judicial Abandonment, 1896–1906

state action doctrine became largely obscured in the twentieth century. The shifts by the Fuller Court play a role in that process.

The Court's approval of legal segregation in *Plessy v. Ferguson* is of course infamous. Writing for the majority, Justice Henry Billings Brown approved an 1890 Louisiana law that required "separate but equal" railroad cars. The Court used the *social rights* category to justify the ruling: "[I]n the nature of things [the Fourteenth Amendment] could not have been intended to abolish distinctions based upon color, or to enforce social, as distinguished from political equality."[12] By naming public accommodation rights as social rights, Justice Bradley's opinion in the *Civil Rights Cases* had given institutional legitimacy to the category. His opinion plays a role in the process of incorporating white supremacy norms into the structure and operation of the states and the nation, but not in the way scholars have imagined. Bradley used the civil/social distinction for one purpose, namely, to distinguish between public accommodation rights and the rights protected by the Civil Rights Act of 1866. He did not say whether segregation laws followed from the distinction. He also said nothing about whether the boundary between the civil and social spheres was permeable. The Fuller Court used the *social rights* category for a different purpose: to declare the boundary between the civil and social realms impermeable, a product of immutable difference. The civil/social distinction could be used to legitimize a more encompassing subjugation and indeed, the distinction was put to exactly that end.

But did the *Civil Rights Cases* nevertheless authorize segregation laws? Was it a short step to *Plessy v. Ferguson*? The *Chicago Tribune* offers yet again a touchstone for considering this question. When the decision in the *Civil Rights Cases* was issued, the *Tribune* printed, nearly verbatim from the Syllabus, the Fourteenth Amendment grounds for invalidating the public accommodation provisions.[13] A nearly identical statement appeared in the *New York Times*.[14] The *Tribune* interpreted this language to mean that local laws authorizing race-based ejections of blacks from public accommodations were unconstitutional. A manager of an inn, the *Tribune* explained, may eject somebody. He acts, however, on his own responsibility and may be sued under the common law. "If he acts without warrant he may be sued for damages incident

---

[12] 163 U.S. at 544.

[13] *Chicago Tribune*, October 16, 1883, p. 1. (The Court holds "That the fourteenth amendment is prohibitory upon States only and that the legislation authorized to be adopted by Congress for enforcing that amendment is not direct legislation on matters respecting which the States are prohibited from making or enforcing certain laws or doing certain acts, but is corrective legislation necessary or proper for counteracting and redressing the effect of such laws or acts; that in forbidding the States, for example, to deprive any person of liberty or property without due process of law, and giving Congress power to enforce the prohibition, it was not intended to give Congress the power to provide due process of law for the protection of life, liberty, and property (which would embrace almost all subjects of legislation), but to provide modes of redress for counteracting the operation and effect of State laws obnoxious to the prohibition.")

[14] *New York Times*, October 16, 1883, p. 2.

188   *Rethinking the Judicial Settlement of Reconstruction*

to the exclusion."[15] The legal "authorizing" of race-based ejections, however, violated principles of equality.

> If a negro be ejected from a hotel, a sleeping-car or a theatre, the courts are open to him to sue for damages just as they would be open to the white man under the same circumstances. *The corporation or individual responsible for the ejection cannot set up the color or race of the negro in justification, for there is no local law authorizing such discrimination, and if there were it would be under the decision held to be unconstitutional and void.*[16]

The *Tribune's* interpretation drives a potential wedge between the *Civil Rights Cases* and *Plessy v. Ferguson*. The corporation responsible for Homer Plessy's ejection from a railroad car, the East Louisiana Railroad, identified his race as justification, pointing to Louisiana's segregation statute[17] as having authorized the ejection. If the *Tribune's* statement is taken to mean that states cannot pass laws stating, literally, "blacks can be ejected from hotels, sleeping-cars, and theaters," then separate-but-equal laws including Louisiana's might pass muster as none of them are so formulated.

Nevertheless, the *Tribune's* conclusion that the *Civil Rights Cases* invalidated laws authorizing race-based exclusions introduces uncertainty into our understanding of the relationship between that decision and *Plessy*.[18] To be sure, the *Tribune* was not looking out on a landscape of segregation laws when it made the statement; legally authorized segregation lay largely in the future. And of course, neither can Bradley's characterization of public accommodation rights as social rights be understood as a rationalization of a Jim Crow regime that did not yet exist. But while these observations would no doubt be conceded by scholars, claims that it was a short step from the *Civil Rights Cases* to *Plessy* ignore the reception history as well as the jurisprudential logic of the *Civil Rights Cases*.

After the Fuller Court approved legal segregation, it issued a series of decisions pertaining to voting rights. In *Giles v. Harris*,[19] the Court washed its hands of supervising state elections, even as race-based denials of voting were taking place on a mass scale. The case stemmed from an action quietly supported by Booker T. Washington, which challenged Alabama's new state

---

[15] *Chicago Tribune*, November 6, 1883, p. 4.

[16] *Chicago Tribune*, October 24, 1883, p. 4. See also the *New York Times*, June 17, 1883, p. 6 ("Should any State by law authorize these distinctions [distinctions between customers made by railroad corporations or proprietors] and lend its power to their enforcement, or should it when appealed to recognize differences in the legal rights of citizens, a different question would arise, and the fourteenth amendment would doubtless be found to apply").

[17] Act of 1890, requiring separate but equal cars.

[18] The *Tribune* states: "In the absence of State violation of the constitutional amendment ... Congress has no authority under the Constitution to enforce by United States courts or by martial power the social privileges of any class of citizens, be they black or white." Whether a segregation law *counts* as authorizing racial discrimination in social privileges, of course, is key. *Chicago Tribune*, October 17, 1883, p. 4.

[19] 189 U.S. 475 (1903).

Definitive Judicial Abandonment, 1896–1906

constitution. Jackson Giles, on behalf of 5,000 others, charged Alabama officials with conspiring to deprive blacks of the right to vote. The remedy they wanted was a Court order requiring that their names be added to the voter registration lists. Justice Oliver Wendell Holmes, writing for the Court, refused. Narrowly constructing Section 1979 of the Revised Statutes, which was originally part of the Klan Act of 1871, Holmes stated:

> The bill imports that the great mass of the white population intends to keep the blacks from voting. To meet such an intent, something more than ordering the plaintiff's name to be inscribed upon the lists of 1902 will be needed. If the conspiracy and the intent exist, a name on a piece of paper will not defeat them. Unless we are prepared to supervise the voting in that state by officers of the court, it seems to us that all that the plaintiff could get from equity would be an empty form. Apart from damages to the individual, relief from a great political wrong, if done, as alleged, by the people of a state and the state itself, must be given by them or by the legislative and political department of the government of the United States.[20]

So precisely the scope of opposition to black rights appears to prevent the Court from responding to it. Recall the Waite Court decision *Reese v. United States*, where the justices declared that race-based interference in voting by state officials violated the Fifteenth Amendment. Court supervision was assumed. In *Giles*, the scale of the violation became the reason for renouncing Court supervision. Justices Brewer, Brown, and Harlan dissented.

In *James v. Bowman*,[21] the Fuller Court applied state action doctrine to the Fifteenth Amendment, rejecting the prosecution of a private individual. This application appears unremarkable by modern standards, but the Court was in fact rejecting the Fifteenth Amendment exemption accepted in *Cruikshank*, *Butler*, and *Yarbrough*. Likewise, the Court ignored two recent lower court decisions, *United States v. Lackey*[22] and *United States v. Miller*,[23] both of which included an affirmation of the Fifteenth Amendment exemption.

James v. Bowman, however, had a transitional character, as there were aspects of the Court's reasoning that contradicted the state action rule. *Bowman* identified two contradictory grounds for voiding the indictment of a private individual under the Fifteenth Amendment. The Court presented a modern state action reading of the *Civil Rights Cases* and applied the state action rule to the Fifteenth Amendment due to the shared "no state" language of the two amendments, reasoning in direct (if not acknowledged as such) opposition to *Cruikshank*. But the Court also explained that the indictment failed to specify a racial motive, reasoning that harkened back to *Cruikshank*, suggesting the presence of a state action/neglect rule. The decision thus presents an internally contradictory use of the state action cases. In the wake of

[20] 189 U.S. at 488.
[21] 190 U.S. 127 (1903).
[22] *United States v. Lackey*, 99 F. 952 (Kentucky, 1900)
[23] *United States v. Miller*, 107 F. 913 (Indiana, 1901).

the *Bowman* decision, a modern reading of the state action rule will be routinely applied to the Fifteenth Amendment.

Abandonment reached the core of the civil rights category in *Hodges v. United States*.[24] The case stemmed from an incident in Arkansas, and it involved the civil rights enumerated in the Civil Rights Act of 1866. An armed white mob threatened Berry Winn and seven other black men with violence if they did not stop work and leave their place of employment, a sawmill. As put in the indictment, Winn and the others were to "cease the free enjoyment of all advantages under [their work] contracts." The indictment charged that such threats were made "because they were colored men and citizens of African descent."[25] The case looks like a textbook violation under Waite Court rules.

The indictment was drawn in part under Section 1977, which guaranteed to all persons the same right to make and enforce contracts "as is enjoyed by white persons." Section 1977 derived from Section 1 of the Civil Rights Act of 1866. The indictment was also drawn under the now-familiar Section 5508, which made it a crime to conspire to deprive any citizen of any right secured by the Constitution or laws of the United States. The Waite Court had repeatedly approved this statute.

Writing for the Court, Justice Brewer recognized that Section 1977 reached private individuals. However, he took this to mean that only the Thirteenth Amendment could authorize the law. "That the Fourteenth and Fifteenth Amendments do not justify the legislation is...beyond dispute."[26] A recent district court decision had said the same thing, that is, that only the Thirteenth Amendment could authorize the Civil Rights Act of 1866.[27] But recall that Justice Bradley had explicitly identified Section 1977 and other statutes that derived from the Civil Right Act of 1866 as valid enforcement legislation under the Fourteenth Amendment.[28] Bradley's presentation of the concept of state neglect occurs in his discussion of the act of 1866. In asserting that only the Thirteenth Amendment could justify Section 1977, Justice Brewer erased this critical dimension of the *Civil Rights Cases* and thus obscured Bradley's construction of "color of law...or custom."

Hodges shifted direction in a second way. Recall that Waite Court justices required indictments drawn under the Thirteenth Amendment to specify a racial motive. Without addressing the old body of case law, Justice Brewer announced that the Thirteenth Amendment could not be limited to race. The language was not so limited and all persons were subject to involuntary servitude. "Slavery or involuntary servitude of the Chinese, of the Italian, of the Anglo-Saxon are as much within its compass as slavery or involuntary

---

[24] 203 U.S. 1 (1906).
[25] 203 U.S. 1, 20 (Harlan, J., dissenting).
[26] 203 U.S. at 14.
[27] *Morris v. United States*, 125 F. Cas. 322, 323 ("The power of Congress to enact [the Civil Rights Act of 1866] must be found in the Thirteenth Amendment, else it does not exist").
[28] 109 U.S. at 17.

Definitive Judicial Abandonment, 1896–1906

servitude of the African."[29] The Thirteenth Amendment, therefore, could not be limited to race-based servitudes.

> If, as we have seen, [the Thirteenth Amendment] denounces a condition possible for all races and all individuals, then a like wrong perpetrated by white men upon a Chinese, or by black men upon a white man, or by any men upon any man on account of his race, would come within the jurisdiction of Congress, and that protection of individual rights which prior to the Thirteenth Amendment was unquestionably within the jurisdiction solely of the States, would by virtue of that Amendment be transferred to the Nation, and subject to the legislation of Congress.[30]

Justice Brewer was of course right about the language of the Thirteenth Amendment. It was not limited to race. But his move raises a federalism problem. Section 1977 identified interference in contract rights as an imposition of involuntary servitude, and so once the Court opened up the coverage of the Thirteenth Amendment (to include involuntary servitude of any sort), what followed was a national police power over contract rights. And the Fuller Court was not prepared to grant the federal government this general police power. The Court escaped the problem by defining slavery and involuntary servitude in more formal master/servant terms. Slavery was "the state of entire subjection of one person to the will of another."[31] This definition severely restricted the reach of the Thirteenth Amendment.[32]

Much of what the Court appeared to give (by attending to the language of the amendment) the Court took back by defining involuntary servitude in formal terms. The white mob's interference in Berry Winn's contract rights would not be recognized as a "badge of slavery" because it was not "entire subjection" within the new meaning of the Thirteenth Amendment.[33] The Civil Rights Act of 1866 emerged from the case severely compromised

---

[29] 203 U.S. at 17. The government agreed. In oral argument before the Court, the attorney general stated, "I can easily rest this case upon the fact that the persons injured were of the colored race, and therefore peculiarly within the protection of the thirteenth amendment. But I have not been able to satisfy my mind that this amendment makes a permanent distinction between negroes and persons of other races. Its benefits extend to all persons of all races." Quoted in Bernstein, "Thoughts on Hodges," 814.

[30] 203 U.S. at 18.

[31] 203 U.S. at 17.

[32] In *Bailey v. Alabama*, 219 U.S. 219 (1911), the Court invalidated an Alabama peonage statute under the Thirteenth Amendment, repeating the statement in *Hodges* that the Thirteenth Amendment was a charter of civil freedom for "all persons of whatever race, color or estate" (219 U.S. at 241). *Bailey*, notably, involved a state law, not private individuals.

[33] The relationship between *Lochner* and *Hodges* is finally getting attention. See Pamela Karlan, "Contracting the Thirteenth Amendment: *Hodges v. United States*," 85 *Boston University Law Review* 783 (2005) and David E. Bernstein, "Thoughts on *Hodges v. United States*," 85 *Boston University Law Review* 811 (2005). Bernstein has noted that the majority may have been concerned that ruling for the government might involve the federal courts in supervising the membership of labor unions (at 817).

regarding its capacity to vindicate those black rights deemed fundamental during Reconstruction.

The Fuller Court thus expanded the breadth of the Thirteenth Amendment (it would now reach an Alabama peonage law, which did meet the formal requirement), but the cost was the depth of the amendment: private race-based interference in contract, property, and the other rights protected by the Civil Rights Act of 1866 could no longer be reached. The Waite Court had constructed the opposite breadth/depth mix: narrow (i.e., limited to race-based interferences) but deep (covering all the rights listed in the Civil Rights Act of 1866).

The underexplored *Hodges* case requires more attention, but it seems relevant that the government was involved at the time in peonage cases in the South involving Italian immigrants. Under Waite Court rules, it would have been impossible to prosecute the peonage cases. Indicting and convicting the mob leader Reuben Hodges, however, would have been utterly conventional.

Justice Harlan's dissent in *Hodges* offers an important lens on the *Civil Rights Cases*. In his dissent, Harlan identified the disagreement between himself and the majority on the constitutionality of the public accommodation provisions. But he also identified a point of consensus: approval for the Civil Rights Act of 1866:

> I participated in the decision of the Civil Rights Cases, but was not able to concur with my brethren in holding the act there involved to be beyond the power of Congress. But I stood with the court in the declaration that the Thirteenth Amendment not only established and decreed universal civil and political freedom throughout this land, but abolished the incidents or badges of slavery, among which, as the court declared, was the disability, based merely on race discrimination, to hold property, to make contracts, to have a standing in court, and to be a witness against a white person.

In listing the rights enumerated in the Civil Rights Act of 1866, Harlan's point was that majority-dissent consensus in the *Civil Rights Cases* pointed to the opposite conclusion in *Hodges*. Centrist and radical Republicans had long agreed that the enumerated rights were "essential for freedom," but the Court in *Hodges* shifted away from that understanding.

RESIDUAL EXPRESSIONS OF WAITE-ERA CONCEPTS

The last remaining judicial expressions of the rights-friendly concepts of the Waite era occurred in federal district courts during the first decade of the twentieth century. These expressions overlap in time with the definitive legal abandonment of blacks by the Fuller Court.

The legal rules articulated in the district cases endorsed federal power to prosecute the Klan in various ways, and a handful of Klansmen went to jail for short periods. The cases did not, of course, alleviate the violence and intimidation of lynch law. Their significance lies not in their practical impact but in

Definitive Judicial Abandonment, 1896–1906

their construction and understanding of Waite-era case law, where they identified the Fifteenth Amendment exemption and the concept of state neglect.

These district judges were Walter Evans, nominated by President William McKinley; Francis E. Baker, nominated by Teddy Roosevelt; Jacob Trieber, also nominated by McKinley and the first Jew on the federal bench; and Thomas Goode Jones, a Democrat appointed by Roosevelt. While the historian Brent AuCoin has brought deserved attention to Trieber and Jones, he presents their decisions as breaks with Waite-era jurisprudence.[34] But the decisions were continuous. Indeed, in an extraordinary decision, *Ex parte Riggins*, Judge Jones gave a detailed map of the structure of Waite-era rights enforcement jurisprudence.

I begin with *United States v. Lackey* (1900), where we find the penultimate expression of Bradley's Fifteenth Amendment exemption. In that case, Judge Evans upheld an indictment against private individuals for their race-based interference in black voting. He turned away the argument that a state action limitation applied to the Fifteenth Amendment. After noting that all the aggrieved persons were "men of color, of the African race" and that the wrongs against them were alleged to be "committed on account of that fact,"[35] the Judge referred explicitly to Bradley's 1874 rule:

> It is urged with much zeal in respect to both indictments that the many adjudged cases which hold that the fourteenth amendment operates only as an inhibition upon the states, and not individuals, in respect to the matters therein embraced, must control the construction of the fifteenth amendment, also, upon the same grounds. The court does not yield to this view, but accepts that of Justice Bradley in passing upon the Cruikshank Case at the circuit in the language previously quoted.[36]

Judge Evans then quoted Bradley's original 1874 statement: "I am inclined to the opinion that congress has the power to secure that right, not only as against the unfriendly operation of state laws, but against outrage, violence, and combinations on the part of individuals, irrespective of state laws."[37] Judge Evans was reversed.[38] It made no difference that he had properly rendered Bradley's original rule.

In *United States v. Miller* (1901), District Judge Baker also cited Justice Bradley for the Fifteenth Amendment exemption: "I think Mr. Justice Bradley right when he said in U.S. v. Cruikshank, 25 Fed. Cas. 707: 'I am inclined to the opinion that congress has the power to secure that right not only against

---

[34] See especially Brent J. AuCoin, *A Rift in the Clouds: Race and the Southern Federal Judiciary, 1900–1910* (2007). For more on Thomas Goode Jones, see also Brent J. AuCoin, "Thomas Goode Jones and African American Civil Rights in the New South," *Historian* 60 (Winter 1998): 257–71.

[35] *United States v. Lackey*, 99 F. 952, 954 (Kentucky, 1900).

[36] Ibid. at 962.

[37] Ibid. at 957.

[38] *Lackey v. United States*, 107 F. 114. See also *Karem v. United States*, 121 F. 250 (1903).

194 · *Rethinking the Judicial Settlement of Reconstruction*

the unfriendly operation of state laws, but against outrage, violence, and combinations on the part of individuals, irrespective of state laws."[39]

In *United States v. Morris* (1903),[40] Judge Trieber upheld charges drawn under Section 5508 (the descendent of Section 6 of the Enforcement Act of 1870) and Section 1978 (which protected property rights against race-based deprivations and descended from Section 1 of the Civil Rights Act of 1866). Judge Trieber ruled that the Civil Rights Act of 1866 protected the right to lease and cultivate lands against interference on account of race. His ruling was continuous with Waite-era doctrine in some ways but discontinuous in others, marking *Morris* as a transitional case. The continuous element pertained to Trieber's view that the Civil Rights Act of 1866 protected black property rights against individual race-based interference. He noted that the indictment was properly drawn because it contained the allegation that the interference had been on account of race,[41] citing for authority both *United States v. Rhodes* and *United States v. Harris*.[42] But he also said that only the Thirteenth Amendment could authorize the Civil Rights Act of 1866.[43] The Fuller Court soon said the same thing.

The most extraordinary decision came from Judge Thomas Goode Jones, a Democrat and former major in the Confederate army. In a pair of decisions – *Ex parte Riggins* (1904)[44] and *United States v. Powell* (1907)[45] – Jones forcefully endorsed federal power to punish mob violence (private individuals) under both the Thirteenth and Fourteenth Amendments, turning away federalism arguments that such prosecutions destroyed state sovereignty.[46] Both cases stemmed from the lynching of Horace Maples, a black prisoner in lawful state custody in Huntsville, Alabama. A white mob set the jail on fire in order to force out Maples, whereupon they hanged him in the town square.[47]

Judge Jones was not a typical Democrat. He was admitted to the Alabama bar in 1866 and elected in 1884 to the state legislature, becoming speaker of

---

[39] *United States v. Miller*, 107 F. 913, 915 (Indiana, 1901).

[40] *United States v. Morris*, 125 F. 322 (E. D. Ark. 1903).

[41] 125 F. at 328.

[42] 125 F. at 325–7, 328.

[43] 125 F. at 323. ("The power of Congress to enact such legislation [Section 1978] must...be found in the thirteenth amendment, else it does not exist. That Congress assumed that its power was derived from that amendment, and not from either of the later amendments, is conclusively shown by the fact that at the time this law was enacted, in 1866, neither the fourteenth nor fifteenth amendment had been ratified, or even submitted by Congress to the states.") Judge Trieber, like other judges at the time, did not observe that the Civil Rights Act of 1866 was reenacted in the Enforcement Act of 1870, which was passed under both the Fourteenth and Fifteenth Amendments.

[44] *Ex parte Riggins*, 134 Fed. 404 (C. C. N. D. Ala. 1904).

[45] *United States v. Powell*, 151 Fed. 648 (C. C. N. D. Ala. 1907).

[46] The prosecution of Riggins and Powell demonstrates that the federal government did not entirely cease enforcing black civil rights.

[47] There were federal prisoners as well state prisoners in the jail, but this played no role in the case.

Definitive Judicial Abandonment, 1896–1906

the Alabama House in 1886. As head of the Alabama state militia in 1883 Jones saved a black man from a Birmingham lynch mob. His actions led to a lifelong friendship with Booker T. Washington who recommended Jones to Republican President Theodore Roosevelt for appointment to the federal bench. With a probable mix of warm appreciation for Jones and cold realism about the state of white America, Washington called Jones "as good a friend to the Negro as any white man in this country."[48]

Jones was elected governor in 1890 with the quiet support of Booker T. Washington but also with a generous helping of fraud. In winning the Democratic nomination, he was the compromise alternative to Reuben Kolb, Alabama's leading populist-coalition leader in the 1890s. There were a substantial number of black voters still on the rolls in the 1890s, and Washington's support might have been critically important.

As governor, Jones had a history of anti-lynching activism. He condemned sheriffs and citizens for tolerating lynching. A law officer, he declared, must be willing to defend his prisoner, incurring or meting out violence if necessary. "Nothing but bloodshed in defense of the prisoner, or an attempt to shed it," he stated, "ever excuses an officer for permitting a mob to take his prisoner."[49] In 1893, Jones asked the legislature to give him authority to issue orders to law officers and to dismiss them if they were negligent in their duties: "The Governor has no power to order any civil officer to go to the scene [of a lynching], investigate it, or to take steps for the apprehension of the criminals." A statute permitting the governor to dismiss negligent officers, Jones believed, "would do more to prevent lynching than any other conceivable measure."[50] The legislature however failed to pass the requested statute, citing a never-before-used part of the criminal code giving the state authority to impeach officers for negligence upon petition by five taxpayers.

Jones did not give up. After his election to the Constitutional Convention of 1891, which surprised him given his anti-lynching record (the purpose of the convention was disfranchisement), Jones managed to convince the convention to pass an article to the constitution granting the governor power to dismiss law officers who neglected their duty to protect prisoners.[51] He even urged authorities to arm prisoners when an attack was imminent and called for severe penalties against citizens who disregarded a sheriff's request to join a posse to pursue lynch mobs. But he could not gain support for these measures.[52]

---

[48] Quoted in AuCoin, *Rift in the Clouds*, 57

[49] *Montgomery Advertiser*, August 28, 1894, p. 7.

[50] *Montgomery Advertiser*, February 7, 1893, p. 7.

[51] AuCoin, "Thomas Goode Jones," 261.

[52] As governor, he also fought (unsuccessfully) to reform the convict leasing system, and he successfully blocked an effort to fund black and white schools according to taxes paid by blacks and whites, arguing that such a funding scheme would substantially harm black education. And though he came close to outlawing debt peonage in Alabama while he was governor, his successor supported new peonage legislation, entrenching the practice.

196   *Rethinking the Judicial Settlement of Reconstruction*

As governor, Jones also sought to prevent disfranchisement attempted through grandfather clauses, poll taxes, and literacy tests, although he did support a "simple" education qualification. In an 1892 message to the legislature, Jones stated:

> The withdrawal from freemen, who have once exercised the right of suffrage, of all political power, in a popular government, which shapes their destinies and makes their laws, is sure to create a servile class. If the number is large the change nurses a cancer on the life of the State. Their resentments and their constant struggle to regain lost rights, which are sure to be aided by some who have political power, will inevitably breed continued and ever increasing discontent and agitation, the magnitude of which, in the end, will bring greater evils to the State than any which the disfranchisement was intended to cure.[53]

Jones lost this fight, and the Constitutional Convention produced the 1901 state constitution, which disfranchised blacks and poor whites. Indeed, John Knox, president of the Alabama Constitutional Convention, opened the convention by giving an address in which he said: "If we would have white supremacy, we must establish it by law – not by force or fraud."[54] The newly passed voter qualifications massively reduced the number of registered black voters. In 1900, the total was about 181,000. By 1903, the number had plummeted to fewer than 5,000.[55]

Jones was threatened with assassination for his efforts against lynching and peonage.[56] He represented a class of elite Democrats who lost to those who were, as Roosevelt put it, "resolute in their intention practically to introduce some form of serfage or slavery."[57] But he should not be mistaken for an exponent of black equality. Jones's efforts against violence, disfranchisement, and peonage coexisted with his paternalist attitudes and a commitment to white rule. And while there remain questions I cannot address here about the failed attempts of elite Democrats like Jones to control the course of southern politics, Jones's decisions in *Riggins* and *Powell* did try unsuccessfully to preserve the Waite Court's rights jurisprudence that was now in the process of being subverted.

In the *Riggins* case, Judge Jones was confronted with the question: did the prisoner, Horace Maples, have any constitutional right to protection from a lynch mob? His clear answer was *yes*. The question, he explained, was "not mooted in either the *Civil Rights Cases* or in *Harris v. United States*, nor was its decision necessary to the judgment in those cases." Those earlier cases were open on the matter.

---

[53] Thomas Goode Jones to Alabama General Assembly, November 16, 1892.
[54] Quoted in Novkov, *Racial Union*, 71.
[55] Ibid. at 74.
[56] Jones played a significant role in *Bailey v. Alabama*, writing what became the brief submitted by the government. See AuCoin, *Rift in the Clouds*, 55–64. See also *The Peonage Cases*, 123 F. 671 (M. D. Ala. 1903).
[57] AuCoin, *Rift in the Clouds*, 58.

Definitive Judicial Abandonment, 1896–1906

U.S. Attorney Thomas Roulhac, conferring with Judge Jones, charged Thomas Riggins and other members of the mob under Section 5508 (again, the descendant of Section 6 of the act of 1870 under which William Cruikshank was prosecuted). The statute punished conspiracies to deprive any citizen of the enjoyment of any right or privilege "secured to him by the Constitution or laws of the United States."

Judge Jones consulted with Circuit Judge David D. Shelby of the Fifth Circuit, who told him, "Write your instructions to the grand jury in such form that they might be reported as authority. In that way, your views would reach the other judges in the circuit, and to some extent mob murder might be checked."[58] After the grand jury returned indictments, Jones assured them:

> In the charge given you to the effect that Congress had the power to deal with offenses by men of one race against men of another race, when the object and intent of the offense was to deprive the member of that race of civil equality before the law, and induced by race prejudice, and not by mere ordinary felonious motive, the court only was stating what has been the settled law of the United States since the great case of *Cruikshank*.[59]

Lackey had cited *Cruikshank* for the rule that the federal government could punish private race-based interference in voting regardless of state behavior. Judge Jones now cited *Cruikshank* as authority to punish a racially motivated lynch mob. What Jones meant by *civil equality* is unclear here. He would soon be more precise.

With indictments returned by the jury, Judge Jones circulated his charge to political leaders, civic leaders, newspaper editors, and federal judges. While he received praise and thanks, he was also attacked.[60] He wrote to President Roosevelt, "Quite a reaction has set in from the...adverse sentiment that politicians have created against the charge of the court." The five wounds he received as a Confederate soldier, he told Roosevelt, had "not shielded [him] from some very mean and base insinuations, upon the part of the element which despises 'justice without respect of person.' "[61]

Thomas Riggins proceeded to challenge the indictment, arguing that Section 5508 was unconstitutional and infringed on the power of states to punish crime. The argument had been brought repeatedly and each time the Court rejected it.[62]

Judge Jones also rejected it. Four aspects of his reasoning are especially relevant for understanding the reception and ultimate eclipse of Waite Court

---

[58] David D. Shelby to Thomas Goode Jones, September 28, 1904, quoted in AuCoin, *Rift in the Clouds*, 65.

[59] Quoted in AuCoin, *Rift in the Clouds*, 68–9.

[60] AuCoin, *Rift in the Clouds*, 69–71.

[61] Thomas Goode Jones to Theodore Roosevelt, October 25 and November 5, 1904, quoted in AuCoin, *Rift in the Clouds*, 71–2.

[62] *United States v. Cruikshank* (1876), *Ex parte Yarbrough* (1884), *United States v. Waddell* (1884), *In re Neagle* (1890), *Logan v. United States* (1892), etc.

jurisprudence on rights enforcement. First, Jones recovered the rules governing congressional enforcement of the Fourteenth Amendment. He grouped the case law into three classes, and assigned cases to each grouping.[63] The first pertained to the "[d]enial by state legislation or hostile acts of state officers of rights secured by the amendment." This class of cases included *Strauder v. West Virginia*,[64] which invalidated a statute excluding blacks from jury service, and *Ex parte Virginia*,[65] which involved a judge excluding all blacks from juries. The second class of cases pertained to "legislation by Congress which confused rights dependent upon the Constitution or laws with rights secured only by state laws, entwining them without distinction in the grasp of a statute whose provisions were incapable of separation, thus vitiating the enactment because broader than the power conferred." Among the cases he referenced was *United States v. Reese*.

The last class of cases pertained to "congressional interference, regardless of fault on the part of the state, by plenary legislation, creating direct rights within the state, to protect a right which is only an immunity to be exempt from invidious discrimination at the hands of the state, and which can never bring any right into being or authorize any action of Congress, unless the state first makes such wrongful discrimination." The cases included *Cruikshank*, *Harris*, and the *Civil Rights Cases*. Judge Jones offered an extended explanation of the rule for which the *Civil Rights Cases* stood:

> The *Civil Rights Cases* involved the power of Congress to secure rights claimed under the recent amendments, by general legislation, "which steps in the domain of local jurisprudence, and lays down rules for the conduct of individuals in society to each other," *without reference to state laws or state action*, concerning equal accommodations on carriers and at inns and places of public entertainment.... It was the plenary power of Congress over state laws and state officers, *when the state was not at fault*, and not auxiliary power of Congress or its right to punish individuals who prevented the enjoyment of a right secured to the citizen under the Constitution and laws of the United States, which was there involved and decided.[66]

Contrary to the traditional understanding of the *Civil Rights Cases*, Jones indicated that the case stood for the rule that Congress may not act directly on

---

[63] *United States v. Powell*, 151 F. at 650–1.

[64] 100 U.S. 303 (1880).

[65] 100 U.S. 339 (1880).

[66] *Ex parte Riggins*, 134 F. 404, 415, emphasis added. See also *United States v. Powell*, 151 Fed. 648, 657, where Judge Jones repeated this understanding of the "test of the bounds of power in Congress to legislate for the protection of rights under the fourteenth amendment." This rule was recognized in the *Civil Rights Cases* and *Harris*. "The limitation upon such exercise of power, save in case of direct wrong by the state, is that Congress must not enter the domain of state power, creating new rights therein, or changing or displacing its laws, or interfering with its authority, or, in other words, substituting the will of Congress for the will of the state, as to its domestic affairs and internal concerns. In this domain Congress is forbidden to enter, save for correction of wrong by the state, and then it can go no further than to cure the particular wrong."

Definitive Judicial Abandonment, 1896–1906　　　　199

individuals without reference to state fault.[67] He also associated the decision with the rule that Congress could enforce *secured* rights only when state rights denials had taken place.

The second relevant aspect of *Riggins* concerns Jones's discussion of the Civil Rights Act of 1866 and the meaning of civil equality. He treated the act of 1866 as Thirteenth Amendment legislation (thought he did not say that authority for the legislation was limited to that amendment), and he identified the act of 1866 as the "standard of freedom" for the former slaves: "[T]he civil rights enjoyed by the dominant race, or, to quote the language of that section 'as is enjoyed by white citizens'... was the standard of the freedom conferred and the measure of the rights which constituted that freedom." The purpose of the act was "to secure and protect the former slave race from the aggressions of the master race." Invoking the civil/political/social typology circulating during Reconstruction and central to the logic in the *Civil Rights Cases*, Jones cautioned, "[t]his civil equality must not be confounded with social or political rights." Did a black prisoner in lawful custody have a constitutional right to be free from race-based violence? Judge Jones answered unambiguously *yes*, because these aggressions involved *civil rights*. "[I]t is quite clear that the right to be free from attacks by members of one race, designed and intended to prevent the other race from enjoying the civil rights which go to make up that freedom, is a right, privilege, or immunity 'accorded by, or arising under, or dependent upon the Constitution,' and that such rights may be protected by Congress."[68]

The third aspect of *Riggins*'s significance lies in Judge Jones's elaboration of the meaning of state fault and "wrongful discrimination" under the equal protection clause. States do their duty when they enforce laws impartially. When they do not enforce laws impartially, he explained, that is wrongful discrimination:

> The equal protection clause makes but one demand upon the state, and gives the citizen a single right only. It is that the state must make and execute its laws fairly and impartially. It must not grant rights to one which, under similar circumstances, it denies to another. This command is fully obeyed when the state passes impartial laws, and *provides proper officers to execute them, and they endeavor to do so*. The constitutional command is only that the state create and *enforce* a legal status.[69]

---

[67] Though it looks similar, this is not Frantz's reading of the *Civil Rights Cases* as Judge Jones made no claim about public accommodation rights. Calling attention to the fourth headnote of Bradley's majority opinion, Jones stated: "The court declined to decide whether [the right to equal accommodations] was given or secured by the fourteenth amendment contenting itself with holding that the interference by the particular statute with state laws went beyond the limits of the evil to be remedied." Jones thus never asserted that the public accommodation provisions would have been valid had they been conditioned on a state violation. 134 F. at 415.

[68] *Ex parte Riggins*, 134 F. at 407–8. As authority for this understanding, Judge Jones cited Bradley's circuit opinion in *Cruikshank*, *United States v. Rhodes*, and the *Civil Rights Cases*.

[69] *Ex parte Riggins*, 134 F. 404, 416, emphasis added.

Judge Jones continued, linking two key dimensions of the state neglect concept:

> No act of a private citizen can defeat the enjoyment of this status, since it can be created only by the exercise of legislative power, and impaired only by acts of officers, those who wield state authority, by refusing to enforce these laws, or enforcing them with uneven hand or vicious purpose.[70]

We find here the last clear expression of the state neglect concept. The passage links together two points. First, private citizens cannot infringe on the right to equal protection. (Jones would later reiterate the point in *Powell*: "It is impossible for private individuals to impair, in the constitutional sense, the enjoyment of the right to 'the equal protection of the laws.' ")[71] Second, such infringement comes about through a state officer's actions or *inactions* – that is, a refusal to enforce laws or unevenness in enforcement. Following closely both Waite's language in *Cruikshank* (the Fourteenth Amendment "adds nothing to the rights of one citizen as against another") and Bradley's language in the *Civil Rights Cases* ("Individual invasion of individual rights is not the subject of the amendment"), Jones's opinions in *Riggins* and *Powell* underscore the dubiousness of traditional readings of state action doctrine. Those readings typically render Waite's and Bradley's statements canonical expressions of the inapplicability of the state neglect concept to state action doctrine. Clearly, Jones found them to be directly on point.

The vision of federalism articulated by Judge Jones was similar to the vision articulated by centrist Republicans during Reconstruction. Jones explained that the Fourteenth Amendment was designed in accordance with the prevalent doctrine of state-oriented federalism. The framers, he explained, gave primacy to the state governments, but they also made the federal government a watchdog, overseeing the states' fulfillment of their duties and ensuring that constitutional rights were being accorded to the people. The fact of lynching in the South was obvious evidence that state governments were not diligent in fulfilling their duties.[72] In his *Riggins* opinion, Judge Jones asserted forcefully that state sovereignty was in no way harmed by such prosecutions. In other contexts, Jones used notions of civil equality to condemn peonage. Indeed, his condemnation of peonage reads like a manual on free labor ideals during the Reconstruction era.

Riggins is important for a fourth and final reason: Judge Jones elaborated an innovative due process theory of prosecution whereby it was unnecessary to charge fault on the part of state officers, that is, in situations where officers protecting black prisoners were overwhelmed by lynch mobs. The due process theory was distinct from his equal protection argument, which relied on Waite-era notions of civil equality and required state fault.

---

[70] Ibid.
[71] *United States v. Powell*, 151 F. 648, 653.
[72] Charge to the grand jury, *Montgomery Advertiser*, October 12, 1904, p. 3.

Definitive Judicial Abandonment, 1896–1906

As Jones explained, the question of whether private violence deprived the prisoner Maples of due process rights "has never been before the Supreme Court."[73] Jones announced that a prisoner had the right to benefit from the operation of a state's established course of judicial procedure, secured by the Constitution, without the interference of private violence. "The right of the citizen to have the duty performed, which Congress is given power to enforce, necessarily carries with it the right to have protection against lawless acts of outsiders which prevent the state from giving them the benefit of due process of law."[74] It did not matter that state officers were not at fault:

> It may be true the state was not at fault; but that does not obliterate the fact that it was prevented from causing to be done the physical and mental acts which alone constitute the discharge of the duty in this case, and that by means of lawless violence, directed at the state and the prisoner alike, the prisoner has been prevented from enjoying the right to have the state do or cause to be done the physical or mental tasks which alone can afford him due process of law.[75]

Judge Jones also made an important acknowledgment: "It is admitted if state officers had participated in mobbing Maples, or conspired in any way to deprive him of the enjoyment of due process of law at the hands of the state, that Congress could legislate against and punish such acts on their part."[76] The participation of state officers in lynching was not uncommon at the time, and *Riggins* offered a coherent theory for prosecuting such officers.

In a few short years, *Riggins* was reversed. One of the members of the Huntsville mob argued that the *Hodges* decision had overruled *Riggins*. In the new case, *United States v. Powell*,[77] Judge Jones conceded that *Hodges* overruled his Thirteenth Amendment argument. He explained, "the Supreme Court has decided the *Hodges* Case, which held in effect contrary to the decision of Justice Bradley in *United States v. Cruikshank*, that the rights and immunities claimed here under the thirteenth amendment are not secured under the Constitution or laws."[78] Together with Justice Harlan, Jones was among a handful of jurists to notice such reversals – put otherwise, to notice the legal dismantling of Waite Court rights jurisprudence.

---

[73] 134 F. at 423.

[74] 134 F. at 414.

[75] 134 F. at 417. Jones made a typical Waite-era move in citing for authority *Prigg v. Pennsylvania*, the pro-slavery decision that Republicans during the Reconstruction era happily referenced as authority for Reconstruction legislation. Stated Jones, "The rule is: When the end is required, the means are given.... All means are 'appropriate' which directly promote the successful discharge of the duty, unless the use of such means be forbidden by some other provisions of the Constitution." See also 134 F. at 410–12.

[76] 134 F. at 420. Jones cited *Ex parte Virginia*. Jones repeats this rule in *Powell*, 151 F. 648, 655–7.

[77] 151 F. 648 (C. C. N. D. Ala. 1907)

[78] 151 F. at 650.

Did *Hodges* also block prosecution of the lynch mob under the Due Process Clause? In *Powell*, Judge Jones wrote sixteen pages, again explaining his due process theory. Horace Maples, Jones reiterated, had a right to protection under the Due Process Clause, even if state officers were not at fault. But in the last paragraph of the opinion, he bowed to *Hodges*. He was obligated to "take the *Hodges* case as a binding authority that no right, privilege, or immunity in respect of due process, at any stage in the duty of affording it, arises under the fourteenth amendment, unless there be denial of the right by the state or its officer." There must, in other words, be fault by the state, and in the *Riggins* case that allegation had not been made. Powell walked free, but since a due process theory predicated on state fault had not been addressed by the fuller court, it remained available for later prosecutions.

A final expression of Waite-era concepts was still to come, this time from the emerging discipline of political science. In 1909, John Mabry Mathews published a history of the Fifteenth Amendment.[79] Mathews quoted what I have termed the Fifteenth Amendment exemption, Bradley's rule that the federal government had the power to prosecute private race-based interferences in voting "irrespective of state laws."[80] Mathews stated,

> The law on the subject [Bradley] conceived to be that when any atrocity was committed, by private combinations, or even by private outrage or intimidation, which was due to the race of the party injured, it might be punished by the laws and in the courts of the United States; but that any outrages, whether against the colored race or the white race, which did not flow from this cause, were within the sole jurisdiction of the States.[81]

The indictment in *Cruikshank* was defective, Mathews explained, "because it did not allege that the acts complained of were done on account of the race of the complainants."[82]

Again we have the contemporaneous understanding of the flaw in the *Cruikshank* decision. Mathews likewise noted that Bradley's Fifteenth Amendment rule was applied in *United States v. Lackey*.[83] But while Mathews quoted and identified Bradley's "irrespective of state laws" language and explained that the *Lackey* case applied it, Mathews did not identify or discuss the declared/created rights distinction that was at the root of Bradley's Fifteenth

---

[79] See the 1909 reading of *Cruikshank* by John Mabry Mathews, *The Legislative and Judicial History of the Fifteenth Amendment* (1909). Mathews had a contemporary, Horace Flack, who also perceived early understandings of the Reconstruction amendments. Flack argued that the Fourteenth Amendment originally applied the Bill of Rights to the states. See Horace E. Flack, *Adoption of the Fourteenth Amendment* (1908).

[80] Mathews, *Legislative History*, 102.

[81] Ibid. at 103.

[82] Ibid. The Court in *Cruikshank*, he notes, did not repeat Bradley's "irrespective of state laws" language. "But it did base its decision on the ground that it had not been shown that the outrages in question had been committed on account of race."

[83] Ibid. at 103, 111.

Definitive Judicial Abandonment, 1896–1906

Amendment rule. Mathews also clearly felt the force of the "no state" language of the Fifteenth Amendment, pointing directly to the Fourteenth Amendment for guidance on rules of construction. "[L]ight upon the construction of the Fifteenth Amendment might have been drawn from the decisions in regard to the analogous prohibitions of the Fourteenth Amendment."[84] Mathews approved the Court's decision in *James v. Bowman*, which he (correctly) identified as the first time the Supreme Court had applied state action limitations to the Fifteenth Amendment.[85] Mathews, then, could perceive the exemption and its origins in Bradley's 1874 opinion, even if he disagreed with it. It would be seventy years before the rule would again be perceived/recovered, this time by legal historian Michael Les Benedict, though even then, the rights distinction underlying the Fifteenth Amendment rule remained unrecognized in Benedict's account.

JUSTICE WOODS AND *UNITED STATES V. HARRIS*, REDUX

I want to return to a question raised by Judge Jones's pair of decisions in *Riggins* and *Powell*. Given that Judge Jones articulated an expansive due process theory about the rights of prisoners against mob violence, can we say that Justice Woods could – and so should – have done the same in *United States v. Harris*? Consider that Judge Jones had access to unambiguous fact situations. The practice of white mobs lynching black prisoners in state custody had become exceedingly common after 1890. Judge Jones was extraordinary in surmounting institutional trends, but he did not need to perceive a future that did not yet exist. The stakes that attached to a due process theory were abundantly clear.

It is possible to view *Harris* as a judicial failure, a lost or refused opportunity to use the law to "do the right thing." But note that this assessment catches Justice Harlan, as well as Justice Woods, in the net as Harlan declined to write a dissenting opinion on the merits. Can we conclude that Harlan's silence indicates a judicial failure and that he should have produced an expansive theory of prisoners' rights similar to the broad theory of civil rights he produced in his *Civil Rights Cases* and *Plessy v. Ferguson* dissenting opinions? From what we know about Harlan, he was committed to black rights and Reconstruction. Perhaps, then, this counterfactual highlights the limited value of interpretations that turn singularly on ideology.

Korematsu v. United States (1944),[86] a paradigmatic example of judicial failure, offers an instructive comparison to *Harris*. The *Korematsu* decision ratified the policy of interning Japanese-Americans during World War II without any individualized inquiry. The justices had knowledge of the facts and the stakes that attached to Korematsu's claims through briefs filed by

[84] Ibid. at 111.
[85] Ibid. at 113.
[86] 323 U.S. 214 (1944).

the Japanese American Citizens League and the ACLU.[87] Both briefs documented that Japanese-Americans were not the threat that General De Witt and the U.S. solicitor general claimed them to be. Justice Frank Murphy made full use of this information in his dissenting opinion. Indeed, the justices had begun to expand civil rights for racial minorities in the early 1940s[88] and likewise had begun to pay attention to race-based denials of due process rights in the 1930s.[89] And ultimately, in 1946, the Court did find that rights had been violated in a case analogous to *Korematsu*.[90] That finding was of course made after the war had ended when even paranoid claims about the Japanese-American threat became discredited.

Given the combination of available facts and case precedent, *Korematsu* exemplifies judicial failure. Woods faced a remarkably different situation, and this should caution us from applying the concept to *Harris*. Jones's due process argument in *Riggins* was an extraordinary feat of jurisprudential reasoning. That Woods was unable or unwilling to perform similar feats in *Harris* means that he was instead rather ordinary. When we assume that failures to act in an extraordinary way constitute a judicial failure, the category ceases to offer any meaningful distinctiveness inasmuch as it encompasses too many cases.

The Fuller Court definitively abandoned blacks at the same time as the Jim Crow regime was instituted. The definitive legal abandonment also parallels the rise of reform-minded Progressives, whose political agenda has long been seen as a reaction to *Lochner*. But so too the oft-noted racism within that reform movement reflects a disregard for black rights wholly consistent with Fuller Court jurisprudence.

Consider the accounts of muckraking journalists like Ray Baker, who emerged to challenge the rule of giant corporations: "the vast majority of Negroes...are still densely ignorant, and have little or no appreciation of the duties of citizenship.... Negroes as a class are today far inferior in education, intelligence, and efficiency to the white people as a class."[91] As Herbert Aptheker has remarked, "the muckrakers tended to ignore the oppression of Black people, while writing reams about bad meat."[92] Progressives like Baker "advocated sweeping reforms to remedy the nation's ills, [but] his laissez-faire attitude toward racial inequality suggests how pervasively racist assumptions characterized the minds" of even liberal whites during this era.[93]

---

[87] Joel Grossman, "The Japanese American Cases and the Vagaries of Constitutional Adjudication in Wartime: An Institutional Perspective," 19 *University of Hawaii Law Review* 649, 684–5 (1997).

[88] *United States v. Classic*, 313 U.S. 299 (1941); *Smith v. Allright*, 321 U.S. 64a (1944).

[89] *Powell v. Alabama*, 287 U.S. 45 (1932); *Norris v. Alabama*, 294 U.S. 587 (1935) (the Scottsboro cases).

[90] *Duncan v. Kahanamoku*, 327 U.S. 304 (1946).

[91] Quoted in Klinkner and Smith, *Unsteady March*, 108.

[92] Aptheker, *Literary Legacy*, 110.

[93] Klinkner and Smith, *Unsteady March*, 109.

Definitive Judicial Abandonment, 1896–1906

During the Progressive era, one could be celebrated as a "people's attorney" while avoiding matters of race and Jim Crow. Such was Louis Brandeis, who rose to prominence during what Bracey and others call "the most vulgar and horrific period of African-American suffering since chattel slavery."[94] While Brandeis "demonstrated profound creativity when crafting opinions in vigorous defense of civil and economic liberties,"[95] he was, at best, ambivalent on race matters. There was great risk associated with public advocacy of black causes at this time even as such advocacy was always possible.[96]

It is hard to know whether Fuller Court justices were aware of Justice Bradley's Fourteenth Amendment authorization of the Civil Rights Act of 1866 in the *Civil Rights Cases* and chose to ignore it or whether they were unaware of the authorization. That the earliest postwar decisions reached by the Salmon P. Chase Court (1864–73) authorized the act of 1866 under the Thirteenth Amendment (as did Bradley himself in his circuit opinion in *Cruikshank*) might be taken as support for the latter option. Still, the text of the *Civil Rights Cases* unambiguously identifies the act of 1866 as authorized by the Fourteenth Amendment, and in an era of judicial training not steeped in the "case method," we have every reason to believe that the justices closely read the original text. And yet, if Fuller Court justices were using Chase Court decisions, they also knew that *Hodges* was reversing them.

It is also plausible that Fuller Court justices consciously disregarded Waite Court constructions of the Fifteenth Amendment. At the time, lower courts were still citing the relevant case law on the Fifteenth Amendment exemption, and so it is hard to imagine blindness on the score. No doubt, the fact that Bradley's rule disregarded the amendment's text made the exemption easier to ignore. Fuller Court justices would likely have cared very little for the Fifteenth Amendment exemption or the Fourteenth Amendment authorization of the act of 1866, both of which contained broad possibilities for protecting black rights.

---

[94] Christopher A. Bracey, "Louis Brandeis and the Race Question," 52 *Alabama Law Review* 859 (2001), 862.

[95] Ibid., 895.

[96] For example, Karl Llewellyn, the Columbia law professor, and Louis Marshall, president of the American Jewish Committee. Bracey, "Louis Brandeis and the Race Question," 881.

8

Twentieth-Century Receptions

The recoveries of the previous chapters make it clear that contemporaneous interpreters of Waite Court decisions saw them as endorsing a concept of state neglect and a broad theory of voting rights enforcement. But by the 1940s – just forty years after Judge Jones traced out the state neglect concept in *Cruikshank*, *Harris*, and the *Civil Rights Cases* – Justice Department attorneys and scholars had come to the conclusion that the decisions contained no such concept. Their readings of the state action cases took place in political, jurisprudential, and cultural contexts that had changed substantially from prior decades. I examine several features of the reconfigured contexts, namely, the institutional establishment of the scientific or "case" method of legal study at the turn of the twentieth century and the establishment of a new rights paradigm during the Progressive and New Deal eras. In focusing on these developments, I suggest in allusive but never conclusive fashion that legal and political practices obscured the intellectual and political contexts of state action cases, leaving the historical language of state action difficult to "read."

Toward this end, I juxtapose two episodes in the reception history of the *Civil Rights Cases* and precursor decisions, one of which is the Justice Department's 1940s effort to prosecute lynching, in which lawyers concluded that a state neglect concept was absent in Waite-era decisions. I contrast that assessment with those given in the early 1920s by supporters of the Dyer Anti-Lynching bill, some of whom perceived the concept of state neglect in those same decisions. Anatomizing the reasoning in both episodes, I track erosion in the capacity to perceive the state neglect concept.

THE CASE METHOD OF LEGAL STUDY

The case method is a particular way of studying law. The method puts an emphasis on classification and inductive reasoning, and it assumes the exclusivity of a few selected judicial opinions as source materials. "The student is not referred to a mass of cases...but a *few classified* cases, selected with a

206

Twentieth-Century Receptions

view to developing the cardinal principles of the topic under consideration."[1] From these few cases, the student is to "extract the underlying principles."[2]

The case method was established for a set of reasons and its institutionalization has drawn the interest of numerous scholars.[3] In its broadest sense, the case method was a dimension of the knowledge revolution that swept educational institutions in the late nineteenth and early twentieth centuries.[4] In her classic study of the origins of American social science, Dorothy Ross connected the emergence of scientific thinking to the crisis of American exceptionalism that gathered force after the Civil War, as rapid industrialization and immigration created massive upheaval.

> On one level, the crisis was connected to the problem of intellectual authority, as science increasingly discredited the apologetic stance and naïve resort to divine providence of the established voices in American culture. On another level, the crisis grew out of the social and political challenges of the Gilded Age, as the Civil War and Reconstruction and then rapid industrialization appeared to test whether America could sustain the principles that defined her place in history.[5]

Responding to the growing crisis, the gentry class – largely northeastern, well educated, liberal or heterodox in religion – presided over a turn toward positivism and historicism. Christopher Langdell's case method was part of this turn[6] and ushered in a new phase of legal scientism.

The first phase of scientism had combined natural law and positive law concepts. Justice Joseph Story is an exemplar of this early notion of legal science. For Story, "natural law reflected the universal reason and moral principles God had built into human nature, while [positive] law reflected the special conditions that had created unique cultures and changing stages of development."[7] As Dorothy Ross explains, this combination carried conviction because "Story appeared to accept, as did most of his contemporaries, the guiding hand of God in the historical process."

---

[1] William A. Keener, "The Inductive Method in Legal Education," 17 *American Bar Association Reports* 473–90 (1894), 481, emphasis in original.

[2] John Chipman Gray, "Methods of Legal Education," 1 *Yale Law Journal* 159–61 (1892), 159.

[3] For an early and sustained study, see William LaPiana, *Logic and Experience: The Origin of Modern American Legal Education* (1994).

[4] G. Edward White, *Tort Law in America: An Intellectual History* (2003), 26.

[5] Dorothy Ross, *Origins of American Social Science* (1991), 53. See also William Wiecek, *The Lost World of Classical Legal Thought* (1998), 64–89, and White, *Tort Law in America*, 20–6.

[6] Christopher Langdell, *Cases on the Law of Contracts* (1871).

[7] Dorothy Ross, "Historical Consciousness in Nineteenth Century America" *American Historical Review* 89 (1984): 920. For discussion of the two phases of scientism in law, see Wiecek, *Lost World of Classical Legal Thought*, 38–41, 89–93, and Christopher Tomlins, "Framing the Field of Law's Disciplinary Encounters," *Law and Society Review* 34. (2000): 914–32.

208   *Rethinking the Judicial Settlement of Reconstruction*

Justice Bradley likewise approached law in a way that exemplified the early phase of legal scientism. Speaking on the "science of law" in an introductory lecture at the University of Pennsylvania in 1884,[8] Bradley explained that "the study and science of law is divided and subdivided, according to the subjects to which it is applied, and these embrace all of the transactions and relations of society."[9] Law was the "expression of man's sense of justice" and was "founded upon immutable and eternal principles."[10] For Justice Bradley as for Justice Story, concepts drawn from the natural law tradition were part of legal science.

In his aforementioned lecture at the University of Pennsylvania, Justice Bradley offered advice on how to study law. His method stands in stark contrast to Langdell's case method. As Bradley explained, in order to study law, "It is not only necessary to know the rule, but to know how to express it in the appropriate language." One had to master rhetorical forms and usage.[11] One of the "best aids" in the study of law, Bradley explained, was to learn the forms of expression of a legal thinker with "pure and accurate diction." He advised students to read the works of a legal thinker and "become so familiar with its contents that, although not absolutely committed to memory, the words and forms of expression will spontaneously suggest themselves whenever you begin to speak or write on the subject.[12] In addition, it was necessary to study civil society which meant studying philosophy, history, and modes of business.[13]

Justice Bradley's prescription to learn "forms of expression" in addition to philosophy, history, and modes of business was strikingly different from the method introduced by Christopher Langdell. When Langdell introduced the case method, he discarded most of the defining commitments of antebellum legal science, especially its natural theology.[14] Prescriptions to learn "forms of expression" were not paramount.

As is clear from the 1884 date that attaches to Justice Bradley's introductory lecture, the early phase of legal science did not suddenly disappear in 1870 when Langdell introduced the case method. Indeed, Langdell's entirely secular

---

[8] Joseph P. Bradley, "Law: It's Nature and Office as the Bond and Basis of Civil Society: Introductory Lecture to the Law Department of the University of Pennsylvania," in *Miscellaneous Writings of the Late Hon. Joseph P. Bradley* (1902), 226–66.

[9] Ibid. at 244.

[10] Ibid. at 246. But law also progressed. "The elasticity and expansibility of law to meet the growing wants of society" was "another proof that jurisprudence is a science" (at 247).

[11] "There is no science in which the words and forms of expression are more important than in law. Precision of definition and statement is a sine qua non. Possessing it, you possess the law; not possessing it, you do not possess the law, but only the power of vainly beating the air with uncertain words which impress nobody, instruct nobody, convince nobody." Ibid. at 256–7.

[12] Ibid.

[13] Ibid. at 263, 265.

[14] Howard Schweber, "The 'Science' of Legal Science: The Model of the Natural Sciences in Nineteenth Century American Legal Education," *Law and History Review* 17 (1999): 455–64.

Twentieth-Century Receptions

conception of law remained an "oddity in the Gilded Age."[15] Langdellian legal science began to take hold at Harvard in the 1870s but not yet elsewhere.

The case method of legal instruction cannot be said to have "won" institutionally until at least the 1890s. Only then did every faculty member at Harvard teach a course from his own casebook.[16] And only then did other leading law schools such as Columbia and Chicago adopt the case method. At the turn of the century, the publication of casebooks multiplied,[17] and by 1915, the case method of legal study was established in nearly all the elite law schools.[18]

The reasons for the institutionalization of the case method are many. The method was responsive to concerns about order and classification, perceived at the time to be of central and pressing importance. It was also embraced by a small group of elites. Harvard held a prominent position in a status hierarchy, and its networks were influential in gaining notice for the case method.[19] The method became linked with rites of professionalization, which helped embed it institutionally.[20] At Harvard and then elsewhere, the process of "becoming a lawyer" became equated with a particular mode of acquiring knowledge, that is, the case method.

The case method played a prominent role in encounters between law and social science. These encounters were moments of rivalry – that is, competition to supply the language of policy making – at a time when the administrative state was being built. "Mostly," Christopher Tomlins concludes, "law wins."[21] He explains that "Langdell's emphasis on the case gave law a sturdily reformed identity as a technically sophisticated and professionalized discourse of decisionmaking, located securely within the control of courts and law schools, an identity with which anyone desirous of implementing some new conception of the state as the regulator and administrator of the social order would surely have to contend."[22]

---

[15] Stephen A. Siegel, "Comment: The Revision Thickens," *Law and History Review* 20 (2002): 636.

[16] Finch on Contracts (1886); Gray on Property (1888); Keener on Quasi-Contracts (1888); Thayer on Evidence (1892); Thayer on Constitutional Law (1895). Harvard Law School Association, *Centennial History of the Harvard Law School, 1817–1917* (Boston: Harvard Law School, 1918).

[17] In 1908, West Publishing Co. entered the trade with their American Casebooks series (James Brown Scott, general editor, St. Paul, 1908).

[18] In 1915, the U.S. Bureau of Education reported, "the case method forms the principal, if not the exclusive, method of teaching in nearly all of the stronger law schools in the country." Schweber, "The 'Science' of Legal Science," 464. On the spread of the case method, see LaPiana, *Logic and Experience*, 148–52.

[19] White, *Tort Law in America*, xxv.

[20] Robert Gordon, "Legal Thought and Legal Practice in the Age of American Enterprise, 1870–1920," in Gerald L. Geison, ed., *Professions and Professional Ideologies in America* (1983). For a summary of the major changes in the practice of law wrought by professionalization, see White, *Tort Law in America*, xxv–xxvi. Professionalization of course was not unique to law schools, and it spread across higher education at the close of the nineteenth century.

[21] Tomlins, "Framing the Field of Law's Disciplinary Encounters," 911.

[22] Ibid. at 929.

The case method thus helped secure law's prominence in the emerging competition with other academic disciplines to structure the state's policy-making discourse.[23] In the face of a serious challenge from the newer social sciences such as sociology, which sought to identify law as something invented in legislatures by sociologically informed legislators, the case method reconstituted the political authority of lawyers and helped secure judicial ascendancy.[24] The case method, finally, met the institutional imperative of law schools: mass producing lawyers adaptable to any local situation in the industrial economy.[25]

Exponents of the case method seized on the *Civil Rights Cases* as a "leading case," for it contains the most extended discussion of state action doctrine, detaching it from surrounding case law. But those cases were critical to understanding the language of state action; approaching the *Civil Rights Cases* in isolation made the decision highly vulnerable to anachronistic interpretations. Its isolation can be seen in the very first constitutional law casebook, the two-volume *Cases on Constitutional Law* (1895) by James Bradley Thayer.[26] A colleague of Langdell's at Harvard, Thayer taught constitutional law twenty-two times between 1870 and 1917. Thayer parted company with Langdell on the role of legislatures in lawmaking, and he did not initially adopt the case method. Thayer came to accept it, however, stating in the Preface to his casebook that he favored the study of cases as the principal method in legal education.

> Dean Langdell's associates have all come to agree with him...that there is no method of preparatory study so good as the one with which his name is so honorably connected – that of studying cases carefully chosen and arranged so at to present the development of principles." (p. vi)

As Thayer explained, he had "selected only the leading titles," giving to these "a fairly full treatment" (p. vii). In Thayer's casebook, Bradley's majority opinion in the *Civil Rights Cases* appeared in full (pp. 554–67). No other state action cases were referenced or excerpted. Thayer's casebook thus exemplifies the practice of isolating the study of the *Civil Rights Cases*.[27]

Following suit was the 1913 casebook of James Parker Hall, professor of law and dean of the University of Chicago Law School. Hall's casebook, part of West Publishing Co.'s "American Casebook Series," includes a three-page

---

[23] Ibid. at 925–9.

[24] See LaPiana, *Logic and Experience*, 161–4 (on how law schools came to connect case method training with the prestige and status of the bar).

[25] Tomlins, "Framing the Field of Law's Disciplinary Encounters," 932.

[26] The 1895 edition was the official edition, though Thayer published an earlier 1894 edition, which he distributed to fellow legal scholars (White 1993). My references are to the official edition. Jay Hook identifies Thayer's casebook on constitutional law as the first, though treatises on constitutional law preceded it. Hook, "A Brief Life of James Bradley Thayer," *Northwestern University Law Review* 88 (1993): 1, 5.

[27] The many editions of Gerald Gunther's *Constitutional Law* (1937–2004) exemplify this practice as well.

Twentieth-Century Receptions

excerpt from the *Civil Rights Cases* that opens a chapter on "Personal and Religious Liberty" (p. 151). The remainder of Bradley's opinion appears later, in the chapter "Fundamental Rights" (pp. 240–8). There Hall added a citation to *Harris* (p. 248), moving closer to today's standard practice of presenting excerpts from precursor cases and excerpts from Bradley's opinion.

Thayer and Hall were not alone in thinking the case method "suited to the subject of constitutional law" (Thayer 1895: v). In its *Centennial History of the Harvard Law School* (1918), the Harvard Law School Association put constitutional law into the same category as contracts, torts, and conflict of laws. These subjects were different from jurisprudence and the philosophy of law both of which "call for abstract courses" and are therefore unfit for the "general professional curriculum" (p. 168). In order for legal instruction to be "effective," the Association explained, it "must be concrete." Like common law (but unlike jurisprudence), constitutional law involved the application of law, and the application of law was what mattered: "Langdell's method requires us to study the applications and to derive our principles by critical investigation of the law in action" (ibid.).

The case method had wide appeal as legal actors of varying jurisprudential persuasions endorsed it. Holmes, for example, became a critic of Langdell, but he defended and practiced the case method.[28] This suggests that the case method had a wide impact: legal actors who disagreed on the nature of law and the role of courts nevertheless agreed on a method of study.

An isolated focus on the *Civil Rights Cases* (and the now-standard excerpts) carried profound consequences. Federal judges in lower court decisions had developed the legal vocabulary of state neglect, including of course Bradley in his circuit opinion in *Cruikshank*. Without studying the lower court opinions as well as the jury cases, which provide a framework for understanding state neglect as a form of state action, Bradley's use of the state neglect vocabulary in the *Civil Rights Cases* (e.g., "shield," "protect," and "excuse") could go unnoticed.

The isolation of the *Civil Rights Cases* also made it difficult to perceive the nineteenth-century notion of a hybrid Constitution. In the *Civil Rights Cases*, Justice Bradley stated, "This court has uniformly held that the national government has the power, whether expressly given or not, to secure and protect rights conferred or guaranteed by the Constitution."[29] An interpreter today will easily "read over" the conferred/guaranteed distinction because the concept of a hybrid constitution and its attendant vocabulary have disappeared. One needs to read enough case law, moreover, to see how the distinction organized the Waite Court's rights jurisprudence, including state action doctrine, the Fifteenth Amendment exemption, and federal elections jurisprudence.

Another nineteenth-century development that served to isolate the *Civil Rights Cases* from surrounding case law was the Circuit Courts of Appeals

---

[28] Oliver Wendell Holmes, *Collected Legal Papers* (1920), 42–3.
[29] 109 U.S. at 34.

212   *Rethinking the Judicial Settlement of Reconstruction*

Act (also known as the Evarts Act) of 1891. Among other things the act created nine new circuit courts, each composed of two circuit judges and one district judge, bringing to an end to the long-standing practice of Supreme Court justices "riding circuit." The significance and authority of circuit decisions declined, and the circuits became the institutional site where conflicting interpretations "pooled," thus signaling the need for resolution by the Supreme Court. The scholarly habit of minimizing circuit opinions might be traced at least in part to the anachronistic assumption that circuit opinions from the 1870s occupied the same institutional position as they did after 1891. As I have emphasized throughout the book, Justice Bradley's 1874 circuit opinion in *Cruikshank* was widely circulated, and courts cited it as an authoritative statement on state action rules.[30] Counsel also cited it for authority.[31] Both the case method and the modern practice of minimizing circuit opinions, however, have directed attention away from the case, as well as from C. J. Waite's circuit opinion in *Butler*, where we find the Fifteenth Amendment exemption clearly articulated.

New decontextualizing practices of legal study took hold just as interest in having those concepts buried became commonplace. This was the era of lynch law, arguably the post–Civil War nadir for black Americans,[32] and the enormous social distance between blacks and whites was expressed in popular,[33] governmental,[34] and academic forms.[35] Many of the South's most oppressive labor laws – vagrancy laws, anti-enticement laws, and contract enforcement laws – were enacted and reenacted during the first decade of the twentieth century. As the new century dawned, the color line became more formal and

---

[30] Recall: *LeGrand v. United States*, 12 F. 577 (1882); *United States v. Harris*, 106 U.S. 629 (1883); *Presser v. Illinois*, 116 U.S. 252 (1886); *United States v. Sanges*, 48 F. 78 (1891); *Green v. Elbert*, 63 F. 308 (1894); *Lackey v. United States*, 99 F. 952 (1900); *United States v. Morris*, 125 F. 322 (1903); *Karem v. United States*, 121 F. 250 (1903); *Ex parte Riggins*, 134 F. 404 (1904); *United States v. Powell*, 151 F. 648 (1907).

[31] *Davis v. Beacon*, 133 U.S. 333 (1890); *Logan v. United States*, 144 U.S. 263 (1892); *James v. Bowman*, 190 U.S. 127 (1903); *Hodges v. United States*, 201 U.S. 1 (1906).

[32] Philip A. Klinkner and Rogers M. Smith, *Unsteady March: The Rise and Decline of Racial Equality in America* (1999), 92–135.

[33] In 1902, Thomas Dixon published his Lost Cause novel, *The Leopard's Spots: A Romance of the White Man's Burden*. He followed that up with the 1906 best-seller *The Clan*, which became the basis for the classic blockbuster film by D. W. Griffith, *Birth of a Nation*, which glorified the Klan.

[34] Republican President William Howard Taft (1908–12), the first Republican presidential candidate to actively campaign in the South, stated publicly that the nation's experiment with black suffrage (i.e., the Fifteenth Amendment) had been a failure, reassuring southern whites that the Fifteenth Amendment did not bar their efforts to prevent "domination by an ignorant electorate." Said Taft to blacks, "Your race is adapted to be a race of farmers, first, last and for all time." Klinkner and Smith, *Unsteady March*, 109.

[35] See, e.g., William Graham Sumner, *Folkways: A Study of the Sociological Importance of Usages, Manners, Customs, Mores, and Morals* (1906). See also William A. Dunning, *Reconstruction, Political and Economic, 1865–1877* (1907), 260–5, and John Burgess, *Reconstruction and the Constitution, 1866–1876* (1902).

Twentieth-Century Receptions

pervasive, and southerners defended segregation and disfranchisement as enlightened alternatives to lynching, violence, and election fraud.[36] It was no doubt convenient to have available an innovation in legal education, practiced by well-respected experts, which helped hide the older legal context of the 1870s and 1880s – a context that gave greater support to black civil and political rights.

THE DYER ANTI-LYNCHING BILL OF 1921: A TRANSITIONAL EPISODE

In the early 1920s, supporters of anti-lynching legislation gave opposing readings of the state action cases. While some did not perceive the concept of state neglect, others read the *Civil Rights Cases* and precursor decisions to embrace the state neglect concept. An episode involving the Dyer Anti-Lynching bill of 1922 is instructive.

The Dyer bill targeted atrocities that took the form of public festivals – a "show."[37] In his brief supporting the bill, Moorfield Storey – the civil rights champion, anti-imperialist, and president and chief counsel of the NAACP – recounted one atrocity that occurred on a Sunday morning in December of 1917.[38] "The details are revolting, and you may ask me why they are recited. Because unless the hideous horror of the disease is brought home to the people of this country, they will not rouse themselves to find the remedy."[39] Photographs and postcards show smiling communities of whites – men, women, and children – posing with the remains of victims.[40]

---

[36] Klarman, "Plessy Era," 912–13.

[37] *Chicago Defender*, July 1, 1922, p. 15.

[38] Storey recounts an episode in the prosperous town of Dyersburg, Tennessee: "The Negro was seated on the ground and a buggy-axle driven into the ground between his legs. His feet were chained together, with logging chains, and he was tied with wire. A fire was built. Pokers and flat-irons were procured and heated in the fire. It was thirty minutes before they were red-hot. His self-appointed executioners burned his eyeballs with red-hot irons. When he opened his mouth to cry for mercy a red-hot poker was rammed down his gullet. Red-hot irons were placed on his feet, black and body, until a hideous stench of burning human flesh filled the Sabbath air of Dyersburg. Thousands of people witnessed this scene. They had to be pushed back from the stake to which the Negro was chained. Roof-tops, second-story windows and porch-tops were filled with spectators. Children were lifted to shoulders, that they might behold the agony of the victim." As reported by the Memphis *News-Scimitar*, "Three and a half hours were required to complete the execution." Storey recounts another episode at Estill Springs, Tennessee, of a black man similarly tortured and burned alive. Moorfield Storey, "Brief in Support of the Dyer Anti-Lynching Bill. Submitted to The Committee on the Judiciary of the United States Senate" (reprinted; New York: National Association for the Advancement of Colored People, 1922), 2–4.

[39] Storey, "Brief in Support of the Dyer Anti-Lynching Bill," 6.

[40] See, e.g., *Without Sanctuary: Lynching Photography in America*, essays by James Allen, Hilton Als, John Lewis, and Leon F. Litwack (2000). See also *Without Sanctuary: Photographs and Postcards of Lynching in America*, http://withoutsanctuary.org.

214   *Rethinking the Judicial Settlement of Reconstruction*

Acts of torture and public spectacle were new on the national American scene. In response, the NAACP began a 1916 anti-lynching drive.[41] Executive secretary of the NAACP Roy Nash observed that while the number of lynchings had decreased from their peak in the early 1890s,[42] lynching had become even more vicious than it had been during the Reconstruction era, expressing sheer antiblack hatred, taking a sadistic form, and encompassing more and more "offenses."[43] The black individuals tortured and murdered, moreover, were not political threats; disfranchisement had been completed. Between 1889 and 1922, a known 3,443 persons, including 64 women, were lynched. In 1921 alone, sixty-four persons were lynched. Four were burned alive.[44] The last years of World War I had seen a renewed wave of violence: the rate of lynching doubled between 1917 and 1918.

The failure of local officials to punish these brutal crimes was well known to observers. Moorfield Storey identified the failures in his brief in support of the Dyer bill.

> [V]ery few instances can be found in which even an attempt has been made to punish the lynchers. Rarely have officers resisted them, and practically no lyncher has been punished. They have made no attempt to conceal their identity. Their neighbors have not condemned them, and they have walked unashamed in the communities where they dwelt.[45]

Scores of newspapers in both North and South condemned the crimes and the failure to prevent to prosecute them.[46] Of course, condemnation of mob violence did not necessarily mean condemnation of Jim Crow. Most of the time, it did not. In the South, elite Democrats sought to maintain white supremacy through legal means, and they struggled against the popular (and then stronger) wing of the party that implicitly and at times overtly endorsed extralegal violence and torture.[47]

In July of 1917, after a racial massacre in East St. Louis left over forty blacks dead, President Woodrow Wilson mustered a public response to mob violence, observing, "It cannot live where the community does not countenance it."[48]

---

[41] The NAACP had organized against lynching from its founding in 1909–10. For an account of these early efforts, see Charles Flint Kellogg, *NAACP: A History of the National Association for the Advancement of Colored People, 1909–1920* (1967), 209–21.

[42] Lynching peaked as the disfranchisement movement took off across the South. Lynching also spread from rural to urban areas in the South and from south to north, as blacks migrated. A massacre in Atlanta (1906) was followed by a massacre in Springfield, Illinois (1908).

[43] Nash to Storey, May 18, 1916. Cited in William B. Hixson, "Moorfield Storey and the Defense of the Dyer Anti-Lynching Bill," *New England Quarterly* 42 (1969): 65–81

[44] Storey, "Brief in Support of the Dyer Anti-Lynching Bill," 1.

[45] Ibid. at 7.

[46] For listings of newspapers, see 62 *Cong. Rec.* 792–4 (January 4, 1922) and 62 *Cong. Rec.* 1275–80 (January 17, 1922). See also the listing in the *Chicago Defender*, January 21, 1922, p. 3.

[47] Nokov, *Racial Union*, 69–74.

[48] Quoted in 62 *Cong. Rec.* 789 (July 26, 1918).

Twentieth-Century Receptions

The first southerner elected president since the Civil War, Wilson was no supporter of black rights.[49] As president of Princeton, Wilson barred the entry of blacks, and as president of the United States, he segregated civil servants in the Treasury, Post Office, and Navy Departments.[50] Under his administration federal patronage for blacks fell to a post–Civil War low. Wilson also famously screened D. W. Griffith's *Birth of a Nation*, the blockbuster film that glorifies the Klan and espouses Lost Cause mythology, at the White House.

The American Bar Association, which was founded in 1878 and excluded blacks from membership in 1912, also spoke out in August of 1917 against mob violations of legal process.[51] The ABA organized a high-profile National Conference on Lynching attended by figures such as Attorney General A. Mitchell Palmer, Charles Evans Hughes, William Howard Taft, Elihu Root, and the governors of eleven states, including Georgia and Tennessee. The conference ended with a declaration urging Congress find a way "to end this scourge."[52]

Leonidas C. Dyer, a Republican congressman from Missouri, sought to confront the problem by focusing on the failure and refusal of state officers to punish the perpetrators of the atrocities. Dyer's district had become home to many refugees who had fled East St. Louis during the city's 1917 massacre. Newly employed blacks in the local war industry, specifically employees at a factory holding a government contract, had been the target of the violence, in which scores of black men, women, and children were murdered. The East St. Louis massacre was just a harbinger of the violence to come.

After the return of black veterans following World War I in the summer and fall of 1919, whites rampaged for days in twenty-five cities across the country, including Chicago (thirteen days), Washington, D.C. (for five days), and Phillips County, Arkansas (three days). Known as Red Summer, John Hope Franklin called it "the greatest period of interracial strife the nation had ever witnessed."[53] In Chicago between 1917 and 1921, whites threw fifty-eight homemade bombs into the homes of newly arrived black families.[54] In 1921, Tulsa saw the worst episode of racial violence in American history. In the racially segregated neighborhood of Greenwood over 300 blacks were murdered, 35 city blocks were burned, and an estimated 10,000 were left homeless.[55]

---

[49] See, e.g., Cleveland M. Green, "Prejudice and Empty Promises: Woodrow Wilson's Betrayal of the Negro, 1910–1919," *Crisis* 87 (1980): 87; Klinkner and Smith, *Unsteady March*, 109–111.

[50] Klarman, "Plessy Era," 915. Washington, D.C., was segregated during the Wilson years and remained so until the Eisenhower administration.

[51] Statement of John R. Shillady, NAACP press release, August 1, 1918, cited in Hixson, "Moorfield Storey," 66.

[52] May 6, 1919, quoted in Hixson, "Moorfield Storey," 66.

[53] John Hope Franklin, *From Slavery to Freedom: A History of Negro Americans* (1967), 480.

[54] Klinkner and Smith, *Unsteady March*, 115.

[55] See Scott Ellsworth, *Death in a Promised Land: The Tulsa Race Riot of 1921* (1982); Albert Brophy and Randall Kennedy, *Reconstructing the Dreamland: The Tulsa Race Riot of 1921* (2002).

The Dyer bill was designed to afford citizens federal protection if states failed to provide it.[56] It provided that if "any State or governmental subdivision thereof fails, neglects, or refuses to provide and maintain protection to the life of any person within its jurisdiction against a mob or riotous assemblage, such State shall by reason of such failure, neglect or refusal be deemed to have denied to such person the equal protection of the laws."[57] The bill provided penalties for individual members of mobs upon a showing that state actors failed to act with "due diligence."[58] Attorney General Harry M. Daugherty[59] and Assistant Attorney General Guy D. Goff supported the bill. Testifying before the Judiciary Committee, Goff stated that it was a rights denial "[i]f the State omits to give or withholds protection through motives of indifference or inability."[60]

The chairman of the House Judiciary Committee, Andrew J. Volstead of Minnesota, explained the decision to make federal punishment contingent on state failure. He pointed specifically to the state action cases:

> A number of statutes were passed shortly after the adoption of the Fourteenth Amendment and held void, but the operation of those statutes did not depend upon any failure of the State to protect the individual. In setting aside those statutes the court repeatedly called attention to that fact.... To avoid the construction that this is direct instead of corrective legislation [the Dyer bill is made] inapplicable to any private person until the State has had a reasonable opportunity to do its duty.[61]

Rep. Volstead reiterated that conclusion in an exchange with Rep. Mann. "I understand the gentleman to say," Mann stated, "that so far as the constitutional power of Congress is concerned we have the power to pass a law to

---

[56] 62 *Cong. Rec.* 796.

[57] Dyer Anti-Lynching bill, 1918, Senate Reports (7951), 67th Congress, 2nd sess., 1921–22, vol. 2, pp. 33–4. The bill made it a felony for any local or state officer who had custody of a prisoner to "fail, neglect, or refuse" to make all reasonable efforts to perform his duty in apprehending or prosecuting members of a lynch mob, providing for a five-year prison term and a $5,000 fine. The county in which the lynching took place, moreover, was liable for a $10,000 penalty, to be paid to the victim's family. Mob violence was defined as a crime "against the peace and dignity of the United States." If victims were transported across county lines, all counties were to be jointly liable for the $10,000 penalty.

[58] Section 4 required that indictments against members of lynch mobs specify that state officers had "failed, neglected, or refused to proceed with due diligence to apprehend and prosecute the participants in the mob."

[59] *Washington Post*, Nov. 17, 1921, p. 6.

[60] 62 *Cong. Rec.* 795. Congressmen made this point continually. See, e.g., 62 *Cong. Rec.* 547 ("by failing to bring to justice the perpetrators of lynchings, clearly they have denied the protection guaranteed by the Constitution").

[61] 62 *Cong. Rec.* 1340. See also 62 *Cong. Rec.* 1341. ("The question is, can Congress act when the State fails to act and fails to protect? The Supreme Court has repeatedly said that the Federal Government occupied toward the State the position of a guarantor. The duty of a guarantor is not to compel his principal to pay, but to pay when his principal makes default.")

Twentieth-Century Receptions

punish any crime." Volstead replied: "Provided you make it dependent upon whether the State fails to perform its duty."[62]

Sen. Little of Kansas made the same point. Responding to Democrats who invoked *Cruikshank*, *Harris*, and the *Civil Rights Cases* as evidence against the constitutionality of the Dyer bill,[63] Sen. Little advanced a different reading of the decisions. Section 5 legislation, Little explained, "must necessarily be predicated upon" state denials. "The present bill is entirely predicated."[64] Little challenged the Democrats' reading of the state action cases. He argued:

> There has never been a law predicated on the fact that a State refuses a man protection. Therefore there has never been a decision that such a law is unconstitutional.... The cases the gentlemen cite are concerning laws which did not contain any provision that the State had refused to do its duty. In those cases, the Supreme Court has frequently said that those laws were unconstitutional because they were not predicated upon the fact that the State had refused to give people protection. The inference is that this bill, which is predicated on the claim that the State had refused to give men equal protection, is constitutional. Therefore, there are many decisions which tend to support the constitutionality of this bill.[65]

Clearly, both Volstead and Little perceived the principle of state neglect in the state action decisions. The Dyer bill passed the House by a vote of 230 to 119,[66] and Republican President Warren G. Harding publicly pledged to sign and enforce the bill if the Senate passed it.[67] But the bill was defeated by what the *Chicago Tribune* characterized as the most efficiently organized and executed filibuster witnessed thus far in the Senate.[68] The same alliance of southern Democrats and western Republicans that had defeated the 1891 Lodge-Hoar elections bill was at work still. While Republican Party platforms in 1924 and 1928 continued to call for anti-lynching legislation, the filibuster remained an effective tool to block such legislation.

---

[62] 62 *Cong. Rec.* 1343.

[63] See, e.g., 62 *Cong. Rec.* 550–3, 802–5, 1702, 1725–6. The case *Ex parte Virginia* was the "only one case that seems to afford any basis for the argument of the proponents of the bill" (62 *Cong. Rec.* 550).

[64] 62 *Cong. Rec.* 1735 (January 25, 1922)

[65] 62 *Cong. Rec.* 1732. See also 62 *Cong. Rec.* 1735.

[66] *Chicago Tribune*, January 27, 1922, p. 5. Eight Democrats and one Socialist joined 221 Republicans in support of the bill; 17 Republicans joined 102 Democrats opposing the bill.

[67] *Chicago Defender*, February 18, 1922, p. 1. ("If the Senate of the United States passes the Dyer anti-lynching bill, it won't be in the White House three minutes before I'll sign it; and having signed it, I'll enforce it.") On April 12, 1922, President Harding told Congress that it "ought to wipe the stain of lynching from the banners of free and orderly representative democracy." 62 *Cong. Rec.* 794 (also at 62 *Cong. Rec.* 1296). The *Chicago Defender* called Harding "indifferent" (September 30, 1922, p. 1).

[68] "The Senate has never witnessed a better organized and executed filibuster." *Chicago Tribune*, November 29, 1922, p. 3, and December 3, 1922, p. 5.

Of particular interest is the bill's failure to specify the covered forms of discrimination in law enforcement. This made it incompatible with the historical articulation of the state neglect concept. In other words, the text of the bill – its failure to identify race as the basis on which the denial of equal protection rested[69] – left it vulnerable to constitutional challenge under the rules given in *Cruikshank.*

The racial dimension of lynching and the state's failure to punish it was obvious to observers. The *Nation* stated,

> The simple facts are that officers make all reasonable efforts to protect their prisoners except against mobs bent on lynching a Negro, and that murder in the South is punished as vigorously as elsewhere, except when murder takes the form of lynching. Who, having regard for reality, will deny that in such a situation, the protection of the laws is not equal – that indeed for one class of citizens it does not exist at all?[70]

Congressmen likewise saw race as the basis for the nonenforcement of laws. Republican Rep. Frank Mondell of Wyoming concluded that if the victim of a mob "is black or brown or yellow, no law is invoked."[71] Perhaps with the 1915 lynching of Leo Frank in mind, Mondell also identified religious prejudice as a cause of lynching.[72] Massachusetts State Attorney General Albert E. Pillsbury also stated, "It is not a race question."[73]

It is impossible to provide a definitive answer about why Republicans did not specify race as a form of covered discrimination. My interest lies in showing that they could deploy the state neglect concept, at least partially, thus laying down a temporal marker by which to track the eroding capacity to perceive the concept in Waite-era jurisprudence.

But there is the intriguing possibility that some of the congressmen *realized* that the concept of state neglect required the federal government to specify race as a covered form of discrimination. One of these congressmen was Rep. Volstead, who cited *United States v. Blackburn* in support of the Dyer bill.[74] The first sentence in *Blackburn* states: "The defendants are indicted for conspiring together and going in disguise on the highway, and on the premises of Lucas and others, for the purpose of depriving them, as a class of persons, *and because of their being colored citizens of the United States of African descent,* of the equal protection of the laws...."[75] After repeating the race

---

[69] This observation is made, as well, in Barbara Holden-Smith, "Lynching, Federalism, and the Intersection of Race and Gender in the Progressive Era," *Yale Journal of Law and Feminism* 8 (1996): 50.

[70] *The Nation,* June 7, 1922.

[71] 62 *Cong. Rec.* 1700 (January 25, 1922).

[72] 62 *Cong. Rec.* 1698.

[73] 62 *Cong. Rec.* 795.

[74] 62 *Cong. Rec.* 1341–2.

[75] *United States v. Blackburn,* 24 F. Cas. 1158, 1159 (District Court, W. D. Missouri), emphasis added.

Twentieth-Century Receptions

requirement four more times in the first paragraph, the author of the opinion, Judge Krekel, states, "Crimes, however, such as these defendants are charged with, when committed without any design to affect particular persons, or a particular class, are punishable under state laws only."[76] In the second paragraph (of what is only a six-paragraph opinion), Judge Krekel repeats three more times that a racial motive is required to bring federal charges under the equal protection clause.

Surely, Rep. Volstead (or his staff) read the six-paragraph *Blackburn* opinion as he represented and cited the decision in support of the Dyer bill. Volstead also makes reference to Justice Bradley's statement in the *Civil Rights Cases* that "allowing persons who have committed certain crimes (horse stealing, for example) to be seized and hung by the posse comitatus without regular trial"[77] is a denial of due process/the Fourteenth Amendment. Rep. Burton likewise pointed to Bradley's statement, suggesting that the due process clause might authorize the Dyer bill.[78]

Putting aside questions about a due process strategy, my point is that Rep. Volstead's own display of evidence raises the likelihood that he knew a racial specification was necessary under Waite Court rules. As a legal matter, the issue was moot because the bill was never passed and so never challenged in Court. But as a historiographical matter, such evidence suggests that full perception of the state neglect concept appears to have been possible in 1922.

The historian Claudine Ferrell suggests that the Republican framers of the Dyer bill shied away from race in order to avoid inflaming southern Democrats, who would have charged them with illegitimate interference in Southern "home rule."[79] Of course, the charges were nonetheless made.

Moorfield Storey provides a pointed contrast to Rep. Volstead. Storey initially expressed the conviction that the Dyer bill was unconstitutional.[80] So, too, Taft's Attorney General George W. Wickersham supported the bill but was "puzzled to know just what line to proceed upon."[81] The authorization problem proved insurmountable to Storey.

While Storey came to support the legislation, it was not because he had solved that problem. According to the historian William B. Hixson, Storey took a step "which in view of his past attitude toward constitutional law was little short of revolutionary. The man who had urged his audiences 'to teach

---

[76] 24 F. Cas. 1159, emphasis added.

[77] Recall *United States v. Harris* (1883), an earlier case involving the mob murder of an individual held in state custody. The author of that decision, Justice William B. Woods, did not make reference to a due process theory of federal rights enforcement.

[78] 62 *Cong. Rec.* 1341. Rep. Burton did likewise (62 *Cong. Rec.* 1283).

[79] Claudine L. Ferrell, *Nightmare and Dream: Antilynching in Congress, 1917–1922* (1986), 201.

[80] Letter from Storey to John R. Shillady, executive secretary of the NAACP, April 3, 1919, quoted in Hixson, "Moorfield Storey," 69.

[81] George W. Wickersham to Storey, January 7, 1921, quoted in Hixson, "Moorfield Storey," 71.

220   *Rethinking the Judicial Settlement of Reconstruction*

respect for the law' came very close to saying that a law should be passed even if it were unconstitutional because of its beneficent effect."[82] Storey stated,

> I observe that after the Lever Act[83] was declared unconstitutional the newspapers consoled themselves by saying that it did a great deal of good while it lasted, and if we can get Congress to pass an anti-lynching statute drawn as nearly as possible to avoid the decisions, it may do some good while it lasts, and even if it is ultimately declared unconstitutional, it will at least have put this country right before the world as not supporting the atrocities which now go unpunished in various states of the Union.[84]

Storey ultimately submitted to Congress a brief supporting the Dyer bill.[85] In correspondence with Wickersham, he argued that blacks were denied rights "not merely because individuals used violence, but because the whole community approves their violence....The Governor of the state, the prosecuting officers, the grand juries, the sheriffs, and all the instrumentalities of the law refuse to operate so as to protect negroes against lynching."[86] While Storey identified failures to protect blacks against lynching, he did not mobilize state action case law to support the bill.

Storey felt legally constrained, and he offered a weakly reasoned argument based on *Logan v. United States* (1892), the case I discussed in Chapter 6 that mapped the distinction between declared and created rights. Using *Logan*, Storey attempted to show that life and liberty were rights "created by" the Constitution and as such within congressional power to enforce.[87] Storey also invoked the notion "peace of the United States" to justify the Dyer bill. He hesitated to use the concept because it had implications he resisted:

> The attempt is made to make [lynching] punishable by the contention that they are offenses against the peace of the United States which the United States may punish. They are not more so than every crime is against the peace of the United States, and if this doctrine were to prevail, the whole criminal law which now leaves these offenses to be dealt with by the states, must be set aside.[88]

But Storey later put these hesitations aside, arguing that the "peace of the United States" doctrine, which had its source in *Ex parte Siebold* (1880), was a source of authority for the Dyer bill.[89] As I explained in Chapter 5, the national police power affirmed in *Siebold* pertained only to rights created

---

[82] Hixson, "Moorfield Storey," 73.

[83] Three sections of the Lever Act, which protected coal miners, were invalidated by a district court on the grounds that they were class legislation (*New York Times*, May 27, 1920, p. 1).

[84] Storey to Wickersham, March 21, 1921, quoted in Hixson, "Moorfield Storey," 73.

[85] Storey, "Brief in Support of the Dyer Anti-Lynching Bill." See also George C. Rable, "The South and the Politics of Anti-lynching Legislation, 1920–1940," *Journal of Southern History* 51 (May 1985): 201.

[86] Storey to Wickersham, January 22, 1921, quoted in Hixson, "Moorfield Storey," 72.

[87] Hixson, "Moorfield Storey," 76.

[88] Storey to John R. Shillady, executive secretary, NAACP, April 3, 1919, quoted in Hixson, "Moorfield Storey," 69.

[89] Storey, "Brief in Support of the Dyer Anti-Lynching Bill," 20–3.

Twentieth-Century Receptions

by the Constitution or federal law, and life and liberty were declared rights secured by the Constitution. Storey was misreading the cases, and even he recognized that the application of the "peace of the United States" concept overthrew the criminal law of the states.

We should perhaps distinguish between what Storey was doing as a lawyer and what he was doing as an historian. As a lawyer, he could frame case precedent in the most advantageous way possible. We should not expect him to be bound by historical meaning. Historical knowledge was nonetheless exerting a force on his reasoning. For Storey, an emerging standard in legal knowledge about state action doctrine maintained the operational utility of a line demarcating *private* from state action: the wrongs of private individuals were essentially and inescapably private action and remained outside federal reach even if these wrongs remained systematically unpunished by states. Storey attributed this conceptualization of private action to the *Civil Rights Cases* and precursor decisions.

As I noted in the Introduction, a distinction between private and state action must be made in order to mobilize the Fourteenth Amendment. The distinction is required by Section 1, which contains the "no state" prohibition. But while it is necessary to demarcate a private realm in order to put the amendment into operation, the text does not identify the boundary, and it is not drawn in nature. The distinction between state and private action will therefore always be constructed. Though a lawyer, Storey was not "free" from history. In constructing the line, he felt compelled to look outside the state action cases for authorization, and what he found did not convince him.

On the Republican side, then, we are left not just with Storey's view that the state action cases deny authority to the Dyer bill. There is also partial and perhaps full perception of the state neglect concept by Volstead and others. The point applies to the Democrats as well, though they welcomed the defeat of the Dyer bill. They stated continually that the state action cases made the bill unconstitutional, citing *United States v. Cruikshank*, *United States v. Harris*, and the *Civil Rights Cases*, as well as Fuller-era decisions such as *Hodges v. United States* and *United States v. Powell*.[90]

Interestingly, some Democrats argued that the Dyer bill was unconstitutional because it did not specify the form of discrimination on which the denial of equal protection rested. "Taking into consideration every provision in the bill," Rep. Buchanan stated, "you cannot deduce therefrom the constitutional and legal definition of the denial by the State or its agents of the 'equal protection of the law.' It ignores the element of discrimination, of unequal treatment, essential to constitute the offense."[91] Rep. Garrett agreed: "The fundamental features of this bill do not in anywise involve the race question."[92] Because

---

[90] See, e.g., 62 *Cong. Rec.* 550–3, 802–5, 1702, 1725–6.
[91] 62 *Cong. Rec.* 464 (December 17, 1921).
[92] 62 *Cong. Rec.* 1731 (January 25, 1922).

no form of discrimination was identified, Rep. Byrnes of South Carolina concluded that the bill was ordinary municipal legislation: "This law does not apply solely to the lynching of Negroes. It applies wherever five or more persons kill a human being."[93] Other Democrats added their assent: a failure to specify the covered form of discrimination made the bill "a municipal code to define offenses and provide for their punishment, which the Supreme Court has said Congress cannot do."[94] Such comments indicate perception of the state neglect concept and the Waite Court's insistence on a racial motive.

Of course, even if the bill contained a racial limitation most Democrats would doubtlessly have asserted its unconstitutionality. Republican Sen. Little identified "the rebel yell"[95] emitting from the other side of the aisle. He was contemptuous of Democratic assertions that federal punishment of unremedied mob violence would destroy states rights. "The gentleman from Maine [Democratic Sen. Hersey] says that if they cannot burn somebody alive they will not have a right left."[96]

A flood of racism and anxiety about race mixing poured forth from Democrats.[97] Rep. Lowrey "found in the Negro a preponderance of the animal [and] reckless indulgence of physical appetites and passions."[98] Democrats expressed and invoked fears of race mixing, repeatedly invoking "black beasts" and the rape of "helpless white women."[99] Rep. Garrett of Tennessee, who led Democratic opposition to the bill, called it "a bill to encourage rape."[100] Naming Reconstruction a "monstrous failure,"[101] Democrats cast blacks in the pre-war era as contented slaves and Reconstruction as the product of vengeful and hate-filled Radical Republicans.

Democratic vitriol was of a piece with contemporaneous politics and culture, which were saturated with Lost Cause mythology. At its height during the period, the mythology was expressed in Dunning School histories of Reconstruction[102] and in political scientists'[103] portraits of Reconstruction

---

[93] 62 *Cong. Rec.* 544.

[94] 62 *Cong. Rec.* 800.

[95] 62 *Cong. Rec.* 1733.

[96] 62 *Cong. Rec.* 1732.

[97] See, generally, Barbara Holden-Smith, "Lynching, Federalism, and the Intersection of Race and Gender in the Progressive Era," *Yale Journal of Law and Feminism* 8 (1996): 31–78.

[98] 62 *Cong. Rec.* 1713.

[99] 62 *Cong. Rec.* 544 (Byrnes); 545, 546 (Answell); 548 (Garrett); 549 (Pou); 1718 (Sisson); 1720 (Connally).

[100] 62 *Cong. Rec.* 548.

[101] 62 *Cong. Rec.* 546.

[102] William A. Dunning, *Reconstruction, Political and Economic, 1865–1877* (1907), 260–5; Claude G. Bowers, *The Tragic Era*, (1929), 405. On the history of Reconstruction historiography, see Foner, *Reconstruction*, xix–xxvii. As an indicator of the extent to whcih the reputation of Reconstruction-era Republicans was changing, favorable treatments of Charles Sumner still appeared in 1892 and 1893. These were soon replaced by negative assessments. See Ronald B. Jager, "Charles Sumner, the Constitution, and the Civil Rights Act of 1875," *New England Quarterly* 42 (1969): 354.

[103] Burgess, *Reconstruction and the Constitution*, viii–ix; George Milton, *The Age of Hate* (1930).

Twentieth-Century Receptions

legislation, both of which drew from Democratic interpretations of the state action cases. William W. Davis, for example, described the Enforcement Acts of 1870 and 1871 as unconstitutional and an abandonment of principle: "The enactment of the law and its enforcement meant the desertion, for the time being, by the national government of certain principles of political procedure which make working democracy in America a practical possibility."[104] Such portraits of the Enforcement Acts helped constitute the political, intellectual, and cultural context in which Volstead and Mondell advanced their state neglect readings of *Blackburn*, *Cruikshank*, and *Harris*. While Volstead and Mondell (and some Democrats) perceived the concept of state neglect, they could not leverage this understanding to win support for the Dyer bill.

THE DECLINE AND COLLAPSE OF *LOCHNER*-ERA JURISPRUDENCE

As Congress debated the Dyer bill, Progressive reformers were in the process of building a new way of thinking about rights and rights enforcement. Progressives criticized *Lochner v. New York* (1905), the landmark Supreme Court decision that invalidated a maximum-hours law passed by the New York legislature.[105] The struggle over *Lochner* was a struggle to define the role of the Supreme Court in reviewing economic regulation. For Progressives, *Lochner* symbolized an activist Court, one that trespassed on the rightful territory of legislatures. Progressives wanted legislatures to control the regulation of labor and business.[106] Legislatures, they argued, could better evaluate facts and call on experts to assess the shifting nature of production and working conditions. Progressives denounced *Lochner* as laissez-faire jurisprudence and heaped disrepute on "freedom of contract," which the *Lochner* Court understood to be a natural law concept.[107]

Lochner-era jurisprudence collapsed under the weight of industrialization and the Depression[108] and a new and rearranged way of thinking about rights emerged in its place. The New Deal Court enshrined the new rights paradigm in a series of decisions between 1936 and 1942.[109]

[104] "The Federal Enforcement Acts," in William A. Dunning, *Studies in Southern History and Politics*, No. 9 (1914).

[105] *Lochner v. New York*, 198 U.S. 45 (1905).

[106] See, e.g., the Brandeis brief in *Muller v. Oregon* (1908), in *Landmark Briefs and Arguments of the Supreme Court of the United Sates: Constitutional Law*, vol. 16 (Washington, DC: University Publications of America, 1975), 63–178.

[107] Roscoe Pound, "Liberty of Contract," 18 *Yale Law Journal* 454, 460–8 (1909). See also Edward S. Corwin, "The 'Higher Law' Background of American Constitutional Law," 42 *Harvard Law Review* 365, 382–3, 395–409 (1929); Charles Haines, *The Revival of Natural Law Concepts* (1930), 143–232; Benjamin Wright, *American Interpretations of Natural Law* (1931), 298–306.

[108] See, e.g., Gillman, *The Constitution Besieged* (1993); Cushman, *Rethinking the New Deal Court* (1998).

[109] *Nebbia v. New York*, 291 U.S. 502 (1934); *West Coast Hotel v. Parrish*, 300 U.S. 379 (1937); *United States v. Carolene Products*, 304 U.S. 144 (1937); *United States v. Darby*, 312 U.S. 100 (1941); *Wickard v. Filburn*, 317 U.S. 111 (1942).

Along with the establishment of the case method, the collapse of *Lochner*-era jurisprudence appears related to erosion in the capacity to "read" the Waite Court's state action decisions. Like Waite-era justices, those who rendered *Lochner* accepted the concept of a hybrid Constitution.[110] With the delegitimation of *Lochner* came the delegitimation of natural rights categories. All rights were now conceptualized as positive or created rights, and the notion of a hybrid Constitution disappeared. Certain terms in the nineteenth-century vocabulary carried over – *civil rights* and *created rights* – but they took on new meanings. The terms as they appeared in Waite Court decisions became alien. There was thus an emergent danger that in reading the opinions the now alien elements would be "dissolve[d] into a misleading familiarity."[111] For most legal actors, the Waite Court's language of state action became readable, if at all, in only partial and inchoate ways.

As I have shown in prior chapters, the *civil rights* category of the Reconstruction and post-Reconstruction eras was part of the tripartite civil/political/social typology. The typology made its final Court appearance in a 1917 case, *Buchanan v. Warley*.[112] In that decision, the Court invalidated a Louisville, Kentucky, ordinance (passed May 11, 1914) that barred whites from selling property to blacks.[113] The Court explained that statutes deriving from the Civil Rights Act of 1866 protected property rights, which were at issue in *Buchanan*. "These enactments did not deal with the social rights of men," the Court explained, "but with those fundamental rights in property which [the act of 1866] was intended to secure upon the same terms to citizens of every race and color."[114] While Democrats in Congress continued to invoke the specter of social equality in debate over the Dyer Anti-Lynching bill, the civil/social distinction[115] passed out of use for the Court during the Progressive era.

Struggle over free expression rights played an important role in the reconceptualization of rights during the period. World War I and the Red Scare brought a new salience to free speech rights, and the Supreme Court sided with legislatures that limited these rights.[116] Some Progressives wanted an

---

[110] *Lochner* combined both positive law and natural law. See Siegel (1990), correcting Pound and Corwin, who miss the nature of the combination. It should be noted, too, that *Lochner* used the concept of a hybrid Constitution and the right to contract in ways that were different from the Waite Court's usage. See Paul Kens, "*Lochner v. New York*: Tradition or Change in Constitutional Law?" 1 *New York University Journal of Law & Liberty* 404 (2005).

[111] Quentin Skinner, *Visions of Politics, vol. I, Regarding Method* (2002), 76.

[112] *Buchanan v. Warley*, 245 U.S. 60 (1917).

[113] The city ordinance barred blacks from occupying houses on blocks where a majority of the houses were occupied by whites, thereby preventing whites on the block from selling property to blacks.

[114] 245 U.S. at 79.

[115] Recall that the *political rights* category declined in use as voting and holding office began the uneven migration to the civil rights, that is, "fundamental" category after 1870; after the migration was complete, the category disappeared.

[116] *Abrams v. United States*, 250 U.S. 616 (1919).

Twentieth-Century Receptions

active, interventionist Court on matters of free speech, which is to say, they wanted the Court to throw out legislation that censored and punished speech. But they also wanted a restrained, noninterventionist Court on matters of business and labor regulation, which is to say, they wanted the Court to sustain such laws. They faced a dilemma in reconciling these positions.[117]

The law professor Zechariah Chafee offered a way out of the dilemma. Chafee's writings during the Progressive era were exemplary of a new and rearranged way of thinking about rights and rights protections, and he offered a new "process-protecting" theory of the First Amendment.[118] Chafee distinguished between (1) rights that protected the political process and (2) economic rights. Rights that protected the political process, he argued, required a higher level of judicial scrutiny and so Court interventions to void speech regulations could be justified. Once the political process was adequately protected, Chafee argued, the Court could then trust legislatures to make decisions on economic rights. Regulation of business and labor thus required a lower level of judicial scrutiny, which justified greater restraint on matters of the economy.

The new approach to rights was laid out by the Court in Justice Stone's famous Footnote Four in *Carolene Products* (1938).[119] There he uses a bifurcated rights paradigm to introduce the idea of "levels of scrutiny": legislation that interfered with fundamental rights – for example, Bill of Rights freedoms and process-protecting rights – was to receive more exacting scrutiny, while legislation involving business and economic regulations would receive what later became known as "rational level" scrutiny.[120] The notion that economic rights were fundamental – which Republicans took for granted during the Civil War and Reconstruction eras[121] – was discarded. Likewise, the references in *Reese* to created rights came to look mundane as it became conventional to view *all* rights as created by the Constitution. That historians view *Reese* as a state action decision is itself evidence that the case is being read in an anachronistic manner.

The steady disappearance of the nineteenth-century intellectual world would likely have been accompanied by a loss of familiarity with its categories

---

[117] On this dilemma confronting Progressives, see Mark A. Graber, *Transforming Free Speech: The Ambiguous Legacy of Civil Libertarianism* (1991).

[118] Chafee, significantly, erased the nineteenth-century conception of free expression rights that was held by "conservative libertarians." See Graber, *Transforming Free Speech*. In the nineteenth-century structure of legal thought, both free expression and freedom of contract were individual rights protected by the due process clause of the Fourteenth Amendment. The destruction of the freedom-of-contract category removed, simultaneously, the conceptualization of free expression rights as protected by the due process clause. Chafee's erasure of conservative libertarian thought no doubt contributed to the erosion of the capacity to read nineteenth-century legal languages.

[119] Footnote four has spawned a massive literature. See, e.g., John Hart Ely, *Democracy and Distrust* (1980).

[120] *Williamson v. Lee Optical*, 348 U.S. 483 (1955).

[121] On the "free labor" ideology of the Republicans, see Eric Foner, *Free Soil, Free Labor, Free Men: The Ideology of the Republican Party Before the Civil War* (1970).

and distinctions. Recognizing the vocabulary of state neglect and the Fifteenth Amendment exemption depended on familiarity with the "forms of expression" that courts had developed in the 1870s and 1880s to talk about state action. When combined with the rise of the case method, a new rights paradigm helped establish a new context for interpreting the state action cases.

Importantly, the establishment of the new rights paradigm in Footnote Four appeared promising for black rights. Justice Stone formulated a concern for "discrete and insular minorities"[122] inducing, it is likely, commitments to the new paradigm. But that bifurcation also posed special problems for black agricultural labor.[123] While rational-level scrutiny for policies pertaining to economic rights was good for industrial labor (because legislative policies protected industrial labor), it was not good for agricultural labor (which was primarily black and Latino) because legislative policies remained oppressive. Indeed, New Deal legislation excluded agricultural labor in order to win southern Democratic support, thus leaving black and Latino agricultural labor outside New Deal worker protections that were now presumed constitutional.

So too the new rights paradigm was indirectly supported by the political strategy of the NAACP. In search of respectability and fearful of anticommunist propaganda in the age of McCarthyism, the NAACP chose not to confront the problems that faced black agricultural labor, directing their energies instead to voting rights, segregation, and industrial labor.[124] Their campaigns bore fruit, but those efforts also helped cement the separation between civil rights and economic rights.

The bifurcation of civil rights and economic rights driven in part by Progressive reformers' criticism of *Lochner* and in part by mainstream black rights organizations carried the implication that the hierarchy of rights that informs the Waite Court's state action/neglect concept would be obscured.

STORYLINES IN THE ACADEMY

The crumbling of *Lochner*-era jurisprudence was accompanied by a burgeoning materialist historiography that took its cue from Justice Holmes's dissenting opinion in *Lochner*. Across history, political science, and law, scholars attributed "laissez-faire" jurisprudence to judicial fears about a rising tide of socialism and the Republican justices' inbred sympathy for the interests of big business and wealthy elites.[125] Tracing this jurisprudence to dissenting

---

[122] Robert Cover, "Origins of Judicial Activism in the Protection of Minorities," in *Narrative, Violence, and the Law: The Essays of Robert Cover* (1993), 13–50.

[123] Goluboff, *Lost Promise of Civil Rights* (2007).

[124] The NAACP chose not to follow the lawyers in the Civil Rights Section of the Justice Department, who brought peonage cases under the Thirteenth Amendment, which combined black civil rights with economic rights. Emphasizing the "openness" of New Deal legal doctrine on worker protections, especially as regarding agricultural labor, Risa Goluboff recovers the creative efforts of the CRS during this time. See Goluboff, *The Lost Promise of Civil Rights* (2007).

[125] Gutavus Myers, *History of the Supreme Court of the United States* (1912); Benjamin Twiss, *Lawyers and the Constitution: How Laissez Faire Came to the Supreme Court* (1942);

Twentieth-Century Receptions

opinions by Justices Bradley and Field in the *Slaughter-House Cases*, scholars paid insufficient attention to Bradley's break from Field in *Munn v. Illinois* and Bradley's dissent in *Chicago, M. & St. P. Ry. Co. v. Minnesota*. Such scholarship introduced Justice Bradley's reputation as a "railroad lawyer," which as I have indicated has had remarkable staying power.[126] Legal scholars embraced the materialists' periodization, for which the Civil War and the New Deal constitutional revolution serve as bookends.[127] Legal scholars also projected the image of a Republican Party unified on economic matters backward onto the Civil War era. Even justices on the Chase Court (1864–73) were pronounced proponents of laissez-faire jurisprudence.[128]

The progressive, materialist literature existed alongside another strand of Reconstruction scholarship. Named after Columbia University professor William A. Dunning, this body of scholarship painted Reconstruction-era Republicans as vengeful incompetents who imposed the horrible mistake of Reconstruction on a beaten but heroic South.[129] Such academic expression of Lost Cause mythology valorized President Andrew Johnson, demonized Charles Sumner and the radical Republicans, and embraced social Darwinism. The overthrow of Reconstruction governments and the return of Democratic rule in the South were celebrated as a return to federalism principles.

Revisionist history of the 1950s and 1960s rescued Reconstruction-era Republicans from both of these strands of scholarship. Recasting Reconstruction as a second American Revolution, scholars recovered antislavery constitutionalism,[130] Radical Republicanism, black agency, and the principled effort to protect black rights.[131] The standard account of Reconstruction by Eric Foner expresses the revisionist consensus.[132]

The historical scholarship of the 1950s and 1960s was corrective in fundamental ways but also left in place anachronisms about the Republican Party

---

Benjamin F. Wright, *Growth of American Constitutional Law* (1942); Arnold M. Paul, *Conservative Crisis and the Rule of Law: Attitudes of the Bar and Bench, 1887–1895* (1969).

[126] Myers, *History of the Supreme Court*, 537; Wright, *Growth of American Constitutional Law*, 95–107. See also Carr (1942: 147) and Hacker (1940: 389). See also Robert G. McCloskey, *The American Supreme Court*, 4th ed. (Chicago: University of Chicago Press, 2005), 81, 82 (describing Bradley as "passionately devoted to the defense of property").

[127] McCloskey, *The American Supreme Court*, 69.

[128] Hyman and Wiecek, *Equal Justice Under Law*, 365 (Chase Court justices "all believed devoutly in laissez-faire economics").

[129] William A. Dunning, *Reconstruction: Political and Economic, 1865–1877*. (1907); William W. Davis, *The Civil War and Reconstruction in Florida* (1913); Walter L. Fleming, *The Civil War and Reconstruction in Alabama* (1905).

[130] Graham, "Our 'Declaratory' Constitution"; Jacobus tenBroek, *Equal Under Law* (1951); William Wiecek, *The Sources of Antislavery Constitutionalism in America, 1760–1848* (Ithaca: Cornell University Press, 1977).

[131] James McPherson, *The Struggle for Equality* (1964); Kenneth Stamp, *The Era of Reconstruction, 1865–1877* (1965); Eric Foner, *Free Soil, Free Labor, Free Men: The Ideology of the Republican Party Before the Civil War* (1970); Foner, *Politics and Ideology in the Age of the Civil War* (1980); William E. Gienapp, *The Origins of the Republican Party, 1852–1856* (1987).

[132] For a brief history of Reconstruction historiography, see Foner, *Reconstruction*, xix–xxvii.

228   *Rethinking the Judicial Settlement of Reconstruction*

and political developments from 1877 to the early 1890s. Indeed, the success of this scholarship reinforced a myth that the "Compromise of 1877" was a political abandonment of blacks and presented the state action decisions as a judicial consolidation of that political abandonment. The abandonment narrative and the materialist narrative about *Lochner* were mutually reinforcing storylines: they both presented the Republican judges of the Reconstruction and post-Reconstruction eras as instrumental actors enforcing the pro-corporate policies of the Republican Party.[133]

THE STRUGGLE TO PROSECUTE LYNCHING AND POLICE BRUTALITY

In the early 1940s, liberal lawyers in the newly created Civil Rights Section (CRS) of the Justice Department[134] sought to revive dormant Reconstruction-era statutes. Police brutality and lynching had become pressing concerns for the Roosevelt administration during World War II when Axis propaganda exploited such incidents.[135] CRS lawyers scoured the state action cases in search of authority to prosecute such violence. Their efforts provide a gauge of the extent to which Waite-era concepts were now obscured. In contrast with nineteenth-century readings of *Cruikshank*, *Harris*, and the *Civil Rights*

---

[133] A long and slowly built line of scholarship has repudiated the "laissez-faire" story of *Lochner*, and my recoveries promise a (re)integrated understanding of the nineteenth century. For *Lochner* revisionism, see Alan Jones, "Thomas M. Cooley and Laissez-Faire Constitutionalism: A Reconsideration," *Journal of American History* 53 (1967): 751–71; Charles McCurdy, "Justice Field and the Jurisprudence of Government-Business Relations: Some Parameters of Laissez Faire Constitutionalism, 1863–1897," *Journal of American History* 61 (1975): 970–1005; Michael Les Benedict, "Laissez Faire and Liberty: A Re-evaluation of the Meaning and Origins of Laissez Faire Constitutionalism," *Law and History Review* 3 (1985): 293–331; William Forbath, "The Ambiguities of Free Labor: Labor and Law in the Gilded Age," *Wisconsin Law Review* (1985): 767–817; Stephen A. Siegel, "Historism in Late Nineteenth Century Constitutional Thought," *Wisconsin Law Review* (1990): 1431; Howard Gillman, *The Constitution Beseiged* (1993); Paul Kens, *Justice Stephen Field* (1997); Barry Cushman, *Rethinking the New Deal Court* (1998); G. Edward White, *The Constitution and the New Deal* (2000); Manuel Cachan, "Justice Stephen Field and 'Free Soil, Free Labor Constitutionalism': Reconsidering Revisionism," *Law and History Review* 20 (2002): 591–76; Lewis A. Grossman, "James Coolidge Carter and Mugwump Jurisprudence," *Law and History Review* 20 (2002): 577–629. This revisionist scholarship is now sufficiently detailed as to generate disagreements among the revisionists. For a summary, see Siegel (2002).

[134] See, generally, Carr, *Federal Protection*, 24–32. John T. Elliff, "Aspects of Federal Civil Rights Enforcement: The Justice Department and the FBI, 1939–1964," in Donald Fleming and Bernard Bailyn, eds., *Perspectives in American History* (1971), 605–73.

[135] Within two days of the 1942 lynching of Cleo Wright in Sikeston, Missouri, German and Japanese radio broadcasters were exploiting the incident for propaganda purposes. Attorney General Francis Biddle authorized an investigation, identifying the lynching as a matter of national importance impacting war morale. Rotnem, "Federal Right Not to be Lynched," 57–8. See, generally, Mary Dudziak, *Cold War Civil Rights: Race and the Image of American Democracy* (2002).

Twentieth-Century Receptions 229

Cases, the government lawyers read the cases to preclude a state neglect conception of state action.

The conclusion was not the result of a shoddy effort.[136] All New Dealers and Democrats, unit lawyers shared a liberal outlook. They had joined the CRS out of a commitment to civil rights.[137] Section Chief Victor Rotnem also had a reputation as an original thinker.[138] In anatomizing the efforts of CRS lawyers, I show the care with which they proceeded. Had they done a cursory reading, their failure to perceive the state neglect concept would be less of a puzzle. The inability of CRS lawyers to perceive the state neglect concept stands in stark contrast to nineteenth-century legal and political actors and to the turn-of-the-century judge Thomas Goode Jones.

It is of course impossible to provide a definitive explanation for an absence. I have offered, suggestively, a discussion of various contexts in which CRS lawyers read the state action cases: an educational context (defined in part by the case method) and an intellectual context (a new rights paradigm and materialist historiography). There was also a jurisprudential context. The 1945 decision *Screws v. United States*[139] – in which even police brutality held an uncertain status as state action – provides a lens through which we can view the failure of CRS lawyers to perceive the state neglect concept. While the *Screws* case, which was brought by the CRS, post-dates the lawyers' canvassing of state action precedent, the Court had already heard and ruled on another case brought by the CRS, the 1941 *Classic* decision.[140] In that case, election officials' misuse of power was held to be state action,[141] though the arguments could be read to suggest division when local law enforcement officers were involved. That division emerged in *Screws*. In short, CRS readings of the state action cases took place in a jurisprudential context in which it was uncertain if even a sheriff's committing a murder would be viewed by the Court as state action.

At the heart of the efforts of CRS lawyers was a pair of Reconstruction-era statutes that had survived the repeal of 1894.[142] The first was the "color of law" statute that I discussed in Chapter 6. Recall that the statute derived from the Civil Rights Act of 1866 and provided punishment for whomever

---

[136] In Circular No. 3356, Supplement No. 1, section lawyers Albert Arent and Irwin L. Langbein laid out the ways in which these two statutes could authorize, among other things, lynching and police brutality. Circular No. 3356, Supplement No. 1, issued May 21, 1940. Michal R. Belknap, ed., *Civil Rights, the White House, and the Justice Department 1945–1968* (1991), 11–51. Supplement No. 2, issued April 4, 1942, supplied a revision, adding recent relevant law. Belknap, *Civil Rights*, 64–86.

[137] Ibid. at 122–3.

[138] Ibid. at 134.

[139] 325 U.S. 91 (1945).

[140] *United States v. Classic*, 313 U.S. 299.

[141] 313 U.S. at 326.

[142] In 1894, Democrats repealed thirty-nine of the Revised Statutes of 1874 that pertained to voting (act of February 8, 1894, 28 Stat. 36). In the Criminal Code of 1909, the remaining provisions were further reduced (act of March 4, 1909, 35 Stat. 1088).

230 *Rethinking the Judicial Settlement of Reconstruction*

"under color of law...or custom willfully subjects any inhabitant to the deprivation of any right secured by the Constitution or federal laws, to different punishments, pains, or penalties on account of alienage, race, or color." In 1939, the statute was codified as Section 52 of the Federal Criminal Code. (It has since been recodified and is known today as Section 242.) The second statue was the "conspiracy" statute, formerly Section 5508, which I discussed in Chapters 5 and 7. The statute, used to prosecute William Cruikshank, A. P. Butler, Jasper Yarbrough, and Eugene Logan, made it a crime to conspire to deprive citizens of any right secured by the Constitution or laws of the United States. In 1939 it was codified as Section 51 of the Federal Criminal Code.[143] (It has since been recodified and is known today as Section 241.)

The question in *Screws* involved the misuse of state-granted power by a local sheriff. Was this *state action* within the meaning of the Fourteenth Amendment? The Waite Court decision *Ex parte Virginia* (1880) was on point:[144] a state judge had misused his office, excluding blacks from juries on the basis of race in violation of the law. The federal government prosecuted him, but he challenged the prosecution, arguing that no state action had occurred. The Court soundly rejected his claim.

> Whoever, by virtue of public position under a State government, deprives another of property, life, or liberty, without due process of law, or denies or takes away the equal protection of the laws, violates the constitutional inhibition; and as he acts in the name and for the State, and is clothed with the State's power, his act is that of the State. This must be so, or the constitutional prohibition has no meaning. Then the State has clothed one of its agents with power to annul or to evade it.[145]

But *Ex parte Virginia* was deemed to carry limited force in 1945. Democrats argued in the 1920s, during congressional debate over the Dyer bill, that a state officers' abuse of his powers was not state action because it violated the laws of his state. Justice Stone cited the 1880 decision in *Classic*,[146] but it was not seen as dispositive.

The *Screws* case involved the beating and murder of Robert Hall, a black man, by Sheriff Claude Screws of Georgia and two deputies. Sheriff Screws

---

[143] The CRS noted that this section would protect against attacks by private persons upon the exercise of collective bargaining rights, as the right to collective bargaining had been acquired through the Wagner Act. Circular No. 3356, Supplement No. 1, pp. 28–9. The CRS emphasized that "ordinary outbreak of ruffian, vigilante, or Ku Klux Klan activity, whether directed against reds, nazis, negroes, soap-box speakers, Jehovah's Witnesses, Jews or Catholics, is not within" this section (at 30). After the Court approved the Wagner Act, the NLRB could more easily handle such cases, and the government used this administrative machinery to handle these sorts of cases.

[144] 100 U.S. 339 (1880). This decision upheld the jury provisions of the Civil Rights Act of 1875.

[145] 100 U.S. at 347. The vote was on party lines, 7–2 (Field and Clifford dissenting).

[146] 313 U.S. at 326.

Twentieth-Century Receptions

arrested Hall on phony charges in an apparent vendetta involving Screws's theft of Hall's pearl-handled revolver and Hall's recourse to legal remedies to secure the return of the gun.

In a set of fractured Court opinions, a trio of Justices (Frankfurter, Jackson, and Roberts) argued bitterly that when Sheriff Screws and the deputies beat Hall to death, it was "a patently local crime" that should not be deemed "under color of law."[147] The trio invoked Dunning School histories of Reconstruction in arguing that Section 52 "has remained a dead letter" over the years. "It is familiar history that much of this legislation was born of that vengeful spirit which to no small degree envenomed the Reconstruction era."[148] Justice Frankfurter again cited Dunning School history in a later case,[149] deeply suspicious of the legitimacy of the Civil Rights Act of 1866 and the Enforcement Acts.

The majority in *Screws*, led by Justice Douglas, was unwilling to follow the trio. Ruling that the federal government could proceed against Sheriff Screws but had to prove "willful intent" to deprive Hall of a specific federal right, the Court ordered a new trial. The government failed to obtain a conviction at retrial,[150] and Claude Screws was later elected to the Georgia state senate. Prosecutions under the "willful intent" standard proved difficult, but the government did win rare convictions.[151]

In CRS publications, Section Chief Victor Rotnem called the meaning of "color of law...or custom" a "troublesome question."[152] In bringing the case against Screws, section lawyers were confident that the phrase was intended to limit the statute to persons occupying public office or persons who exercise governmental powers.[153] As they saw it, the statute was designed to punish public officials who intentionally misused their powers to deprive any inhabitant of rights secured by the Constitution.[154] They thought it might possibly apply to individuals impersonating officers, but this was "highly conjectural."[155] As Attorney General Francis Biddle stated, "The word 'color' seems to clearly include pretended authority."[156] But he was sure that the section "would be

---

[147] See also *Snowden v. Hughes*, 321 U.S. 1 (1944) (Frankfurter, J., concurring).

[148] 325 U.S. at 140.

[149] See *Collins v. Hardyman*, 341 U.S. 651 (1951). On the influence of Dunning School history on Charles Fairman's classic study of Fourteenth Amendment history, which argued that the amendment did not originally incorporate the Bill of Rights, see Brandwein, *Reconstructing Reconstruction*, 115–16. See also William Forbath, "Charles L. Black, Jr.: Lincoln, the Declaration, and the 'Grisly, Undying Corpse of States Rights': History, Memory, and Imagination in the Constitution of a Southern Liberal," 92 *Georgetown Law Review* 716–17, 733–5.

[150] Carr, *Federal Protection*, 114.

[151] For the rare victory, see *Crews v. United States*, 160 F. 2d 746 (5th Cir. 1947). On *Crews*, see Carr, *Federal Protection*, 174–5.

[152] Rotnem, "Clarifications," 257.

[153] Francis Biddle, Circular No. 3356, Supplement No. 2 (April 4, 1942), 77.

[154] Rotnem, "Clarifications," 252, 259. Biddle, Supplement No. 2, 80. See also Robert K. Carr, "*Screws v. Georgia*: The Police Brutality Case," *Cornell Law Quarterly* 31 (1946): 50 (Section 52 "is concerned with the action of public officers").

[155] Rotnem, "Clarifications," 259; Biddle, Supplement No. 2, 80.

[156] Biddle, Supplement No. 2, 81.

232   *Rethinking the Judicial Settlement of Reconstruction*

inapplicable to private citizens alone."[157] In none of the section's discussions of the meaning of "color of law...or custom" was there mention of Justice Bradley's construction of the phrase in the *Civil Rights Cases*.

CRS lawyers noted the "close connection [of the Civil Rights Act of 1866] with the Fourteenth Amendment."[158] "The legislative history of this statute," the lawyers explained, "discloses that it was originally framed to enforce against the agents of the several states the inhibitions imposed on the states by the Fourteenth Amendment." Understanding the basis for this conclusion is difficult as the citation contains an error and is not on point.[159]

On the question of whether private individuals could be charged under Section 52, Section Chief Rotnem gave a clear answer: only if they participated or cooperated with a public official to deprive an individual of a federally secured right. He stated, "Though private individuals cannot by themselves violate Section 52, yet if they cooperate with a public official to accomplish the deprivation of Federally secured rights, they may be made defendants in an indictment" based on Section 52.[160] On the question of what Section 52 meant by "custom," Rotnem said it was not clear. All of his examples, however, included the behavior of state officers.[161]

Attorney General Francis Biddle and Section Chief Rotnem were both keenly aware of the problem of state failure to punish Klan violence and other forms of mob intimidation. Taking an analytic rather than an historical approach, they asserted that an approach based on the equal protection clause "appears to be the strongest basis for attacking state inaction."[162]

> [I]f it could be established that a police officer ordinarily stopped street brawls that occurred in his presence or that were reported to him, but refused to intercede in cases of assaults on union organizers or Jehovah's Witnesses

---

[157] Circular No. 3356, Supplement No. 1 (May 21, 1940). Michal R. Belknap, ed., *Civil Rights, The White House, and the Justice Department 1945–1968* (1991), 42; see also p. 26 (Section 242 "is, subject to fairly speculative exceptions, restricted to cases where public officials are defendants").

[158] Belknap, *Civil Rights*, 42.

[159] There is an incorrect citation to "91 Cong. Globe 3672 and 3690" followed by "Enforcement Act of May 31, 1870; Secs. 16 and 17." Sections 16 and 17 reenacted the Civil Rights Act of 1866. There was no ninety-first volume of the *Congressional Globe*. Page 3690 of volume 41 (41st Congress, 2nd sess.) marks the passage of the Enforcement Act of 1870 in the Senate (but says nothing about the meaning of Sections 16 and 17. Page 3672 contains discussion on a Senate bill to empower Congress to regulate federal elections (and so is not on point).

[160] Rotnem, "Clarifications," 259.

[161] For example, he said the term should embrace "de facto officers. It should also embrace persons engaging in practices that have official sanction, or are recognized as law. Typical of such practices is the brutal 'kangaroo court' that exists in many local jails throughout the country, or the custom of excluding qualified Negroes from juries, or from voters' lists." Rotnem, "Clarifications," 259. See also Biddle, Supplement No. 2, 81.

[162] Biddle, Supplement No. 2, 85; Rotnem, "Clarifications," 260. For the suggestion that dereliction in the performance of official duties can violate the due process and equal protection clauses, they both cite W. W. Willoughby, *Constitutional Law of the United States*, 2nd ed. (1929), 1934–5.

Twentieth-Century Receptions

or political opponents, it is felt that this would constitute a denial of equal protection in violation of Section 52.[163]

Rotnem explained that "inaction" was a misnomer: "Actually some positive act is usually involved such as a refusal to give police protection, or the turning away from an attack when the officer knows it is going on."[164] Rotnem was proceeding by analytic reason, and his logic was sound. My point is that he did not rest his argument on case law.

The scholarship of Robert K. Carr, who supported and chronicled the efforts of CRS lawyers, showed the same pattern.[165] A widely respected academic, Carr was a professor of government at Dartmouth, served as the executive secretary of President Truman's Committee on Civil Rights, and was the principal author of the committee's report.[166] Carr had a strong commitment to rights enforcement, and he asserted more forcefully than CRS lawyers that Congress intended for enforcement legislation to reach private individuals.[167] Treating in one breath the Civil Rights Act of 1866, the Ku Klux Klan Act of 1871, and the Civil Rights Act of 1875, Carr stated, "It is clear that...Congress intended to...provid[e] federal protection of the rights of individuals against interferences either by public officers or by private individuals."[168] But as I explained in Chapter 2, the intent to provide protection against private interference could take one of two forms: (1) a more radical form in which federal jurisdiction was plenary and not contingent on state denials, and (2) a centrist form in which federal punishment of individuals was corrective and contingent on state denials of rights. Carr advanced a plenary enforcement theory, a view I challenged earlier.

While Carr found ample authority for the federal prosecution of private individuals in Section 51, CRS attorneys struggled with precedent and ultimately disregarded two decisions that were perceived as insurmountable. The struggle is apparent in their response to the 1942 lynching of Cleo Wright by a white mob in Sikeston, Missouri.

After the murder became fodder for Axis propaganda, Attorney General Biddle authorized a federal grand jury to consider charges against the mob. Wright was in state custody at the time, and the Sikeston police "failed

---

[163] Victor W. Rotnem, "Clarifications of the Civil Rights Statutes," *Bill of Rights Review* 2 (1941): 252–61, 260; Biddle, Supplement No. 2, 85.

[164] Rotnem, "Clarifications," 260; Biddle, Supplement No. 2, 86.

[165] Robert K. Carr, *Federal Protection of Civil Rights: Quest for a Sword* (1947).

[166] *To Secure These Rights* (1947).

[167] Carr quotes Horace E. Flack, *The Adoption of the Fourteenth Amendment* (1908), 277 ("according to the purpose and intention of the Amendment as disclosed in the debates in Congress and in the several State legislatures and in other ways, Congress had the constitutional power to enact direct legislation to secure the rights of citizens against violation by individuals as well as by States"). Quoted in Carr, *Federal Protection*, 36.

[168] Carr, *Federal Protection*, 39. Carr also notes the "unfriendly attitude of [scholar] Charles Warren toward this legislation" in Charles Warren, *The Supreme Court in United States History* (1922).

completely to cope with the situation." After the federal grand jury reported that the lynching did not constitute a federal crime,[169] Rotnem and the CRS took up the question of whether lynching a person in lawful state custody was a federal crime under Section 51, the conspiracy statute. Section lawyers advanced a due process theory of prosecution: individuals had a right to trial in the criminal courts of the state, and the taking and lynching of a person in custody is a denial of prisoner's due process rights.[170]

Section lawyers argued that because the *Civil Rights Cases* was not a due process case, it did not block the prosecution.[171] But there was another problem: the general language of Bradley's majority opinion, not to mention the "no state" language of the Fourteenth Amendment, applied to the due process clause as well as to the equal protection clause. The right to trial was secured against deprivation by states, and the due process theory advanced by CRS lawyers did not have state fault as an element.

The problem led Rotnem to frame the *Civil Rights Cases* in terms of private rights: the public accommodation provisions at issue were flawed legislation because they created a new private right (equal access to public accommodations), and only the states could create new private rights. It was enough, Rotnem asserted, for the Court to invalidate the legislation on this narrow ground. The general language of the opinion (which stated, e.g., that "individual invasion of individual rights was not the subject matter of the Amendment") was therefore unnecessary, that is, was *dictum*. "It was not necessary to invalidate the act in question...on the broad ground that the direction of permissible legislation under the Fourteenth Amendment may not in any case be against individual action or conduct."[172] Rotnem attempted to circumvent (already canonical) language by arguing, "The general language in the *Civil Rights Cases* was unnecessary to the decision...and should be regarded as dictum."[173] Presenting the *Civil Rights Cases* as standing for the rule that Congress could not create new private rights, Rotnem framed the prosecution of the Sikeston mob as consistent with that rule. Prosecuting the Sikeston mob did not create a new private right, therefore, but rather turned on the existing right to due process.

But Rotnem saw no way around *United States v. Harris*. This case presented a perfectly analogous situation "on all fours with the Sikeston affair."[174] Rotnem's solution was to declare that *Harris* lacked authority. "The Precedents are Not Necessarily the 'Law.'"[175] He noted that punishing

---

[169] Rotnem "Federal Civil Right," 58. See also Dominic J. Capeci, Jr., "The Lynching of Cleo Wright: Federal Protection of Constitutional Rights during World War II," *Journal of American History* 72 (1986): 859–87.

[170] Rotnem, "Federal Civil Right," 60–1.

[171] Ibid. at 65–6.

[172] Ibid. at 67.

[173] Ibid.

[174] Ibid. at 71. Carr, too, perceived this case as an obstacle (*Federal Protection*, 41–2, 167).

[175] Ibid. at 64–7.

Twentieth-Century Receptions

the mob in *Harris* would not have created any new private right (because, again, individuals already had due process rights). This distinguished *Harris* from the *Civil Rights Cases* (because individuals did not already have public accommodation rights), but *Harris* posed insurmountable difficulties and so remained immovable.

So too did *Powell v. United States*,[176] the follow-up case to *Riggins*. Recall that in *Powell*, Judge Jones articulated the no-fault due process theory. Rotnem felt justified in ignoring *Powell* because the case invalidated, without comment and on the sole authority of *Hodges*, a due process prosecution of a mob that had lynched a state prisoner.[177] (It is unclear if Rotnem realized that *Powell* blocked only the no-fault due process theory, leaving available the fault-based due process theory.)

As Rotnem presented it, *Harris* and *Powell* provided the only basis for rejecting the prosecution of the Sikeston mob, and the two cases made for a slim foundation. In rejecting them, Rotnem advanced his theory of Section 51. Robert Carr, viewing the same evidence, concluded there were "constitutional difficulties" with a Section 51 prosecution of the Sikeston mob, but noted that these "have not deterred the CRS from a vigorous and continuing attempt" to prosecute lynching cases.[178]

In addition to such moves, CRS attorneys made a deliberate and reluctant choice to leave unpunished lynching – where black victims were not in state custody and where state officers did not participate – unprosecuted. They perceived *Cruikshank* as controlling on the matter: "The Court in *Cruikshank*... dismissed general counts drawn on the due process and equal protection clauses of the Fourteenth Amendment with the remark – which is still sound constitutional law – that the Amendment 'adds nothing to the rights of one citizen as against another.' "[179] But *Cruikshank* did not demand such a conclusion. Neither did *Harris* or the *Civil Rights Cases*.

The dominant models of legal decision making in political science, which hold that political ideology or regime interests determine choices, cannot explain the deliberate choice of liberal CRS attorneys to leave most lynching unprosecuted. CRS attorneys felt legally constrained by their understanding of *Cruikshank*, and they abided the belief that they lacked authority to bring such prosecutions. We must turn to a constitutive conception of institutions in order to explain their behavior. Standard knowledge about the *Cruikshank* decision – namely, that it established a rigid boundary around "private action" – helped define a legal terrain that favored opponents of black civil rights.

---

[176] 212 U.S. 564 (1909).

[177] "Federal Civil Right," 72. Rotnem viewed *Hodges* as a "wholly distinguishable" case because it did not involve a prisoner in state custody. Carr, too, noted that *Hodges* and *Powell* presented "very different problems" (*Federal Protection*, 167).

[178] Carr, *Federal Protection*, 168–9.

[179] Circular No. 3356, Supplement No. 1, 32.

236   *Rethinking the Judicial Settlement of Reconstruction*

In 1960s civil rights decisions, lower federal courts used analytic reason rather than case law to extend the meaning of state action. Holding officers and/or city governments civilly liable for police failures to protect civil rights protesters from violence, courts made the protesters' exercise of constitutional rights under the First Amendment and the Commerce Clause the trigger for federal protection.[180]

In a case involving the failure of Montgomery, Alabama, police to protect Freedom Riders from the Klan, for example, a district court ruled that the students had the right to protection from violence when they were exercising their right to travel in interstate commerce.[181] Other cases involved Section 1983, the civil counterpart to Section 242. Section 1983 also contains the "color of law" language from the Civil Rights Act of 1866.[182] Lower courts ruled that Section 1983 permitted civil suits against officials and/or city governments for failures to protect individuals who were exercising their First Amendment rights to free speech and assembly. Marchers from Selma to Montgomery, for example, had a right to police protection when exercising their rights of speech and assembly.[183] A body of case law at the district and circuit levels thus held that protesters exercising contitutional rights had the right to police protection against violent and disorderly retaliation at the hands of those who disagreed with them.[184] Courts also ruled that the failure of local officials to grant a parade permit to Vietnam War protesters who sought to gather to petition the Government for redress of their grievances violated Section 1983.[185]

There was an irony in the lower courts' use of analytic reason to derive a state neglect concept. The turn to analytic reason appears to be an attempt to escape history, that is, the conventional understanding of case precedent, but

---

[180] *United States v. U.S. Klans, Knights of Ku Klux Klan et al.*, 194 F. Supp. 897, 901–2 (1961); *Cottonreader v. Johnson*, 252 F. Supp. 492 (M. D. Ala. 1966); *Wolin v. Port of New York Authority*, 392 F. 2d 83 (1968); *Smith v. Ross*, 482 F. 2d 33, 37 (6th Cir. 1973); *Glasson v. City of Louisville*, 518 F. 2d 899 (1975); *Dunlap v. City of Chicago*, 435 F. Supp. 1295 (1977). I am indebted to Don Herzog for bringing these cases to my attention. See Don Herzog, "The Kerr Principle, State Action, and Legal Rights," 105 *Michigan Law Review* 1 (2006).

[181] *United States v. U.S. Klans, Knights of Ku Klux Klan et al.*, 194 F. Supp. 897, 901–2 (1961). The court also added, though without elaboration, "The failure of the defendant law enforcement officers to enforce the law in this case clearly amounts to unlawful state action in violation of the Equal Protection Clause of the Fourteenth Amendment.... The willful and deliberate failure on the part of the law enforcement officers was also unlawful in that it deprived the student-passengers and other passengers of their right without due process of law." 194 F. Supp. 897, 902.

[182] 42 U.S.C. 1983. According to the statute, persons who "under color of law...or custom" deprived individuals of rights secured by the Constitution are liable for civil damages.

[183] *Williams v. Wallace*, 240 F. Supp. 100 (1965).

[184] See the cases cited above in note 180, which expanded the definition of state action to include a circumscribed conception of state neglect (failure to protect individuals exercising consititutional rights under the First Amendment and the commerce clause) and which are therefore civil rights victories.

[185] *Hurwitt et al. v. City of Oakland*, 247 F. Supp. 995 (1965).

Twentieth-Century Receptions

Justice Bradley's construction of "color of law...or custom" actually provided a more encompassing conceptualization of the state neglect concept: Bradley's construction was not limited to deprivations of constitutional rights such as free speech and assembly. The historical argument was not only adequate to justify the court's outcome, it justified even more expansive federal power.

Robert Carr's view of federal power to enforce civil rights exemplifies a perspective that was just emerging in the academy. Assessing the failure of federal civil rights enforcement during Reconstruction, Carr gave three reasons for its failure: the Court's invalidation of key provisions of Reconstruction legislation, the growing disinterest of Congress, and the reluctance of Justice Department officials to use the power that remained to them.[186] As summary indicators of the now obscured concepts of the Waite Court, I want to identify each of these reasons.

For Carr, the Court's jurisprudence lacked muscle. It was a weak jurisprudence, unable to underwrite effective enforcement for a trio of reasons: state action doctrine, which he characterized as applying to the Fourteenth and Fifteenth Amendments;[187] the racial limitation of the Fifteenth Amendment;[188] and the Court's narrow construction of the Thirteenth Amendment.[189] Carr missed all of the Waite Court's legal concepts that I have elaborated and discussed.

Carr also accepted myths about political development during the Reconstruction and post-Reconstruction eras. For evidence of growing disinterest in Reconstruction he cited the statutory revision of 1874. Like Attorney General Francis Biddle, Carr presented the statutory revision as a purposeful concealment of the scheme for protecting civil rights.[190] He did not take account of evidence that complicated or undermined that conclusion: the revision was part of the "rationalization" of statutes that was typical of the era and the Senate committee that did the revision was chaired by George S. Boutwell, a friend of civil rights enforcement. Boutwell was among the prosecutors in the impeachment trial of Andrew Johnson and later president of the American Anti-Imperialist League.

---

[186] Carr, *Federal Protection*, 41.

[187] "[T]he Court was influenced by a firm belief that the rights covered by the Fourteenth and Fifteenth Amendments are ones that Congress may safeguard only against action by agencies of state government and not against action by private persons" (ibid. at 42).

[188] "[T]he Court insisted that the Fifteenth Amendment, while protecting the right to vote in both federal and state elections against state interference, authorizes Congress to provide such protection only against interferences based upon the race, color, or previous condition of servitude of the voter" (ibid. at 43).

[189] "[T]he Thirteenth Amendment does establish rights the Congress may protect against private as well as public threats. [T]he Court said that these rights – to be free from slavery and involuntary servitude – must be narrowly defined and do not include any right to be free from mere acts of discrimination based upon color." Carr cited the *Hodges* case for this doctrine (ibid. at 44).

[190] Ibid. at 46.

Carr's evidence for congressional disinterest included the 1879 Democratic attempt to repeal voting rights statutes and their 1894 success on this score. But Democrats had always opposed Reconstruction legislation; they were able to pass repealing legislation in 1879 (which President Hayes vetoed numerous times) because they had gained control of both houses of Congress in the election of 1878. Recall that Republicans rebounded in the 1880 election after Hayes renounced his reconciliation policy and that federal civil rights enforcement resurged during the first half of the decade. Enforcement was not vigorous, but it was not dead. The repeal in 1894, finally, is part of the political context for the Fuller Court cases. Initiating what would become a standard interpretation, Carr perceived a seamlessness between the Waite and Fuller eras.

Following on the heals of Carr's account was C. Vann Woodward's highly influential *The Strange Career of Jim Crow*. Woodward provided a brief description of constitutional development during Reconstruction that would become the backbone of the abandonment narrative:

> The cumulative weakening of resistance to racism was expressed...in a succession of decisions by the United States Supreme Court between 1873 and 1898 that require no review here. In the Slaughter House Cases of 1873 and in United States v. Reese and United States v. Cruikshank in 1876, the court drastically curtailed the privileges and immunities recognized as being under federal protection. It continued the trend in its decision on the Civil Rights Cases of 1883 by virtually nullifying the restrictive parts of the Civil Rights Act. By a species of what Justice Harlan in his dissent described as 'subtle and ingenious verbal criticism,' the court held that the Fourteenth Amendment gave Congress power to restrain states but not individuals from acts of racial discrimination and segregation. The court, like the [Republican Party], was engaged in a bit of reconciliation – reconciliation between federal and state jurisdiction, as well as between North and South, reconciliation also achieved at [black] expense.[191]

Woodward's account of the judicial settlement of Reconstruction quickly became academic orthodoxy, and its distorted renderings of state action doctrine and political development were transported into the legal literature on Reconstruction. My book has been an effort to correct those distortions and reorient our understanding of that settlement and the Court's relationship to the political branches.

I have focused throughout on assumptions about what follows from racism, showing how such assumptions lead to a misapprehension of the state action cases and the opportunities they provide for federal rights enforcement. In the twentieth century, the standard reading of state action doctrine has been seized upon by opponents of anti-lynching legislation, segregationists, and

---

[191] C. Vann Woodward, *The Strange Career of Jim Crow*, 3rd ed. (New York: Oxford University Press, 1974), 71. See also C. Vann Woodward, *Reunion and Reaction: The Compromise of 1877 and the End of Reconstruction* (New York: Oxford University Press, 1966 [1951]), 245.

Twentieth-Century Receptions

opponents of black suffrage. Acceptance of the standard reading by liberal lawyers and anti-racist scholars shows that political ideology did not control or determine this reading. A complete account of the rise of distorted knowledge about the state action cases must explain this acceptance.

But liberals' assessments of the *Civil Rights Cases* are not static, and critics of Rehnquist Court federalism jurisprudence have rejected the Court's standard reading of that 1883 decision.[192] State action doctrine carries renewed importance in constitutional law today, and an invigorated challenge to standard knowledge about the Waite Court's state action decisions is taking place in a changing jurisprudential context.

---

[192] Post and Siegel, "Federal Antidiscrimination Legislation after *Morrison* and *Kimel*" (2000).

9

Conclusion

I want to end by offering some brief comments and cautions about the applicability of Waite-era legal concepts to current constitutional disputes. I want first to reiterate, in no uncertain terms, that no originalist assumptions reside here.[1] My goal has been to supply a better account of constitutional development during the Reconstruction and post-Reconstruction eras and to examine the legal and political dimensions of Supreme Court decision making at this time. I have also tried to underscore how possibilities for argumentation have been opened up or closed down by historical processes. Such arguments create space for analytic reason to enter Fourteenth Amendment jurisprudence but the creation of such space has not been my driving objective.

The recovery of the concept of state neglect opens avenues for precedent-based argumentation in constitutional law today, but the concept was undertheorized and underelaborated. While Justice Bradley outlined the basic structure of the concept of state neglect, neither he nor anybody else provided answers to a number of critical questions: By what criteria was state neglect to be established? How were actions "on account of race" to be determined? Did state duties evolve, and how might new duties become established? Could the concept of state neglect be extended to cover other status-based failures? These are open questions that history cannot answer.

And that is unsurprising. The failure to address these threshold questions is a function of the problem that Republicans confronted. The failure to punish Klan violence against blacks and white Republicans – the problem for which the concept of state neglect was a remedy – was massive, systematic, and enduring. There was simply no need to confront threshold questions at that time. Political retrenchment, moreover, occurred, and so the Court did not get the repeat opportunities that were necessary for the consideration of threshold questions. Today, threshold questions would arise immediately, as

---

[1] The assumptions that animate originalism have been soundly critiqued elsewhere. See, e.g., Jack Rakove, *Original Meanings: Politics and Ideas in the Making of the Constitution* (1996).

240

Conclusion 241

would questions about extension of the concept. The recoveries here therefore cannot be the last word on contemporary legal disputes. In short, the state neglect concept determines no legal results today.

There is perhaps a more basic question: if the concept of state neglect is based within an intellectual universe that has disappeared, can judges just pick it up? The recovery of this old conceptual apparatus carries tremendous significance as a matter of constitutional history and development, but its contemporary legal relevance is not obvious. Today, after all, the administrative state is expansive.[2] In today's context, the idea that states have affirmative duties creates extensive legal obligations, and hence expansive correlative rights. This creates the potential for a flood of federal rights claims. At the same time, the Court's own development of state action doctrine in the twentieth century has not completely precluded a state neglect reading of the *Civil Rights Cases*.

On the problem of applying historical legal concepts today, consider applying the Fifteenth Amendment exemption. Few scholars or jurists, I imagine, would seek to apply the concept. The notion of a hybrid Constitution is gone and the text of the amendment would be experienced today as an insuperable barrier to the application of the rule, regardless of the fact that jurists for a period of time found it acceptable.

The concept of state neglect is more "transportable" across centuries even though it has natural law content. But that is because certain formulations are supported by the application of analytical reason in today's context. Contemporary jurists such as Richard Posner have given analytical support for the idea that discrimination in providing protection against private violence can violate the equal protection clause.[3] Murkiness and incoherence has marked the twentieth-century development of state action doctrine[4] but Posner's formulation remains analytically compelling.

Regarding doctrinal developments pertaining to federal prosecutions of individuals, current doctrine permits the federal government to prosecute private individuals under the Fourteenth Amendment if *state action* is deemed to occur. In *United States v. Price*, the Court ruled that the "joint participation" of law enforcement officers in a conspiracy to murder civil rights workers in Mississippi established state action, permitting the federal government to

---

[2] During the Waite era, the administrative state was in its infancy. See Stephen Skowronek, *Building a New American State: The Expansion of National Administrative Capacities, 1877–1920* (1982).

[3] See, e.g., *Bowers v. DeVito*, 686 F.2d 616, 618 (1982) (Posner, J.) ("It is monstrous if the state fails to protect its residents against...predators, but it does not violate the due process clause of the Fourteenth Amendment." However, "Discrimination in providing protection against private violence could of course violate the equal protection clause of the Fourteenth Amendment.")

[4] The law professor Charles Black famously observed that state action doctrine is a "conceptual disaster area." Charles L. Black, Jr., "Foreword: 'State Action,' Equal Protection, and California's Proposition 14," 81 *Harvard Law Review* 69, 87 (1967).

prosecute private individuals who were co-conspirators.[5] While this was a victory for civil rights at the time, the strong implication of *Price* was that absent the participation of the state officers, the federal government could not have prosecuted the private individuals.

In *United States v. Guest*, the Court lowered the bar when it came to defining state action. Here the Court ruled that the false reports of law enforcement officers established state action, even though the reports were peripheral to a private conspiracy to deprive blacks of the equal enjoyment of public accommodations. "In a variety of situations," Justice Stewart explained, "the Court has found state action of a nature sufficient to create rights under the Equal Protection Clause even though the participation of the State was peripheral, or its action was only one of several co-operative forces leading to the constitutional violation."[6] According to Justice Stewart, it was not necessary to plumb the meaning of "leading to." Avoiding confrontation with the *Civil Rights Cases*, Justice Stewart asserted that *Guest* "requires no determination of the threshold level that state action must attain in order to create rights under the equal protection clause."[7]

Critics charged that the Warren Court was disturbing the clear and settled meaning of the *Civil Rights Cases*. Professor Charles L. Black took note of them. "[A] feeling persists, and is passionately expressed that massive Doric columns are falling. Connected with this is another feeling...that the certain is being abandoned for the uncertain, the clear for the unclear."[8] Black asserted that the *Civil Rights Cases* was not the Doric column that the critics imagined and that Justice Bradley's continual references to state action "of some kind" did not provide a clear and certain definition of state action.

The critics were not mollified but they were no doubt relieved when the Court directly addressed the question of state inaction in *DeShaney v. Winnebago County Dept. of Social Services* (1989).[9] Here, the Supreme Court ruled that the failure of state authorities to protect a boy who was in danger from his father was not a state denial of due process (state action) under the Fourteenth Amendment. While the Department of Social Services had knowledge of the danger, the Court ruled there was no duty to protect the boy from dangers the state did not create. According to the Court, the Department of Social Services did not render the boy more vulnerable to dangers from the father. The situation involved private violence, and state and local governments had no duty to protect their citizens from private violence. The state's failure to

---

[5] *United States v. Price*, 383 U.S. 787, 794 (1966). ("Private persons, jointly engaged with state officials in the prohibited action, are acting 'under color' of law for purposes of the statute. To act 'under color' of law does not require that the accused be an officer of the State. It is enough that he is a willful participant in joint activity with the State or its agents.")

[6] *United States v. Guest*, 383 U.S. 745, 755 (1966).

[7] 383 U.S. at 755–6.

[8] Black, "'State Action,' Equal Protection, and California's Proposition 14," 88–9.

[9] 489 U.S. 189 (1989).

Conclusion 243

intervene, therefore, was not "encouragement" or "facilitation" within the meaning of state action.

But *DeShaney* did not involve an equality-of-rights claim, which matters. It matters, too, in the more recent case *Town of Castle Rock v. Gonzales* (2005).[10] In *Castle Rock*, the Court ruled that the repeated failure of the police to enforce a restraining order did not give rise to a due process claim under the Fourteenth Amendment.[11] The police clearly knew that a particular man had a history of domestic violence but they failed to protect the woman and her family, and the husband killed the children. The plaintiff argued that the police had a duty under the due process clause to enforce the restraining order but the Supreme Court rejected the claim, 7–2, with Justices Souter and Breyer voting with the majority.

The recovery of the state neglect concept could provide a precedent-based Section 1983 claim against the police if it could be established that the police provided less protection to victims of domestic violence compared to other kinds of violence. A court would have to extend the concept of state neglect. But the possibility of an equality-based claim is opened up for the first time.

In a Rehnquist Court decision, *United States v. Morrison*, the state neglect concept could provide guidance for rewriting the statute. While there was testimony during congressional hearings that states were failing to provide adequate remedies for gender-based violence, the statute was general and not predicated on state neglect. The concept of state neglect, it certainly appears, would require that the statute be so predicated. Standards of proof, moreover, would remain a difficult matter. Would evidence of the practice of state neglect need to be established district by district? That, of course, would be an immense burden. State by state? And then how would an insufficient remedy be measured? And how many instances of providing an insufficient remedy need to be identified? The threshold questions that Republicans never asked during Reconstruction would have to be asked now, and it is unclear what standards are both efficacious (so that they would have real-world impact) and enforceable by courts.

These difficulties aside, the recovery of the state neglect concept would certainly provide a rejoinder to Chief Justice Rehnquist, who criticized the statute in *Morrison* because it did not target state officials. This aspect of the law, he stated, weighed against its Section 5 validity: "Sect. 13981 visits no

---

[10] 543 U.S. 748 (2005).

[11] *Gonzales v. City of Castle Rock*, 366 F. 3d 1093 (10th Cir. 2004). This case required the court to decide whether a court-issued domestic restraining order, whose enforcement was mandated by a state law, created a property interest protected by the due process clause of the Fourteenth Amendment. "At issue here is whether Ms. Gonzales' [procedural] due process rights, pursuant to the Fourteenth Amendment, were violated when the officers failed to enforce her restraining order against her husband" (366 F. 3d at 1098). While the circuit court ruled, en banc, that such a procedural right existed, the court affirmed the earlier dismissal of a substantive due process claim under the rule in *DeShaney* that the state does not have an affirmative duty to protect individuals from private third-party violence.

consequence whatever on any Virginia public official involved in investigating or prosecuting Brzonkala's assault. The section is, therefore, unlike any of the § 5 remedies that we have previously upheld."[12] The recovery of the concept of state neglect would turn aside this objection, rendering it invalid.

As much as liberal critics of the Rehnquist/Roberts Court might welcome the recovery of the concept of state neglect, it is no silver bullet. Its recovery, moreover, comes with the loss of a story about judicial villains and heroes of the Reconstruction era that has been a mainstay of liberal scholarship for over a half-century.

---

[12] 529 U.S. at 626–7. For approved remedies he cited *Katzenbach v. Morgan*, 384 U.S. 641; *South Carolina v. Katzenbach*, 383 U.S. 301; and *Ex parte Virginia*, 100 U.S. 339.

Bibliography

Cases Cited

Abrams v. United States, 250 U.S. 616 (1919)
Adamson v. California, 332 U.S. 46 (1947)
Bailey v. Alabama, 219 U.S. 219 (1911)
Baldwin v. Franks, 120 U.S. 678 (1887)
Bell v. Maryland, 378 U.S. 226 (1964)
Blanchard v. Kansas, 16 F. 444 (1883)
Bowers v. DeVito, 686 F. 2d 616 (1982)
Boyd v. United States, 116 U.S. 616 (1884)
Bradwell v. Illinois, 83 U.S. 130 (1873)
Brown v. Board of Education, 347 U.S. 483 (1954)
Buchanan v. Warley, 245 U.S. 60 (1917)
Campbell v. Holt, 115 U.S. 620 (1885)
Carey v. Washington, 5 F. Cas. 62 (1836)
Charge to Grand Jury–Civil Rights Act, 30 F. Cas. 1005, 1006–7 (C. C. W. D. Tenn.) (1875)
Civil Rights Cases, 109 U.S. 3 (1883)
Collins v. Hardyman, 341 U.S. 651 (1951)
Cottonreader v. Johnson, 252 F. Supp. 492 (M. D. Ala.) (1966)
Crews v. United States, 160 F. 2d 746 (5th Cir. 1947)
Davis v. Beacon, 133 U.S. 333 (1890)
DeShaney v. Winnebago County Dept. of Social Services, 489 U.S. 189 (1989)
Dunlap v. City of Chicago, 435 F. Supp. 1295 (1977)
Ex parte McIllwee, 16 F. Cas. 147 (C. C. D. Va.) (1870)
Ex parte Riggins, 134 F. 404 (C. C. N. D. Ala.) (1904)
Ex parte Siebold, 100 U.S. 371 (1880)
Ex parte Virginia, 100 U.S. 339 (1880)
Ex parte Wells, 29 F. Cas. 633 (No. 17,386) (C. C. D. La.) (1878)
Ex parte Yarbrough, 110 U.S. 651 (1884)
Gaughan v. Northwestern Fertilizing Co., 10 F. Cas. 91 (Case No. 5,272) (C. C. N. D. Ill.) (1873)
Glasson v. City of Louisville, 518 F. 2d 899 (1975)
Green v. Elbert, 63 F. 308 (1894)

246   *Bibliography*

Griffin's Case, 11 F. Cas. 7 (Case No. 5,815) (C. C. D. Va.) (1869)
Hague v. CIO, 307 U.S. 496, 513 (1939)
Harrison v. Hadley, 11 F. Cas. 649 (D. D. E. D. Ark.) (1873)
Hodges v. United States, 203 U.S. 1 (1906)
Holden v. Hardy, 169 U.S. 366 (1898)
Home Tel. & Tel. Co. v. Los Angeles, 227 U.S. 278, 287 (1913)
Hornbuckle v. Toombs, 85 U.S. 648 (1873)
Hurwitt et al. v. City of Oakland, 247 F. Supp. 995 (1965)
In re Brosnahan, 18 F. 62 (1883)
In re Hobbs, 12 F. Cas. 262 (Case No. 6,550) (C. C. N. D. Ga.) (1871)
In re Lindauer, 15 F. Cas. 550 (C. C. S. D. N.Y.) (1870)
In re Turner, 24 F. Cas. 337 (Case No. 14,247) (C. C. D. Md.) (1867)
James v. Bowman, 190 U.S. 127 (1903)
Karem v. United States, 121 F. 250 (1903)
Katzenbach v. Morgan, 384 U.S. 641 (1966)
Kellogg v. Warmouth, 14 F. 257 (Case No. 7,667) (C. C. D. La.) (1872)
Korematsu v. United States, 323 U.S. 214 (1944)
Leavenworth v. United States, 92 U.S. 733 (1875)
LeGrand v. United States, 12 F. 577 (1882)
*Live-Stock Dealers' & Butchers' Assn. v. Crescent City Live-Stock Landing &
   Slaughter-House Co.* 15 F. Cas. 649 (Case No. 8,408) (C. C. D. La.) (1870)
Lochner v. New York, 198 U.S. 45 (1905)
Logan v. United States, 144 U.S. 263 (1892)
Luther v. Borden, 48 U.S. 1 (1849)
Marsh v. Burroughs, 16 F. Cas. 800 (Case No. 9,112) (C. C. S. D. Ga.) (1871)
Monroe v. Pape, 365 U.S. 167 (1961)
Munn v. Illinois, 94 U.S. 113 (1877)
Neal v. Delaware, 103 U.S. 370 (1880)
Nebbia v. New York, 291 U.S. 502 (1934)
Norris v. Alabama, 294 U.S. 587 (1935)
Oregon v. Mitchell, 400 U.S. 112 (1970)
Pace v. Alabama, 106 U.S. 583 (1883)
Peonage Cases, 123 F. 671 (M. D. Ala.) (1903)
People v. Salem, 20 Mich. 487 (1870)
Plessy v. Ferguson, 163 U.S. 537 (1896)
Powell v. Alabama, 287 U.S. 45 (1932)
Presser v. Illinois, 116 U.S. 252 (1886)
Prigg v. Pennsylvania, 41 U.S. [16 Pet.] 618 (1842)
Scott v. Sandford, 60 U.S. 393, 407 (1857)
Screws v. United States, 325 U.S. 91 (1945)
Shelley v. Kraemer, 334 U.S. 1 (1948)
Slaughter-House Cases, 83 U.S. 36 [16 Wall.] (1873)
Smith v. Allwright, 321 U.S. 649 (1944)
Smith v. Ross, 482 F. 2d 33, 37 (6th Cir. 1973)
Snowden v. Hughes, 321 U.S. 1 (1944)
South Carolina v. Katzenbach, 383 U.S. 301 (1966)
State v. Gibson, 36 Ind. 389 (1871).
Strauder v. West Virginia, 100 U.S. 303 (1880)
Swafford v. Templeton, 185 U.S. 487 (1902)
Town of Castle Rock v. Gonzales, 545 U.S. 748 (2005)

Bibliography

United States v. Blackburn, 24 F. Cas. 1158 (District Court, W. D. Missouri)
United States v. Buntin, 10 Fed. 730 (S. D. Ohio) (1882)
United States v. Butler, 25 Fed. Cas. 213 (Case No. 14,700) (C. C. D. S.C.) (1877)
United States v. Canter, 25 F. Cas. 281 (C. C. S. D. Ohio) (1870)
United States v. Carolene Products, 304 U.S. 144 (1937)
United States v. Classic, 313 U.S. 299 (1941)
United States v. Clayton, 25 F. Cas. 458 (C. C. E. D. Ark.) (1871)
United States v. Collins, 25 F. Cas. 545 (Case No. 14,837) (C. C. S. D. Ga.) (1873)
United States v. Cruikshank, 25 F. Cas. 707 (Case No. 14,897) (1874)
United States v. Cruikshank, 92 U.S. 542 (1876)
United States v. Crosby, 25 F. Cas. 701 (Case No. 14,893) (C. C. S.C.) (1871)
United States v. Darby, 312 U.S. 100 (1941)
United States v. Given, 25 Fed. Cas. 1324 (Case No. 15,210) (C. C. D. Del.) (1873)
United States v. Goldman, 25 F. Cas. 1350 (1879)
United States v. Guest, 383 U.S. 745 (1966)
United States v. Hall, 26 F. Cas. 79 (Case No. 15,282) (C. C. S. D. Ala.) (1871)
United States v. Harris, 106 U.S. 629 (1883)
United States v. Lackey, 99 F. 952 (District Court, Kentucky) (1900)
United States v. Miller, 107 F. 913 (District Court, Indiana) (1901)
United States v. Morris, 125 F. 322 (1903)
United States v. Morrison, 529 U.S. 598 (2000)
United States v. Munford,16 F. 223 (C.C. E. D. Va.) (1883)
United States v. Petersburg Judges of Elections, 27 Fed. Cas. 506 (1874)
United States v. Powell, 151 F. 648 (1907)
United States v. Price, 383 U.S. 787 (1966)
United States v. Reese, 92 U.S. 214 (1876)
United States v. Rhodes, 27 F. Cas. 785 (Case No. 16,151) (C. C. D. Ky.) (1867)
United States v. Sanges, 48 F. 78 (1891)
United States v. Stone, 188 F. 836 (D. Md. 1911)
United States v. Sutherland, 37 F. Supp. 344 (N. D. Ga.) (1940)
United States v. U.S. Klans, Knights of Ku Klux Klan et al., 194 F. Supp. 897 (1961)
United States v. Waddell, 112 U.S. 76 (1884)
United States v. Yarbrough, 110 U.S. 651 (1884)
Virginia v. Rives, 100 U.S. 313 (1880)
West Coast Hotel v. Parrish, 300 U.S. 379 (1937)
Wickard v. Filburn, 317 U.S. 111 (1942)
Wiley v. Sinkler, 179 U.S. 58 (1900)
Williams v. Wallace, 240 F. Supp. 100 (1965)
Williamson v. Lee Optical, 348 U.S. 483 (1955)
Wolin v. Port of New York Authority, 392 F. 2d 83 (1968)
Yick Wo v. Hopkins, 118 U.S. 356 (1884)

Statutes Cited

Civil Rights Act of 1866, 14 Stat. 27
Enforcement Act of 1870, 16 Stat. 140
Enforcement Act of 1871, 17 Stat. 13
Civil Rights Act of 1875, 18 Stat. 335
Circuit Courts of Appeal Act of 1891, 26 Stat. 826
Civil Rights Repeal Act of 1894, 28 Stat. 36

Bibliography

References

Allen, James, Hilton Als, John Lewis, and Leon F. Litwack (2000) *Without Sanctuary: Lynching Photography in America*. Santa Fe, NM: Twin Palms.

Amar, Akhil Reed (2000) "The Supreme Court, 1999 Term Foreword: The Document and the Doctrine." 114 *Harvard Law Review* 26.

  (1998) *The Bill of Rights: Creation and Reconstruction*. New Haven, CT: Yale University Press.

Angle, Paul M., ed. (1958) *Created Equal? The Complete Lincoln-Douglas Debates of 1858*. Chicago: University of Chicago Press.

Aptheker, Herbert (1989) *The Literary Legacy of W. E. B. DuBois*. White Plains, NY: Krause Publications.

AuCoin, Brent J. (2007) *A Rift in the Clouds: Race and the Southern Federal Judiciary, 1900–1910*. Fayetteville: University of Arkansas Press.

  (1998) "Thomas Goode Jones and African American Civil Rights in the New South." *Historian* 60: 257–71.

Balkin, Jack M. (2001) *What Brown v. Board of Education Should Have Said*. New York: New York University Press.

Ball, Terence, and J. G. A. Pocock (1988) *Conceptual Change and the Constitution*. Lawrence: University Press of Kansas.

Belknap, Michael R., ed. (1991) *Civil Rights, the White House, and the Justice Department 1945–1968*. New York: Garland.

Bell, Derrick (1992) *Race, Racism and American Law*. Boston: Little, Brown.

Belz, Herman (1976) *A New Birth of Freedom: The Republican Party and Freedmen's Rights, 1861–1866*. Westport, CT: Greenwood Press.

Benedict, Michael Les (2006) *Preserving the Constitution: Essays on Politics and the Constitution in the Reconstruction Era*. New York: Fordham University Press.

  (1992) "The Slaughterhouse Cases." In Kermit L. Hall, ed., *The Oxford Companion to the Supreme Court*. New York: Oxford University Press.

  (1985) "Laissez Faire and Liberty: A Re-evaluation of the Meaning and Origins of Laissez Faire Constitutionalism." *Law and History Review* 3: 293–331.

  (1978) "Preserving Federalism: Reconstruction and the Waite Court." *Supreme Court Review* 1978: 39–79.

  (1974) "Preserving the Constitution: The Conservative Basis of Radical Reconstruction." 61 *Journal of American History* 65–90.

Benesh, Sara C. (2002) *The U.S. Court of Appeals and the Law of Confessions: Perspectives on the Hierarchy of Justice*. New York: LFB Scholarly Publishing.

Bensel, Richard (2000) *The Political Economy of American Industrialization, 1877–1900*. New York: Cambridge University Press.

  (1984) *Sectionalism and American Political Development, 1880–1980*. Madison: University of Wisconsin Press.

Bernstein, David E. (2005) "Thoughts on Hodges v. United States." 85 *Boston University Law Review* 811.

Black, Charles L., Jr. (1967) "Foreword: 'State Action,' Equal Protection, and California's Proposition 14." 81 *Harvard Law Review* 69.

Blight, David (2001) *Race and Reunion: The Civil War in American Memory*. Cambridge, MA: Harvard University Press.

Bowers, Claude G. (1929) *The Tragic Era: The Revolution After Lincoln*. New York: Houghton Mifflin.

Bibliography

Bracey, Christopher A. (2001) "Louis Brandeis and the Race Question," 52 *Alabama Law Review* 859.

Bradley, Charles, ed. and comp., William Draper Lewis, and Anthony Q. Keasbey (1902) *Miscellaneous Writings of the Late Hon. Joseph P. Bradley*. Newark, NJ: L. J. Hardham.

Brandwein, Pamela (2007) "A Judicial Abandonment of Blacks? Rethinking the 'State Action' Cases of the Waite Court." *Law & Society Review* 41: 343–86.

(2006) "The *Civil Rights Cases* and the Lost Language of State Neglect." In Ronald Kahn and Ken I. Kersch, eds., *The Supreme Court and American Political Development*. Lawrence: University Press of Kansas.

(2006) "Studying the Careers of Knowledge Claims: Bringing Science Studies to Legal Studies." In Dvora Yanow and Peregrine Schwartz-Shea, eds., *Interpretation and Method: Empirical Research Methods and the Interpretive Turn*. Armonk, NY: M. E. Sharpe.

(2004) Review of Labbé, Ronald M., and Lurie, Jonathan, *The Slaughterhouse Cases: Regulation, Reconstruction, and the Fourteenth Amendment*, and Ross, Michael A., *Justice of Shattered Dreams: Samuel Freeman Miller and the Supreme Court during the Civil War Era*. H-Law, H-Net Reviews. May 2004. URL: http://www.h-net.org/reviews/showrev.php?id=9267.

(2000) "Slavery as an Interpretive Issue in the Reconstruction Debates." *Law & Society Review* 34: 315–66.

(1999) *Reconstructing Reconstruction: The Supreme Court and the Production of Historical Truth*. Durham, NC: Duke University Press.

(1996) "Dueling Histories: Charles Fairman and William Crosskey Reconstruct 'Original Understanding'." *Law & Society Review* 30: 289–334.

Brophy, Albert, and Randall Kennedy (2002) *Reconstructing the Dreamland: The Tulsa Race Riot of 1921*. New York: Oxford University Press.

Burgess, John W. (1902) *Reconstruction and the Constitution, 1866–1876*. New York: C. Scribners Sons.

Burns, James MacGregor (2009) *Packing the Court: The Rise of Judicial Power and the Coming Crisis of the Supreme Court*. New York: Penguin.

Cachan, Manuel (2002), "Justice Stephen Field and 'Free Soil, Free Labor Constitutionalism': Reconsidering Revisionism." *Law and History Review* 20: 541–76.

Calhoun, Charles W. (2006) "*Conceiving a New Republic: The Republican Party and the Southern Question, 1869–1900*." Lawrence: University Press of Kansas.

(2005) *Benjamin Harrison*. New York: Henry Holt.

Capeci, Dominic J., Jr. (1986) "The Lynching of Cleo Wright: Federal Protection of Constitutional Rights during World War II." *Journal of American History* 72: 859–87.

Carr, Robert K. (1947) *Federal Protection of Civil Rights: Quest for a Sword*. New York: Rinehart & Company.

(1946) "*Screws v. Georgia*: The Police Brutality Case." *Cornell Law Quarterly* 31: 48–67.

Chafee, Zechariah, Jr. (1920) *Freedom of Speech*. New York: Harcourt.

Chandler, William E. (1878) *Letters of Mr. William E. Chandler Relative to the So-Called Southern Policy of President Hayes*. Concord, NH: Monitor and Statesman Office.

Chin, Gabriel J. (2004) "Reconstruction, Felon Disenfranchisement and the Right to Vote." 92 *Georgetown Law Journal* 259.

250 *Bibliography*

Collingwood, R. G. (1939) *An Autobiography*. New York: Oxford University Press.

Collins, Michael (1996) "Justice Bradley's Civil Rights Odyssey Revisited." 70 *Tulane Law Review* 1979.

Cortner, Richard C. (2001) *Civil Rights and Public Accommodations: The Heart of Atlanta Motel and McClung Cases*. Lawrence: University Press of Kansas.

Corwin, Edward S. (1948) *Liberty Against Government*. Baton Rouge: Louisiana State University Press.

(1929) "The 'Higher Law' Background of American Constitutional Law." 42 *Harvard Law Review* 365.

Cottrol, Robert J. (2005) "Civil Rights Cases." In Kermit L. Hall, ed., *The Oxford Companion to the Supreme Court*, 2nd ed. New York: Oxford University Press.

Cover, Robert M. (1993) "Origins of Judicial Activism in the Protection of Minorities." In *Narrative, Violence, and the Law: The Essays of Robert Cover*. Ann Arbor: University of Michigan Press.

Cresswell, Stephen (1987) "Enforcing the Enforcement Acts: The Department of Justice in Northern Mississippi, 1870–1890." *Journal of Southern History* 53: 421–40.

Curtis, Michael Kent (2003) "John A. Bingham and the Story of American Liberty: The Lost Cause Meets the 'Lost Clause.'" 36 *Akron Law Review* 617.

(1986) *No State Shall Abridge: The Fourteenth Amendment and the Bill of Rights*. Durham, NC: Duke University Press.

Cushman, Barry (1998) *Rethinking the New Deal Court: The Structure of a Constitutional Revolution*. New York: Oxford University Press.

Dahl, Robert A. (1967) "Decision Making in a Democracy: The Supreme Court as a National Policy Maker." 6 *Journal of Public Law* 279.

Davis, Elmer H. (1921) *History of the New York Times, 1851–1921*. New York: The New York Times.

Davis, William W. (1914) "The Federal Enforcement Acts." In William A. Dunning, *Studies in Southern History and Politics*, No. 9. New York: Columbia University Press.

(1913) *The Civil War and Reconstruction in Florida*. New York: Columbia University Press.

Divine, Robert A. (2005) *The American Story*. New York: Penguin.

Dixon, Thomas (1906) *The Leopard's Spots: A Romance of the White Man's Burden, 1865–1900*. New York: A. Wessels Company.

Dow, Douglas C. (2008) "Decline as a Form of Conceptual Change: Some Considerations on the Loss of the Legal Person." *Contributions to the History of Concepts* 4: 1–26.

Du Bois, W. E. B. (1922 [1935]) *Black Reconstruction in America*. New York: Atheneum.

(1923) "On Being Crazy." *Crisis* 26: 55.

Dudziak, Mary (2000) *Cold War Civil Rights: Race and the Image of American Democracy*. Princeton, NJ: Princeton University Press.

Dunning, William A. (1907) *Reconstruction, Political and Economic, 1865–1877*. New York: Harper & Row.

Dykstra, Robert (1993) *Bright Radical Star: Black Freedom and White Supremacy on the Hawkeye Frontier*. Cambridge, MA: Harvard University Press.

Eisenberg, Theodore (2000) "Color of Law." In Leonard W. Levy and Kenneth L. Karst, eds., *Encyclopedia of the American Constitution*. New York: Macmillan.

Elliff, John T. (1971) "Aspects of Federal Civil Rights Enforcement: The Justice Department and the FBI, 1939–1964." In Donald Fleming and Bernard Bailyn, eds., *Perspectives in American History*. Boston: Little, Brown.

Bibliography

Ellsworth, Scott (1982) *Death in a Promised Land: The Tulsa Race Riot of 1921.* Baton Rouge: Louisiana State University Press.

Ely, John Hart (1980) *Democracy and Distrust.* Cambridge, MA: Harvard University Press.

Epp, Charles R. (1998) *The Rights Revolution: Lawyers, Activists and Supreme Courts in Comparative Perspective.* Chicago: University of Chicago Press.

Epps, Garrett (2006) *Democracy Reborn: The Fourteenth Amendment and the Fight for Equal Rights in Post-Civil War America.* New York: Henry Holt.

Epstein, Lee, and Jack Knight (1998) *The Choices Justices Make.* Washington, DC: Congressional Quarterly Press.

Epstein, Lee, and Thomas Walker (2004) *Constitutional Law for a Changing America.* Washington, DC: Congressional Quarterly Press.

Ewick, Patricia, and Susan S. Silbey, (1998) *The Common Place of Law.* Chicago: University of Chicago Press.

Ezell, John S. (1968) "The Civil Rights Act of 1875." *Mid-America: An Historical Review* 50: 251.

Fairman, Charles (1987) *Reconstruction and Reunion, 1864–88,* Volume 2. New York: Macmillan.

    (1956) "Joseph P. Bradley." In Allison Dunham and Philip B. Kurland, eds., *Mr. Justice.* Chicago: University of Chicago Press.

    (1953) "The So-Called Granger Cases, Lord Hale and Justice Bradley." 5 *Stanford Law Review* 587.

    (1950) "What Makes a Great Justice? Mr. Justice Bradley and the Supreme Court, 1870–1892." 30 *Boston University Law Review* 46.

    (1949) "Does the Fourteenth Amendment Incorporate the Bill of Rights?" 2 *Stanford Law Review* 5.

    (1949) "The Education of a Justice: Justice Bradley and Some of His Colleagues." 1 *Stanford Law Review* 217.

    (1941) "Mr. Justice Bradley's Appointment to the Supreme Court and the Legal Tender Cases" (pts. 1 and 2). 54 *Harvard Law Review* 977.

Ferrell, Claudine L. (1986) *Nightmare and Dream: Antilynching in Congress, 1917–1922.* New York: Garland.

Finch, Gerard Brown (1886) *A Selection of Cases on the English Law of Contract.* London: C. J. Clay.

Flack, Horace E. (1908) *The Adoption of the Fourteenth Amendment.* Baltimore: Johns Hopkins University Press.

Fleming, Walter L. (1905) *The Civil War and Reconstruction in Alabama.* New York: Columbia University Press.

Foner, Eric (1988) *Reconstruction: America's Unfinished Revolution, 1863–1877.* New York: Harper & Row.

    (1980) *Politics and Ideology in the Age of the Civil War.* New York: Oxford University Press.

    (1970) *Free Soil, Free Labor, Free Men: The Ideology of the Republican Party Before the Civil War.* New York: Oxford University Press.

Forbath, William E. (2004) "Charles L. Black, Jr.: Lincoln, the Declaration, and the 'Grisly, Undying Corpse of States' Rights': History, Memory, and Imagination in the Constitution of a Southern Liberal." 92 *Georgetown Law Journal* 709.

    (1985) "The Ambiguities of Free Labor: Labor and Law in the Gilded Age." *Wisconsin Law Review* 1985: 767.

Franklin, John Hope (1967) *From Slavery to Freedom: A History of Negro Americans.* New York: Knopf.

Frantz, Laurent B. (1964) "Congressional Power to Enforce the Fourteenth Amendment Against Private Acts." 73 *Yale Law Journal* 1353.

Friedman, Barry (2009) "Reconstructing Reconstruction: Some Problems for Originalists (and Everyone Else, Too)." 11 *Journal of Constitutional Law* 1201–38.

Friedman, Leon, and Fred Israel, eds. (1969) *The Justices of the United States Supreme Court, 1789–1969: Their Lives and Major Opinions,* vol. 2, pp. 1182–94 [Joseph P. Bradley]. New York: Chelsea House.

Garfield, James A. (1879) "Symposium on Negro Suffrage: Ought the Negro to Be Disenfranchised? Ought He To Have Been Enfranchised?" *North American Review* 268: 244–50.

Garth, Bryant G. (2000) "James Willard Hurst as Entrepreneur for the Field of Law and Social Science." 18 *Law and History Review* 37–58.

Gienapp, William E. (1987) *The Origins of the Republican Party, 1852–1856.* New York: Oxford University Press.

Gillette, William (1979) *Retreat from Reconstruction, 1869–79.* Baton Rouge: Louisiana State Univ. Press.

Gillman, Howard (2002) "How Political Parties Can Use the Courts to Advance Their Agendas: Federal Courts in the United States, 1875–1891." 96 *American Political Science Review* 511–24.

(1993) *The Constitution Besieged: The Rise and Demise of Lochner Era Police Powers Jurisprudence.* Durham, NC: Duke University Press.

Goldman, Robert M. (2001) *"A Free Ballot and a Fair Count": The Department of Justice and Enforcement of Voting Rights in the South, 1877–1893.* New York: Fordham University Press.

Goldstein, Leslie Friedman (2007) "The Specter of the Second Amendment: Rereading Slaughterhouse and Cruikshank." *Studies in American Political Development* 21: 131–48.

Goluboff, Risa (2007) *The Lost Promise of Civil Rights.* Cambridge, MA: Harvard University Press.

Gordon, Robert (1983) "Legal Thought and Legal Practice in the Age of American Enterprise, 1870–1920." In Gerald L. Geison, ed., *Professions and Professional Ideologies in America.* Chapel Hill: University of North Carolina Press.

Graber, Mark A. (1991) *Transforming Free Speech: The Ambiguous Legacy of Civil Libertarianism.* Berkeley: University of California Press.

Graham, Howard Jay (1954) "Our Declaratory Fourteenth Amendment." 7 *Stanford Law Review* 3.

Gray, John Chipman (1892) "Methods of Legal Education." 1 *Yale Law Journal* 139–61.

(1888) *Select Cases and Other Authorities on the Law of Property.* Cambridge, MA: Charles W. Sever.

Greeley, Horace (1893) *Proceedings of the First Three Republican Conventions of 1856, 1860, and 1864.* Minneapolis, MN: C. W. Johnson.

Green, Cleveland M. (1980) "Prejudice and Empty Promises: Woodrow Wilson's Betrayal of the Negro, 1910–1919." *Crisis* 87: 380.

Gressman, Eugene (1952) "The Unhappy History of Civil Rights Legislation." 50 *Michigan Law Review* 1323.

Grossman, James R. (1989) *Land of Hope: Chicago, Black Southerners, and the Great Migration.* Chicago: University of Chicago Press.

Bibliography

Grossman, Joel (1997) "The Japanese American Cases and the Vagaries of Constitutional Adjudication in Wartime: An Institutional Perspective." 19 *University of Hawaii Law Review* 649.

Grossman, Lewis A. (2002) "James Coolidge Carter and Mugwump Jurisprudence." *Law and History Review* 20: 577–629.

Gudridge, Patrick O. (1989) "Privileges and Permissions: The Civil Rights Act of 1875." *Law & Philosophy* 8: 83.

Guterl, Matthew Pratt (2001) *The Color of Race in America, 1900–1940.* Cambridge, MA: Harvard University Press.

Haakonssen, Knud (1991) "From Natural Law to the Rights of Man: A European Perspective on American Debates." In Michael J. Lacey and Knud Haakonssen, eds., *A Culture of Rights: The Bill of Rights in Philosophy, Politics, and Law.* New York: Cambridge University Press.

Hacker, Louis M. (1940) *The Triumph of American Capitalism: The Development of Forces in American History to the End of the Nineteenth Century.* New York: Simon & Schuster.

Haines, Charles Grove (1930) *The Revival of Natural Law Concepts.* Cambridge, MA: Harvard University Press.

Hall, James Parker (1913) *Cases on Constitutional Law.* St. Paul: West Publishing.

Hall, Kermit L. (2005) *The Oxford Companion to the Supreme Court,* second edition. New York: Oxford University Press.

Harper, Frances Ellen Watkins (1893) *Iola Leroy; or Shadows Uplifted.* Philadelphia: Garrigues Bros.

Harris, Robert J. (1960) *Quest for Equality.* Baton Rouge: Louisiana State University Press.

Herzog, Don (2006) "The Kerr Principle, State Action, and Legal Rights." 105 *Michigan Law Review* 1.

Hirshson, Stanley P. (1962) *Farewell to the Bloody Shirt: Northern Republicans and the Southern Negro, 1877–1893.* Chicago: Quadrangle Books.

Hixson, William B. (1969) "Moorfield Storey and the Defense of the Dyer Anti-Lynching Bill." *New England Quarterly* 42: 65–81.

Hogue, Arthur R., ed. (1951) *Charles Sumner, An Essay by Carl Schurz.* Urbana: University of Illinois Press.

Holden-Smith, Barbara (1996) "Lynching, Federalism, and the Intersection of Race and Gender in the Progressive Era." 8 *Yale Journal of Law and Feminism* 50.

Holmes, Oliver Wendell (1920) *Collected Legal Papers.* New York: Harcourt, Brace & Co.

Holt, Michael F. (2008) *By One Vote: The Disputed Presidential Election of 1876.* Lawrence: University Press of Kansas.

Hook, Jay (1993) "A Brief Life of James Bradley Thayer." 88 *Northwestern University Law Review* 1.

Hyman, Harold M., and William M. Wiecek (1982) *Equal Justice Under Law.* New York: Harper & Row.

Jager, Ronald B. (1969) "Charles Sumner, the Constitution, and the Civil Rights Act of 1875." *New England Quarterly* 42: 365.

Jones, Alan (1967) "Thomas M. Cooley and Laissez-Faire Constitutionalism: A Reconsideration." *Journal of American History* 53: 751–71.

Kaczorowski, Robert (2004) "The Supreme Court and Congress's Power to Enforce Constitutional Rights: A Moral Anomaly." 73 *Fordham Law Review* 154.

(1989) "The Enforcement Provisions of the Civil Rights Act of 1866: A Legislative History in Light of Runyon v. McCrary." 98 *Yale Law Journal* 565.

(1987) *The Politics of Judicial Interpretation: The Federal Courts, the Department of Justice, and Civil Rights.* New York: Oceana.

Kahn, Ronald, and Ken Kersch (2006) *The Supreme Court and American Political Development.* Lawrence: University Press of Kansas.

Karlan, Pamela (2005) "Contracting the Thirteenth Amendment: Hodges v. United States." 85 *Boston University Law Review* 783.

Katz, Ellen D. (2003) "Reinforcing Representation: Congressional Power to Enforce the Fourteenth and Fifteenth Amendments in the Rehnquist and Waite Courts." 101 *Michigan Law Review* 2341.

Keener, William A. (1894) "The Inductive Method in Legal Education." 17 *American Bar Association Reports* 473–90.

(1893) *A Treatise on the Law of Quasi-Contracts.* New York: Baker, Voorhis and Co.

Kellogg, Charles Flint (1967) *NAACP: A History of the National Association for the Advancement of Colored People, 1909–1920.* Baltimore: Johns Hopkins University Press.

Kelly, Alfred H. (1966) "Comment on Harold M. Hyman's Paper." In Harold M. Hyman, ed., *New Frontiers of the American Reconstruction.* Urbana: University of Illinois Press.

Kennedy, Randall (1997) *Race, Crime and the Law.* New York: Pantheon.

Kens, Paul (2005) "Lochner v. New York: Tradition or Change in Constitutional Law?" 1 *NYU Journal of Law & Liberty* 404.

(1997) *Justice Stephen Field: Shaping Liberty from the Gold Rush to the Gilded Age.* Lawrence: University Press of Kansas.

Kersch, Ken I. (2005) *Constructing Civil Liberties: Discontinuities in the Development of American Constitutional Law.* New York: Cambridge University Press.

Klarman, Michael J. (2004) *From Jim Crow to Civil Rights: The Supreme Court and the Struggle for Racial Equality.* New York: Oxford University Press.

(1998) "The Plessy Era." 1998 *Supreme Court Review* 303.

Klinkner, Philip A., and Rogers M. Smith (1999) *Unsteady March: The Rise and Decline of Racial Equality in America.* Chicago: University of Chicago Press.

Kousser, J. Morgan (1999) *Colorblind Injustice: Minority Voting Rights and the Undoing of the Second Reconstruction.* Chapel Hill: University of North Carolina Press.

(1974) *The Shaping of Southern Politics: Suffrage Restriction and the Establishment of the One-Party South, 1880–1910.* New Haven, CT: Yale University Press.

Kurland, Philip B., and Gerhard Casper, eds. (1975) *Landmark Briefs and Arguments of the Supreme Court of the United States: Constitutional Law.* Washington, DC: University Publications of America.

Labbe, Ronald, and Jonathan Lurie (2003) *The Slaughterhouse Cases: Regulation, Reconstruction, and the Fourteenth Amendment.* Lawrence: University Press of Kansas.

Lamoreaux, Naomi R. (1985) *The Great Merger Movement in American Business, 1895–1904.* Cambridge: Cambridge University Press.

Lane, Charles (2008) *The Day Freedom Died: The Colfax Massacre, the Supreme Court, and the Betrayal of Reconstruction.* New York: Henry Holt.

Bibliography

Langdell, Christopher (1871) *Cases on the Law of Contracts*. Boston: Little, Brown.

LaPiana, William P. (1994) *Logic and Experience: The Origin of Modern American Legal Education*. New York: Oxford University Press.

Larson, Henrietta (1968) *Jay Cooke: Private Banker*. New York: Greenwood Press.

Lash, Joseph P. (1975) *From the Diaries of Felix Frankfurter*. New York: Norton.

Levy, Leonard W. (2000) "The Civil Rights Cases." In Leonard W. Levy and Kenneth L. Karst, eds., *Encyclopedia of the American Constitution*. New York: Macmillan.

(2000) "United States v. Cruikshank." In Leonard W. Levy and Kenneth L. Karst, eds., *Encyclopedia of the American Constitution*. New York: Macmillan.

Lofgren, Charles A. (1987) *The Plessy Case: A Legal-Historical Interpretation*. New York: Oxford University Press.

Logan, Rayford W. (1965) *The Betrayal of the Negro: From Rutherford B. Hayes to Woodrow Wilson*. New York: Collier.

(1954) *The Negro in American Life and Thought, The Nadir, 1877–1901*. New York: Dial Press.

Lopez, Ian F. Haney (1996) *White By Law: The Legal Construction of Race*. New York: New York University Press.

Lurie, Jonathan (1986) "Mr. Justice Bradley: A Reassessment." *16 Seton Hall Law Review* 343.

Madison, James (1988) "Memorial and Remonstrance," point 4, reprinted in Robert S. Alley, *Supreme Court on Church and State*. New York: Oxford University Press.

Magrath, Peter C. (1963) *Morrison R. Waite: The Triumph of Character*. New York: Macmillan.

Maltz, Earl (2003) *The Fourteenth Amendment and the Law of the Constitution*. Durham, NC: Carolina Academic Press.

Mathews, John Mabry (1909) *The Legislative and Judicial History of the Fifteenth Amendment*. Baltimore: Johns Hopkins University Press.

McCloskey, Robert G. (1951) *American Conservatism in the Age of Enterprise*. Cambridge, MA: Harvard University Press.

McConnell, Michael W. (1995) "Originalism and the Desegregation Decisions." *81 Virginia Law Review* 94.

McCurdy, Charles (1975) "Justice Field and the Jurisprudence of Government-Business Relations: Some Parameters of Laissez Faire Constitutionalism, 1863–1897." *Journal of American History* 61: 970–1005.

McMahon, Kevin J. (2004) *Reconsidering Roosevelt on Race*. Chicago: University of Chicago Press.

McPherson, James (1988) "Reconstruction Reconsidered" (book review). *The Atlantic* 261 (no. 4) (April 1988): 75–7.

(1964) *The Struggle for Equality: Abolitionists and the Negro in the Civil War and Reconstruction*. Princeton, NJ: Princeton University Press.

Mertz, Elizabeth (2007) *The Language of Law School: Learning to Think Like a Lawyer*. New York: Oxford University Press.

Metzger, Gillian E. (2005) "Facial Challenges and Federalism." *105 Columbia Law Review* 873.

Michelman, Frank I. (1989) "Conceptions of Democracy in American Constitutional Argument: The Case of Pornography Regulation." *56 Tennessee Law Review* 291.

Miller, Loren (1966) *The Petitioners*. New York: Pantheon.

Milton, George F. (1930) *The Age of Hate: Andrew Johnson and the Radicals*. New York: Coward-McCann Inc.

Mohamed, A. N. (1998) "Attitudes of Northern Papers toward the Egalitarian Laws of Reconstruction." *Newspaper Research Journal*, 19.3: 47(1). *General OneFile*, Gale, University of Michigan - Ann Arbor, 30 Nov. 2008. <http://find.galegroup.com.proxy.lib.umich.edu/itx/infomark.do?&contentSet=IAC-Documents&type=retrieve&tabID=T002&prodId=ITOF&docId=A53521781&source=gale&srcprod=ITOF&userGroupName=lom_umichanna&version=1.0>.

Murphy, L. E. (1927) "The Civil Rights Act of 1875." 12 *Journal of Negro History* 113.

Murphy, Walter, James Fleming, and William Harris (1986) *American Constitutional Interpretation*. New York: Foundation Press.

Myers, Gustavus (1912) *History of the Supreme Court of the United States*. Chicago: C. H. Kerr.

Novkov, Julie (2008) *Racial Union: Law, Intimacy, and the White State in Alabama, 1865–1954*. Ann Arbor: University of Michigan Press.

  (2006) "*Pace v. Alabama*: Interracial Love, the Marriage Contract, and Postbellum Foundations of the Family." In Ronald Kahn and Ken Kersch, eds., *The Supreme Court and American Political Development*. Lawrence: University Press of Kansas.

O'Brien, David M. (2000) *Storm Center: The Supreme Court in American Politics*. New York: Norton.

Orren, Karen, and Stephen Skowronek (1996) "Institutions and Intercurrence: Theory Building in the Fullness of Time." In Ian Shapiro and Russell Hardin, eds. *Political Order: Nomos XXXVIII*. New York: New York University Press.

Parker, Cortlandt (1892) "Mr. Justice Bradley of the United States Supreme Court." 11 *Proceedings of the New Jersey Historical Society* 158 (2d ser. 1892).

Paul, Arnold M. (1969) *Conservative Crisis and the Rule of Law: Attitudes of the Bar and Bench, 1887–1895*. Ithaca, NY: Cornell University Press.

Perman, Michael (2001) *Struggle for Mastery: Disfranchisement in the South, 1888–1908*. Chapel Hill: University of North Carolina Press.

Peskin, Allan (1973) "Was There a Compromise?" *Journal of American History* 50: 63–75.

Pierce, Edward L. (1893) *Memoir and Letters of Charles Sumner*, vol. 4. Boston: Roberts Brothers.

Pierson, Paul (2000) "Increasing Returns, Path Dependence, and the Study of Politics." *American Political Science Review* 94: 253–4.

Pocock, J. G. A. (2009) *Political Thought and History: Essays on Theory and Method*. New York: Cambridge University Press.

  (1985) *Virtue, Commerce, and History: Essays on Political Thought and History*. New York: Cambridge University Press.

Polakoff, Keith Ian (1973) *The Politics of Inertia: The Election of 1876 and the End of Reconstruction*. Baton Rouge: Louisiana State University Press.

Porter, Kirk H., ed. (1956) *National Party Platforms, 1840–1956*. Urbana: University of Illinois Press.

Post, Robert C., and Reva Siegel (2000) "Equal Protection of the Law: Federal Antidiscrimination Legislation after Morrison and Kimel." 110 *Yale Law Journal* 441.

Pound, Roscoe (1909) "Liberty of Contract." 18 *Yale Law Journal* 454.

Bibliography

Powe, Lucas A., Jr. (2000) *The Warren Court and American Politics.* Cambridge, MA: Harvard University Press.

Primus, Richard A. (1999) *The American Language of Rights.* New York: Cambridge University Press.

Rable, George C. (1985) "The South and the Politics of Anti-lynching Legislation, 1920–1940." *Journal of Southern History* 51: 201.

Rakove, Jack. (1996) *Original Meanings: Politics and Ideas in the Making of the Constitution.* New York: Knopf.

Reed, Thomas B. (1890) "Federal Control of Elections." *North American Review* 150: 6 (June): 671.

Report of the Joint Select Committee to Inquire into the Condition of Affairs in the Late Insurrectionary States; made to the two houses of Congress February 19, 1872, 13 vols. New York: AMS Press, 1968

Richardson, Leon Burr (1940) *William E. Chandler, Republican.* New York: Dodd, Mead and Co.

Ritter, Gretchen (2006) *The Constitution as Social Design: Gender and Civic Membership in the American Constitutional Order.* Stanford, CA: Stanford University Press.

Roediger, David (1999) *The Wages of Whiteness: Race and the Making of the American Working Class.* New York: Verso.

Ross, Dorothy (1991) *Origins of American Social Science.* New York: Cambridge University Press.

 (1984) "Historical Consciousness in Nineteenth Century America." *American Historical Review* 89: 4.

Ross, Michael A. (2003) *Justice of Shattered Dreams: Samuel Freeman Miller and the Supreme Court during the Civil War Era.* Baton Rouge: Louisiana State University Press.

Rossiter, Clinton (1951) *The Supreme Court and the Commander in Chief.* Ithaca, NY: Cornell University Press.

Rotnem, Victor W. (1943) "The Federal Civil Right Not to Be Lynched." *Washington University Law Quarterly* 28: 57–73.

 (1942) "Clarifications of the Civil Rights Statutes." 2 *Bill of Rights Review* 252–61.

Scaturro, Frank J. (2000) *The Supreme Court's Retreat From Reconstruction.* Westport, CT: Greenwood Press.

Scheppele, Kim Lane (2004) "Constitutional Ethnography: An Introduction." 38 *Law and Society Review* 389.

Schweber, Howard (1999) "The 'Science' of Legal Science: The Model of the Natural Sciences in Nineteenth-Century American Legal Education." 17 *Law and History Review* 421–66.

Scott, John A. (1971) "Justice Bradley's Evolving Concept of the Fourteenth Amendment." 25 *Rutgers Law Review* 552–69.

Scott, Rebecca J. (2008) "Public Rights, Social Equality, and the Conceptual Roots of the Plessy Challenge." 106 *Michigan Law Review* 777.

 (2005) *Degrees of Freedom: Louisiana and Cuba after Slavery.* Cambridge, MA: Harvard University Press.

Segal, Jeffrey A., and Harold J. Spaeth (1993) *The Supreme Court and the Attitudinal Model.* Cambridge: Cambridge University Press.

(2002) *The Supreme Court and the Attitudinal Model Revisited.* Cambridge: Cambridge University Press.

Siegel, Stephen A. (2002) "Comment: The Revision Thickens." 20 *Law and History Review* 631.

(1990) "Historism in Late Nineteenth Century Constitutional Thought." 1990 *Wisconsin Law Review* 1431.

Silbey, Joel H. (1991) *The American Political Nation, 1838–1893.* Stanford, CA: Stanford University Press.

Simpson, Brooks D. (1998) *The Reconstruction Presidents.* Lawrence: University Press of Kansas.

Skinner, Quentin (2002) *Visions of Politics, Vol. I, Regarding Method.* Cambridge: Cambridge University Press.

(2001) *The History of Political Thought in National Context,* ed. D. Castiglione and I. Hampsher-Monk. Cambridge: Cambridge University Press.

(1989) "Language and Political Change." In Terence Ball, James Farr, and Russell L. Hanson, eds., *Political Innovation and Conceptual Change.* Cambridge: Cambridge University Press.

(1988) "Meaning and Understanding in the History of Ideas." In J. Tully, ed., *Meaning and Context: Quentin Skinner and His Critics.* Princeton, NJ: Princeton University Press.

Skowronek, Stephen (1982) *Building a New American State: The Expansion of National Administrative Capacities, 1877–1920.* Cambridge: Cambridge University Press.

Smith, Rogers M. (1997) *Civic Ideals: Conflicting Visions of Citizenship in U.S. History.* New Haven, CT: Yale University Press.

(1988) "Political Jurisprudence, the 'New Institutionalism' and the Future of Public Law." 82 *American Political Science Review* 89–108.

Spauling, Norman (2003) "Constitution as Countermonument: Federalism, Reconstruction, and the Problem of Collective Memory." 103 *Columbia Law Review* 1992.

Stampp, Kenneth M. (1965) *The Era of Reconstruction, 1865–1877.* New York: Vintage

Stanley, Amy Dru (1998) *From Bondage to Contract: Wage Labor, Marriage, and the Market in the Age of Slave Emancipation.* Cambridge: Cambridge University Press.

Stone, Geoffrey, Louis Seidman, Cass Sunstein, and Mark Tushnet (1996) *Constitutional Law.* Boston: Little, Brown.

Storey, Moorfield (1922) *Brief in Support of the Dyer Anti-Lynching Bill. Submitted to the Committee on the Judiciary of the United States Senate.* New York: National Association for the Advancement of Colored People.

Sumner, Charles (1883) *The Works of Charles Sumner,* vol. 14. Boston: Lee and Shepard.

Sumner, William Graham (1906) *Folkways: A Study of the Sociological Importance of Usages, Manners, Customs, Mores, and Morals.* New York: Dover Publications.

tenBroek, Jacobus (1951) *Equal Under Law.* New York: Collier.

Thayer, James Bradley (1895) *Cases on Constitutional Law.* Cambridge, MA: Charles W. Sever.

(1892) *Select Cases on Evidence at the Common Law.* Cambridge, MA: Charles W. Sever.

Bibliography

Tomlins, Christopher (2000) "Framing the Field of Law's Disciplinary Encounters." 34 *Law and Society Review* 911–72.

Trelease, Allen W. (1971) *White Terror: The Ku Klux Klan Conspiracy and Southern Reconstruction*. New York: Harper & Row.

Tribe, Laurence H. (2000) *American Constitutional Law,* 3rd ed. New York: Foundation Press.

Tushnet, Mark (1987) "The Politics of Equality in Constitutional Law: The Equal Protection Clause, Dr. Du Bois, and Charles Hamilton Houston." 74 *Journal of American History* 884–90.

Twiss, Benjamin (1942) *Lawyers and the Constitution: How Laissez Faire Came to the Supreme Court*. Princeton, NJ: Princeton University Press.

Urofsky, Melvin I., and Paul Finkelman (2002) *A March of Liberty: A Constitutional History of the United States, Volume 1*. New York: Oxford University Press.

Valelly, Richard M. (2009) "The Reed Rules and Republican Party Building: A New Look." *Studies in American Political Development* 23:115–42.

  (2007) "Partisan Entrepreneurship and Policy Windows: George Frisbie Hoar and the 1890 Federal Elections Bill." In S. Skowronek and M. Glassman, eds., *Formative Acts: American Politics in the Making*. Philadelphia: University of Pennsylvania Press.

  (2004) *The Two Reconstructions: The Struggle for Black Enfranchisement*. Chicago: University of Chicago Press.

Wang, Xi (1997) *The Trial of Democracy: Black Suffrage and Northern Republicans, 1860–1910*. Athens: University of Georgia Press.

Warren, Charles (1922) *The Supreme Court in United States History*. Boston: Little, Brown.

Welch, Richard E., Jr. (1971) *George Frisbie Hoar and the Half-Breed Republicans*. Cambridge, MA: Harvard University Press.

Welke, Barbara (1995) "When All the Women Were White, and All the Blacks Were Men: Gender, Class, Race, and the Road to Plessy, 1855–1914." *Law and History Review* 13: 261–316.

Wells-Barnett, Ida B. (1962) *On Lynching: Southern Horrors, A Red Record*. New York: Arno Press.

Wendt, Lloyd (1979) *Chicago Tribune: The Rise of a Great American Newspaper*. Chicago: Rand McNally.

White, G. Edward (2003) *Tort Law in America: An Intellectual History*. Oxford University Press.

  (2000) *The Constitution and the New Deal*. Cambridge, MA: Harvard University Press.

  (1993) "Revisiting James Bradley Thayer." 88 *Northwestern University Law Review* 48.

Whiteside, Ruth Ann (1981) *Justice Joseph P. Bradley and the Reconstruction Amendments*. Ph.D. dissertation, Rice University, Department of History.

Whittington, Keith E. (2007) *Political Foundations of Judicial Supremacy: The Presidency, the Supreme Court, and Constitutional Leadership in U.S. History*. Princeton, NJ: Princeton University Press.

Wiecek, William M. (1998) *The Lost World of Classical Legal Thought: Law Ideology in America, 1886–1937*. New York: Oxford University Press.

Williams, Lou Faulkner (1996) *The Great South Carolina Ku Klux Klan Trials, 1871–1872*. Athens: University of Georgia Press.

Willoughby, W. W. (1929) *Constitutional Law of the United States*, 2nd ed. New York: Baker, Voorhis and Co.

Wilson, Charles Erwin (1947) *To Secure These Rights: The Report of President Harry S. Truman's Committee on Civil Rights*. New York: Simon & Schuster.

Wilson, James Grant, and John Fiske, eds. (1891) *Appleton's Cyclopaedia of American Biography, Vol. 1*. New York: D. Appleton and Co., 352–3.

Woodward, C. Vann (1951) *Origins of the New South, 1877–1913*. Baton Rouge: Louisiana State University Press.

(1966 [1951]) *Reunion and Reaction: The Compromise of 1877 and the End of Reconstruction*. New York: Oxford University Press.

(1950) *The Strange Career of Jim Crow*. New York: Oxford University Press.

Wright, Benjamin F. (1942) *Growth of American Constitutional Law*. Boston: Houghton Mifflin.

(1931) *American Interpretations of Natural Law: A Study in the History of Political Thought*. New York: Russell and Russell.

Zuckert, Michael P. (1986) "Congressional Power under the Fourteenth Amendment: The Original Understanding of Section 5." 3 *Constitutional Commentary* 123.

Index

abandonment narrative, 1–7, 129, 139, 228, 238

Akerman, Amos T., 31, 32, 49

allegiance, as basis for protection, 29, 53

Alabama, 33, 139, 143, 188, 194, 195

American Anti-Imperialist League, 237

American Bar Association, 215

American Civil War, 144, 207, 214
  contested meaning, 34
  lost cause mythology, 8, 144, 186, 222, 227

American exceptionalism, 207

anti-lynching activism, 195.
    See also Dyer anti-lynching bill

antislavery, 91
  multiple meanings of, 61, 62

Aptheker, Herbert, 204

Arkansas, 140, 215

Arthur, Chester, 2, 12, 21, 88, 142, 143, 144, 153, 169, 180

Article 1, Section 4, 2, 12, 16, 57, 93, 120, 125–6, 132–3, 143, 146, 152. *See also Siebold, Ex parte*; *Yarbrough, Ex parte*

Atlantic Monthly, 143

Baker, Francis E., 193

Baker, Ray, 204

Ballard, Bland, 44, 108–10, 113, 157

Ballinger, William Pitt, 58

Baltimore *Gazette*, 136

Bayard, Thomas F., 127, 134, 135

Beckwith, James, 106, 112

Bell, Derrick, 4

Bell v. Maryland, 178

Benedict, Michael Les, 15, 121, 203

Bensel, Richard, 142

Biddle, Francis, 231, 232, 233, 237

Bill of Rights, application to states, 39, 56, 57

Bingham, John A., 34, 38, 43

Birth of a Nation, 215

Black, Charles L., 242

Black Codes, 28, 162

Blaine, James G., 141

Blair, Francis P., 43

Blyew v. United States, 79

Bond, Hugh L., 22, 49, 51, 93, 116

Boutwell, George S., 237

Bouvier's Law Dictionary, 66

Bradley, Joseph P., 3, 6, 7, 13, 14, 39, 46, 57, 60, 61, 78, 79, 88–93.
    See also Civil Rights Cases; *Siebold, Ex parte*
  and Compromise of 1877, 6, 92
  and legal scientism, 208
  and *United States v. Hall*, 48
  dissent in *Slaughter-House Cases*, 53, 97, 168
  reputation as railroad lawyer, 6, 25, 89, 90, 227

Brooks, James, 65

Brown v. Board of Education, 169, 170

Buchanan v. Warley, 224

Burchard, Horatio C., 41

Bush, David, 146
"business affected with a public interest," 80
Butler, Benjamin F., 33, 44, 65, 66, 138

Cain, Richard H., 81
Calhoun, Charles M., 14
Calhoun, John C., 90, 170
Campbell, John A., 112
Carpenter, Matthew H., 65, 66, 69, 77, 172
Carr, Robert K., 233, 237, 238
case method, 206–13
Castle Rock v. Gonzales, 243
Chafee, Zechariah, 225
Chamberlain, David, 131, 145
Chandler, William E., 140, 152
Chase, Salmon P., 205
Chicago & St. P. Railway v. Minnesota, 89, 227
Chicago Tribune, 76, 137
   on Bradley, 92
   on Civil Rights Act of 1875, 67, 76, 77, 84
   on *Civil Rights Cases*, 12, 14, 167, 168, 171, 172, 174, 175, 178, 187
   on *Cruikshank*, 12, 98, 106, 113, 126
   on Enforcement Act of 1870, 44
   on filibuster of Dyer bill, 217
   on Garfield, 45
   on Klan violence, 33, 45, 138, 139
   on Lincoln, 77
   on Taft's circular, 136–9
Christian Recorder, 54, 83, 84, 85, 86, 173, 176, 177
Circuit Court of Appeals Act of 1891 (Evarts Act), 212
citizenship, rights of, 63. *See also* equal protection clause; Fourteenth Amendment
   national vs. state citizenship, 3, 55–9
civil rights, 13, 14
   as a natural law construct, 96
   as distinct from political rights, 29, 30
   as distinct from social rights, 14, 29, 31, 58, 60–86, 104, 161, 163
civil/political/social rights typology, 70–4, 101, 186, 190, 199, 224

Civil Rights Act of 1866, 2, 13, 14, 18, 19, 23, 27, 28, 35–7, 46, 62, 63, 71, 79, 83, 101, 110, 119, 121, 186, 187, 190, 191, 194, 199, 224
Civil Rights Act of 1870. *See* Enforcement Act of 1870
Civil Rights Act of 1871. *See* Enforcement Act of 1871
Civil Rights Act of 1875, 3, 6, 27, 161, 178–80. *See also Civil Rights Cases*; Republicans, dispute (intra-party) over public accommodation rights
   as special legislation, 173–7
   legislative history (Supplementary Civil Rights Bill), 61–70
   preamble, 175–6
Civil Rights Cases, 2–6, 12, 14, 17, 19, 20, 24, 30, 85, 151, 154, 196, 198, 205. *See also* state action doctrine
   and canonical language, 167, 200
   and Civil Rights Act of 1866, 102, 161–5
   and "color of law ... or custom," 161–5, 190, 237
   and due process clause, 159
   and hybrid Constitution, 180–2
   and legislative history of the Civil Rights Act of 1875, 60–1, 69–70
   and Rehnquist Court federalism jurisprudence, 239
   relationship to *Plessy v. Ferguson*, 18, 86, 187
   and the case method, 210, 211
   interpreted by CRS lawyers, 206, 234
Civil Rights Section (CRS), 23, 228–35
Civil War. *See* American Civil War
Clarkson, James S., 182
Colfax (Louisiana) massacre, 87, 119
Collingwood approach, 28, 30
Colored Men's National Convention, 84
Compromise of 1877, 5, 6–8, 26, 139, 140. *See also* Woodward, C. Vann
   as a myth, 8, 26, 228
conferred rights, 148, 149. *See also* created rights
Connecticut, 118, 143
Cooke, Jay, 68, 117
Cooley, Thomas, 29
Cooley, William H., 65

Index

Congress, U.S., 4, 25, 30, 31, 36, 38, 45, 50, 62, 67, 79, 90, 97, 98, 101, 113, 122, 126, 163, 165. *See also* Dyer anti-lynching bill
Constitution, U.S. *See* Fifteenth Amendment; Fourteenth Amendment; Thirteenth Amendment
Cornell, Alonzo B., 141
Cottrol, Robert, 4
created rights, 15, 37, 95, 121, 125, 150, 220, 225. *See also* conferred rights; hybrid constitution
Curtis, George Ticknor, 134, 135

Dahl, Robert, 21
Daugherty, Harry M., 216
Davis, Elmer, 76
Declaration of Independence, 63
declared rights, 96. *See also* secured rights
Delaware, 65
Democrats and Democratic Party, 2, 3, 5, 10, 21, 28, 29, 43, 44, 91, 103, 110, 133
  and Civil Rights Act of 1866, 28
  and Klan, 43, 131, 133, 134, 145
  and race mixing, 222
  briefs in *Cruikshank*, 112–15
  control of House in 1874, 9, 68, 118, 170
  defeat of Lodge bill, 182
  denouncing Taft's circular, 133
  elite, conservative Democrats, 194–6, 214
  opposition to Dyer bill (interpreting state action cases), 217, 221, 222
  opposition to public accommodation rights, 65, 72
  opposition to Taft circular (interpreting *Cruikshank* and *Reese*), 126, 127, 134
  repeal effort of 1878–79, 141, 238
  repeal of Reconstruction statutes in 1894, 150–1, 185, 238
Depression (following Panic of 1873), 8, 54, 68, 117
DeShaney v. Winnebago Cty. Dept. of Social Services, 242

Devens, Charles, 141, 144
disenfranchisement movement, 185, 212, 213
Dodge, Grenville, 182
Douglas, William O., 178, 231
Douglass, Frederick, 3, 170, 171
Dred Scott v. Sandford, 73, 112
due process clause, 159, 219, 234, 242, 243
due process theory of prisoners' rights, 156, 200–4
Dunning School historiography, 26, 222, 223, 227, 231
Dyer anti-lynching bill, 206, 213–23

East St. Louis massacre, 215
Economic Panic of 1873, 8, 9, 54, 68, 117, 129
Edmunds, George F., 52, 91
elections, 9, 10, 51
  election of 1874, 68, 69, 118, 129, 170
  election of 1876, 117, 118, 151
  election of 1878, 141, 147, 238
  election of 1880, 141, 142, 238
  election of 1888, 182
election fraud, 10, 141, 213. *See also Siebold, Ex parte*
election violence, 9, 10, 87, 88, 140, 141, 143, 148, 153. *See also United States v. Butler; United States v. Cruikshank; Yarbrough, Ex parte*
electoral federalism. *See Siebold, Ex parte; United States v. Butler; Yarbrough, Ex parte*
Ellenton (South Carolina) massacre. *See United States v. Butler*
emancipation, 61, 62, 71, 79
Emmons, Halmer H., 60–1, 86, 108, 111, 113
Enforcement Act of 1870, 9, 15, 27, 33, 39, 47, 223
  at issue (Section 6) in *Cruikshank*, 94, 95, 105, 111, 119, 121, 135
  at issue (Sections 3 and 4) in *Reese*, 122–5, 134
Enforcement Act of 1871 (Klan Act), 9, 27, 34, 40–4, 52, 54, 69, 103, 109, 137, 154, 157, 189, 223
Epp, Charles, 30

equality. *See* civil rights, as distinct from social rights; civil/political/social typology

equal protection, deprivations of, 29, 30, 40–2, 46. *See also* equal protection clause; state neglect, as a practice

equal protection clause, 59, 101, 103, 104, 105, 107, 109, 115, 119, 120, 155, 158, 199, 241. *See also* state action, as including concept of state neglect

  and Dyer anti-lynching bill, 218–19

  interpretation by CRS lawyers, 232

Evans, Walter, 193

Evarts, William M., 132

Ezell, John, 67, 81

Fairman, Charles, 88, 89

federal elections jurisprudence, 116. *See also* Article 1, Section 4; Taft, Alphonso, 1876 circular to federal marshals

Federal Elections bill of 1890. *See* Lodge elections bill of 1890

federal marshals, 122. *See also* Taft, Alphonso, 1876 circular to federal marshals

federalism, 31, 58, 69, 103, 200

Ferrell, Claudine, 219

Ferry, Orris S., 65

Field, David Dudley, 112–14, 119

Field, Stephen J., 112, 186, 227

Fifteenth Amendment, 2, 3, 10, 11, 39, 46, 47, 57, 61, 71, 93, 102, 109, 116, 122–6, 152, 163. *See also United States v. Butler*; *Yarbrough, Ex parte*

  exemption from state action doctrine, 11, 12, 15–17, 20, 49, 98–101, 169, 189, 202, 205

filibuster, 217

First Amendment, 56, 224, 225, 236

Florida, 139

Footnote Four, 225, 226

Foner, Eric, 4, 91, 227

Fortune, T. Thomas, 85

Fourteenth Amendment, 2, 3, 4, 5, 11, 35, 39, 46, 100. *See also* equal protection clause; state action doctrine

John Bingham as author, 38

prototype, 38–9, 43

state/private distinction as constructed, 22, 24, 221

Foushee, Matthew, 122

Frankfurter, Felix, 90, 231

Franklin, John Hope, 215

Frantz, Laurent B., 124, 178, 180

free labor, 70, 71, 73

Freedmen's Bureau, 28, 54

Frelinghuysen, Frederick T., 13, 81, 91

Fugitive Slave Act of 1850, 37

fugitive slave clause, 94

Fuller (Melville) Court, 18, 186–92, 204, 205, 238

Garfield, James A., 9, 12, 21, 40–2, 45, 69, 81, 88, 140–4, 153

Garner, William, 122

Georgia, 138, 143, 230

Giles v. Harris, 188–9

Goff, Guy D., 216

Goldberg, Arthur, 178

Goldman, Robert, 141, 151

Goldstein, Leslie, 59, 123

Graham, Howard Jay, 96, 97

Grant, Ulysses S., 6, 12, 21, 33, 34, 49, 60, 68, 75, 76, 88, 91, 118, 121, 128, 131, 133, 137, 153

granted rights. *See* created rights; hybrid constitution

Gray, Horace, 186. *See also Logan v. United States*

Hall, James Parker, 210

Hall, John Jr., 47

Hall, Robert, 230

Hampton, Wade, 139, 186

Harding, Warren G., 217

Harlan, John Marshall, 2, 7, 14, 19, 80, 154, 186, 189, 203

  dissent in *Civil Rights Cases*, 85, 86, 174

  dissent in *Hodges v. United States*, 192, 201

Harper, Francis E. W., 86

Harper's Weekly, 66

Harris, R. G., 154–6

Harrison, Benjamin, 153, 182

Index

265

Harvard Law School, 25, 54, 209, 211
Hayes, Rutherford B., 5, 6, 12, 88, 137, 139, 140, 143, 153
  acknowledging failure of conciliation policy, 140–1
  recommitment to rights enforcement, 141
  vetoes of repealer legislation, 141
Hirshson, Stanley, 129
Hixson, William B., 219
Hoar, George F., 41, 182
Hodges v. United States, 2, 18, 184, 190–2, 201, 205
Holmes, Oliver Wendell, 189, 226
Hunt, Ward, 123
hybrid constitution, 15, 94–7, 98, 224, 241. *See also Logan v. United States*
Hyman, Harold M., 92, 96, 140, 186

Indiana, 64, 83, 143
Iowa, 58
Independent, 44, 78, 127, 134, 135, 138
Ingersoll, Robert G., 171
industrialization, 25, 80–1, 207, 223

Jackson, Andrew, 90
Jackson, F. M., 84
James v. Bowman, 18, 189, 203
Jim Crow, 2, 3, 7, 8, 139, 170, 186, 204, 212
Johnson, Andrew, 91, 227, 237
Jones, John (county commissioner), 84
Jones, Thomas Goode, 159, 193–6, 203, 229. *See also Riggins, Ex parte*; *United States v. Powell*
jurisprudence building, 19, 160
jury rights, 74
Justice Department, 25, 54, 126, 130, 143, 206

Kaczorowski, Robert, 34, 38
Kansas City *Times*, 142
Kentucky, 44, 85, 109
Kolb, Reuben, 195
Korematsu v. United States, 203–4
Kousser, J. Morgan, 10, 184
Krekel, Arnold, 106, 107, 108, 113, 219

Ku Klux Klan, 2, 4, 5, 9, 11–13, 23, 28, 29, 30, 31–4, 49, 54, 57, 74, 87, 119, 131, 143, 148, 170, 192, 232
Ku Klux Klan Act of 1871. *See* Enforcement Act of 1871

"laissez-faire" constitutionalism, 25, 89, 223, 226
Lamar, L. Q. C., 186
Langdell, Christopher, 54, 207, 208, 209, 211
legal science, 54. *See also* case method
Levy, Leonard, 4
Lincoln, Abraham, 21, 25, 70, 77, 90, 106, 109
Lochner v. New York, 25, 89, 204, 223, 224, 226, 228. *See also* "laissez-faire" constitutionalism
Lodge, Henry Cabot, 182
Lodge elections bill of 1890, 7, 8, 10, 184, 185, 217
Logan, John A., 65, 140
Logan v. United States, 149, 180–2, 220
Louisiana, 5, 55, 56, 82, 87, 131, 139, 141, 143
Lurie, Jonathan, 79, 89, 92
Lynch, John R., 82
lynching, 10, 213, 214, 233, 235. *See also* Dyer anti-lynching bill; Ku Klux Klan

Magrath, C. Peter, 25, 90
Maine, 63
Maples, Horace, 194, 196, 202
Marr, Robert H., 113
Martin, J. Sella, 84
Maryland, 138, 140
Massachusetts, 67
Mathews, John Mabry, 41, 42, 202, 203
McKinley, William, 193
Medill, Joseph, 77, 137
Merrill, Lewis, 32, 33
Miller, Samuel F., 13, 53, 58, 112. *See also Slaughter-House Cases*; *Yarbrough, Ex parte*
miscegenation, 72, 83. *See also* race mixing
Missouri, 106, 233
Mississippi, 82, 118

Index

Mondell, Frank, 218
Morrill, Lot M., 63, 64, 86, 91
Morton, Levi P., 182
Morton, Oliver P., 44, 64, 127
Munn v. Illinois, 89
Murray, William A., 54, 155, 156, 158

NAACP, 214, 226
Nation, 77, 78, 129, 218
natural law tradition, 10, 25, 54, 96,
    207, 223
Neal v. Delaware, 165–6
Nelson, Levi, 116, 117
New Deal, 25, 206, 223, 226
New Jersey, 89
New Orleans, 55, 80, 82, 84, 113
New Orleans *Picayune*, 98, 106
newspapers, 33, 35, 44, 66, 75, 126,
    138, 173, 214. *See also* specific
    newspapers
New York, 65, 143
New York *Globe*, 85
New York Stock Exchange, 68
New York *Sun*, 44, 134
New York Times, 33, 75, 76, 77, 106,
    127, 136, 138, 156, 176
New York Tribune, 67, 176
North Carolina, 140, 143

Ohio, 64, 143
Overton, William J., 154

Panic of 1873. *See* Economic Panic of
    1873
peonage, 185–6
Pettigrew, William, 47
Phillips, Samuel F., 115
Phillips, Wendell, 140
Pierce, Edward, 67, 168
Pierrepont, Edward, 118
Pierson, Paul, 19
Pillsbury, Albert E., 218
Platt, James H., 52
plenary enforcement theory, 34–7, 38,
    42, 126, 233
Plessy v. Ferguson, 2, 7, 18, 140, 172,
    184, 187, 188
police powers, 80, 148, 191
Pool, John, 39, 40, 42

Posner, Richard, 241
Prigg v. Pennsylvania, 35–7, 94–5
Primus, Richard, 74
privileges or immunities clause, 63
Progressives, 204, 205, 223
public accommodation rights. *See* Civil
    Rights Act of 1875; *Civil Rights
    Cases*; social rights
"public rights," 82–3

Quay, Matthew, 182

race mixing, 31, 65, 72, 73, 81, 222
railroads, 25, 31, 45, 68, 89, 90, 117, 185
Rainey, Amzi, 49
Rainey, Joseph, 62
rape, 165, 222
Raymond, Henry J., 76
Reconstruction Act of 1867, 28
Reconstruction amendments. *See*
    Fifteenth Amendment; Fourteenth
    Amendment; Thirteenth
    Amendment
Red Summer, 215
Reese, Hiram, 122
Republicans and Republican Party, 2, 3,
    5, 6, 7, 8, 16. *See also* civil rights;
    civil/political/social typology; social
    rights
  belief in white superiority, 2, 3
  centrists, 14, 29, 31, 44, 45, 58, 59,
    60, 61, 91
  defeat in the congressional election of
    1874, 89
  definitive abandonment of blacks, 18,
    183–6
  dispute (intra-party) on federalism, 103
  dispute (intra-party) on public
    accommodation rights, 14, 60–86
  election of 1876, 118
  election of 1880, 141
  factionalism, 9, 117, 142, 151, 152
  federalism, 31, 38, 39, 131
  party building in the South, 10, 19,
    117, 129, 130, 143, 144, 152, 153,
    182
  platforms, 82, 217
  post-*Cruikshank* rights enforcement,
    10

Index

program of Reconstruction, 9, 19, 130, 183
radicals, 14, 29, 61
voting rights enforcement (late 1870s, 1880s), 7, 9, 10, 19, 142, 143, 151–3
Rehnquist Court, 23, 24, 239, 243
Revels, Hiram, 62
Riggins, Ex parte, 18, 193, 194, 196–201
Robinson, Jackie, 170
Roosevelt, Franklin, 228
Roosevelt, Theodore, 193, 195, 197
Ross, Dorothy, 207
Ross, Michael A., 55, 58, 59
Rotnem, Victor, 229, 231, 232, 233, 234
Roulhac, Thomas, 197
Rutgers University, 92

Saulsbury, Eli, 65
Saunders, Berry, 148
Schurz, Carl, 65
Scofield, Glenni, 82
Scott, John A., 103, 104
Scott, Rebecca, 82
Screws v. United States, 229, 230, 231
Scribner's Monthly, 75
secured rights, 15, 149. *See also* declared rights; hybrid constitution
segregation (formal), 18. *See also Civil Rights Cases*, and relationship to *Plessy*; *Plessy v. Ferguson*
Shelby, David D., 197
Sherman, John, 64, 142
Siebold, Ex parte, 9, 16, 17, 20, 21, 80, 88, 130, 147–8, 153, 160, 169, 181, 220
Skinner, Quentin, 28, 43
Slaughter-House Cases, 13, 20, 39, 53, 55–7, 59, 114, 115
slavery, 61, 63, 191. *See also* antislavery; emancipation
Smith, Gerrit, 44
Smith, Robert R., 154
social Darwinism, 172, 186
social rights, 3, 14, 31, 33, 51, 60–86, 104, 163, 186, 187. *See also* civil rights, as distinct from social rights
South and southern states, 142.
    See also Ku Klux Klan; White Leagues

South Carolina, 5, 32, 44, 48, 54, 81, 93, 131, 138, 139, 141, 143, 145
Speer, Emory, 143
Stanton, Henry B., 44
state action doctrine, 3, 4, 10, 11, 15, 22–4. *See also Civil Rights Cases*; "under color of law … or custom"; *United States v. Cruikshank*
as including concept of state neglect, 11–14, 29, 30, 95, 97–8, 103, 110, 161–70
and the *Slaughter-House Cases*, 55–7
conventional legal-historical view, 1–7, 10, 11
principles of state neglect concept, 29, 30, 53, 54
language/vocabulary of state neglect concept, 29, 31, 34, 39–54, 158
state neglect concept as undertheorized, 24, 30, 167, 240, 241, 243
twentieth-century doctrinal development, 241–4
state neglect, practice of, 14, 28, 29, 31–4, 240
State v. Gibson, 83
Storey, Joseph, 36, 37, 95, 207
Storey, Moorfield, 213, 219–21
Strauder v. West Virginia, 198
Strong, William, 51, 165
suffrage. *See* federal elections; voting
Sumner, Charles, 75, 82, 85, 91, 121, 227. *See also* Civil Rights Act of 1875, legislative history
Swayne, Noah, 47

Taft, Alphonso, 16, 17, 155
1876 circular to federal marshals, 16, 17, 26, 130–9, 144
Taft, William Howard, 130
Talbot, Nancy, 47
tariff, 142
Tennessee, 140
Texas, 143
Thayer, James Bradley, 210
Thirteenth Amendment, 19, 63, 101–4, 111, 157, 163, 190–2, 201
Tilden, Samuel, 118, 137, 138
Tillman, Alexander, 116, 117

Tillman, Ben, 186
To Secure These Rights (President's
 Committee on Civil Rights), 233
Tomlins, Christoper, 209
Trieber, Jacob, 193, 194
Trumbull, Lyman, 35, 37
Tucker, William A., 154
Tulsa riot of 1921, 215
Tushnet, Mark, 70
Tweed, William M. "Boss," 76

"under color of law ... or custom" 13,
 23, 26, 37, 190, 236. *See also Civil
 Rights Cases*
 codified as Section 52/242 (Federal
 Criminal Code), 230, 232
 codified as Section 1983 (U.S.C.), 243
 interpreted by CRS lawyers, 231, 232
United States v. Blackburn, 106, 108,
 218
United States v. Butler, 12, 15, 107,
 145–7, 149, 152, 160, 189, 212
United States v. Classic, 229, 230
United States v. Crosby, 49, 50
United States v. Cruikshank, 2, 17, 87,
 88, 144, 145, 155, 181, 198, 200–2
 circuit opinion of 1874, 12, 15–18, 80,
 86, 88, 93–108, 125, 149, 150, 167,
 180, 189, 193, 212
 C. J. Waite's shorthand, 16, 88, 118,
 119–22, 153
 early reception, 130–53
 interpreted by CRS lawyers, 235
 political and economic context, 117,
 118, 129
United States v. Given, 51
United States v. Goldman, 150
United States v. Guest, 242
United States v. Hall, 47
United States v. Harris, 2, 20, 24, 54,
 109, 153–60, 181, 196, 198, 203–4
 interpreted by CRS lawyers, 234, 235
United States v. Lackey, 18, 189, 193,
 197, 202
United States v. Miller, 189, 193
United States v. Morris, 194
United States v. Morrison, 24, 243, 244
*United States v. Petersburg Judges of
 Elections*, 50–1

United States v. Powell, 200–2
 interpreted by CRS lawyers, 235
United States v. Price, 241, 242
United States v. Raines, 124
United States v. Reese, 16, 17, 20,
 122–6, 144, 145, 149,
 153, 157, 189, 198, 225
 early reception, 130–53
United States v. Rhodes, 47
United States v. Waddell, 181
University of Chicago Law School,
 210
University of Pennsylvania, 166, 208

Valelly, Richard M., 10, 19, 131, 150,
 151
violence. *See also* election violence;
 Ku Klux Klan; lynching;
 White Leagues
 antiblack, 28, 71, 215, 233, 240
 against civil rights protesters, 236
 against white Republicans, 12, 240
Virginia, 138, 140
Virginia, Ex parte, 181, 198, 230
Virginia *Star*, 85
Virginia v. Rives, 165–6
Volstead, Andrew J., 216, 218, 219
voting rights. *See* Article 1, Section 4;
 Fifteenth Amendment

Wade, Benjamin, 140
Waite, Morrison, 12, 15, 105, 107.
 See also United States v. Butler;
 United States v. Cruikshank; *United
 States v. Reese*
Wang, Xi, 151
Warren, Earl, 178
Washington, Booker T., 195.
 See also Giles v. Harris
Washington Post, 33, 173
Welke, Barbara, 72
Wells, P. M. (Perry McDonald),
 154, 155
White, Horace, 137
White Leagues, 9, 87, 106, 131, 146.
 See also Ku Klux Klan
Whiteside, Ruth Ann, 91, 106
Whittington, Keith, 22
Wickersham, George W., 219, 220

Index

Wiecek, William M., 92, 96, 140, 186
Williams, George H., 106, 111, 115
Williams, Lou Faulkner, 50, 87, 146, 154
Wilson, James F., 36, 37
Wilson, Woodrow, 214, 215
Winn, Berry, 190
Woods, William B., 48, 150, 168, 203–4. *See also United States v. Harris*

Woodward, C. Vann, 5, 6, 26, 238
and "Compromise of 1877," 129, 139
World War I, 214, 224
World War II, 228

Yale Law Journal, 178
Yarbrough, Ex parte, 9, 15, 16, 17, 20, 21, 59, 88, 130, 143, 148–51, 153, 160, 169, 181, 189

For EU product safety concerns, contact us at Calle de José Abascal, 56–1°, 28003 Madrid, Spain or eugpsr@cambridge.org.

www.ingramcontent.com/pod-product-compliance
Ingram Content Group UK Ltd.
Pitfield, Milton Keynes, MK11 3LW, UK
UKHW040414060825
461487UK00006B/510